DORLING KINDERSLEY *TRAVEL GUIDES*

MILAN
& THE LAKES

DK

DORLING KINDERSLEY
LONDON • NEW YORK • SYDNEY • DELHI • PARIS
MUNICH • JOHANNESBURG
www.dk.com

A DORLING KINDERSLEY BOOK

www.dk.com

Produced by Fabio Ratti
Editoria Libraria e Multimediale
Milan, Italy

PROJECT EDITORS Barbara Cacciani, Giovanni Francesio
EDITORS Emanuela Damiani, Mattia Goffetti,
Alessandra Lombardi, Marco Scapagnini
DESIGNERS Oriana Bianchetti, Silvia Tomasone

Dorling Kindersley Ltd
PROJECT EDITOR Fiona Wild
SENIOR ART EDITOR Marisa Renzullo
DTP DESIGNERS Maite Lantaron, Samantha Borland,
Sarah Meakin
PRODUCTION Marie Ingledew

CONTRIBUTOR
Monica Torri

ILLUSTRATORS
Giorgia Boli, Alberto Ipsilanti,
Daniela Veluti, Nadia Viganò

ENGLISH TRANSLATION
Richard Pierce

Film output by Quadrant Typesetters, London

Reproduced by Lineatre, Milan

Printed and bound by
L. Rex Printing Company Limited, China

First published in Great Britain in 2000 by
Dorling Kindersley Ltd,
80 Strand, London WC2R 0RL

Copyright 2000 © Dorling Kindersley Ltd

ISBN 0 7513 1177 4

CONTENTS

HOW TO USE THIS
GUIDE 6

Statue, entrance to the Pinacoteca
di Brera *(see pp114–7)*

INTRODUCING MILAN AND THE LAKES

PUTTING MILAN ON
THE MAP *10*

THE HISTORY
OF MILAN *14*

MILAN AT
A GLANCE *26*

MILAN THROUGH
THE YEAR *36*

Naviglio Grande, in the southern
district of Milan *(see p89)*

Leonardo da Vinci's *Last Supper*, in Santa Maria delle Grazie *(see pp72–3)*

MILAN AREA BY AREA

HISTORIC CENTRE *42*

The Pirelli Building is the tallest in Milan *(see p118)*

NORTHWEST MILAN *60*

SOUTHWEST MILAN *76*

SOUTHEAST MILAN *92*

NORTHEAST MILAN *104*

THE LAKES OF NORTH ITALY

INTRODUCING THE LAKES *126*

LAKE MAGGIORE *130*

LAKE COMO *136*

LAKE GARDA *142*

THE MINOR LAKES *150*

TRAVELLERS' NEEDS

WHERE TO STAY *154*

WHERE TO EAT *164*

BARS & CAFÉS *176*

SHOPS & MARKETS *180*

ENTERTAINMENT *188*

Shopping in Via Montenapoleone *(see p106–7)*

SURVIVAL GUIDE

PRACTICAL INFORMATION *192*

TRAVEL INFORMATION *206*

STREET FINDER *216*

GENERAL INDEX *230*

ROAD MAP

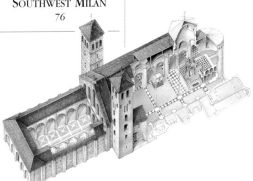

Sant'Ambrogio Basilica dates from the 4th century *(see pp84–7)*

HOW TO USE THIS GUIDE

THIS GUIDE helps you to get the most out of your visit to Milan and the lakes of Northern Italy by providing detailed descriptions of sights, practical information and expert advice. *Introducing Milan*, the first chapter, sets the city in its geographical and historical context, and *Milan at a Glance* provides a brief overview of the architecture and cultural background. *Milan Area by Area* describes the main sightseeing areas in detail, with maps, illustrations and photographs. A special section is dedicated to the lakes of Northern Italy, which are all within easy travelling distance of Milan's city centre. Information on hotels, restaurants, bars, cafés, shops, sports facilities and entertainment venues is covered in the chapter *Travellers' Needs*, and the *Survival Guide* section contains invaluable practical advice on everything from personal security to using the public transport system. The guide ends with a detailed Street Finder map and a map of the public transport network in Milan.

FINDING YOUR WAY AROUND THE SIGHTSEEING SECTION

The city of Milan is divided into five sightseeing areas, each with its own colour-coded thumb tab. Each area has its own chapter, which opens with a numbered list of the sights described. The lakes of Northern Italy are covered in a separate chapter, also colour coded. The chapter on the lakes opens with a road map of the region. The major sights are numbered for easy reference.

1 Introduction to the Area
On this page the major sights are numbered, listed by category and plotted on an area map, which also shows where public transport stops, taxi ranks and car parks are located.

A locator map shows where you are in relation to the other areas of the city.

Each area has a colour-coded thumb tab.

Locator map

The area shaded pink is shown in greater detail on the Street-by-Street map.

2 Street-by-Street Map
This gives a bird's-eye view of the most interesting parts of each sightseeing area. The numbering of the sights ties in with the area map on the preceding page as well as with the fuller descriptions provided on the pages that follow.

A suggested route for a walk covers the most interesting streets in the area.

MILAN AREA BY AREA

The five coloured areas shown on this map *(see pp12–13)* correspond to the main sightseeing areas of Milan – each of which is covered by a full chapter in the *Milan Area by Area* section *(see pp40–123)*. These areas are also highlighted on other maps, for example in the section *Milan at a Glance (see pp26–35)*. The colours on the margins of each area correspond to those on the colour-coded thumb tabs.

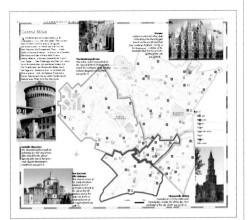

Numbers refer to each sight's position on the area map and its place in the chapter.

Practical information provides everything you need to know to visit the sights, including map references to the *Street Finder (see pp216–29)*.

3 Detailed Information on Each Sight

All the most important monuments and other sights are described individually. They are listed in order, following the numbering on the area map. The key to the symbols used is shown on the back flap for easy reference.

The story boxes discuss particular aspects of the places described.

Stars indicate the features you should not miss.

4 The Top Sights

All the most important sights are described individually in two or more pages. Historic buildings and churches are dissected to reveal their interiors, and museums and galleries have colour-coded floorplans to help you locate the major works on exhibit.

The Visitors' Checklist provides all the practical information needed to plan your visit.

INTRODUCING
MILAN

ALLI LETTORI·

Quanto la nobiliſſima Città di Milano ſia bella, grande, forte, e populata, e
d'acque, per le quali anco uengono barche, abondantiſſima, e'l d'ogni ſorti d'arti
piena, e d'il ſuo territorio fertiliſſimo. Ciaſcuno che l'habbia uiſte, ò prattica, ò
che leggera chi di eſſa ne hà ſcritto facilmente lo può ſapere e però qui ſi laſia
di narrarlo, ma ſolo ſi metterà nell'altro ſpatio quello che di eſſa più
notabile ne appare.

PUTTING MILAN ON THE MAP 10-13
THE HISTORY OF MILAN 14-25
MILAN AT A GLANCE 26-35
MILAN THROUGH THE YEAR 36-39

Putting Milan on the Map

M ILAN IS THE CAPITAL OF LOMBARDY (LOMBARDIA), the most densely populated and
economically developed region in Italy. The population of Milan is over
1,300,000 (second only to Rome). This figure does not include the many people
who live in the suburbs – which have spread outwards over the years – who
depend on the city both for work (there are large numbers of commuters) and
entertainment. The city lies in the middle of the Po river valley (Valle Padana)
and has always been a key commercial centre. Today it forms part of an
industrial triangle with the cities of Turin and Genoa. Milan's position makes it
an ideal starting point for visits to the Alpine lakes. Lake Maggiore and Lake
Como are close to Milan, whereas Lake Garda is
further east, with the western shore part of
Lombardy, the eastern
part of the Veneto.

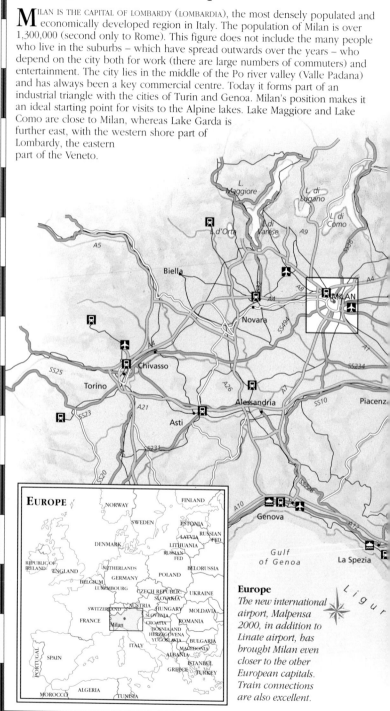

Europe
*The new international
airport, Malpensa
2000, in addition to
Linate airport, has
brought Milan even
closer to the other
European capitals.
Train connections
are also excellent.*

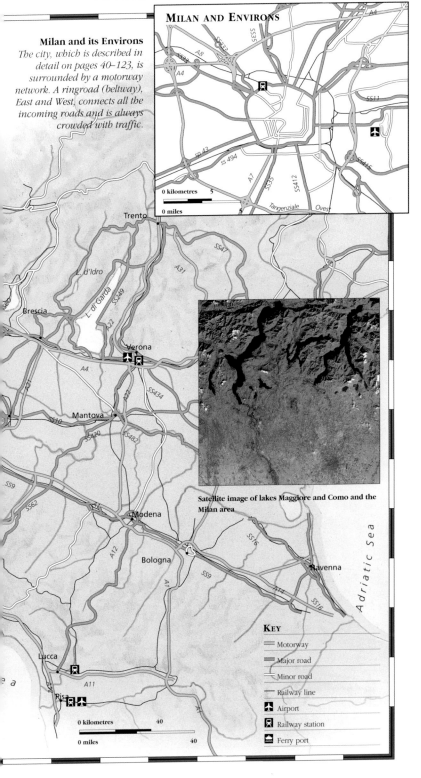

MILAN AND ENVIRONS

Milan and its Environs

The city, which is described in detail on pages 40–123, is surrounded by a motorway network. A ringroad (beltway), East and West, connects all the incoming roads and is always crowded with traffic.

0 kilometres   5

0 miles   5

Tangenziale   Ovest

Trento

L. d'Idro

L. di Garda

Brescia

Verona

Mantova

Satellite image of lakes Maggiore and Como and the Milan area

Modena

Bologna

Ravenna

Lucca

Pisa

0 kilometres   40

0 miles   40

KEY

Motorway

Major road

Minor road

Railway line

Airport

Railway station

Ferry port

Adriatic Sea

Central Milan

ALTHOUGH MILAN is a major city in all respects, it is comparatively small. The city has been divided into five areas in this guide. The historic centre, which you can visit on foot, takes in the Duomo and Teatro alla Scala; in the northwestern district are the Castello Sforzesco and Santa Maria delle Grazie, whose refectory houses Leonardo da Vinci's famous *Last Supper*. Sant'Ambrogio and San Lorenzo lie in the southwest; the southeast boasts the Ca' Granda, now the university. The large northeastern district includes the Brera quarter, with its famous art gallery, Corso Venezia and the so-called Quadrilateral, with its designer shops.

Via Montenapoleone
This is the most famous street in the area known as the "Quadrilateral", where the leading fashion designers are located (see pp 106–7).

Castello Sforzesco
The Visconti built this fortress in 1368 and it was later rebuilt by the Sforza dynasty, creating one of Europe's most elegant Renaissance residences (see pp64–7).

| 0 metres | 600 |
| 0 yards | 600 |

San Lorenzo alle Colonne
This church is one of the Early Christian basilicas built for Sant'Ambrogio (St Ambrose) in the 4th century. It is the only one that still preserves some of its original parts (see pp80–81).

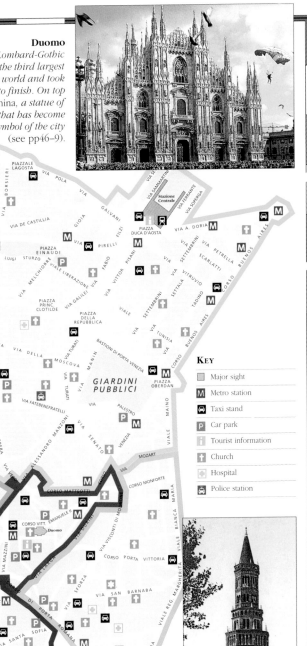

Duomo
Milan's Lombard-Gothic cathedral is the third largest church in the world and took four centuries to finish. On top is the Madonnina, a statue of the Madonna that has become a symbol of the city (see pp46–9).

KEY

	Major sight
M	Metro station
	Taxi stand
P	Car park
i	Tourist information
	Church
	Hospital
	Police station

Abbey of Chiaravalle
The abbey, founded in 1135 by Cistercian Benedictines, lies 7 km (4 miles) southeast of Milan (see pp102–3).

THE HISTORY OF MILAN

A CCORDING TO *the words of a 17th-century ambassador, "Milan never fails to be a great city, and when it declines it soon becomes great again". The sentiments encapsulate one of the characteristics of the city – its ability to rise from the ruins of wars, epidemics, sieges and bombings suffered over the centuries, and to regain dynamism and prosperity once more.*

THE PREHISTORIC AND ROMAN CITY

In the 3rd–2nd millennium BC, the area covered by Milan today was inhabited by the Ligurians. It was later settled by Indo-European populations and then, in the 5th century BC, by the Etruscans. Around the lakes, archaeologists have unearthed fascinating pre-Roman objects that reveal the presence of a Celtic civilization in the 9th–6th centuries BC. Milan itself was founded in the early 4th century BC when the Gallic Insuber tribes settled there.

Slab with a relief of the half-woolly boar, once the city emblem

The origins of the city are somewhat obscure, as is its name, which most scholars say derives from *Midland* (or "middle of the plain"), while others say it derives from *scrofa semilanuta* (half-woolly boar), the city emblem in ancient times. In 222 BC the Romans, led by the consuls Cnaeus Cornelius Scipio and Claudius Marcellus, defeated the Celts and conquered the Po river valley and its cities. Milan soon became a flourishing commercial centre and in the Imperial era attained political and administrative independence. In AD 286 it became the capital of the Western Roman Empire (until 402) and was the residence of Emperor Maximian. By the late Imperial era Milan was the most important city in the West after Rome and it became a leading religious centre after Constantine's Edict of Milan in 313, which officially recognized Christianity as a religion. Sant'Ambrogio (Ambrose) exerted great influence at this time. He was the first great figure in Milan's history: a Doctor of the Church, he built four basilicas (San Simpliciano, Sant'Ambrogio, San Lorenzo, San Nazaro) and was a leading opponent of the Arian heresy (which denied the divinity of Christ). Sant'Ambrogio was the first in a long series of bishops who ran the city's affairs in the early Middle Ages. Roman Milan was a substantial size: the Republican walls, enlarged to the northeast during the Imperial Age, defined an area that was roughly the same size as the present-day city centre.

TIMELINE

14th–3rd century BC		2nd–1st century BC	1st–2nd century AD	3rd–4th century AD
4th century BC Foundation of *Mediolanum* by Gallic Insubers	**191 BC** Through an alliance, Milan becomes an integral part of Roman world	**89 BC** Milan becomes Latin colony	**15 BC** Milan capital of IX Augustan region **AD 286** Maximian makes Milan Imperial capital	*Sant'Ambrogio*
222 BC Cnaeus Cornelius Scipio conquers Milan		**55–50 BC** Virgil attends School of Rhetoric in Milan *Virgil*	**49 BC** *Lex Roscia* confers Roman citizenship on Milan	**AD 313** With the Edict of Milan, Constantine grants Christians religious freedom	**AD 374** Sant'Ambrogio (340–397) is made Bishop of Milan

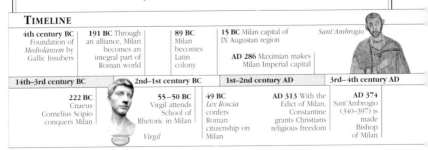

◁ **The *Sforza Altarpiece* (1494), now in the Brera art gallery, with portraits of Beatrice d'Este and Lodovico il Moro**

THE EARLY MIDDLE AGES AND THE COMMUNE OF MILAN

The 5th and 6th centuries marked a period of decline for Milan. In 402 it lost its status as Imperial capital, was sacked by Attila's Huns in 452, conquered by the Germanic Eruli in 476 and then by Ostrogoths in 489. During the war between the Greek Byzantines and Goths, the city, allies of the former, was attacked by the Goths and utterly destroyed. Reconstruction began in 568, when the city was reconquered by the Byzantine general Narses, who was forced to cede it to the Lombards in the following year. Milan was then ruled by the city of Pavia. The few remaining citizens, led by their bishop Honorius, fled to Liguria: what had been one of the most prosperous cities in the Western Roman Empire was reduced to ruins in the 6th and 7th centuries. The Edict of Rothari of 643 describes in detail Lombard administrative structures of the time.

Emperor Frederick Barbarossa at the Battle of Legnano (1176) in a 1308 miniature

In 774, the Franks defeated the Lombards and conquered Northern Italy. The archbishops regained power and there was a revival of the economy with the rise of an artisan and merchant class, which in the 11th century led to the birth of the commune. After centuries in which Monza and Pavia had been the focal points of Lombardy, Milan was once again the political centre of the region. The aristocrats and mercantile classes struggled for power in the 11th century, but then joined forces

King Rothari proclaims his edict (643), miniature, *Codex Leg..m Longobardorum*

to defend the city against the emperor. Once again the city was led by a series of archbishops, some of whom, such as Ariberto d'Intimiano (1018–45), were both bishops and generals. In 1042 the free commune of Milan was founded and a new city wall built. It was demolished in 1162 when, after a siege, the Milanese were forced to open their gates to Frederick Barbarossa: for the second time the city was burned to the ground. Milan and other northern communes together formed the Lombard League, which defeated Barbarossa's troops at Legnano in 1176. Seven years later the Treaty of Constance sanctioned the freedom of these communes.

TIMELINE

c.491 Invasion of Burgundians | 569 Invasion of Alboin's Lombards | 570 Entire Po river valley under Lombard dominion | 616 Theodolinda, wife of Authari and then of Agilulf, heads regency | *Agilulf and Theodolinda*

400 — 500 — 600 — 700 — 800 — 900

452 Milan is sacked by Attila | 539 The Goths exterminate the local population | 591 Agilulf is elected King of Italy in the Roman circus | 643 Edict of Rothari | 824 Milan becomes powerful under its bishops who, defying the Church of Rome, defend the Ambrosian rite

In the 13th century, Milan created a formidable canal network, the Navigli, which linked the city to Ticino in Switzerland. However, power struggles among the leading families sapped the strength of the entire city and fore-shadowed its decline.

THE GREAT DYNASTIES

In 1277 at Desio, the Visconti, under Archbishop Ottone, overthrew the Torriani family. The Visconti then summoned the leading artists of the time, including Giotto, to Milan to embellish the city and its palazzi, and they commissioned new buildings such as the Castello and the Duomo (see pp46–9). The height of Visconti power was achieved under Gian Galeazzo, who became duke in 1395 and undertook an ambitious policy of expansion. Milan soon ruled most of Northern Italy and even controlled some cities in Tuscany, but the duke's dream of a united Italy under his lead came to

Coat of arms of the Visconti family

an end with his death in 1402. The Visconti dynasty died out in 1447 and for three years the city enjoyed self-government under the Ambrosian Republic. In 1450 the condottiere Francesco Sforza initiated what was perhaps the most felicitous period in the history of Milan: he abandoned the Visconti expansionist policy and secured lasting peace for the city, which flourished and grew to a population of 100,000. The Visconti castle was rebuilt and became the Castello Sforzesco (see pp64–7), while architects such as Guiniforte Solari and Filarete began work on the Ospedale Maggiore, better known as Ca' Granda (see p97). However, Milan's cultural golden age came with Lodovico Sforza, known as "il Moro" (1479–1508). He was an undisciplined politician but a great patron of the arts. His policy of alliances and strategic decisions marked the end of freedom for Milan, which in 1499 fell under French dominion, yet during his rule Milanese arts and culture were second only to Medici Florence. From 1480 on, great men such as Bramante and Leonardo da Vinci were active in Milan. The former restored numerous churches and designed Santa Maria delle Grazie (see p71), in whose refectory Leonardo painted The Last Supper (see pp72–3), one of his many master-pieces. Leonardo also worked on major city projects such as the Navigli network of canals.

Milan in a 15th-century print

		1277 Rise of the Visconti	1447–50 Ambrosian Republic	1482–99 Leonardo da Vinci in Milan
1038 Archbishop Ariberto d'Intimiano leads Milanese against Corrado II and uses Carroccio cart with city banner as symbol of Milan	1158 Barbarossa lays siege to Milan. In 1162 the city is destroyed by Imperial troops	1395 Gian Galeazzo Visconti becomes duke		1499 Lodovico cedes duchy to Louis XII

00	1100	1200	1300	1400	1500
57 The Pataria vement abuses e clergy	1154 Frederick Barbarossa suppresses commune at Roncaglia	1176 Lombard League defeats Barbarossa at Legnano	*Frederick Barbarossa*	1450 Rise of the Sforza 1494 Lodovico il Moro rules	1525 Sforza return to power 1535 Charles V takes over duchy

The Visconti and Sforza

THE PERIOD of the *Signorie*, or family lordships, from the late 13th to the early 16th century, was one of the most successful in the history of Milan. The Visconti dynasty succeeded – especially during Gian Galeazzo's rule – in expanding the city's territories, albeit for a brief span of time. The Sforza dukedom is best known for the cultural and artistic splendour commissioned by Lodovico il Moro, who invited the leading artists and architects of the time to his court.

Gian Galeazzo imprisoned his uncle Bernabò in 1385 and became sole ruler of Milan. He was made a duke by Emperor Wenceslaus ten years later.

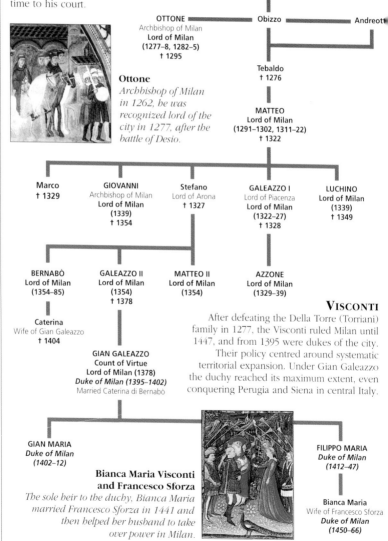

Ottone
Archbishop of Milan in 1262, he was recognized lord of the city in 1277, after the battle of Desio.

Umberto
† before 1248

OTTONE
Archbishop of Milan
**Lord of Milan
(1277–8, 1282–5)
† 1295**

Obizzo

Andreot

Tebaldo
† 1276

**MATTEO
Lord of Milan
(1291–1302, 1311–22)
† 1322**

**Marco
† 1329**

GIOVANNI
Archbishop of Milan
**Lord of Milan
(1339)
† 1354**

Stefano
Lord of Arona
† 1327

GALEAZZO I
Lord of Piacenza
**Lord of Milan
(1322–27)
† 1328**

**LUCHINO
Lord of Milan
(1339)
† 1349**

**BERNABÒ
Lord of Milan
(1354–85)**

**GALEAZZO II
Lord of Milan
(1354)
† 1378**

**MATTEO II
Lord of Milan
(1354)**

**AZZONE
Lord of Milan
(1329–39)**

Caterina
Wife of Gian Galeazzo
† 1404

GIAN GALEAZZO
Count of Virtue
Lord of Milan (1378)
Duke of Milan (1395–1402)
Married Caterina di Bernabò

VISCONTI

After defeating the Della Torre (Torriani) family in 1277, the Visconti ruled Milan until 1447, and from 1395 were dukes of the city. Their policy centred around systematic territorial expansion. Under Gian Galeazzo the duchy reached its maximum extent, even conquering Perugia and Siena in central Italy.

GIAN MARIA
*Duke of Milan
(1402–12)*

FILIPPO MARIA
*Duke of Milan
(1412–47)*

Bianca Maria Visconti and Francesco Sforza

The sole heir to the duchy, Bianca Maria married Francesco Sforza in 1441 and then helped her husband to take over power in Milan.

Bianca Maria
Wife of Francesco Sforza
*Duke of Milan
(1450–66)*

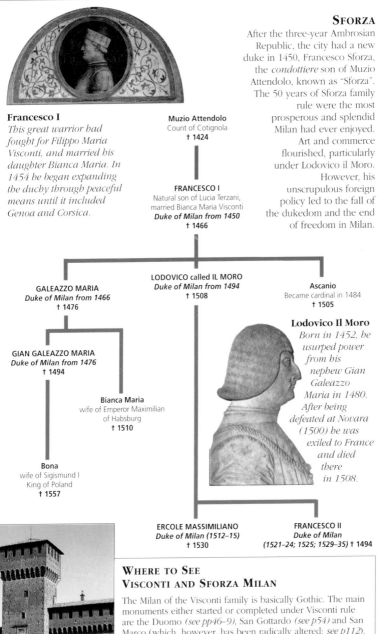

SFORZA

After the three-year Ambrosian Republic, the city had a new duke in 1450, Francesco Sforza, the *condottiere* son of Muzio Attendolo, known as "Sforza". The 50 years of Sforza family rule were the most prosperous and splendid Milan had ever enjoyed. Art and commerce flourished, particularly under Lodovico il Moro. However, his unscrupulous foreign policy led to the fall of the dukedom and the end of freedom in Milan.

Francesco I
This great warrior had fought for Filippo Maria Visconti, and married his daughter Bianca Maria. In 1454 he began expanding the duchy through peaceful means until it included Genoa and Corsica.

Muzio Attendolo
Count of Cotignola
† 1424

FRANCESCO I
Natural son of Lucia Terzani, married Bianca Maria Visconti
Duke of Milan from 1450
† 1466

GALEAZZO MARIA
Duke of Milan from 1466
† 1476

LODOVICO called IL MORO
Duke of Milan from 1494
† 1508

Ascanio
Became cardinal in 1484
† 1505

GIAN GALEAZZO MARIA
Duke of Milan from 1476
† 1494

Bianca Maria
wife of Emperor Maximilian of Habsburg
† 1510

Lodovico Il Moro
Born in 1452, he usurped power from his nephew Gian Galeazzo Maria in 1480. After being defeated at Novara (1500) he was exiled to France and died there in 1508.

Bona
wife of Sigismund I
King of Poland
† 1557

ERCOLE MASSIMILIANO
Duke of Milan (1512–15)
† 1530

FRANCESCO II
*Duke of Milan
(1521–24; 1525; 1529–35)* † 1494

The Castello Sforzesco is one of the symbols of the Signoria period in Milan.

WHERE TO SEE VISCONTI AND SFORZA MILAN

The Milan of the Visconti family is basically Gothic. The main monuments either started or completed under Visconti rule are the Duomo *(see pp46–9)*, San Gottardo *(see p54)* and San Marco (which, however, has been radically altered: *see p112*). Under the Sforza family there was a transition from Gothic to Renaissance architecture, as can be seen in San Pietro in Gessate *(see p99)* and especially in Santa Maria delle Grazie, where Leonardo painted *The Last Supper (see pp71–3)*. The Ospedale Maggiore, or Ca' Granda *(see p97)* was designed by Filarete for Francesco Sforza, and the Castello Sforzesco *(see pp64–7)* was built by the Visconti but enlarged and embellished by the Sforza, hence the name.

FRANCE AND SPAIN

The Renaissance petered out in the 16th century and was followed by a long period of decline. Milan was greatly affected by the loss of political and military importance on the part of the Italian states, now battlefields for other European powers, and because of its wealth and strategic position the city was a key target. The presence of foreign troops was so common that it

Charles V in a portrait by Titian (1532–3)

gave rise to a bitterly sarcastic proverb: "Franza o Spagna purché se magna" (France or Spain, it doesn't matter, as long as we have something on our platter). When Francesco Sforza died in 1535, Emperor Charles V appointed a governor for Milan and the city thus officially became an Imperial province. However, the city nonetheless con-

tinued to thrive and the population grew to 130,000. Its territory expanded and from 1548 to 1560 new city walls were built (called the Spanish walls) corresponding to today's inner ring road. The walls were the most important public works undertaken during Spanish rule. All that is left now is Porta Romana arch, though not in its original position. Many Baroque buildings, such as Palazzo Durini and those facing Corso di Porta Romana, were also built in this period. Among the leading figures in Spanish Milan was San Carlo Borromeo (1538–84), cardinal and archbishop of Milan, patron of the arts and benefactor, who rebuilt many churches and was one of the leading figures in the Counter Reformation. His nephew Federico (1564–1631) was also later archbishop of Milan and was immortalized in Manzoni's novel *I Promessi Sposi (The Betrothed)*, a wide-ranging portrait of Milan under Spanish rule. Economic and social decline reached its lowest point with the 1630 plague, which brought the city's population down to 60,000.

ENLIGHTENMENT MILAN

Spanish rule ended in 1706, when during the War of Spanish Succes-

Title page of a rare 1827 edition of Manzoni's novel

ALESSANDRO MANZONI'S *THE BETROTHED*

Considered one of the greatest novels in Italian literature and a masterpiece of 19th-century European narrative, *The Betrothed (I Promessi Sposi)* is also a splendid portrait of Milan under Spanish rule in the 1600s. Manzoni rewrote it several times and had three different editions published (1820, with the title *Fermo e Lucia*, 1827 and 1840). The novel is set in 1828–31 and portrays different phases of Milanese life. In chapter 12 the hero Renzo is involved in the bread riots (in Corso Vittorio Emanuele, a plaque marks the site of the bakery), while from chapter 31 onwards there are vivid descriptions of the city devastated by the plague of 1630.

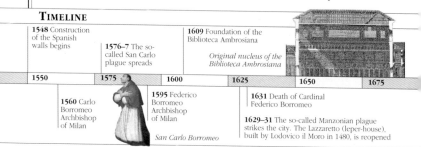

TIMELINE

1548 Construction of the Spanish walls begins

1576–7 The so-called San Carlo plague spreads

1609 Foundation of the Biblioteca Ambrosiana

Original nucleus of the Biblioteca Ambrosiana

1550	1575	1600	1625	1650	1675

1560 Carlo Borromeo Archbishop of Milan

San Carlo Borromeo

1595 Federico Borromeo Archbishop of Milan

1631 Death of Cardinal Federico Borromeo

1629–31 The so-called Manzonian plague strikes the city. The Lazzaretto (leper-house), built by Lodovico il Moro in 1480, is reopened

French troops at the city walls

The leading architect of the time was Giuseppe Piermarini, who designed the Teatro alla Scala *(see pp52–3)*, rebuilt Palazzo Reale in a Neo-Classical style, planned the urban renewal of the historic centre and designed the Corso Venezia gardens. The city's flourishing cultural life did not diminish even when the Austrians had to flee from Napoleon's troops in 1796. As the capital of the short-lived Cisalpine Republic, Milan was the setting for Napoleon's coronation in the Cathedral (1804) and witnessed the construction of various new building projects, including the Foro Bonaparte, the Arena and the Arco della Pace. After Napoleon's defeat, the Congress of Vienna handed Milan back to the Habsburgs, whose government, however, was quite different

Maria Theresa of Austria

sion Austrian troops occupied the city. Milan remained part of the Austro-Hungarian Empire until 1859, except for the Napoleonic period and the Cinque Giornate rebellion *(see pp22–3)*. Economic and, in particular, cultural revival marked the 18th century. Milan was one of the capitals of the Enlightenment, encouraged by Maria Theresa's wise administration (1740–80). From June 1764 to May 1766 a group of Milanese intellectuals, including Cesare Beccaria and the Verri brothers, published the periodical *Il Caffè*, influencing Italian cultural life by propounding the ideas of the French "Encyclopedists".

from the one under Maria Theresa. There were many abortive revolts, and Milan became one of the focal points of Romanticism and the struggle for Italian independence and unity as propounded in the local periodical *Il Conciliatore*. The publication was repressed by censors and its main exponents (Pellico, Confalonieri and Maroncelli) were imprisoned. The independence movement continued to grow, with the help of the operas of Verdi, and reached its peak with the revolt known as the *Cinque Giornate di Milano*, when the Milanese succeeded, albeit briefly, in driving the Austrian troops out of the city.

Abbé Longo, Alessandro Verri, Giovanni Battista Biffi and Cesare Beccaria, the founders of *Il Caffè*

Eugene of / drives out last sh governor		**1778** Inauguration of La Scala opera house	**1796** French troops enter Milan		**1848** Cinque Giornate revolt
	1740 Beginning of Maria Theresa's rule in Milan		**1805** Italic Kingdom proclaimed	**1820** Pellico imprisoned by Austrians	**1848** Radetzky again occupies Milan
1725	**1750**	**1775**	**1800**	**1825**	**1850**
1714 Treaty of Utrecht: Lombardy ceded to Austria	*Cesare Beccaria*	**1764–66** Pietro Verri publishes *Il Caffè*	**1818** *Il Conciliatore* published	**1839** Cattaneo founds *Il Politecnico*	**1859** Milan liberated by French-Piedmontese troops
		1764 Cesare Beccaria publishes *On Crimes and Punishment*	**1797** Cisalpine Republic	**1849** Austria-Piedmont peace treaty	

The Cinque Giornate Revolt

The Italian flag in 1848

THIS HISTORIC EVENT was preceded by the "smoking strike", held during the first three days of 1848, when the Milanese refused to buy tobacco as a protest against Austrian taxation. The "Five Days" revolt began on 18 March 1848. Clashes initially broke out after a demonstration and continued in a disorderly fashion for two days, during which the Austrians, led by Field Marshal Radetzky, were initially besieged inside the Castello Sforzesco. Then, after the formation of a War Council and a Provisional Government on 22 March at Porta Tosa, the Imperial troops were defeated and driven out of Milan.

Carlo Cattaneo (1801–69)
Cattaneo was one of the leaders in the Cinque Giornate, and later went into exile in Switzerland.

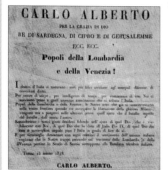

Carlo Alberto's Proclamation
With this declaration, Carlo Alberto, king of Sardinia, put himself at the head of the revolt. Yet when the opportune occasion arose he failed to attack the Austrians and in August 1848 he was forced to cede Milan to the Austrian Radetzky.

Behind the barricades were people from all social classes, demonstrating the unity of the Milanese in the battle for independence.

The Austrian Army
Field Marshal Radetzky had some 74,000 men (about a third of them Italians) at his disposal, divided into two army corps. The first and larger one was stationed in Milan.

PORTA TOSA

This painting by Carlo Canella, now in the Museo di Milano, represents the *Battle at Porta Tosa*, when the Milanese dealt the final blow to the Austrian troops on 22 March. After this historic event, the city gate, which is situated in the eastern part of the city, was renamed Porta Vittoria (Victory Gate).

Pasquale Sottocorno
Despite being crippled, this 26-year-old shoemaker managed to set fire to the military engineers' building where the enemy troops were barracked, and capture the hospital of San Marco, which was another Austrian stronghold.

ABITANTI DELLA LOMBARDIA!

Alla testa del prode e vittorioso mio esercito sono entrato sul vostro suolo come il liberatore vostro da una dominazione rivoluzionaria e tirannica. Molti di voi, sedotti da perfide suggestioni, hanno dimenticato i sacri doveri verso il legittimo loro Sovrano. Tornate devoti sotto lo scettro benigno del nostro Imperatore e Re. Io vi offro la mano a sincera conciliazione.

Abitanti la Lombardia, ascoltate il benevolo mio consiglio. Confidenti accogliete le brave mie Truppe. Esse guarentiranno al cittadino pacifico ogni maggior sicurezza della persona e della proprietà, ma contro chi si ostinasse nel cieco delirio della ribellione procederanno irremissibilmente con tutta la severità della legge marziale.

A voi sta la scelta; a me l'impegno di esattamente adempire la mia parola.

Dal Quartier-Generale di Valleggio 27 Luglio 1848.

RADETZKY

The Austrians, forced into retreat

The Austrians Return
After he had defeated King Carlo Alberto at Custoza (25 July), Radetzky returned to Lombardy, as announced in this proclamation of 27 July. He recaptured Milan on 6 August.

Over 1,600 barricades were set up throughout the city during the insurrection.

The Soldier's Widow
In Italy the struggle for independence was closely linked to Romanticism, as can be seen in works dating from this period, such as this 1851 sculpture by Giovanni Pandiani.

THE CINQUE GIORNATE REVOLT

Radetzky

	18 March	19 March	20 March	21 March	22 March
		The revolt spreads throughout the city and barricades are built everywhere		Radetzky proposes an armistice but is rejected	
	Demonstration in the Monforte district for freedom of the press and the establishment of a Civil Guard. Radetzky is besieged in the Castello Sforzesco		Formation of the War Council and Provisional Government		The Imperial troops suffer defeat in the last battle at Porta Tosa (renamed Porta Vittoria) and abandon Milan

Guardia Nobile helmet

MILAN AFTER ITALY'S UNIFICATION

In 1861 the population of Milan was 240,000, which shows how much the city had grown under Austrian rule. However, the real demographic explosion was yet to come. Although Milan did not become the political capital after the unification of Italy, it became the economic and cultural capital of the country. Infrastructures created by the Austrians were exploited to the full and by 1920 the city had developed into an industrial metropolis. Business was thriving, *Corriere della Sera*, the leading Italian daily newspaper, was founded, the city increased in size and the population exploded (there were 850,000 inhabitants in 1923). This over-rapid growth inevitably brought major social consequences: the first trade

A Corriere della Sera poster

union centre was founded, and socialist groups grew in strength. Strikes and demonstrations became more and more frequent, and social tensions exploded in 1898, when a protest against the high cost of living was violently repressed by cannon fire,

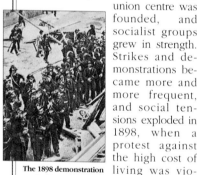

The 1898 demonstration quelled by Bava Beccaris

on the orders of General Bava Beccaris. The early 20th century witnessed the rise of an important avant-garde movement in Milan (the second in the city after the Scapigliatura movement of the second half of the 19th century): Futurism, which was founded by Filippo Tommaso Marinetti (a plaque in Corso Venezia commemorates the event). The Futurists were not only important from an artistic standpoint, but also because their ideas and actions fitted in perfectly with the cultural temper of the times, characterized by the pro-intervention attitude regarding World War I and then the rise of Fascism. In fact, Fascism and Mussolini had a very close relationship with Milan. The original nucleus of the movement was founded in Milan in 1919. In 1943, after the fall of the regime and the foundation of the Repubblica Sociale puppet government, Milan – severely damaged by bombing raids – was the last large Italian city to remain under the control of the remaining Fascists and the Germans. On 26 April 1945, the story of Mussolini and Italian Fascism played out its final moments in Milan: the corpses of il Duce, his mistress Claretta Petacci and some party officials were put on display in Piazzale

Milan after the 1943 bombings

TIMELINE

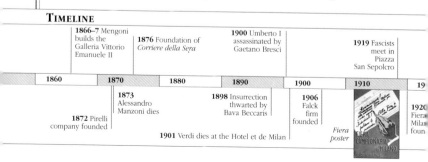

1866–7 Mengoni builds the Galleria Vittorio Emanuele II

1876 Foundation of *Corriere della Sera*

1900 Umberto I assassinated by Gaetano Bresci

1919 Fascists meet in Piazza San Sepolcro

1860   1870   1880   1890   1900   1910   19

1873 Alessandro Manzoni dies

1872 Pirelli company founded

1898 Insurrection thwarted by Bava Beccaris

1901 Verdi dies at the Hotel et de Milan

1906 Falck firm founded

Fiera poster

1920 Fiera Milan foun

Loreto, exactly the same place where some partisans had been executed a few weeks earlier.

THE POSTWAR PERIOD

On 11 May 1946, Arturo Toscanini conducted a concert to celebrate the re-opening of the Teatro alla Scala, which had been destroyed by bombs during the war.

Logo of Teatro alla Scala

This historic event demonstrated the desire for recovery and recon-struction that characterized postwar Milan. The linchpin of an industrial triangle with Turin and Genoa, Milan now had 1,800,000 inhabitants. This period of secure growth, disturbed only by student protests in 1968, ended on 12 December 1969, when the explosion of a terrorist bomb in a bank in Piazza Fontana, causing a massacre, began the long, grim period of terrorist activity. The 1980s saw the development of the fashion industry that has made Milan one of the world leaders in this field. The most recent significant event in the city's history was the 1992 anti-corruption investigations which forced many members of the ruling parties to step down from power.

PRESENT-DAY MILAN

Thanks to its dynamic life, productivity and inventive capacities, Milan today is a leading European city, but it still has many problems: the decline in population, now 1.36 million, is proof of the growing dissatisfaction with a city that is considered, for example, unsuitable for children. The rapid increase in commuter traffic has not been matched by adequate long-distance public transport, which is why the city is frequently blocked by heavy traffic on weekdays. Last, although Milan is probably the most multi-cultural city in Italy, clandestine immigration causes its own social problems. Despite this, Milan is an avant-garde city by all standards, a financial, professional and cultural leader in Italian life.

THE GROWTH OF MILAN

This map shows the growth of Milan from the original Roman city to the present-day metropolis.

KEY

- The Roman city
- The medieval city
- Up to the 18th century
- The 19th century
- The early 20th century
- Present-day Milan

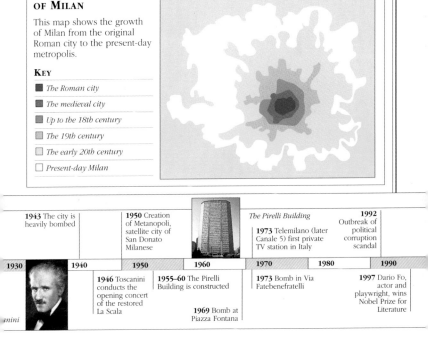

1943 The city is heavily bombed

1950 Creation of Metanopoli, satellite city of San Donato Milanese

The Pirelli Building

1973 Telemilano (later Canale 5) first private TV station in Italy

1992 Outbreak of political corruption scandal

1930 | 1940 | 1950 | 1960 | 1970 | 1980 | 1990

1946 Toscanini conducts the opening concert of the restored La Scala

1955–60 The Pirelli Building is constructed

1969 Bomb at Piazza Fontana

1973 Bomb in Via Fatebenefratelli

1997 Dario Fo, actor and playwright, wins Nobel Prize for Literature

...anini

MILAN AT A GLANCE

NE OF THE MANY CLICHÉS about Milan is that it is a practical, industrious, even drab city, wholly dedicated to work and the world of commercial gain. In fact, besides being a leading metropolis in Europe from a financial standpoint and in terms of productivity, it is also rich in history and culture, architecture and art. The historic centre has no single dominating architectural style, and the buildings are perhaps more varied than any other city centre in Italy. The museums and galleries are among the finest in Northern Italy, and many of the leading figures in the fields of Italian art, design, culture and politics were either born in Milan or achieved success here. The following eight pages will provide brief descriptions of some of the major aspects of the city, while below is a selection of top attractions that no visitor to Milan should miss.

MILAN'S TOP TEN ATTRACTIONS

Ca' Granda
See p97

Teatro alla Scala
See pp52–3

Pinacoteca Ambrosiana
See pp56–9

Sant'Ambrogio
See pp84–7

San Lorenzo alle Colonne
See pp80–1

Abbazia di Chiaravalle
See pp102–3

Duomo
See pp46–9

Castello Sforzesco
See pp64–7

Pinacoteca di Brera
See pp114–7

The Last Supper
See pp72–3

◁ **Statues decorating the exterior of the Duomo**

Famous Residents and Visitors

M ANY LEADING FIGURES in Italian cultural
life are connected in some way
with Milan, from intellectuals, journalists
and politicians to composers, writers and
poets. The Italian novelist Alessandro
Manzoni was born in Milan, and many
other artists have been drawn here,
hoping to make their fortune (an
illustrious example is Giuseppe Verdi) or,
more simply, to find work. One of the
most widespread, and perhaps most
accurate, sayings about Milan is that it
is an open, receptive city ready to give
strangers and foreigners a sincere, if
brusque, welcome.

**Carlo Emilio Gadda
(1893–1973)**
*Milanese by birth,
Gadda was one of the
great 20th-century
authors. One of his
major works, L'Adalgi
celebrates the lives of
middle-class Milanese
and ends with the her
cleaning the tombs in
the Monumental
Cemetery.*

**Giorgio Strehler
(1921–97)**
*In 1947 the great
Trieste-born director
founded the Piccolo
Teatro della Città di
Milano with
Paolo Grassi. It
was the first
permanent
theatre in Italy.*

NORTHWEST
(see pp60–75)

Leonardo da Vinci (1452–1519)
*In 1482 Lodovico il Moro invited
Leonardo da Vinci to his court in
Milan, where he remained for
almost 20 years. He left a number
of works, including the*
Codex Atlanticus, *now in the
Biblioteca Ambrosiana and* The
Last Supper, *in Santa Maria delle
Grazie (see pp72–3).*

SOUTHWE
(see pp76–9

0 metres	700
0 yards	700

Benito Mussolini (1883–1945)
*In 1919, in Milan's Piazza San Sepolcro, Mussolini
founded the* Fasci Nazionali di Combattimento, *the first
nucleus of the future Fascist movement. On 16 December
1944 Mussolini gave his last speech at the Teatro Lirico in
Milan. A few months later, on 26 April 1945, his corpse
was hung upside down in Piazzale Loreto.*

Giuseppe Verdi (1813–1901)

Born in Busseto, in the province of Parma, Verdi moved to Milan at a very early age. His third opera, Nabucco *(1842), brought him fame. He died at the Hotel et de Milan, which he had made his home.*

Alessandro Manzoni (1785–1873)

Manzoni wrote what is considered the greatest Italian novel, The Betrothed, *as well as plays and poetry. His house in Piazza Belgioioso (see p51) is open to the public.*

Cesare Beccaria (1738–94)

A leading exponent of the Enlightenment movement in Milan, Beccaria wrote its most representative work, On Crimes and Punishment. *In the square named after him is a monument in his honour.*

NORTHEAST
(see pp104–23)

SOUTHEAST
(see pp92–103)

ORIC
RE
42–59)

The Verri Brothers

Pietro (1728–97) and Alessandro (1741–1816) Verri met other noted Enlightenment figures at the Caffè Greco, opposite the Duomo, where they conceived the influential periodical Il Caffè.

Carlo Porta (1775–1821)

A poet who wrote in Milanese dialect, Porta offered a vivacious description of the society of his time in his satirical poems. There is a monument in his honour in Piazza Santo Stefano, which was the setting for one of his best-known works, Ninetta del Verzee.

Milan's Best: Churches and Basilicas

T HE CHURCHES OF MILAN are built in two basic architectural styles: Lombard Romanesque, which can be seen elsewhere in the region, and the Counter Reformation Mannerism of Milan under the Borromeos. The only exception is the magnificent Duomo, a splendid example of Lombard Gothic. There are very few examples of older styles. This is partly the result of destructive invasions and time, but is mostly due to the fact that the city is built just above the water table, and older buildings had to be demolished to make way for new ones.

Santa Maria delle Grazie
Besides being home to Leonardo's Last Supper, this church designed by Solari and Bramante, is a marvellous example of Renaissance architecture (see pp71–3).

Basilica of Sant'Ambrogio
The famous church founded by Sant'-Ambrogio has a long architectural history, culminating in the restoration carried out to repair damage caused by the bombs of World War II (see pp84–7).

NORTHWEST
(see pp60–75)

SOUTHW
(see pp76

Basilica of San Lorenzo
This late 4th-century basilica still has some original architectural elements, such as the columns that surround the courtyard (see pp80–81).

Basilica of Sant'Eustorgio
Inside this 9th-century basilica are several aristocratic chapels, including the Cappella Portinari, one of the great examples of Renaissance architecture in Milan (see p90).

San Marco

The basic structure is 13th-century Romanesque, while the Neo-Gothic façade was built in 1871. The three statues depicting San Marco between Sant'Ambrogio and Sant'Agostino (above) are works of the Campionese school (see p112).

San Fedele

This typical example of Counter Reformation architecture was begun in 1569. Pellegrini's original design was completed by Bassi, who built the façade, and by Richini (see p50).

RTHEAST
pp104–23)

ORIC
RE
59)

SOUTHEAST
(see pp92–103)

Duomo

Milan's cathedral is the third largest church in the world (see pp46–9). It was begun by the Visconti family in 1386 and finished by Napoleon in 1805 – over four centuries later.

| 0 metres | 700 |
| 0 yards | 700 |

Basilica of San Nazaro Maggiore

Founded by Sant'Ambrogio towards the end of the 4th century, the basilica has been altered many times, but recent restoration work has revived its original austere beauty. Don't miss the Trivulzio Chapel (see p96).

Milan's Best: Buildings and Gardens

Cᴵᴠɪᴄ ᴀʀᴄʜɪᴛᴇᴄᴛᴜʀᴇ in Milan suffered the same fate as religious architecture: the sequence of destruction wrought by successive waves of invaders meant constant rebuilding, to the detriment of the works of the past. Nonetheless, the city has emerged enriched, as can be seen in the splendid Baroque buildings in the city centre, the Neo-Classical examples in Corso Venezia, and the late 19th-century Art Nouveau architecture. With all its buildings Milan may seem to have little greenery, but in fact there are landscaped gardens, court-yards and public parks which stand comparison with any northern European city.

Art Nouveau detail, Casa Galimberti (see p119)

Castello Sforzesco and Parco Sempione
Behind the fortress built by the Visconti and enlarged by the Sforza (see pp64–7), is the Parco Sempione, the largest park in Milan (see p68).

NORTHWEST
(see pp60–75)

Casa degli Omenoni
This was the residence of the sculptor Leone Leoni (1509–90), who built it in 1565. The eight telamones, called omenoni *by the Milanese, are by Antonio Abbondio (see p51).*

SOUTHWEST
(see pp76–91)

Parco delle Basiliche
This park lies between the basilicas of Sant'Eustorgio and San Lorenzo, hence its name (it is also called Piazza della Vetra). Part of the park was created from land which had been bombed during World War II (see p82).

Palazzo della Ragione
Construction of this splendid example of Romanesque civic architecture began in 1228. Inside is the huge Sala della Ragione (see p54).

Stazione Centrale
The grandiose central railway station was opened in 1931, after almost 20 years of construction work (see p119). Nearby is the Pirelli Building (1955–60), Milan's tallest skyscraper (see p118).

Giardini Pubblici
The public gardens were designed by Piermarini (late 18th century) and house exotic plants, museums and a Planetarium (see pp120–21).

Palazzo Serbelloni
One of the most imposing examples of Milanese Neo-Classical architecture (1793) stands in elegant Corso Venezia (see pp122–3). Napoleon, Metternich and Vittorio Emanuele II were guests here.

NORTHEAST
(see pp104–23)

**ORIC
[RE**
p42–59)

SOUTHEAST
(see pp92–103)

| 0 metres | 600 |
| 0 yards | 600 |

Torre Velasca
A symbol of postwar Milan, this tower was built during the "economic boom" of the late 1950s. It is 106 m (348 ft) high and is based on medieval towers (see p96).

Ca' Granda
Francesco Sforza commissioned this building in the second half of the 15th century as a city hospital (Ospedale Maggiore). It is now the University. Three building phases can be seen: dating from the 15th century, 17th century, and late 18th and early 19th centuries (see p97).

Milan's Best: Museums and Galleries

17th-century clock,
Museo della Scienza
e della Tecnica

BESIDES HOUSING priceless works of art, the museums and art galleries of Milan also reflect the history of the city. The Pinacoteca di Brera was founded at the height of the Enlightenment period and the Ambrosiana is the result of the patronage of religious art by the Borromeo family. The Castello Sforzesco collections date from the period of the *Signorie*, while the Galleria d'Arte Moderna is a sign of civic commitment to fine arts. Last, the Museo Bagatti Valsecchi and Poldi Pezzoli, private collections, are typical manifestations of the Milanese love of art.

Pinacoteca di Brera
One of Northern Italy's largest art galleries has works from the 14th to the 19th century. Above, Pietà *by Giovanni Bellini (see pp114–7).*

Musei del Castello
The Castello Sforzesco museums are rich in sculpture, furniture and applied arts and also include a gallery with works by great artists, such as this Madonna and Child with the Infant St John the Baptist *by Correggio (see pp64–7).*

NORTHWEST
(see pp60–75)

Museo Nazionale della Scienza e della Tecnica
The Science and Technology Museum has wooden models of Leonardo's inventions and a section given over to clocks, computers and means of communication and transport (see p88).

SOUTH
(see pp7

Pinacoteca Ambrosiana
This art gallery was founded by Cardinal Federico Borromeo in the 17th century to provide models for the students at the Fine Arts Academy. The collections include works by artists such as Caravaggio and Raphael (see pp56–9), while the Biblioteca Ambrosiana (library) contains the precious Codex Atlanticus *by Leonardo da Vinci.*

Museo Poldi Pezzoli
Together with the many works by Italian artists in this splendid residence-cum-museum (see p108) is Lucas Cranach's Portrait of Martin Luther.

Galleria d'Arte Moderna
The imposing Villa Reale (see p121) houses 19th-century Italian art collections, the Museo Marini, the Vismara Collection and the Grassi Collection. Right, Matilda Juva Branca *(1851) by Francesco Hayez.*

NORTHEAST
(see pp104–123)

Museo Bagatti Valsecchi
This marvellous example of a 19th-century private residence contains 16th-century handicrafts, furniture, arms, ivory pieces, paintings and ceramics (see p109).

Museo del Duomo
The Duomo Museum was founded in 1953 and holds fine sculptures and other objects representing the religious history of Milan. Right, the 16th-century Ambrosian Monstrance, *made of rock crystal and precious stones (see p49).*

ORIC
RE
42–59

SOUTHEAST
(see pp92–103)

Civico Museo d'Arte Contemporanea
On the second floor of Palazzo Reale, now under restoration (see p54), this museum has a good Futurist collection and works by famous artists such as Picasso and Klee. The sculpture collection is also important, and includes this Woman at the Mirror *by Lucio Fontana (1934).*

0 metres 700
0 yards 700

MILAN THROUGH THE YEAR

MILAN OFFERS a range of different events and attractions at different seasons of the year, from traditional to commercial. The city's citizens are still attached to traditional religious celebrations such as the Carnevale Ambrosiano (Milanese Carnival) or the festivities that take place around 7 December, the Festival of Sant'Ambrogio, the city's patron saint. This is also the date of opening night at La Scala, the world-famous opera house. Such traditional and characteristic festivities alternate with other events that are perhaps more in keeping with the image of a modern, industrial city. Among these are Fashion Week, one of the world's top fashion shows, held twice a year, and SMAU, an important international multimedia and communications technology trade show.

Private courtyards in Milan, open to the public in the spring

SPRING

AFTER THE LONG Milanese winter, local inhabitants welcome the arrival of spring with a sigh of relief. The pleasant spring breezes clear the air of the notorious Milanese smog and the city seems to take on different colours. On very clear days, if you look northwards you will see the peaks of the Alps, which are still covered with snow – one of the finest views the city affords at this time of year.

Towards the end of spring, the clear weather may very well give way to showers and even violent storms, which may blow up in the space of just a few hours, causing problems with city traffic.

This is the season when tourist activity resumes at the lakes. Boat services start up again and the water becomes a major weekend attraction for the Milanese once more.

MARCH

MODIT-Milanovendemoda *(beginning of month)*. The autumn-winter collections of the leading international and Italian fashion designers go on show.
Milano–SanRemo *(third Sat)*. Part of the city centre hosts the start of this prestigious inter-national bicycle race.
Oggi Aperto *(third weekend)*. Monuments and historic buildings usually closed to the public are now open.
BIT. The Fiera (Milan's Exhibition Centre) hosts an international tourist trade show.

APRIL

Fiera dei Fiori *(Mon after Easter)*. In and around Via Moscova, near the Sant'Angelo Franciscan convent, is this fair devoted mainly to flower growing.
Bagutta-Pittori all'Aria Aperta *(third week)*. The famous Via Bagutta plays host to a fascinating outdoor

The Fashion Week, held in March

exhibition for artists' work.
Stramilano *(mid-Apr)*. This celebrated marathon is for professionals and amateurs alike and attracts an average of 50,000 competitors every year.

MAY

Milano Cortili Aperti. The courtyards of the city's private residences are open to the public.
Pittori sul Naviglio. Outdoor art display along the Alzaia Naviglio Grande canal *(see p89)*.
Estate all'Idroscalo. Near Linate airport, the Milan seaplane airport inaugurates its summer season with sports events, water entertainment and concerts.
Sagra del Carroccio. At Legnano, 30 km (19 miles) from Milan, there is a commemoration of the battle of 1176, when the Lombard League defeated Emperor Frederick Barba-rossa: parades in costume and folk festivities and events.

The March Milan–SanRemo race, opening the Italian cycling season

AVERAGE DAILY HOURS OF SUNSHINE

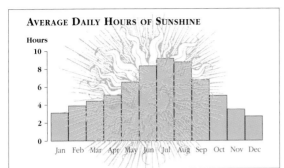

Hours

Jan Feb Mar Apr May Jun Jul Aug Sep Oct Nov Dec

Sunshine Hours
The hours of sunshine in Milan are in line with the Mediterranean average. However, in autumn and winter the weather can be very foggy, which is a typical feature of the climate in the Po river valley, exacerbated by city pollution. The lakes, surrounded by the Alps, are more shaded in the morning and evening.

Parco Sempione, a major venue for summer entertainment

SUMMER

JUNE IS ONE OF the most pleasant months to visit Milan because the climate is mild and the programme of cultural and sports events is truly packed. In July the torrid, muggy summer heat (the temperature may be as high as 40° C/104° F), together with the heavy traffic, can make sightseeing quite uncomfortable.

In August, most of the factories and offices close for the summer holidays and the empty city is an unusual and, in some respects, quite pleasant sight. The same streets that were crowded a week earlier are now quiet, even restful.

Despite the exodus, many events, both cultural and recreational, are held in Milan during the summer.

This is the busiest season for visiting the lakes of Northern Italy, but also the sunniest. Even at the peak of the summer heat, the water can have a cooling effect.

JUNE

Festa del Naviglio *(first Sun)*. You can find everything under the sun at this festival, held in the atmospheric setting of the illuminated Navigli canals: street artists and performers, concerts, sports, an antiques market, handicrafts, regional cooking.
Milano d'Estate *(Jun–Aug)*. This marks the beginning of summer entertainment in the city (concerts, exhibits, various cultural events), which takes place in the Parco Sempione.
Sagra di San Cristoforo *(third Sun)*. The patron saint of travellers, St Christopher, is celebrated along the Naviglio, in the square facing the church. In the evening decorated barges glide along the canals.
Estate all'Umanitaria. The Humanitarian Association organizes a festival of cinema, dance, music, theatre and cartoons and shows for children.

Fotoshow. An interesting video, photography and optics show in the Fiera (Exhibition Centre) pavilions.
Orticola. Flower growing and garden furnishings show and market in the Porta Venezia public gardens *(see p120)*.
Sagra di San Giovanni. At Monza, a few miles north of Milan, the patron saint's feast day is celebrated with sports and cultural events, some of which are held at a splendid venue – the park at the Villa Reale.

JULY AND AUGUST

Festival Latino-Americano. The Forum di Assago hosts this lively festival of Latin-American music, handicrafts and cuisine.
Arianteo. At the Rotonda della Besana *(see p100)*, the Anteo motion-picture theatre organizes a series of outdoor showings, which includes all the most important films featured in Milan's cinemas and theatres during the year.

The Festa del Naviglio, marking the beginning of summer events

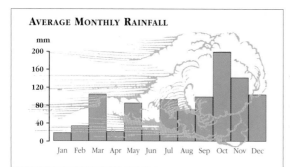

AVERAGE MONTHLY RAINFALL

mm
200
160
120
80
40
0
Jan Feb Mar Apr May Jun Jul Aug Sep Oct Nov Dec

Rainfall
The average monthly rainfall in the Milan area can vary quite considerably during the year. The wettest season is certainly autumn, when it may rain for several days without a break. In late spring and summer the average rainfall level may increase because of unexpected storms.

AUTUMN

SEPTEMBER IN MILAN really gives you the impression of life beginning anew. In general, by the last week of August the Milanese have returned from holiday, but it is only in September that things get back into full swing. As far as the weather is concerned, fog and rain alternate with lovely clear days with that typical "Lombard sky" which Alessandro Manzoni, in *The Betrothed*, described as being "so beautiful when it is beautiful, so blue, so serene".

A Ferrari in action at Monza

SEPTEMBER

Premier league football (soccer).
Early September marks the resumption of the Italian football season. Two of the leading Italian teams are based in Milan: Inter and Milan. They are arch rivals and the local championship is always a major event here.
Panoramica di Venezia *(early Sep)*. Milan cinemas show films from the Venice Film Festival while they are being screened there.
Gran Premio di Monza. One of the top motor racing circuits, the Grand Prix of Italy, often crucial to the outcome of the Formula One competition.

OCTOBER

Fiera di Chiaravalle *(first Mon)*. This famous fair is held in the shade of the *ciribiciaccola* (as the Milanese call the bell tower of the Chiaravalle Cistercian abbey, *see pp102–3*). The fair features music, dancing and an outdoor art exhibition.
SMAU *(first week)*. International multimedia show held in the Fiera

The Fiera, host to both SMAU and fashion shows

Exhibition Centre: IT, from computers for offices to CD-Roms and Virtual Reality.
MODIT-Milanovendemoda *(beginning of month)*. The second major fashion show for leading Italian and international fashion designers. The spring-summer collections in various show-rooms and the Fiera pavilions.

NOVEMBER

Premio Bagutta. Milan's most important literary prize is awarded.

PUBLIC HOLIDAYS

New Year's Day (1 Jan)
Epiphany (6 Jan)
Easter Sunday and Monday
Liberation Day (25 Apr)
Labour Day (1 May)
Ferragosto (15 Aug)
All Saints' Day (1 Nov)
Sant'Ambrogio (Milan's Patron Saint) (7 Dec)
Immaculate Conception (8 Dec)
Christmas (25 Dec)
Santo Stefano (26 Dec)

San Siro stadium, packed with fans at the beginning of the season

AVERAGE MONTHLY TEMPERATURE

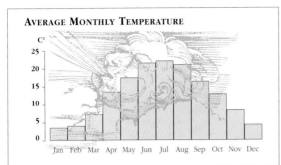

Temperature
Milan is inland and there are big differences in temperature between winter and summer. The winters can be very cold indeed, particularly in December and January, typical of continental Europe, while there may be torrid heat in summer. The climate is always very humid.

WINTER

CHARACTERIZED by severe cold (heavy snowfall is not rare), the Milanese winter is "warmed up" by a rich and fascinating programme of cultural events, major holidays and special occasions. The city becomes especially lively around the feast day of Sant'Ambrogio (St Ambrose), the local patron saint, and then for Christmas, which is preceded by the usual shopping sprees in the city-centre shops. On the cultural side, the theatres of Milan present a high-quality theatre season, headed by the world-famous Piccolo Teatro.

Christmas decorations in the Galleria Vittorio Emanuele II

DECEMBER

Festa di Sant'Ambrogio
(7 Dec). This is the locals' favourite holiday, just before Immaculate Conception *(8 Dec)*. Sant'Ambrogio is celebrated with many events: the jam-packed **Fiera degli Oh bej Oh bej**, a street fair featuring antiques as well as a

Typical antiques stalls at the Oh bej Oh bej fair

vast assortment of articles. It is held in the streets around the basilica of Sant'Ambrogio *(see pp84–7)*.
La Scala. The season at the world-famous opera house *(see pp52–3)* starts on 7 December. The opening night is, of course, a major cultural event, and it is also an important occasion in the Milanese social calendar.
Piccolo Teatro. Milan's other famous theatre, founded by Paolo Grassi and world-class director Giorgio Strehler, also inaugurates its programme of plays on 7 December.

JANUARY

Corteo dei Re Magi *(6 Jan)*.
A traditional procession with a *tableau vivant* of the Nativity goes from the Duomo to Sant'Eustorgio.
Fiera di Senigallia *(every Sat all year long)*. Along the Darsena is a colourful market offering ethnic handicrafts, records and bicycles.
Mercato dell'Antiquariato di Brera *(third Sat of month, all year)*. Stalls with antiques, books, postcards, jewellery.

FEBRUARY

Carnevale Ambrosiano.
The longest carnival in the world ends on the first Saturday of Lent. Floats and stock Milanese characters such as Meneghin and Cecca, take part in a parade to Piazza del Duomo, which is filled with children throwing confetti everywhere.

Taking part in the Carnevale Ambrosiano in Piazza del Duomo

MILAN AREA
BY AREA

HISTORIC CENTRE 42–59
NORTHWEST MILAN 60–75
SOUTHWEST MILAN 76–91
SOUTHEAST MILAN 92–103
NORTHEAST MILAN 104–123

HISTORIC CENTRE

HE AREA AROUND the Duomo was the religious centre of Milan in the 4th century. Up to the 14th century it was the site of the basilicas of Santa Tecla and Santa Maria Maggiore and the Early Christian baptisteries, San Giovanni alle Fonti and Santo Stefano. These were all demolished to make room for the new cathedral. The political and administrative centre of the city was the nearby Palazzo della Ragione. At that time Milan was only slightly larger than the present-day historic centre; in fact, what is today Piazza della Scala was on the edge of town. Piazza del Duomo was the focus of small businesses until the 18th

Leonardo da Vinci, in Piazza della Scala

century, and a stage for the city's major religious and civic ceremonies. In the 19th century it became the nucleus from which avenues radiated. In the 1860s the decaying dwellings and the shops around the Duomo were demolished to make way for the construction of the then futuristic Galleria, the symbol of Milan after the unification of Italy. The damage caused by bombs in World War II created large empty areas later occupied by many modern buildings. The Historic Centre is always thronging with visitors, drawn by the world-famous churches, museums and galleries and also by the excellent shops.

SIGHTS AT A GLANCE

Streets, Squares and Historic Buildings
Casa degli Omenoni **6**
Casa Manzoni and Piazza Belgioioso **7**
Galleria Vittorio Emanuele II **2**
Palazzo Borromeo **14**
Palazzo Marino **4**
Palazzo Reale **10**

Piazza del Liberty and Corso Vittorio Emanuele II **8**
Piazza Mercanti **11**

Churches
Duomo pp46–9 **1**
San Fedele **5**
San Giorgio al Palazzo **15**
San Gottardo in Corte **9**

San Sepolcro **13**
Santa Maria presso San Satiro **16**

Galleries
Pinacoteca Ambrosiana pp56–9 **12**

Theatres
Teatro alla Scala pp52–3 **3**

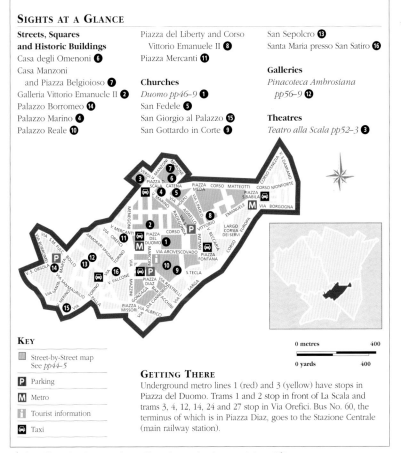

KEY

▪ Street-by-Street map See pp44–5

P Parking

M Metro

i Tourist information

🚕 Taxi

0 metres 400
0 yards 400

GETTING THERE
Underground metro lines 1 (red) and 3 (yellow) have stops in Piazza del Duomo. Trams 1 and 2 stop in front of La Scala and trams 3, 4, 12, 14, 24 and 27 stop in Via Orefici. Bus No. 60, the terminus of which is in Piazza Diaz, goes to the Stazione Centrale (main railway station).

◁ **The Galleria Vittorio Emanuele II, Milan's elegant "drawing room" since 1867**

Street-by-Street: Piazza del Duomo

PIAZZA DEL DUOMO, designed by Giuseppe Mengoni and opened in 1865 after protracted difficulties, is the ideal starting point for a visit to Milan's historic centre. The area is packed with visitors fascinated by the "great machine of the Duomo", as Alessandro Manzoni describes the cathedral in *The Betrothed*. There are numerous spots where the Milanese like to meet for an apéritif on Sunday morning. Young people prefer to go to Corso Vittorio Emanuele II, which has most of the cinemas as well many shops and department stores.

Sculpture, Casa degli Omenoni

San Fedele
This church, a typical example of Counter Reformation architecture, is popular with the old Milanese aristocracy ⑤

Casa degli Omenoni

★ **Teatro alla Scala**
This was the first monument in Milan to be rebuilt after the 1943 bombings ③

Palazzo Marino

Piazza Mercanti

Zucca in Galleria is a popular café, decorated with mosaics and décor dating from 1921.

★ **Galleria Vittorio Emanuele II**
The Galleria was one of the first iron and glass constructions in Italy ②

0 metres   100
0 yards   100

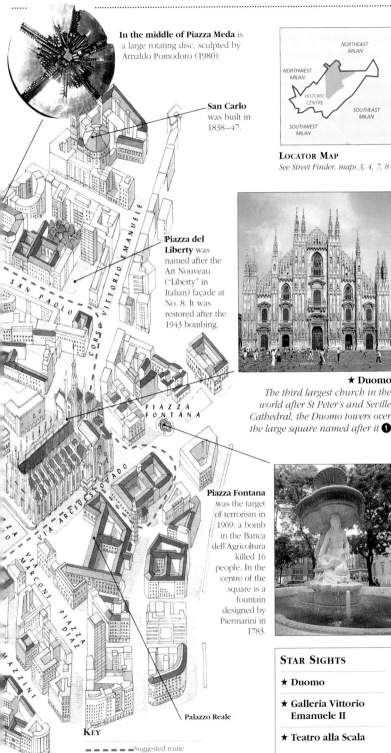

In the middle of Piazza Meda is a large rotating disc, sculpted by Arnaldo Pomodoro (1980).

San Carlo was built in 1838–47.

LOCATOR MAP
See Street Finder, maps 3, 4, 7, 8

Piazza del Liberty was named after the Art Nouveau ("Liberty" in Italian) façade at No. 8. It was restored after the 1943 bombing.

★ **Duomo**
The third largest church in the world after St Peter's and Seville Cathedral, the Duomo towers over the large square named after it ❶

PIAZZA FONTANA

Piazza Fontana was the target of terrorism in 1969: a bomb in the Banca dell'Agricoltura killed 16 people. In the centre of the square is a fountain designed by Piermarini in 1783.

Palazzo Reale

KEY

------ Suggested route

STAR SIGHTS

★ **Duomo**

★ **Galleria Vittorio Emanuele II**

★ **Teatro alla Scala**

Duomo ❶

Statue in the interior

THE CONSTRUCTION OF THE DUOMO began in 1386, with the city's bishop, Antonio da Saluzzo, as its patron. Duke Gian Galeazzo Visconti invited Lombard, German and French architects to supervise the works and insisted they use Candoglia marble, which was transported along the Navigli canals. The official seal AUF *(ad usum fabricae)*, stamped on the slabs, exempted them from customs duty. The cathedral was consecrated in 1418, yet remained unfinished until the 19th century, when Napoleon, who was crowned King of Italy here, had the façade completed.

La Madonnina
The 4.16-m (14-ft) gilded statue of the Madonna was sculpted by Giuseppe Bini in 1774.

Flying buttresses

★ **Stained Glass Windows**
Most of the windows depict scenes from the Bible, and date from the 19th century. The oldest one – the fifth in the right-hand aisle – dates back to 1470–75 and depicts the life of Christ, while the newest one (the seventh) dates from 1988.

★ **Trivulzio Candelabrum**
This masterpiece of medieval goldsmithery was donated in 1562 by Gian Battista Trivulzio. On the pedestal there are fantastic monsters and figures representing arts, crafts and the virtues.

Crypt

THE BUILDING OF MILAN CATHEDRAL

1300	1400	1500	1600	1700	1800	1900
1386 The first stone of the Duomo is laid		**1567** Pellegrino Tibaldi ("il Pellegrini") redesigns the presbytery	**1656** Carlo Buzzi continues façade in Gothic style	**1774** The Madonnina is placed on the tallest spire		**1838–65** The Bertinis make the apse windows
	1418 Pope Martin V consecrates the high altar	**1500** Central spire inaugurated *Martin V*	**1617** Francesco Maria Richini begins work on the façade		**1813** Façade completed with Gothic spires	**1981–4** Presbytery piers restored

★ Roof Terraces
The view of the city from the roof terraces is simply unforgettable. You can also have a close-up look at the central spire. The roof bristles with spires, the oldest of which dates from 1404.

VISITORS' CHECKLIST

Piazza del Duomo. **Map** 7 C1.
02-86 46 34 56. 1, 3 Duomo.
50, 60. 1, 2, 3, 12, 14, 15, 24, 27. 6:45am–7pm. 7, 7:30, 8, 9, 10, 11am, 12:45, 5:30, 6:15pm daily (5, 6pm sun, hols).
Baptistery/Digs 9:45am–12:45pm, 2–5:45pm. **Treasury** 9am–noon, 2:30–6pm. **Roof Terraces** 9am–4:30pm (summer 5:30pm).

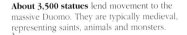

About 3,500 statues lend movement to the massive Duomo. They are typically medieval, representing saints, animals and monsters.

A plaque confirms that the Duomo is dedicated to Maria Nascente.

The Interior
The five aisles in the nave are separated by 52 piers, whose capitals are decorated with statues.

Main entrance

STAR FEATURES

★ **Stained Glass Windows**

★ **Trivulzio Candelabrum**

★ **Roof Terraces**

The Doors
The five doors were made from 1840 to 1965. Right, The Flagellation *by Ludovico Pogliaghi, a bronze relief in the central door.*

Exploring the Duomo

Statue of Sant'Ambrogio

So THAT THE Duomo could be built, a great Jubilee was proclaimed in 1390 in order to urge the Milanese to contribute money and manual labour to carry out the work. The initial plan was to build it in fired bricks, as the excavations in the northern sacristy have revealed, but in 1387 Duke Gian Galeazzo Visconti, who wanted the cathedral to be seen as a great symbol of his power, demanded that marble should be used instead and that the architectural style should be International Gothic. Building continued over five centuries, resulting in the obvious mixture of styles that characterizes the cathedral.

The presbytery, with the small ciborium dome in the foreground

THE FAÇADE

UP TO THE FIRST level of windows the façade is Baroque. It was completed in the 19th century with Neo-Gothic ogival windows and spires, revealing the difficulties entailed in building the Duomo.

THE INTERIOR

TALL CROSS VAULTS cover the interior and the five aisles in the nave are separated by 52 piers (for the 52 weeks of the year). The capitals on the piers are decorated with statues of saints. Behind the façade, embedded in the floor, is a meridian ①, installed in 1786 by the Brera astronomers. It marked astronomical noon, thanks to a ray of sunlight that enters from the first bay of the south aisle on the right-hand side.

This is a good starting point for a visit to the Duomo. To the right is the sarcophagus of Archbishop Ariberto d'Intimiano ②, bearing a copy of the crucifix that he donated to the San Dionigi monastery (the original is in the Museo del Duomo). Next to this, on the left, is a plaque with the date of the foundation of the cathedral. The corresponding stained glass window, executed in the old mosaic technique, relates the *Life of St John the Evangelist* (1473–7). The stained glass windows in the next three bays, showing episodes from the Old Testament, date from the 16th

Stained glass window, detail

century. In the fifth bay there is a stained glass window executed between 1470 and 1475 that illustrates the *Life of Christ* ③. Compare this with the other window in the seventh bay – it was made in 1988 and is dedicated to Cardinals Schuster and Ferrari ④. The presbytery ⑤ is constructed in the style imposed in 1567 by Pellegrini who, at the request of San Carlo Borromeo, made this part of the Duomo the Lombard model of a typical Counter Reformation church. In the middle, under the ciborium behind the altar, is the Tabernacle ⑥, donated by Pius IV to his nephew San Carlo (St Charles). In front of them are two 16th-century gilded copper pulpits ⑦ with

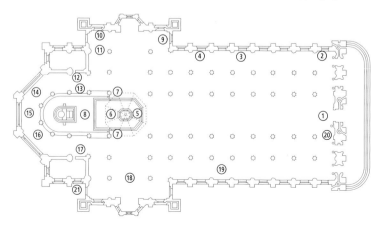

THE HOLY NAIL OF THE CROSS

Tabernacle of the Nail of the Cross

In the vault above the choir, a red light marks the location of the niche where a nail from Christ's Cross has been kept since 1461. The nail, which was once kept in the early medieval Santa Maria Maggiore, is in the shape of a horseshoe and was found by St Helena and later given to her son, Emperor Constantine. It was later donated to Sant'Ambrogio and carried by San Carlo in procession during the 1576 plague. It is shown to the public every 14 September, when the Bishop of Milan is raised up to the level of the niche which holds the nail in a kind of decorated balcony, drawn by invisible pulleys.

episodes from the Old and New Testaments, surmounted by the organs painted by Giovanni Ambrogio Figino, Camillo Procaccini and Giuseppe Meda.

Behind the altar is an extraordinary wooden choir with the *Life of Sant'Ambrogio* ⑧, carved in 1572–1620. In the right-hand transept is the funerary monument of Gian Giacomo Medici ⑨, the brother of Pope Pius IV, which was once attributed to Michelangelo but is in fact the work of Leone Leoni (1560–63). Past the chapel dedicated to St John the Good, Bishop of Milan in the 7th century, above the side entrance is the splendid stained glass window of St Catherine of Alexandria ⑩, designed by the Arcimboldi brothers in 1556. A little further on is the strange statue of the flayed St Bartholomew ⑪, signed and dated 1562 by Marco d'Agrate.

At the beginning of the ambulatory there is a *Deposition* on the southern door of the sacristy ⑫ (1393), dedicated to the "Mysteries of the Virgin Mary". Steps ⑬ lead to the crypt (1606), where San Carlo Borromeo is buried, the Duomo Treasury, with its exceptional collection of church vestments and objects, and the Coro Jemale, a small 16th-century room decorated with fine stuccowork (don't miss the relief sculpture cycle of the *Life of the Virgin Mary*, a 17th-century masterpiece). The apse is illuminated by the

Chalice in the Duomo Treasury

three huge 19th-century stained glass windows by the Bertini brothers with episodes from the Old ⑯ and New ⑭ Testaments and the Apocalypse ⑮. The ambulatory ends at the northern portal of the sacristy ⑰, with *Christ the Lord and Judge* (1389). The left-hand transept is dominated by the 5-m (16-ft) bronze Trivulzio Candelabrum ⑱, a 12th-century masterpiece by the goldsmith Nicola da Verdun. The candelabrum carries scenes from the Old Testament and the Three Wise Men riding towards the enthroned Virgin. Going down the north aisle, you will see the Chapel of the Crucifix ⑲ carried by San Carlo in procession during the 1576 plague. Behind this is a window with a depiction of the *Discovery of the True Cross by St Helena* (1570–77). To the left of the entrance, steps lead down to the

remains of an Early Christian apse of Santa Tecla and an octagonal baptistery ⑳ where, according to tradition, Sant'Ambrogio (St Ambrose) baptized St Augustine in AD 387. From San Carlo's feast day to Epiphany, the *Quadroni di San Carlo* go on display in the nave. These paintings, the work of leading 17th-century Lombard artists, depict the story of the life and miracles of San Carlo.

ROOF TERRACES

ON THE WAY TO the lift ㉑ which goes up to the roof, you should go to the apse to admire the central stained glass window, designed by Filippino degli Organi in 1402. From the roof there is a magnificent view of the city and the mountains to the north, as well as the Duomo spires and statues and even the buttresses below.

MUSEO DEL DUOMO

THE CATHEDRAL MUSEUM, founded in 1953, is at No. 15 Via Arcivescovado. It houses paintings, sculptures, religious objects and stained glass windows from the Duomo. Among the best works on display are the 15th-century *St Paul the Hermit*, Tintoretto's *Christ among the Doctors* (1530) and a wooden model of the Duomo, begun in 1519. Rooms 18 and 19 document the difficult restoration of the four central piers (1981–4).

One of the exhibition rooms in the Museo del Duomo

Palazzo Marino, the Town Hall since 1860, and the 1872 statue of Leonardo da Vinci on the right

Galleria Vittorio Emanuele II ❷

Piazza della Scala, Piazza del Duomo.
Map 7 C1. **M** *1, 3 Duomo.*

THE GALLERIA is an elegant arcade lined with cafés, shops, bookshops and a famous restaurant, Savini *(see p166)*. Work began in 1865, overseen by the architect Giuseppe Mengoni, and it was opened two years later by the king, Vittorio Emanuele II, after whom it was named. The gallery was designed to connect Piazza del Duomo and Piazza della Scala, and formed part of an ambitious urban renewal project. On the floor in the central octagonal area, directly under the 47-m (154-ft) high glass dome, is the heraldic symbol of the Savoy family, a white cross on a red ground. Around it are the arms of four major Italian cities: the bull of Turin, the wolf of Rome, the lily of Florence and the red cross on a white ground (Milan). On

the vault are mosaics of Asia, Africa, Europe and America.

Teatro alla Scala ❸

See pp52–3.

Palazzo Marino ❹

Piazza della Scala. **Map** 3 C5.
M *1, 3 Duomo.* ⬛ *to the public.*

THIS PALAZZO WAS designed in 1558 by Galeazzo Alessi for the banker Tommaso Marino, but remained un-finished until 1892, when Luca Beltrami completed the façade. From Via Marino on the right you can see the richly decorated, porticoed courtyard of honour.

According to tradition the palazzo, home of Milan Town Hall since 1860, was the birthplace of Marianna de Leyva, the famous nun of Monza described by Alessandro Manzoni in *The Betrothed* as the "Signora".

San Fedele ❺

Piazza San Fedele. **Map** 3 C5. 🛈 *02-72 00 80 27.* **M** *1, 3 Duomo.* 🚋 *1, 2.* 🚌 *61.* ⏱ *8:30am–2:30pm, 4–7pm Mon–Fri;* ✝ *8, 11am, 12:45, 5:30pm Mon–Fri; 8, 11am, 6.30pm pre-hols; 9:30, 11am, 6:30, 8:30pm hols.*

THIS CHURCH is the Milanese seat of the Jesuit Order, commissioned by San Carlo Borromeo from Pellegrino Tibaldi in 1569. The work was continued by Martino Bassi and the dome, crypt and choir were designed by Francesco Maria Richini (1633–52). With its austere architecture and nave without aisles, this is a typical model of a Counter Reformation church. The interior has three interesting paintings. Near the first altar on the right is *St Ignatius's Vision* by Giovan Battista Crespi, known as "il Cerano" (c.1622). A *Transfiguration* by Bernardino Campi (1565) is in the atrium after the second altar on the left; Ciampi also painted the *Blessed Virgin and Child*, by the second altar (left). These last two works came from Santa Maria della Scala, which was demolished to make room for La Scala opera house *(see pp52–3)*.

The wooden furniture is also worth a closer look: the confessionals (1596) have scenes from the life of Christ carved by Giovanni Taurini, and the cupboards in Richini's sacristy (1624–28) are by Daniele Ferrari (1639). A statue of the writer Alessandro Manzoni, whose death cert-ificate is kept in San Fedele, stands in the square.

Galleria Vittorio Emanuele II, inaugurated in 1867

Casa degli Omenoni ❻

Via Omenoni 3. **Map** 3 C5. Ⓜ *1, 3 Duomo.* ⬤ *to the public.*

EIGHT TELAMONES, which the Milanese call *omenoni*, are the most striking feature of this house-cum-studio, built by the sculptor Leone Leoni in 1565. The artist collected many works of art, including paintings by Titian and Correggio and Leonardo da Vinci's famous *Codex Atlanticus (see p59).*

A reference to Leoni can be seen in the relief under the cornice, in which Calumny is torn up by lions *(leoni).*

The entrance to the Casa degli Omenoni

Casa Manzoni and Piazza Belgioioso ❼

Via Morone 1. **Map** 4 D5. 🄲 *02-86 46 04 03.* Ⓜ *3 Montenapoleone.* 🚋 *1, 2.* 🚌 *61.* ⬤ *9am–noon, 2–4pm Tue–Fri.* ⬤ *Sat, Mon, hols.*

THIS IS THE HOUSE where Italian author Alessandro Manzoni lived from 1814 until his death in 1873 after a fall

Part of the façade of Palazzo Liberty, at No. 8 Piazza del Liberty

on the steps of San Fedele. The perfectly preserved interior includes Manzoni's studio on the ground floor, where he received Garibaldi in 1862 and Verdi in 1868. Next to this is the room where poet and author Tommaso Grossi had his notary office, while on the first floor is Manzoni's bed-room. The house is now the seat of the National Centre for Manzoni Studies, which was founded in 1937. It includes a library with works by Manzoni and critical studies of his oeuvre, as well as the Lombard Historical Society Library with over 40,000 volumes. The brick façade overlooks Piazza Belgioioso, named after the palazzo at No. 2 (closed to the public). This monu-mental palazzo was designed by Piermarini in 1777–81 for Prince Alberico XII di Bel-gioioso d'Este. The façade bears heraldic emblems. In the interior a fresco by Martin Knoller represents the apotheosis of Prince Alberico.

The *Omm de preja* statue

Piazza del Liberty and Corso Vittorio Emanuele II ❽

Map 8 D1. Ⓜ *1, 3 Duomo, 1 San Babila.* 🚋 *23.* 🚌 *61, 65, 73.*

ONCE PAST THE ARCH at the end of Piazza Belgioioso, go through Piazza Meda (1926) and past Corso Matteotti, which was built in 1934 to link Piazza della Scala with Piazza San Babila, and then go down Via San Paolo, which will take you to Piazza del Liberty. This small square owes its name to the Art Nou-veau (Liberty) façade on No. 8, restored by Giovanni and Lorenzo Muzio in 1963 with architectural elements from the Trianon café-concert, a building dating from 1905 which was moved from Corso Vittorio Emanuele II.

Go along Via San Paolo to reach Corso Vittorio Emanuele II. This is Milan's main commercial street, and was once called "Corsia dei Servi" (Servants' Lane). It follows the course of an ancient Roman street and in 1628 was the scene of bread riots, described by Manzoni in *The Betrothed*. Near San Carlo al Corso, at No. 13 is the *Omm de preja* (local dialect for *uomo di pietra* or "man of stone") statue, a copy of an ancient Roman work. It is also called "Sciur Carera", a misspelling of the first word of a Latin inscription under the statue *(carere debet omni vitio qui in alterum dicere paratus est).*

Casa Manzoni, now home to the National Centre for Manzoni Studies

Teatro alla Scala ❸

Poster for Turandot

O NE OF THE world's most famous opera houses was built by Giuseppe Piermarini in 1776–8. It owes its name to the fact that it stands on the site of Santa Maria della Scala, a church built in 1381 for Regina della Scala, the wife of Bernabò Visconti. On 3 August 1778 the theatre opened with a performance of an opera by Antonio Salieri. La Scala was badly bombed in 1943, and rebuilt three years later. The traditional gala opening night of the opera season always takes place on 7 December, the feast day of Sant'Ambrogio, Milan's patron saint.

Teatro alla Scala in 1852, **by Angelo Inganni**

The chandelier, made of Bohemian crystal (1923), holds 383 lightbulbs.

The boxes were like small living rooms where romantic trysts and parlour games were arranged.

★ **Museo del Teatro**
The theatre museum was founded in 1913 and boasts a fine collection of sculpture, original scores, paintings and ceramics related to the history of La Scala as well as of theatre in general.

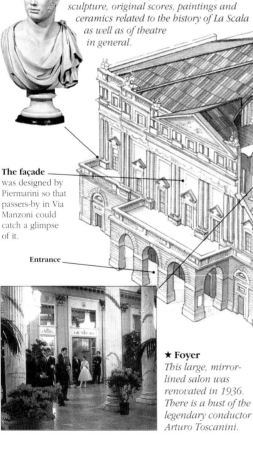

The façade was designed by Piermarini so that passers-by in Via Manzoni could catch a glimpse of it.

Entrance

★ **Foyer**
This large, mirror-lined salon was renovated in 1936. There is a bust of the legendary conductor Arturo Toscanini.

STAR FEATURES
★ **Auditorium**
★ **Foyer**
★ **Museo del Teatro**

THE BALLET SCHOOL

La Scala's Ballet School was founded in 1813.
Originally there were 48 students who studied
dance, mime or specialist disciplines. At the end
of an eight-year course, the best students were
awarded merits of distinction and became part of
the theatre's *corps de ballet* with an annual stipend
of 3,000 lire. This rigorously disciplined

Students at the school has produced such artists as Carla
Ballet School Fracci and Luciana Savignano.

A tank filled with water,
placed over the wooden
vault, was ready for use in
case of fire.

**Dressing
rooms**

**The orchestra
pit** was introduced in
1907. Before then the
orchestra played behind
a balustrade on the same
level as the stalls.

Stage
*This is one of the largest stages
in Italy, measuring 1,200 sq m
(13,000 sq ft).*

★ Auditorium
*Made of wood covered with red velvet
and decorated with gilded stuccowork,
the interior boasts marvellous acoustics
and has a seating capacity of 2,015.*

The entrance to the church of San Gottardo in Corte

San Gottardo in Corte ⑨

Via Pecorari 2. **Map** 8 D1. 02-86 46 45 00. **M** 1, 3 Duomo. 12, 23, 27. 54, 60, 65. 8am– noon, 2–5:45pm.

AZZONE VISCONTI, lord of Milan, ordered the construction of this church in 1336 as the ducal chapel in the Broletto Vecchio (Courthouse) courtyard. The interior was rebuilt in Neo-Classical style by Piermarini. On the left-hand wall is a *Crucifixion* by the school of Giotto. Azzone Visconti's funerary monument, executed by Giovanni di Balduccio, is in the apse: the reclining statue of Visconti is flanked by the figures of two women. The octagonal brick bell tower with small stone arches and columns is a masterpiece by Francesco Pecorari (c.1335).

Palazzo Reale ⑩

Piazza del Duomo. **Map** 7 C1. 02-87 54 01, 02-87 56 72. **M** 1, 3 Duomo. 15, 23, 27. 54, 60, 65. **CIMAC** 02-655 14 45. 10am–1pm, 2:30–6:30pm Mon, Wed–Fri; 10am–6:30pm Sat, Sun. Tue, 1 Jan, Easter, 1 May, 15 Aug, 25 Dec.

THE BUILDING was the seat of the commune administration in the 11th century and was drastically rebuilt by Azzone Visconti in 1330–36. At the height of its importance it was the headquarters of the lords of Milan. Galeazzo Maria Sforza's decision to move the ducal palace marked the beginning of the slow decline of the Palazzo Reale. In 1598 it housed the first permanent theatre in Milan. Made of wood, it was rebuilt in 1737. This is where Mozart played a recital

Unique Forms of Continuity in Space (1913) by Umberto Boccioni

as a child, before the terrible 1776 fire that destroyed it.

The present Neo-Classical appearance of Palazzo Reale dates from 1778, when Giuseppe Piermarini made it into a residence for Archduke Ferdinand of Austria. The interior once contained furniture by the famous cabinet-maker Maggiolini and was frescoed by Martin Knoller

and Giuliano Traballesi, becoming a model for aristocratic Milanese homes.

In 1920 Vittorio Emanuele III granted the place temporarily to the city of Milan, and in 1965 the city purchased it to use as offices and museums and for temporary shows. Since 1983 the **Civico Museo d'Arte Contemporanea (CIMAC)** has been housed on the second floor of Palazzo Reale. There are two sections. The first begins with the famous Futurist sculpture *Unique Forms of Continuity in Space*, by Umberto Boccioni, and features 20th-century Italian art to the post-World War II period, including many works by Balla, Funi, Sironi, Modigliani, Carrà, Morandi, Arturo Martini and Fontana. Metaphysical painting is represented mainly by De Chirico. A second section features Italian art from the 1950s to the 1980s, and includes works by Alberto Burri, Piero Manzoni, Vedova and Tancredi, and also includes the Jucker Collection, which was purchased in 1992.

Piazza Mercanti ⑪

Map 7 C1. **M** 1 Cairoli–Cordusio.

THIS CORNER of medieval Milan was the seat of public and civic activities and also housed the prison. Palazzo della Ragione was built in 1233 by the chief magistrate (and virtual ruler) Oldrado da Tresseno, who is portrayed in a relief by Antelami on the side facing the square. This courthouse is also known as "Broletto Nuovo" to distinguish it from the older Broletto Vecchio near Palazzo Reale. Markets were held under the porticoes, while the Salone dei Giudici on the first floor was used as the law court. In 1773 another storey was added to house the notarial archive.

Palazzo Reale, now used as a venue for temporary exhibitions

The well in Piazza Mercanti and, on the left, Palazzo delle Scuole Palatine

On one side of the square is the Loggia degli Osii, built by Matteo Visconti in 1316. The façade is decorated with the arms of the districts of Milan and statues of the Virgin Mary and saints (1330). Next is the Palazzo delle Scuole Palatine (1645), the façade of which bears statues of St Augustine and the Latin poet Ausonius. The Palazzo dei Panigarola (to the right), which was rebuilt in the 15th century, was used to register public documents.

In the centre of the square is a 16th-century well. In Via Mercanti is the Palazzo dei Giureconsulti, dominated by the Torre del Comune, built by Napo Torriani in 1272. At the foot of this tower is a statue of Sant'Ambrogio.

Pinacoteca Ambrosiana ⓬

See pp56–9.

San Sepolcro ⓭

Piazza San Sepolcro. **Map** 7 B1.
Ⓜ 1, 3 Duomo. 🚋 2, 3, 12, 14, 19, 24, 27. 🛅 5pm pre-hols; noon (winter), 5pm hols. Ⓧ

SAN SEPOLCRO WAS founded in 1030 in the area of the ancient Roman Forum and rebuilt in 1100 at the time of the second Crusade, in which many Milanese took part. The Neo-Romanesque façade was built in 1897, while the interior is basically Baroque. There are two terracotta groups by Agostino De Fondutis (16th century) depicting *Christ Washing His Disciples' Feet* and *The Flagellation of Christ with Caiaphas and St Peter.* The only remaining part of the 1030 church is the Romanesque crypt, with a sculpture group of the *Deposition* by the De Fondutis school in the apse.

Palazzo Borromeo ⓮

Piazza Borromeo 7. **Map** 4 D4.
Ⓜ 1 Cordusio. 🚋 2, 3, 12, 14, 19, 24, 27. 🛅 50, 54.
🕐 courtyard only.

THIS PRESTIGIOUS early 15th-century residence was badly damaged by the 1943 bombings and the only remaining original architectural element is the ogival portal, with leaf decoration and the coat of arms of the Borromeo family. The partly rebuilt second court-

The Borromeo family coat of arms with the motto *Humilitas*

yard has porticoes on three sides and on the fourth, between the brick windows, is the original decoration with the family motto *Humilitas.* This courtyard leads to the 15th-century Sala dei Giochi, which is decorated with frescoes of the games played by the aristocracy of the time, including the *Game of Tarot* by a painter known as the Master of the Borromeo Games. The red background is the result of a chemical reaction which changed the original blue of the sky.

San Giorgio al Palazzo ⓯

Piazza San Giorgio 2. **Map** 7 B1.
🕐 02-86 08 31. 🚋 2, 3, 14, 20.
🕐 8am–7pm. 🛅 6pm pre-hols; 11am, 6pm hols; 8am, 6pm Mon–Fri.

FOUNDED IN 750, this church was named after an ancient Roman *palatium* which stood here. It was radically changed in 1623 and 1800–21 by the architects Richini and Cagnola respectively, and little remains of the original or Romanesque (1129) structures. The third chapel in the right-hand aisle contains paintings by Bernardino Luini (1516) with scenes from the Passion. On the vault there is a fresco of the Crucifixion, painted with more subtle colours.

Santa Maria presso San Satiro ⓰

Via Torino 9. **Map** 7 B1.
🕐 02-87 46 83. Ⓜ 1, 3 Duomo.
🚋 2, 3, 12, 14, 15, 24. 🛅 50, 54.
🕐 8.30–11.30am, 3.30–5.30pm.
🛅 6pm pre-hols; 11am, 6pm hols; 7:45am, 6pm Mon–Fri.

THE ORIGINAL NUCLEUS of this church, founded by archbishop Ansperto da Biassono, dates from 876. The only remnant is the Sacello della Pietà (chapel of pity), which was altered by Bramante in the 15th century, and the Lombard Romanesque bell tower. In 1478 Bramante was asked to rebuild the church to salvage a 13th-century fresco on the façade, which was said to have miraculous powers. Bramante set it on the high altar, solving the problem of lack of space by creating a sort of *trompe l'oeil* apse of only 97 cm (38 in) with stuccowork and frescoes. The transept leads to the Chapel of San Satiro with a terracotta *Pietà* (c.1482). Don't miss the octagonal baptismal font decorated by De Fondutis, in the right-hand aisle.

Pinacoteca Ambrosiana ⓬

THE AMBROSIANA ART GALLERY was founded in 1618 by
Cardinal Federico Borromeo, the cousin of San
Carlo and his successor in charge of the archdiocese
of Milan. A true art connoisseur, Borromeo planned
the gallery as part of a vast cultural project which
included the Ambrosiana Library, opened in 1609, and
the Accademia del Disegno (1620) for the training of
young Counter Reformation artists. The gallery, founded to provide inspiration for emerging artists, held
172 paintings – some of which already belonged to
Borromeo, while others were purchased later after
painstaking research by the cardinal. The collection
was then enlarged thanks to private donations.

★ **Portrait of a Musician**
*This is the only Milanese
wood panel painting by
Leonardo da Vinci. The
subject is Franchino
Gaffurio, the
Sforza court
composer.*

Adoration of the Magi
*Cardinal Borromeo considered this painting by
Titian (purchased in 1558) a treasure trove for
painters "for the multitude of things therein".*

STAR EXHIBITS

★ **Portrait of a Musician**

★ **Cartoon for the
School of Athens**

★ **Basket of Fruit**

★ **Madonna del
Padiglione**

The Library is on
the ground floor.

★ **Madonna
del Padiglione**
*The recent
restoration of this
work by Botticelli
has revealed its
masterful and
elegant brushwork.*

GALLERY GUIDE

The most famous works are held in the Borromeo Collection, which was subsequently enriched with important 15th–16th-century paintings and sculptures. The Galbiati wing contains 16th–20th-century paintings, a collection of objects, the Sinigaglia Collection of miniature portraits and scientific instruments belonging to the Museo Settala.

San Sepolcro was annexed to the gallery in 1928.

Centrepiece with Fishing Scene
This is part of the prestigious collection of Neo-Classical gilded bronze objects donated to the Ambrosiana by Edoardo De Pecis in 1827.

KEY

☐ Borromeo Collection and 15th–16th-century paintings

☐ Galbiati Wing

☐ De Pecis Collection & 19th century

☐ Sculpture

☐ Museo Settala

★ Basket of Fruit
Caravaggio painted this extraordinarily realistic work around 1594. The fruit alludes to the symbolism of the Passion of Christ.

★ Cartoon for the School of Athens
This was a preparation for the painting now in the Vatican. Raphael used the faces of contemporary artists – Leonardo, for instance, appears in the guise of Aristotle.

Exploring the Pinacoteca Ambrosiana

AFTER SEVEN YEARS of painstaking restoration work, the Pinacoteca was reopened in October 1997. It is housed in a palazzo originally designed by Fabio Mangone in 1611. It was enlarged in the 19th century and again in 1932, when San Sepolcro was added. The new rooms were inaugurated on the third centenary of the death of Federico Borromeo, when about 700 paintings were exhibited, arranged in rows or set on easels. Today the Pinacoteca, whose collections are even larger thanks to donations, has 24 rooms and is one of Milan's finest museums.

18th-century silver stoup

Portrait of a Young Man, a copy of Giorgione's work

THE BORROMEO COLLECTION, 15TH–16TH-CENTURY PAINTINGS

YOUR VISIT BEGINS in the atrium, which has plaster casts of Trajan's Column, narrating the emperor's victories against the Dacians; on the staircase there are other casts of the *Laocoön* and Michelangelo's *Pietà*. Rooms 1, 4, 5, 6 and 7 house the Borromeo Collection, which boasts many of the best-known works in the gallery. Room 1, which features Venetian and Leonardo-esque painting, opens with the *Holy Family with St Anne and the Young St John the Baptist* by Bernardino Luini (c.1520). Next to this is Titian's *Adoration of the Magi* (1559–60), which is

still in its original frame bearing the carved initials of Henry II of France and his wife, who commissioned the work. The main scene is at the far left, while animals and minor figures fill the right-hand half of this original composition. On the opposite wall is a series of portraits, including *Profile of a Lady* by Ambrogio De Predis, and those of *The Young St John the Baptist* and *Bene-dictory Christ* by Luini, ending with Titian's *Man in Armour.* Rooms 2 and 3 have works acquired after 1618. One is Leonardo da Vinci's *Portrait of a Musician* with its innovative three-quarter profile position and intense expression; it was probably painted in early 1485. Next to this masterpiece is Botticelli's *Madonna del Padiglione,* with its many symbols of the Virgin Mary, and *Sacred Conversation* by Bergognone (c.1485). Another unmissable work is *Adoration of the Child,* by the work-shop of Domenico Ghirlandaio. Room 3 features 15th–16th-

Adoration of the Child, Domenico Ghirlandaio's workshop

century Leonardo-esque and Lombard paintings, among which is Salaino's *St John the Baptist,* whose finger pointing upwards alludes to the coming of Christ. Next to this are three works by Bartolomeo Suardi, better known as "il Bramantino". In his *Madonna of the Towers* (which may have had an anti-heretic function), next to the Virgin are an un-recognizable St Ambrose and St Michael Archangel kneeling and offering a soul to the Christ Child. Room 4 has copies from Titian and Giorgione and the *Rest on the Flight into Egypt* by Jacopo Bassano (c.1547). In room 5 is a Raphael masterpiece, a study for *The School of Athens,* the only great Renaissance cartoon that has come down to us. It was purchased by Cardinal Borromeo in 1626. Raphael executed the cartoon in 1510 as a study for the marvellous fresco in the Vatican. The architectonic setting and figure of Heraclitus (portrayed with Michelangelo's face), which were added after the fresco was completed, are not seen in the cartoon.

One of the most famous works in the museum, *Basket of Fruit,* is in room 6. Cara-vaggio painted it in the late

Holy Family with St Anne and the Young St John the Baptist by Bernardino Luini

1500s on a used canvas. The withered leaves represent the vanity of beauty.

The large body of Flemish paintings in the Borromeo Collection is on display in room 7, where you can compare the works of Paul Bril and Jan Brueghel. Interesting works by the latter are *The Mouse with Roses* and *Allegories of Water and Fire*, which Napoleon removed and took back to France. They were later returned.

THE GALBIATI WING

THE SALA DELLA MEDUSA and the Sala delle Colonne feature Renaissance paintings and a collection of objects, the most curious of which are Lucrezia Borgia's blonde hair and Napoleon's gloves.

A short passageway leads to the Spiriti Magni courtyard, decorated with statues of illustrious artists. The three rooms that follow feature 16th-century Italian and Venetian paintings, including an *Annunciation* by Bedoli (room 10), the *Portrait of Michel de l'Hospital* by Giovan Battista Moroni (1554) and Moretto's altarpiece, *Martyrdom of St Peter of Verona* (c.1535, room 12). This

Lucrezia Borgia's hair

latter room, known as the "exedra room", is decorated with a mosaic reproducing a miniature by Simone Martini from the volume of Virgil annotated by Petrarch in the Biblioteca Ambrosiana.

Italian and Flemish painting of the 16th and 17th centuries is on display in the Sala Nicolò da Bologna, on the upper floor, along with an unfinished *Penitent Magdalen* (1640–42) by Guido Reni. Seventeenth-century Lombard painting is on display in rooms 14, 15 and 16. Among the interesting works are *Still Life with Musical Instruments* by Evaristo Baschenis (room 14) and Morazzone's *Adoration of the Magi* (room 15), while the following room has

works by Francesco Cairo and Daniele Crespi, as well as *Magdalen* by Giulio Cesare Procaccini. Paintings by Magnasco, Magatti, Fra Galgario and Londonio represent 18th-century Italian art in room 17, but the jewels are two works by Tiepolo on the wall near the entrance.

DE PECIS COLLECTION AND 19TH CENTURY

ROOMS 18 AND 19 form the largest section of the Pinacoteca Ambrosiana, donated by Giovanni Edoardo De Pecis in 1827. This collection consists mostly of Italian and Flemish paintings and includes a series of small Neo-Classical bronze pieces and a *Self Portrait* by sculptor Antonio Canova, inspired by Roman portraiture. The exhibition in this wing ends with a selection of 19th- and early 20th-century canvases, including works by Andrea Appiani (*Portrait of Napoleon*), Mosè Bianchi and Francesco Hayez. Emilio Longoni is represented with his masterpiece *Locked out of School* (1888). Room 21 has 15th–17th-century German and Flemish art as well as the

Dantesque Stained Glass by Giuseppe Bertini, the Duomo master glassblower. It was executed in 1865 and depicts the author of the *Divine Comedy* surrounded by his characters and with the Virgin Mary above him.

Funerary monument by il Bambaia

SCULPTURE

ROOM 22 IS given over to sculpture. There are ancient Roman, Romanesque and Renaissance pieces as well as the highly elegant bas-reliefs by Agostino Busti – known as "il Bambaia" – sculpted for the tomb of Gaston de Foix around 1516.

MUSEO SETTALA

THE FINAL ROOM contains the rich collection purchased by the Ambrosiana gallery in 1751. It had been collected a century earlier by Manfredo Settala, an eccentric lover of scientific instruments, exotic animals, semi-precious stones, fossils, furniture, paintings and books – forming a sort of "museum of wonders".

BIBLIOTECA AMBROSIANA

Virgil illuminated by Simone Martini

This was one of the first libraries open to the public. It boasts over 750,000 printed volumes, 2,500 of which are incunabulae, and 35,000 manuscripts. Among them is the 5th-century *Ilias Picta*, a copy of Virgil's book annotated by Petrarch and illuminated by Simone Martini; a volume of Aristotle with annotations by Boccaccio; as well as Arab, Syrian, Greek and Latin texts. The Ambrosian Library also has over 1,000 pages of Leonardo da Vinci's *Codex Atlanticus*, purchased in 1637, removed by Napoleon in 1796 and only partly returned in 1815. The Library opened in 1609, already equipped with shelves and wooden footstools to protect readers from the cold floors.

NORTHWEST MILAN

IN THE 14TH CENTURY, when the construction of the Castello Sforzesco began, this district stood outside the city walls and was covered in woods. After the demolition of the Spanish walls around the Castello in the early 19th century, a new plan for the area was drawn up (but only partly realized). The aim was to transform the zone into a monumental quarter by building the Arco della Pace and a number of

The personification of a river, part of the Arco della Pace (Arch of Peace)

elegant buildings, which were to be used as offices, luxury residences, markets and theatres. By the end of the century, Via Dante, which leads to the Castello and is lined with fine buildings, was complete, as was the Corso Magenta residential district around Santa Maria delle Grazie. Two historic theatres can also be found in northwest Milan: Dal Verme (1872) and the Piccolo Teatro, which was founded in 1947.

GETTING THERE
The Fiera (Amendola, Lotto) and Castello (Cairoli) are served by metro lines 1 and 2. A number of tramlines pass Piazza Cordusio (No. 24 goes to Santa Maria delle Grazie or San Siro stadium).

KEY
- Street-by-Street map *See pp62–3*
- **P** Parking
- **M** Metro
- Taxi

0 metres 400
0 yards 400

SIGHTS AT A GLANCE

Parks and Gardens
Parco Sempione ②

Streets, Squares and Historic Buildings
Arco della Pace ⑤
Arena Civica ④
Castello Sforzesco pp64–7 ①
Certosa di Garegnano ⑩
Corso Magenta ⑫

Corso Sempione ⑦
Palazzo Litta ⑬
Piazza Affari ⑱
Piazza Cordusio ⑰
Via Brisa ⑯

Public Buildings
Acquario Civico ③
Fiera di Milano ⑧
Meazza (San Siro) Stadium ⑨

Churches
San Maurizio ⑮
Santa Maria delle Grazie pp71–3 ⑪

Museums
Civico Museo Archeologico ⑭
Triennale di Milano ⑥

◁ **The Salone degli Specchi in Palazzo Litta, a fine example of the 18th-century Lombard style**

Street-by-Street: Around the Castello Sforzesco

Visconti coat of arms

THE CASTELLO SFORZESCO and Sempione park today are the result of late 19th-century landscaping and restoration. Architect Luca Beltrami managed to thwart attempts to demolish the castle by converting it into a museum centre. He restored many of its original elements. In the early 1800s, the Arco della Pace and the Arena were built in the Parco Sempione, which was landscaped as an "English" garden by Emilio Alemagna. To mark the 1906 opening of the Galleria del Sempione, an International Exposition was held, featuring new products which later became household names in Italy.

Arena Civica
This amphitheatre, built in 1806, was used for boating displays, when it was filled with water from the Naviglio canals ❹

★ Parco Sempione
The 47-hectare (116-acre) English-style garden was designed by Emilio Alemagna in 1893. It contains a number of historic buildings and monuments ❷

Corso Sempione
Napoleon built this avenue leading to the Castello, modelling it on the Champs-Elysées in Paris ❼

PIAZZALE SEMPIONE

★ Arco della Pace
Modelled on the triumphal arch of Septimius Severus, the Arch of Peace was built to celebrate Napoleon's victories. However, it was inaugurated by Francis I in memory of the peace declared in 1815 ❺

STAR SIGHTS
★ Castello Sforzesco
★ Parco Sempione
★ Arco della Pace

VIALE BYRON

VIALE MALTA

VIALE BAR

VIALE ALEMAGNA

Acquario Civico
The Civic Aquarium was built in 1906 as an exhibition and educational centre. The building still has its original decoration of tiles and reliefs **3**

The Foro Buonaparte
is a semicircular boulevard lined with imposing late 19th-century buildings.

LOCATOR MAP
See Street Finder, maps 2–3

KEY

- - - - - - Suggested route

Via Dante, one of the city's most elegant streets, is a pedestrian precinct, and one of the few in Milan where you can sit and have a drink outdoors.

★ Castello Sforzesco
The castle, a symbol of Milan, was initially the palace of the Visconti, who built it in 1368 and named it Castello di Porta Giovia, and then the Sforza, who embellished it, turning it into a magnificent Renaissance residence **1**

Triennale di Milano
The Palazzo dell'Arte holds architecture and design shows. The Triennale show features decorative art, fashion and handicrafts **6**

| 0 metres | 400 |
| 0 yards | 400 |

Castello Sforzesco ❶

Umberto I, the Filarete Tower

Bᵁⁱᴸᵀ ⁱⁿ 1368 ʙʏ Galeazzo II Visconti as a fortress, the Sforza castle was enlarged in the 14th century by Gian Galeazzo and then by Filippo Maria, who transformed it into a splendid ducal palace. It was partly demolished in 1447 during the Ambrosian Republic. Francesco Sforza, who became lord of Milan in 1450, and his son Lodovico il Moro made the castle the home of one of the most magnificent courts in Renaissance Italy, graced by Bramante and Leonardo da Vinci. Under Spanish and Austrian domination, the Castello went into gradual decline, as it resumed its original military function. It was saved from demolition by the architect Luca Beltrami, who from 1893 to 1904 restored it and converted it into an important museum centre.

★ **Trivulzio Tapestries**
The 12 tapestries designed by Bramantino, depicting the months and signs of the zodiac, are masterpieces of Italian textile art.

The Torre Castellana was where Lodovico il Moro kept his treasury. It was "guarded" by a figure of Argus, in a fresco by Bramante at the Sala del Tesoro entrance.

The Cortile della Rocchetta was the last refuge in the event of a siege. Its three porticoes, formerly frescoed, were designed by Filarete, Ferrini and Bramante. The oldest wing (1456–66), opposite the entrance to the Corte Ducale, was the apartment of Lodovico and his wife before he became duke.

The holes in the castle walls, now used by pigeons, were made to anchor the scaffolding used for maintenance work.

Porta Vercellina
Only ruins remain of the great fortified structure that once protected the gate of Santo Spirito.

Cappella Ducale
The Ducal chapel still has the original frescoes painted in 1472 by Stefano de Fedeli and Bonifacio Bembo for Galeazzo Maria Sforza. On the vault is a Resurrection and on the wall to the left of the entrance is an Annunciation *with saints looking on.*

VISITORS' CHECKLIST

Piazza Castello. **Map** 3 B5.
☎ 02-62 08 39 40.
Ⓜ 1 Cairoli–Cadorna, 2 Lanza–Cadorna. 🚋 1, 3, 4, 12, 14, 27. 🚌 43, 57, 61, 70, 94.
Castello ◯ 9am–5:30pm daily.
Musei Civici ◯ 9am–5:30pm Tue–Sun. ● 1 Jan, Easter, 1 May, 25 Dec. ♿ some rooms only. 🏪🏠 📷

Ducal court

★ **Sala delle Asse**
This pergola, painted to look like an open air space, was the work of Leonardo (1498). The room owes its name to the planks (asse) once thought to cover the walls.

STAR FEATURES

★ **Rondanini Pietà**

★ **Sala delle Asse**

★ **Trivulzio Tapestries**

The Filarete Tower collapsed in 1521 when the gunpowder kept there exploded. It was rebuilt in 1905 by Luca Beltrami, who worked from Filarete's original design for the central castle tower.

★ **Rondanini Pietà**
Michelangelo's final work was altered at least three times and eventually left unfinished. Christ's arm on the left and a different angle for Mary's face, visible from the right, are part of the first version.

Exploring the Civic Museums in the Castello Sforzesco

SINCE 1896, THE CASTELLO SFORZESCO has housed the Civic Museums with one of the largest collections of art in Milan. The Corte Ducale houses the Raccolte di Arte Antica and the art and sculpture gallery as well as the furniture collection, while the Rocchetta holds decorative arts (ceramics, musical instruments and gold) and the Trivulzio Tapestries. The archaeological museum, the stamp collections and the Achille Bertarelli Collection, with about 700,000 prints and books, are also here. Major institutions are also housed here such as the Art Library, Trivulziana Library, Drawing Collection and School of Applied Industrial Art.

Relief of the Three Magi, School of Antelami (12th century)

CIVICHE RACCOLTE D'ARTE ANTICA

THE DISPLAYS making up the collections of Ancient Art are arranged in chronological order in rooms facing the Corte Ducale, where the 14th-century Pusterla dei Fabbri postern, rebuilt after being demolished in 1900, has 4th–6th-century sculpture. In room 1 ① is the Sarcophagus of Lambrate (late 4th century) and a bust of the Empress Theodora (6th century). Room

2 ② features Romanesque and Campionese sculpture, with a fine early 12th-century telamon. The relief of the Three Magi is by the school of Benedetto Antelami, the great 12th-century sculptor and architect. The main attraction, however, is the *Mausoleum of Bernabò Visconti*, sculpted by Bonino da Campione in 1363 for the lord of Milan. He is portrayed on horseback between Wisdom and Fortitude, while on the sarcophagus are *Scenes from the Passion*. Room 3 ③ has a window with a 14th-century Tuscan *Benedictory Christ*. Room 4 ④ is given over to Giovanni di Balduccio, with fragments

The *Mausoleum of Bernabò Visconti*

from the façade of Santa Maria di Brera (14th century). A passage leads to the Cappelletta ⑤, dominated by a 14th-century wooden Crucifix.

Room 6 ⑥ features reliefs from the Porta Romana (1171) narrating the *Return of the Milanese after Being Driven out of Town by Barbarossa* and *St Ambrose Expelling the Arians*. In room 7 ⑦ is the *Gonfalone* (Standard) of Milan designed by Giuseppe Meda in 1566, with scenes from Sant'Ambrogio's life. On the walls are 17th-century Flemish tapestries. The Sala delle Asse ⑧ is known for its fine fresco decoration on the vault, designed by Leonardo in 1498, which, despite its poor condition, is a good example of Sforza decoration. From here you go to the bridge over the moat ⑨ ⑩, with lunettes painted by Bernardino Luini with portraits of the Sforza. Next is the Sala dei Ducali ⑪, named after the arms of Galeazzo Maria Sforza, with Lodovico's set above. Here the early 15th-century sculpture is dominated by Agostino di Duccio's relief of *St Sigismund on a Journey* from the Malatesta Temple in Rimini. Left, is the

PLAN OF THE CASTELLO SFORZESCO

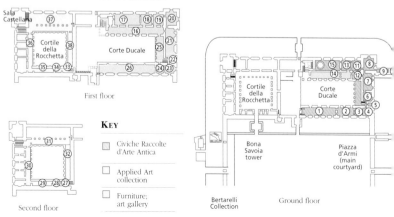

First floor

Second floor

KEY

☐ Civiche Raccolte d'Arte Antica

☐ Applied Art collection

☐ Furniture; art gallery

Bona Savoia tower

Bertarelli Collection

Cortile della Rocchetta

Corte Ducale

Piazza d'Armi (main courtyard)

Ground floor

The armour collection in the Sala Verde

door to the Cappella Ducale ⑫, with a braided Virgin, *Madonna del Coazzone*, a 15th-century work attributed to Pietro Antonio Solari. On the vault is a *Resurrection* painted around 1472 by Bonifacio Bembo and Stefano de' Fedeli. Late 15th-century sculpture is featured in the Sala delle Colombine ⑬, with the Visconti coat of arms and motto, *A Bon Droit*. One of the finest works here is Antonio Mantegazza's *Kneeling Apostles*. The 1463 portal displayed in the Sala Verde ⑭ is attributed to Michelozzo. This room also has some fine armour.

The last room, the Sala degli Scarlioni ⑮, boasts two world-famous sculptures: Gaston de Foix's funerary monument with marvellous reliefs, and Michelangelo's *Rondanini Pietà*. The former is by Agostino Busti, known as "il Bambaia", and commemorates the death on the battlefield of the young captain of the French troops in 1512. Behind a partition is Michelangelo's unfinished masterpiece, which he was working on until a few days before his death in 1564 (he had begun it in 1552–3): the standing Mother of Christ supporting the lifeless body of her Son. The exit route goes through the Cortile della Fontana, where the only original window left in the castle can be seen. It was used by Beltrami as a model in his restoration of the Castello.

FURNITURE COLLECTION AND PINACOTECA

FOUR ROOMS on the first floor house 15th–18th-century furniture. Of particular interest are the Torrechiara Choir (15th century) ⑯, the Passalacqua casket ⑱ (1613) and a chest of drawers by Giuseppe Maggiolini ⑲. Room 17 ⑰ has a reconstruction of an interior with frescoes from the Castello di Roccabianca with the *Stories of Griselda* (1460), inspired by a story by Boccaccio. The Belgioioso collection of 17th-century Flemish paintings is on display in room 18.

The art gallery begins at the Sala Nuziale ⑳, with 14th- and 15th-century Italian paintings, including Mantegna's *Madonna in Glory*

Madonna in Glory and Saints, by Andrea Mantegna

and *Saints* (1497), which you can compare with a *Madonna and Child*, an early work by Giovanni Bellini. Don't miss the two *Saints* by Carlo Crivelli (c.1479).

Fifteenth-century Lombard painting ㉑ is perhaps best represented by Vincenzo Foppa and by Bramantino's *Deposition* (1513). There are also many works by Leonardo-esque painters (Marco d'Oggiono, Cesare da Sesto), together with Correggio *(see pp32–3)* and Romanino.

A room of Mannerist art ㉒ leads to room 23 ㉓, with episodes from the history of the Milanese church by Procaccini, Morazzone, Ambrogio Figino and Cerano. Room 24 ㉔ features 17th-century Lombard art (Giovanni Battista Trotti, Bernardino Campi and Fede Galizia). The permanent collection of portraits (Room 25 ㉕) boasts masterpieces such as *Poet Laureate* (c.1475) attributed to Giovanni Bellini, *Portrait of Giulio Zandemaria* by Correggio (1521), *Young Man* by Lotto and canvases by Titian and Fra Galgario. Room 26 ㉖ has some fine 17th- and 18th-century works.

APPLIED ART COLLECTION

RETURN TO THE entrance for access to the first floor to see the collection of old musical instruments ㊱ ㊳, which includes a 1671 Stradivarius violin. Between these two rooms is the large Sala della Balla (ballroom) ㊲ with the splendid Trivulzio Tapestries of the months (1503–09) designed by Bramantino. On the 2nd floor (rooms 28–32) is a large collection of fine Italian and European glass, ceramics, majolica and porcelain, and collections of costumes, ivory works, gold jewellery and scientific instruments. Lastly, in the basement, is the Archaeological Museum: the *Ritrovare Milano* section featuring Roman objects, a Prehistoric section, and an Egyptian section with funerary cult objects including a tomb dating from c.640 BC.

Parco Sempione **2**

Piazza Castello–Piazza Sempione
(Eight entrances around perimeter).
Map 2 F3–4, 3 A3–4. **M** 1 Cadorna,
Cairoli, 2 Lanza, Cadorna. **R** Ferrovie
Nord, Cadorna. **T** 1, 3, 4, 12, 14,
27, 29, 30. **B** 43, 57, 61, 70, 94.
O 6:30am–8pm Nov–Feb; 6:30am–
9pm Mar–Apr; 6:30am–10pm May;
6:30am–11:30pm Jun–Sep;
6:30am–9pm Oct.

ALTHOUGH IT COVERS an area
of about 47 ha (116
acres), this park occupies
only a part of the old Visconti
ducal garden, enlarged by the
Sforza in the 15th century to
make a 300-ha (740-acre)
hunting reserve. The area was
partly abandoned during
Spanish rule, and in the early
1800s part of it was used to
create a parade ground
extending as far as the Arco
della Pace. The present-day
layout was the work of Emilio
Alemagna, who in 1890–93
designed it along the lines of
an English garden. In World
War II the park was actually
used to cultivate wheat but
after the reconstruction
period it returned to its former splendour as a favourite
haunt of the locals, especially
in spring and summer, when
it plays host to numerous
entertainment events.

Standing among the trees,
you can see the monument to
Napoleon III (designed by
Francesco Barzaghi), De
Chirico's Metaphysical construction *Mysterious Baths*,
the sulphur water fountain
near the Arena and the Torre
del Parco, a tower made of
steel tubes in 1932 after a
design by Gio Ponti.

Acquario Civico **3**

Via Gadio 2. **Map** 3 B4. **C** 02-86 46
20 51. **M** 2 Lanza. **T** 3, 4, 12, 14.
B 43, 57, 70. **O** 9:30am–5:30pm
Tue–Sun. **✔** by appt (02-89 01 07
95).

THE CIVIC AQUARIUM was built
by Sebastiano Locati for
the 1906 National Exposition,
and it is the only remaining
building. Its 36 tanks
house about 100
species (fish,
crustaceans,
molluscs and
echinoderms)
typical of the
Mediterranean
sea and Italian
freshwater
fauna. There are
also rare kinds
of tropical fish
on display.

**Sea creature decorating the
façade of the Aquarium**

The
aquarium museum is also
home to the Hydrobiological
Station, which has a library
specializing in the subject.
The aquarium building itself
(1906) is a fine example of
Art Nouveau architecture and
is decorated with Richard-
Ginori ceramic tiles and
statues of aquatic animals,
dominated by Oreste Labò's
statue of Neptune.

Arena Civica **4**

Via Legnano, Viale Elvezia. **Map** 3
A–B3. **M** 2 Lanza. **T** 3, 4, 12, 14.
B 43, 57, 70. **O** for exhibitions
and events only.

THIS IMPRESSIVE Neo-Classical
amphitheatre, designed in
1806 by Luigi Canonica, was
– together with the Arco della
Pace, Caselli Daziari and Foro
Buonaparte – part of the project to transform the Castello
Sforzesco area into a monumental civic centre.
Napoleon was
present at the
Arena inaugura-
tion, and it was
the venue for
various cultural
and sports
events, from
horse and mock-
Roman chariot races
to hot-air
balloon launch-
ings, mock
naval battles
and festivities. With a seating
capacity of 30,000, it has also
been a football stadium, but
San Siro *(see p70)* is now the
more important ground. The
Arena is now mainly a venue
for athletics (it has a 500-m,
1,640-ft track) and concerts.

View of the Parco Sempione: in the foreground, the artificial lake and in the background, the Arco della Pace

Arco della Pace ❺

Piazza Sempione. **Map** 2 F3. 🚋 *1, 29, 30.* 🚌 *61.* 🎫 *ascent to the top (Associazione Amici Arco della Pace).* 📞 *02-669 22 51.*

WORK ON MILAN'S MAJOR Neo-Classical monument was begun by Luigi Cagnola in 1807 to celebrate Napoleon's victories. It was originally called the Arch of Victories, but building was interrupted and not resumed until 1826 by Francis I of Austria, who had the subjects of the bas reliefs changed to commemorate the peace of 1815 instead. The Arch of Peace was inaugurated on 10 September 1838 on the occasion of Ferdinand I's coronation as ruler of the Lombardy–Veneto kingdom. The arch is dressed in Crevola marble and decorated with bas reliefs depicting episodes of the restoration after Napoleon's fall. On the upper level are personifications of the rivers in the Lombardy–Veneto kingdom: the Po, Ticino, Adda and Tagliamento.

From the top there is a magnificent view of the Castello and Corso Sempione and a close view of the huge bronze Chariot of Peace, by Abbondio Sangiorgio, surrounded by four Victories on horseback. The chariot originally faced France, but when Milan was ceded to Austria, it was turned to face the centre of the city.

Tree-lined Corso Sempione

Triennale di Milano ❻

Viale Alemagna 6. **Map** 3 A4. 📞 *02-72 43 41.* Ⓜ *1–2 Cadorna.* 🚌 *43, 61, 94.* 🚉 *Ferrovie Nord, Cadorna.* 🕐 *10am–8pm Tue–Sun.* ⬤ *1 Jan, Easter, 1 May, 15 Aug, 25 Dec.* 📷 🎫 *(depending on event).* ♿ 🛗 💻 ⛲

THE TRIENNALE Decorative Arts Show is housed in the Palazzo dell'Arte, on the southwestern side of the Parco Sempione. The Palazzo was built by Giovanni Muzio in 1932–3 as a permanent site for the International Exhibition of Decorative Arts. The Triennale show was founded in 1923 to foster the development of Italian arts and handicrafts against a background of their international counterparts. In addition, the Milan Triennale has always played a primary role in promoting architectural development.

Obelisk in front of the Palazzo dell'Arte

Art exhibitions, conferences and occasional lectures on the themes of art and architecture are held in the building. Alongside the exhibition space stands the Teatro dell'Arte, which was redesigned in 1960.

Corso Sempione ❼

Map 2 D1, E2, F3. 🚋 *1, 19, 29, 30, 33.* 🚌 *57, 61, 94.*

MODELLED ON the grand boulevards of Paris, Corso Sempione was the first stage of a road built by Napoleon to link the city with Lake Maggiore, Switzerland and France via the Simplon Pass. The first section, starting at the Arco della Pace, is pedestrianized. The Corso is lined with late 19th-century and early 20th-century houses and is now the main thoroughfare in a vast quarter. The initial stretch (towards the park) is considered an elegant area, with good shops, the headquarters of some Milanese banks and Italian State Radio and TV, RAI (at No. 27). Opposite, at No. 36, is a residence designed by Giuseppe Terragni and Pietro Lingeri in 1935, one of the first examples of Rationalist architecture in Milan.

The semicircular Via Canova and Via Melzi d'Eril cross the Corso, every angle of which offers a different view of the Arco della Pace.

The horses on the Arco della Pace, each cast in one piece

Fiera di Milano  ❽

Largo Domodossola 1. **Map** 1 C3.
📞 02-499 71. 📠 02-49 97 76 05.
Ⓜ 1 Amendola Fiera, Lotto. 🚊 19,
27. 🚌 48, 68, 78. Shuttle from
Linate airport. ATM circle line buses
(free). 🚪 for exhibitions only.

San Siro Stadium, now named after footballer Giuseppe Meazza

THE FIERA CAMPIONARIA, or
Trade Fair, was founded
in 1920 to stimulate the
domestic market in postwar
Italy. It was originally located
along the ramparts of Porta
Venezia and in 1923 was
moved to the parade ground
behind the Castello Sforzesco.
It was fitted out with permanent pavilions and buildings, many of which were
damaged or destroyed in
World War II. Some
original Art Nouveau
buildings have
survived at the
entrance in Via
Domodossola and the
Palazzo dello Sport
(sports arena, 1925).
The Fiera di Milano
has become a symbol
of Milanese industriousness
and spirit of enterprise.

Fiera di Milano logo

In 1985 the Trade Fair
became a bona fide Exhibition Centre, and now hosts 78
specialist international shows
attracting 2.5 million visitors
and 31,000 exhibitors every
year. It is now one of the
leading exhibition centres in
Europe in terms of turnover.
The old main entrance to the
Fiera faces Piazza Giulio
Cesare, which is dominated
by a Four Seasons fountain,
placed there in 1927.

Meazza (San Siro) Stadium ❾

Via Piccolomini 5. 📞 02-40 09 21 75
or 02-48 70 71 23. Ⓜ 1 Lotto (**Map**
1 A2); shuttle bus. 🚊 24.

NAMED AFTER Giuseppe
Meazza, the famous foot-
baller who played for the
local teams, Inter and Milan,
Italy's top stadium is
commonly known as
San Siro, after the
surrounding district.
It was built in 1926,
rebuilt in the 1950s
with a capacity of
85,000, and then
renovated in 1990,
when another ring of
tiers and a roof were added
(see Entertainment pp194–5).
In 1999 a gigantic sculpture of
a horse, Il Cavallo, designed
over 500 years earlier by
Leonardo da Vinci but never
built, was placed between
San Siro stadium and the
nearby San Siro racetrack.

Certosa di Garegnano ❿

Via Garegnano 28. 📞 02-38 00 63
01. 🚊 14. 🕐 7:30am–noon,
3–6pm. ✝ 6pm pre-hols;
7:30, 8:45, 10 & 11:30am,
4:30 & 5:30pm.

THE CHURCH that
forms the heart of
this important Car-
thusian monastery,
dedicated to Our
Lady of the Assump-
tion, was founded in
1349 by Archbishop
Giovanni Visconti.
Sadly, the Certosa is
well-known because
the main cloister was
ruined by the con-
struction of the A4
motorway. The

courtyard is of impressive
size, with the monks' houses,
each with a kitchen garden,
around the sides. The rules
imposed by the semi-closed
order required each monk
to live independently. The
complex was rebuilt in late
Renaissance style in 1562; the
façade, completed in 1608,
was decorated with obelisks
and statues, crowned by a
statue of Our Lady. A porticoed atrium with an exedra-
shaped vestibule provides a
harmonious introduction to
the complex.

Vincenzo Seregni designed
the interior in the 1500s. The
aisleless nave is crowned by a
barrel vault flanked by blind
arcades. The church is famous
for the frescoes by Daniele
Crespi, a leading 17th-century
Lombard artist. He reputedly
painted the entire cycle (The
Legend of the Foundation of
the Order) to thank the Car-
thusian monks for offering
refuge after he had been
charged with murder. The
cycle begins by the first arch
on the right, continues on
the wall behind the façade,
designed by Simone Peter-
zano, and is resumed on the
vault, where there are four
medallions. In the first bay on
the left Crespi included a self-
portrait of himself as a servant
blowing a horn and added
the date (1629) and his
signature in a scroll.

Simone Peterzano painted
the frescoes in the presbytery
and apse (1578), with scenes
from the life of Mary. The
chapel on the right has two
macabre 17th-century paintings informing novices of
the various forms of torture
they might encounter while
spreading Christianity. On
leaving, don't miss the 14th-
century cloister on the right,
the only surviving part of the
original monastery.

Façade of the Certosa di Garegnano (1608)

Santa Maria delle Grazie ⓫

Piazza Santa Maria delle Grazie.
Map 2 F5. 02-48 01 42 48. M
1, 2 Cadorna, 1 Conciliazione. 24.
7:30am–noon, 3–7pm.
6:30pm pre-hols; 8, 9:30, 10:30 &
11:30am, 6:30pm hols.

CONSTRUCTION OF this famous church was begun in 1463. Designed by Guiniforte Solari, it was completed in 1490. Two years later Lodovico il Moro asked Bramante to change the church into the family mausoleum: Solari's apse section was demolished and then replaced by a Renaissance apse. After il Moro lost power in 1500, the Dominicans continued to decorate the church, later assisted by the court of Inquisition, which had moved here in 1558. Restoration was undertaken only in the late 19th century. In 1943 a bomb destroyed the main cloister, but the apse and the room containing Leonardo's *Last Supper* were miraculously left intact, and restoration work has continued since then. On the exterior, Solari's wide brick façade is worthy of note. The doorway was designed by Bramante; it is preceded by a porch supported by Corinthian columns and the lunette has a painting by Leonardo da Vinci with the Madonna between Lodovico and his wife, Beatrice d'Este. The sides and poly-gonal apse are also of interest. As you enter the church you notice the difference between Solari's nave, which echoes Lombard Gothic architecture – entirely covered with frescoes and with ogival arches – and Bramante's design for the apse, which is larger, better lit and is almost bare of decoration. The two parts of the church reflect Bramante's impact on Milanese culture; he introduced the Renaissance style that dominated Tuscany and Umbria in the early 15th century. The all-pervasive painting decoration of the aisle walls is by Bernardino Butinone and Donato Montorfano (1482–6). The Della Torre chapel is the first one in the right-hand aisle: the altar has a 15th-century fresco and to the left is the tomb of Giacomo Della Torre, with bas-relief sculpture by the Cazzaniga brothers (1483). The fourth chapel, dedicated to Santa Corona, has frescoes by Gaudenzio Ferrari. In the next chapel is a *Crucifixion* by Giovanni Demio (1542).

The apse, decorated only with graffiti to maintain the purity of the architectural

The nave of Santa Maria delle Grazie

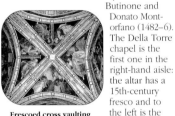

Frescoed cross vaulting in Santa Maria delle Grazie

volumes, is a perfect cube crowned by a hemisphere. It was built to house the tomb of Lodovico il Moro and Beatrice d'Este, sculpted by Cristoforo Solari, but the work never reached Santa Maria delle Grazie (it is now in the Charterhouse of Pavia). The decoration of the dome is rich in Marian symbols, while the Doctors of the Church appear in the roundels in the pendentives. The carved and inlaid wooden stalls of the choir are lovely; above them on the walls are figures of Dominican saints.

A door on the right leads to the small cloister known as Chiostrino delle Rane because of the frogs *(rane)* in the central basin. The cloister leads to the old sacristy, with its painted wardrobes, one of which conceals a secret underground passageway, used by Lodovico to come from the Castello on horseback. Back in the church, the chapels in the north aisle begin with the Madonna delle Grazie chapel, with Cerano's *Madonna Freeing Milan of the Plague* (1631) on the entrance archway. The altarpiece, *Madonna delle Grazie*, dates from the 15th century. The sixth chapel has a *Holy Family with St Catherine* by Paris Bordone, and the first chapel contains the cloak of St Catherine of Siena.

The façade of Santa Maria delle Grazie, designed by Guiniforte Solari

Leonardo da Vinci's *Last Supper*

Lodovico il Moro

T HIS MASTERPIECE was painted for Lodovico il Moro in the refectory of Santa Maria delle Grazie in 1495–7. Leonardo depicts the moment just after Christ has uttered the words, "One of you will betray me". The artist captures their amazement in facial expressions and body language in a remarkably realistic and vivid *Last Supper*. It is not a true fresco, but was painted in tempera, allowing Leonardo more time to achieve the subtle nuances typical of his work. The room was used as a stable in the Napoleonic era and was badly damaged by bombs in 1943. Fortunately, the work was saved because it was protected by sand bags.

Jesus Christ
The isolated, serene figure of Christ contrasts with the agitated Apostles. Half-closed lips show he has just spoken.

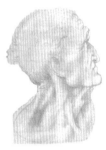

Judas
Unable to find a truly evil face for Judas, Leonardo drew inspiration from that of the prior in the convent, who kept on asking when the work would be finished.

The Last Supper is famous for the gesturing hands of the Apostles, which are so harmonious and expressive that critics have said they "speak".

The Apostle Andrew, with his arms upraised, expresses his horror at Christ's words.

The Crucifixion by Montorfano
The Dominicans asked Donato Montorfano to paint a fresco of the Crucifixion on the opposite wall to depict Christ's sacrifice. In this dense composition the despairing Magdalen hugs the cross while the soldiers on the right throw dice for Christ's robe. On either side of the work, under the cross, Leonardo added the portraits – now almost invisible – of Lodovico il Moro, his wife Beatrice and their children, signed and dated (1495).

THE RESTORATION

It was not the humidity but the method used by Leonardo, *tempera forte*, that caused the immediate deterioration of the *Last Supper*. As early as 1550 the art historian Vasari called it "a dazzling blotch" and regarded it as a lost work. There have been many attempts to restore the *Last Supper*, beginning in 1726, but in retouching the picture further damage was done. The seventh and most recent restoration ended in spring 1999: although it lacks the splendour of the original, it is at least authentic.

Material used for restoration

VISITORS' CHECKLIST

Piazza Santa Maria delle Grazie 2.
Map 2 F5. 02-498 75 88.
1, 2 Cadorna. 24.
9am– 7:15pm Tue–Fri, Sun; 9am–
11pm Sat. 1 Jan, Easter, 1
May, 15 Aug, 25 Dec.

The tablecloth, plates and bowls were probably copied from those in the convent to give the impression that Christ was at table with monks.

Sketches of the Apostles
Leonardo used to wander around Milan in search of faces to use for the Apostles. Of his many sketches, this one for St James is now in the Royal Library in Windsor.

CHRIST AND THE APOSTLES

1 Christ
2 Thomas
3 James the Greater
4 Philip
5 Matthew
6 Thaddaeus
7 Simon
8 John
9 Judas
10 Peter
11 Andrew
12 James the Lesser
13 Bartholomew

Corso Magenta 🔟

Map 3 A5. **Ⓜ** *1 Conciliazione, 1, 2 Cadorna.* 🚋 *18, 19, 24.*

THIS STREET is fascinating, with its elegant shops and historic buildings making it one of the loveliest and most elegant quarters in Milan. At No. 65, just past Santa Maria delle Grazie, is a building incorporating the remains of the Atellani residence, decorated by Luini, where Leonardo da Vinci stayed while working on the *Last Supper*. Piero Portaluppi carried out the work on No. 65 in 1919. In the garden at the back there are some vines, said to be the remains of the vineyard that Lodovico il Moro gave to the great artist. The next building (No. 61), Palazzo delle Stelline, originally a girls' orphanage, is now a convention centre. At the corner of Via Carducci, which was constructed over the original course of the Naviglio canal, stands the Bar Magenta *(see p178)*, a pleasant café with vintage décor. The medieval city gate, the Porta Vercellina, once stood at this junction.

Pastry shop sign in Corso Magenta

Palazzo Litta 🔟

Corso Magenta 24. **Map** 3 A5. **Ⓜ** *1, 2 Cadorna.* 🚋 *18, 19, 24, 27.* 🚌 *50, 54, 58.* ⏰ *during cultural events only.*

CONSIDERED one of the most beautiful examples of 18th-century Lombard architecture, this palazzo was first built in 1648 for Count Bartolomeo Arese by Francesco Maria Richini. At the end of the century the interior was embellished and in 1763 the pink façade was built at the request of the heirs, the Litta Visconti Arese. The façade,

The Sala Rossa in Palazzo Litta, with mementoes of Napoleon's visit here

by Bartolomeo Bolli, is late Baroque, the door flanked by large telamones. Since 1905 the building has housed the State Railway offices.

Inside is a number of sumptuous rooms looking onto a 17th-century courtyard. The broad staircase, designed by Carlo Giuseppe Merlo in 1740 and decorated with precious marble and the family coat of arms (a black and white check), has a double central flight. It leads up to the *piano nobile*, where one of the rooms is named the Sala Rossa (Red Room) after the colour of its wall-paper (a copy of the original). Set in the floor is a pearl, there to commemorate a tear said to have been shed during a meeting between the Duchess Litta and Napoleon.

The next room is the Salone degli Specchi, which seems to be enlarged to infinity by the large mirrors *(specchi)* on the walls. The vault decoration is by Martin Knoller. The Salotto della Duchessa is the only room in the palazzo which still has its original 18th-century wall-paper. The Teatro Litta stands to the left of the palazzo, the oldest theatre in the city.

Civico Museo Archeologico 🔟

Corso Magenta 15. **Map** 3 A5. 📞 *02-86 45 00 11.* **Ⓜ** *1, 2 Cadorna.* 🚋 *18, 19, 24, 27.* 🚌 *50, 54, 58.* ⏰ *9am–5:30pm Tue–Sun.* ♿ *(phone ahead).* 🚫

THE ARCHAEOLOGICAL MUSEUM is well worth a visit for the finds and to see the only remaining part of the city's Roman walls. At the entrance visitors are greeted by a huge stone from the Val Camonica *(see p151)* with Bronze Age engravings. Further on is a model of Milan in Roman times. The visit begins in a hall on the right, with clay objects, including a collection of oil lamps. This is followed by Roman sculpture. One of the most interesting pieces in the series of portraits dating from Caesar's era to late antiquity (1st–4th century AD), is the *Portrait of Maximin* (mid-3rd century AD). At

Roman sarcophagus of a lawyer, on display in the Civico Museo Archeologico

the end of this room is a huge fragment of a torso of Hercules from the Milanese thermae, dating from the first half of the 2nd century AD. Behind this are some 3rd-century AD floor mosaics found in Milanese houses.

By the window are two of the most important works in the museum: the Parabiago Patera and the Diatreta Cup. The Patera is a gilded silver plate with a relief of the triumph of the goddess Cybele, mother of the gods, on a chariot pulled by lions and surrounded by the Sun and Moon and sea and Zodiac divinities (mid-4th century AD). The marvellous Diatreta Cup, also dating from the 4th century AD, comes from Novara and consists of a single piece of coloured glass, with finely wrought, intricate decoration. Winding around the cup is the inscription *Bibe vivas multis annis* ("Drink and you will live many years"). To the left of the entrance are 6th-century Lombard finds. The entrance hall leads to a second courtyard, where you will see the Torre di Ansperto, a Roman tower from the ancient Maximinian walls. The basement contains a collection of Attic red- and black-figure vases and the museum display ends with a fine collection of Etruscan pieces.

Stela with portraits, Museo Archeologico

San Maurizio ⑮

Corso Magenta. **Map** 3 A5.
☏ 02-86 66 60 (Santa Maria alla Porta). Ⓜ 1, 2 Cadorna.
🚊 18, 19, 24, 27. 🚌 50, 54, 58. 🕐 4–6pm Mon–Fri, 10:30–11:30am Sun. ✝ 6pm Mon–Fri, 10:30 am (Greek–Albanian) Sun.

IN 1503 GIAN GIACOMO Dolcebuono began construction of this church, which was intended for the most powerful closed order of Benedictine nuns in Milan, with one hall for the public and another for the nuns. In the first hall, to the right of the altar, is the opening through which the nuns receive the Body of Christ. Most of the decoration was done by Bernardino Luini. He painted the frescoes in the first hall, including the *Life of St Catherine* (third chapel to the right) and those on the middle wall. The second chapel on the right was decorated by Callisto Piazza, the chapels to the left by pupils of Luini. On the altar is an *Adoration of the Magi* by Antonio Campi. The middle wall of the second hall, occupied by the choir, has frescoes by Foppa, Piazza, an *Annunciation* attributed to Bramantino and *Episodes of the Passion*. Concerts are held here in the winter.

The Roman ruins in Via Brisa

Via Brisa ⑯

Map 7 B1. Ⓜ 1, 2 Cadorna.
🚊 18, 19, 24, 27. 🚌 50, 54, 58.

EXCAVATIONS CARRIED OUT after the 1943 bombing of this street revealed Roman ruins which were probably part of Maximin's imperial palace: the foundation of a round hall surrounded by apsidal halls and preceded by a narthex. Note the columns that raised the pavement to allow warm air to pass into the palace.

Piazza Cordusio ⑰

Map 7 C1. Ⓜ 1 Cordusio. 🚊 18, 19, 24, 27. 🚌 50, 58, 60.

THIS OVAL-SHAPED piazza was named after the *Curtis Ducis*, the main seat of the Lombard duchy. The area, Milan's financial district, was laid out from 1889 to 1901. Buildings include Luca Beltrami's Assicurazioni Generali building, Casa Dario, and the main offices of Credito Italiano, designed by Luigi Broggi.

Piazza Affari ⑱

Map 7 B1. Ⓜ 1 Cordusio. 🚊 18, 19, 24, 27. 🚌 50, 58, 60.

THE HEART OF the financial district, this square was laid out in 1928–40 to house the city's markets (especially farm produce). The Borsa Valori, Italy's most important Stock Exchange, stands here. Founded in 1808, it is housed in a building designed by Paolo Mezzanotte in 1931. Ruins of a 1st-century BC Roman theatre were found in the basement area.

The Milan Stock Exchange in Piazza Affari, built in 1931

SOUTHWEST MILAN

ELIGIOUS COMPLEXES once covered this district, preventing further building until the early 19th century. The suppression of the monasteries in the late 18th century paved the way for the urbanization of the area between the medieval and Spanish walls, crossed by two large avenues, Corso Italia and Corso di Porta Ticinese. Beyond Porta Ticinese, which leads to the southern part of Milan, is Corso San Gottardo. The area is bordered by the inner ring

Vault mosaic, Sant'Ambrogio

road, which follows the course of the medieval walls, and the outer ring road, which replaced the Spanish walls. Further on is the Naviglio canals quarter, with the Naviglio Grande and the Pavese, the last vestiges of what was once a major network for communications and commerce. Barges used the Naviglio Grande to transport the Candoglia marble used to build the Duomo and, in the 1950s, the material for postwar reconstruction.

SIGHTS AT A GLANCE

Churches
San Bernardino alle Monache ❺

San Lorenzo alle Colonne pp80–81 ❶

San Paolo Converso ⓫

San Vittore al Corpo ❽

Sant'Alessandro ⓬

Sant'Ambrogio pp84–7 ❻

Sant'Eustorgio ❾

Santa Maria presso San Celso ❿

Streets, Squares and Historic Buildings
Largo Carrobbio and Via Torino ❸

Piazza della Vetra and medieval Porta Ticinese ❷

Via Circo ❹

Museums and Galleries
Museo Nazionale della Scienza e della Tecnica ❼

KEY

☐ Street-by-Street map
  See pp78–9

🅿 Parking

Ⓜ Metro

🚕 Taxi

GETTING THERE
Sant'Ambrogio is served by bus No. 94 (which continues to San Lorenzo) and by metro line 2. Trams 3, 9, 15, 29 and 30 go to the Navigli, and No. 3 is connected to Via Torino by Nos. 2 and 14. Metro line 3 (Missori stop), tram 15 and bus 65 all stop at Corso di Porta Romana.

◁ The antiques market, held on the towpath of the Naviglio Grande on the last Sunday of every month

Street-by-Street: From Sant'Ambrogio to San Lorenzo

SITUATED JUST OUTSIDE the Roman walls, this area was occupied by Early Christian cemeteries and Imperial Age buildings such as the Arena and Circus. Though little remains of this ancient heritage, it is however significant, particularly the columns of the triumphal entrance to the basilica of San

Statue, Università Cattolica

Lorenzo. Nine kings of Italy were crowned in Sant'Ambrogio in the 9th–15th centuries and four were buried here. Napoleon came here in 1805, and Ferdinand of Austria in 1838, after their respective coronations in the Duomo. On the feast day of Sant'Ambrogio, 7 December, the *Oh bej Oh bej* fair is held in the streets.

Via Circo
The remains of an ancient Roman circus, used for public spectacles, were found in this street ❹

Cloister of Santa Maria Maddalena al Cerchio

The Università Cattolica (1921) is located in the monastery and cloisters of old Sant'Ambrogio, built by Bramante in 1497.

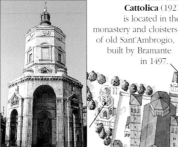

The Tempio della Vittoria (1930), designed by Giovanni Muzio, commemorates the 10,000 Milanese who perished in World War I.

San Bernardino alle Monache
This church was rebuilt in 1450 for Franciscan nuns. The façade is decorated with majolica hollows ❺

★ **Sant'Ambrogio**
Founded by Sant'Ambrogio in the 4th century, this church contains masterpieces such as the San Vittore mosaics and the Golden Altar ❻

| 0 metres | 100 |
| 0 yards | 100 |

Largo Carrobbio
The name of the crossroads at the end of Via Torino derives from quadrivium, *meaning a place where four streets converge* ❸

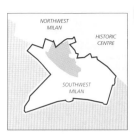

LOCATOR MAP
See Street Finder, map 7, 8

A tower from the Roman Porta Ticinese is hidden in the courtyard of a building between Via del Torchio and Via Medici.

In Largo Carrobbio the small deconsecrated church of San Sisto houses the Museo Messina.

Piazza della Vetra
From this square there are spectacular views of the apses of San Lorenzo and Sant'Eustorgio. Until 1840 the piazza was the scene of executions ❷

KEY

– – – – Suggested route

STAR SIGHTS

★ **San Lorenzo alle Colonne**

★ **Sant'Ambrogio**

The 16 Corinthian columns may have come from a 2nd– 3rd-century AD pagan temple.

Medieval Porta Ticinese

★ **San Lorenzo alle Colonne**
This superb 4th-century basilica consists of a main domed section linked to a series of minor buildings, dating from different periods ❶

San Lorenzo alle Colonne ❶

DATING FROM THE 4th century, San Lorenzo is one of the oldest round churches in Western Christendom and may have been the ancient Imperial palatine chapel. The plan, with exedrae and women's galleries, is unlike Lombard architecture and reveals the hand of Roman architects and masons. After several fires the church was reconstructed in the 11th and 12th centuries and was again rebuilt after the dome collapsed in 1573, but the original quatrefoil plan has been preserved.

Fresco, Cappella di San Sisto

Cappella di San Sisto
This chapel was frescoed by Gian Cristoforo Storer in the 17th century.

A bas relief above the entrance depicts San Lorenzo, who was burnt over live coals in the 3rd century (a recurring symbol in the church).

Main entrance

★ Roman Columns
The 16 Corinthian columns, from the 2nd–3rd century, were part of an unidentified temple and were placed in their present location in the 4th century.

Statue of Constantine
This bronze work is a copy of a Roman statue of the emperor who issued the Edict of Milan in AD 313, bringing persecution of Christians to an end.

The dome, the largest in Milan, is supported by an octagonal tambour lit by eight large windows. It was rebuilt by Martino Bassi after it collapsed in 1573.

An upside-down column symbolizes Christianity rising from the ruins of paganism.

VISITORS' CHECKLIST

Corso di Porta Ticinese 39. **Map** 7 B2. *02-89 40 41 29.* **M** *3 Missori.* *3.* *94.* *9am–6pm daily.* *6am, 6pm Mon–Fri; 6pm pre-hols; 9:30, 11:30am, 4pm (in Philippine language), 6pm hols.* **Cappella di Sant'Aquilino** *9am–6:30pm daily.* (donation).

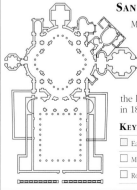

★ **Cappella di Sant'Aquilino**
This 5th-century chapel has mosaics from the same period: Elijah on the Chariot of Fire *and* Christ with the Apostles. *The entire chapel was once decorated with mosaics.*

Byzantine sarcophagus

Behind the altar, steps lead to the crypt, which has stones taken from the amphitheatre and used for compacting the earth.

The 17th-century presbyteries, designed by Trezzi and Richini, were originally designed to join up with the columns so as to revive the pattern of the ancient quadriporticus.

SAN LORENZO

Most of the walls, towers and three chapels date from the late 4th century. The upper parts of the towers are Romanesque. The dome was built in the late 1500s and the façade in 1894 by Cesare Nava.

KEY

☐ Early Christian

☐ Medieval and modern

☐ Romanesque

STAR FEATURES

★ **Roman Columns**

★ **Cappella di Sant'Aquilino**

Piazza della Vetra, linking San Lorenzo to Sant'Eustorgio

Piazza della Vetra and medieval Porta Ticinese ❷

Map 7 B2. 🚇 *2, 3, 14.* 🚌 *94.*

THE VAST AREA of greenery dominated by a column bearing the statue of San Lazzaro (1728) is also called Parco delle Basiliche, because it lies between the basilicas of San Lorenzo and Sant'Eustorgio. The name "Vetra" seems to derive from the Latin *castra vetera*, which probably alluded to the Roman military camps positioned here to defend the nearby imperial palace. The name was also given to a canal that was once on the northern side of the square and was lined with tanners' workshops (the tanners were

Detail of the tabernacle of Porta Ticinese: *Madonna and Child with St Ambrose* **by Giovanni di Balduccio's workshop**

called *vetraschi*). Until 1840 the square was used for the public hangings of condemned commoners, while nobles were decapitated in front of the law court, the Broletto *(see p54)*.

During the Roman era there was a small port here, at the point where the Seveso and Nirone rivers converged in the navigable Vettabbia canal.

This square is worth visiting just for the magnificent view of the apses of the basilicas. In the 12th century, when the city walls were enlarged to include San Lorenzo, the Roman gate at present-day Largo Carrobbio was replaced by the "new" medieval Porta Ticinese. A moat ran around the new walls and along present-day Via Molino delle Armi, which was named after the water mills *(molini)* used mostly to forge weapons.

Porta Ticinese was remodelled after 1329 by Azzone Visconti and decorated with a tabernacle of the *Madonna and Child with St Ambrose Proffering the Model of the City* by the workshop of Giovanni di Balduccio (14th century). This city gate – the only one, along with Porta Nuova on Via Manzoni, still standing – was fortified with two towers in 1865.

Largo Carrobbio and Via Torino ❸

Map 7 B2. 🚇 *2, 3, 14.* **Museo Messina** Via San Sisto 10. 📞 *02-86 45 30 05.* ⏰ *9am–5:30pm Tue–Sun.* 🚫 *1 Jan, Easter, 1 May, 15 Aug, 25 Dec.* 🚫 ♿

THE VAST Carrobbio square, which connects Via Torino and Corso di Porta Ticinese, was either named after the *quadrivium*, a crossroads of four streets, or after *carrubium*, a road reserved for carts. One of the towers flanking the Roman Porta Ticinese is still standing at the corner of Via Medici and Via del Torchio. The name of the gate derived from the fact that it opened onto the road for Pavia, which in ancient times was called *Ticinum*. At the junction with Via San Sisto is the deconsecrated 17th-century church of San Sisto. In 1976 it became the museum-studio of sculptor Francesco Messina (who died in 1990) and now houses a collection of his bronze and

Female nude by Francesco Messina (1967)

coloured plaster sculpture pieces and graphic art.

Largo Carrobbio is at one end of Via Torino, a major commercial street that developed after the merger of the old city districts, which were filled with the work-shops of oil merchants, silk weavers, hatters and famous armourers – as can be seen by the names of some streets.

The 16th-century Palazzo Stampa, built by Massimiliano Stampa, stands in Via Soncino. When the Sforza dynasty died out in 1535, Stampa intro-duced Spanish dominion to the city by hoisting the flag of Charles V on the Castello Sforzesco in exchange for land and privileges. The imperial eagle still stands on the palazzo tower, over the bronze globe representing the dominions of Charles V.

The cloister at Santa Maria Maddalena al Cerchio

Via Circo ❹

Map 7 B1. 🚋 *2, 3, 14.*

THE AREA EXTENDING from Largo Carrobbio to Corso Magenta is very rich in 3rd- and 4th-century ruins, particularly mosaics and masonry, much of it now part of private homes. This was the period when the Roman emperor Maximian lived in Milan: his splendid palace was near Via Brisa. In order to create a proper imperial capital, he built many civic edifices to gain the favour of the Milanese: the Arena, the thermae and the huge Circus used for two-horse chariot races. The Circus, 505 m

(1,656 ft) long, was one of the largest constructions in the Roman Empire. The only remaining parts are the end curve, visible at the junction of Via Cappuccio and Via Circo, and one of the entrance towers, which became the bell tower of San Maurizio in Corso Magenta.

The Circus, active long after the fall of the Roman Empire, was the venue of the corona-tion of the Lombard king Adaloaldo in 615, while in the Carolingian period it became a vineyard, as the place name of nearby Via Vigna indicates. At No. 7 Via Cappuccio, the 18th-century Palazzo Litta Biumi has incorporated, to the left of the central court-yard, the delightful 15th-century nuns' convent Santa Maria Maddalena al Cerchio, which has been partly rebuilt. Its name, a corruption of the Latin *ad circulum*, refers to the Circus over which it was built. The hood of the nuns' habit *(cappuccio)* is probably the origin of the name of the street where the convent is located. Further along, at No. 13, is Palazzo Radice Fossati (a private house), of medieval origin, with a 13th-century portal and 18th-century frescoes inside.

On Via Sant'Orsola you come to Via Morigi, named after a famous Milanese family who once lived here; all that remains of their residence is a 14th-century tower with a small loggia. The nearby square is domi-nated by the 14th-century Torre dei Gorani, another tower crowned by a loggia with small stone columns.

Fifteenth-century frescoes by the school of Vincenzo Foppa

San Bernardino alle Monache ❺

Via Lanzone 13. **Map** 7 A1.
📞 *02-645 19 48 (Amici di San Bernardino cultural association).*
🚋 *2, 3, 14.* ⬤ *for restoration.*

THE CHURCH IS the only remaining building in a Franciscan nuns' convent dating from the mid-15th century and attributed to the Lombard architect Pietro Antonio Solari. The church was named after the preacher Bernardino da Siena, whose relics are kept here. It was partly rebuilt in 1922. The narrow, elegant brick façade is decorated with majolica bowls and a fine elaborate cornice with small arches.

The interior houses fine 15th-century frescoes painted by the school of Vincenzo Foppa, and others dating from the early 16th century. The church is under restoration and will be re-opened to the public in the future.

Part of the curve of the Circus built by the Roman emperor Maximian in the late 3rd century AD

Sant'Ambrogio ❻

Detail of the apse mosaic

THE BASILICA WAS BUILT by Bishop Ambrogio (Ambrose) in AD 379–86 on an Early Christian burial ground as part of a programme to reorganize the Christian face of Milan. The church was dedicated to Ambrogio, a defender of Christianity against Arianism, after his burial here. The Benedictines began to enlarge it in the 8th century, then in the following century Archbishop Anspert built the atrium, which was rebuilt in the 12th century. In the 11th century, reconstruction of the entire church began. The dome collapsed in 1196, and the vaults and pulpit were rebuilt. In 1492 the Sforza family asked Bramante to restructure the rectory and the Benedictine monastery. Sadly, the basilica was badly damaged by bombs in 1943.

The Canons' bell tower was erected in 1124 to surpass in height and beauty the campanile of the nearby Benedictines.

The Capitals
The columns are enlivened by Bible stories and fantastic animals symbolizing the struggle between Good and Evil. Some date from the 11th century.

Anspert's Atrium (11th century) was used by local people as a refuge from danger before the city walls were built.

The Interior
The solemn proportions typical of Lombard Romanesque characterize the interior. The nave is covered by ribbed cross vaulting supported by massive piers.

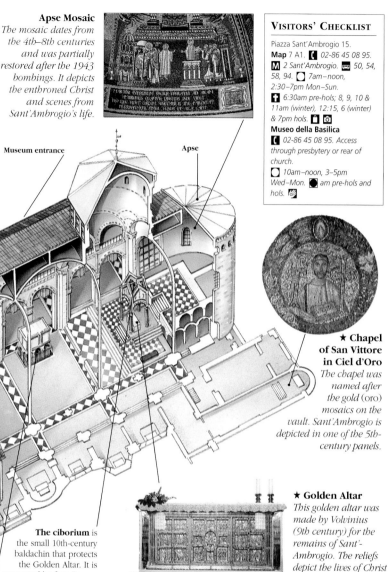

Apse Mosaic
The mosaic dates from the 4th–8th centuries and was partially restored after the 1943 bombings. It depicts the enthroned Christ and scenes from Sant'Ambrogio's life.

Museum entrance

Apse

VISITORS' CHECKLIST

Piazza Sant'Ambrogio 15.
Map 7 A1. 02-86 45 08 95.
2 Sant'Ambrogio. 50, 54, 58, 94. 7am–noon, 2:30–7pm Mon–Sun.
6:30am pre-hols; 8, 9, 10 & 11am (winter), 12:15, 6 (winter) & 7pm hols.
Museo della Basilica
02-86 45 08 95. *Access through presbytery or rear of church.*
10am–noon, 3–5pm Wed–Mon. *am pre-hols and hols.*

★ **Chapel of San Vittore in Ciel d'Oro**
The chapel was named after the gold (oro) mosaics on the vault. Sant'Ambrogio is depicted in one of the 5th-century panels.

★ **Golden Altar**
This golden altar was made by Volvinius (9th century) for the remains of Sant'-Ambrogio. The reliefs depict the lives of Christ (front) and Ambrogio (to the rear).

The ciborium is the small 10th-century baldachin that protects the Golden Altar. It is supported by four Roman porphyry columns and decorated with stuccowork.

★ **Sarcophagus of Stilicho**
Situated under the pulpit, this 4th-century masterpiece has a wealth of relief figures with religious significance. It is traditionally referred to as the tomb of the Roman general Stilicho, but probably contained the remains of the emperor Gratian.

STAR FEATURES

★ **Golden Altar**

★ **Chapel of San Vittore in Ciel d'Oro**

★ **Sarcophagus of Stilicho**

Exploring Sant'Ambrogio

Papal statue

THE FACT THAT the church of Sant'Ambrogio houses the remains of the city's patron saint, the church's founder, makes it a special place for the Milanese. Most of its present-day appearance is the result of rebuilding in the 10th and 12th century by the Benedictines from the nearby monastery, who made it a model of Lombard Romanesque religious architecture. All that remains of the 4th-century basilica are the triumphal arch and its columns, which became part of the apse. In 1937–40 and in the post-war period the Romanesque structure and delicate colours were restored. From the Pusterla (gate) there is a marvellous view of the church, with its two bell towers and atrium, flanked by the rectory and museum.

PUSTERLA DI SANT'AMBROGIO

THE PUSTERLA di Sant'-Ambrogio, one of the minor gates on the medieval walls, is a good starting point for a visit to the church. Rebuilt in 1939, it houses a museum with old weapons and instruments of torture.

A decorated capital in the atrium

ANSPERT'S ATRIUM

JUST BEFORE THE atrium, to the left, is the isolated Roman Colonna del Diavolo (Devil's Column), with two holes halfway up which, according to tradition, were made by the Devil's horns while he was tempting Sant'Ambrogio. The present-day atrium, with its blind arches, dates from the 12th century and replaced one built by Archbishop Anspert in the 9th century. This large courtyard acts as an entrance foyer for the church proper and sets off the façade.

A row of piers (some Roman) with sculpted capitals continues into the basilica. The rhythmic pattern of the arches, half-columns and small suspended arches, as well as the proportions, match those in the church, creating a harmonious continuity between exterior and interior. The atrium houses finds and tombstones from this area, which was once an Early Christian cemetery. The fourth side of the atrium, or narthex, has five bays and is part of the façade, which has an upper loggia with five arches. In the narthex is the main portal (8th–10th centuries), with small columns with figures of animals and the Mystic Lamb, while its wooden wings (1750) have reliefs of the *Life of David*.

The atrium, with finds and tombstones from the surrounding area

THE INTERIOR

THE NAVE PROVIDES the best view of the interior, revealing the basilica in all its splendour. The nave has two side aisles divided by arcades supporting the women's galleries with piers with carved capitals. At the beginning of the nave is the Serpent's Column, said to have been erected by Moses in the desert. Beside it, to the left, excavations show the level of the original 4th-century floor.

The pulpit (or ambo) is made of pieces saved when the dome collapsed in 1196. This magnificent monument is decorated with an eagle and a seated man, symbols of the evangelists John and Matthew. Underneath is the sarcophagus of Stilicho (4th century) with reliefs representing (going clockwise) *Christ Giving the Law to St Peter*, four scenes from the Old Testament, *Christ among the Apostles* and the *Sacrifice of Isaac*. Under the octagonal cupola is the ciborium (10th century), the heart of the basilica, supported by columns taken from the 4th-century ciborium. Its painted stucco sides depict various episodes: on the front is *Christ Giving the Keys to St Peter and the Law to St Paul*. The ciborium acts as a baldachin for the Golden Altar, an embossed work that Archbishop Angilberto commissioned from Volvinius in the 9th century. On the back, a silver relief narrates the *Life of Sant'Ambrogio* and has the artist's signature. On the same side, two small doors allowed the faithful to worship the body of St Ambrose, once kept under the altar. The front is made of gold and jewels, and narrates the *Life of Christ*. Behind the ciborium is the wooden choir with the *Life of Sant'Ambrogio* (15th century) and, in the middle, the bishop's throne (4th and 9th centuries), also used

The Serpent's Column, at the beginning of the nave

by the kings of Italy crowned here. Part of the large mosaic in the apse dates from the 6th and 8th centuries. The scene on the left, a *Benedictory Christ*, is of the same period, while the one on the right is the result of 18th-century and postwar reconstruction.

Next to the presbytery is the stairway to the crypt, decorated with stucco (c.1740). Under the Golden Altar, an urn (1897) has the remains of saints Ambrogio, Gervasio and Protasio. Back upstairs, at the end of the south aisle is the stunning San Vittore in Ciel d'Oro Sacellum, the 4th-century funerary chapel of the martyr, which was later incorporated into the basilica. The 5th-century mosaics on the walls show various saints, including Saints Ambrogio, Gervasio and Protasio.

The Risen Christ by Bergognone (c.1491)

THE SOUTH AISLE

RETURNING TO the entrance in the south aisle, you will see the monks' chapels, built in different eras. St George's chapel – sixth from the entrance – houses an altarpiece of the *Madonna and Child with the Infant St*

John the Baptist by Bernardo Lanino, who frescoed the *Legend of St George* on the sides (1546). The Baroque chapel of the Holy Sacrament, the fifth, contains the frescoes *The Death of St Benedict* by Carlo Preda and *St Bernard* by Filippo Abbiati (17th and 18th century respectively).

In St Bartholomew's chapel (the second) are the *Legends of Saints Vittore and Satiro* (1737) by Tiepolo, detached from the San Vittore Sacellum; they demonstrate the cultural openness of the Cistercians, who commissioned the work. The altarpiece in the second chapel, *The Virgin Mary with St Bartholomew and St John the Baptist*, is attributed to Gaudenzio Ferrari, as is the 1545 *Deposition* in the next chapel, which also has frescoes by Luini on the pillars.

THE NORTH AISLE

GO UP THIS aisle from the baptistery (first chapel), which has a porphyry font by Franco Lombardi with the *Conversion of St Augustine* (1940), the saint baptized by Sant'Ambrogio in Milan. It is

dominated symbolically by Bergognone's *The Risen Christ* (c.1491).

In the third chapel is an interesting painting by Luini, a *Madonna with Saints Jerome and Rocco*.

MUSEO DELLA BASILICA

AT THE END OF THE north aisle you come out into the Portico della Canonica, the presbytery portico, which was left unfinished by Bramante (1492–4) and rebuilt after World War II. The columns of the central arch, sculpted to resemble tree trunks, are unusual. The entrance to the Basilica Museum, with six rooms featuring objects and works of art from the church, is here. Among the most interesting pieces are a 12th-century multicoloured tondo of St Ambrose; a cast of Stilicho's sarcophagus; St Ambrose's bed; fragments of the apse mosaics and four wooden panels from the 4th-century portal. The museum also has a *Triptych* by Bernardo Zenale (15th century) and *Christ among the Doctors* by Bergognone. In the garden opposite is St Sigismund's oratory, already famous by 1096, with 15th-century frescoes and Roman columns.

Plaque of the Università Cattolica del Sacro Cuore

UNIVERSITÀ CATTOLICA DEL SACRO CUORE

ON THE RIGHT-HAND side of the church (entrance at No. 1 Largo Gemelli), in the former Benedictine monastery, is the university founded by padre Agostino Gemelli in 1921. Its two cloisters, with Ionic and Doric columns, were two of the four Bramante had designed in 1497. In the refectory is *The Marriage at Cana* by Callisto Piazza (1545).

Old motion picture camera, the Science and Technology Musuem

Museo Nazionale della Scienza e della Tecnica ❼

Via San Vittore 21. **Map** 6 F1.
🅒 02-48 55 51. Ⓜ 2 Sant'-
Ambrogio. 🚌 50, 54, 58, 94. ◐
9:30am–4:50pm Tue–Fri; 9:30am–
6:20pm Sat, hols. ⬤ Mon not hols.
🈳♿🈂🈂🈂🈂 (book at Ufficio
Didattico). Library, lecture rooms.

THE SCIENCE and Technology Museum is housed in the former Olivetan monastery of San Vittore (16th century) – partly designed by Vincenzo Seregni – which became a military hospital and then a barracks after monasteries were suppressed in 1804. It was badly damaged in World War II, was restored, and in 1947 became the home of the museum. In the two courtyards surrounded by the old section of the museum, you can see part of the foundation of the San Vittore fortress and that of the octagonal mausoleum of Emperor Valentinian II, both ancient Roman.

The museum boasts one of the world's leading science and technology collections. The vast exhibition space is housed in different buildings. The former monastery contains the technological sections on metallurgy, casting and transport, as well as science sections featuring physics, optics, acoustics and astronomy. Another section shows the development of calculation, from the first mechanical calculating machine, invented by Pascal

in 1642, to IBM computers. There is also a section on time measurement, with a reconstruction of a 1750 watchmaker's workshop. The printing section is also worth a visit: it shows the 1810 automatic inking method by which 800 sheets an hour could be printed, and also has the father of the modern typewriter (1855).

The cinema photography section shows how the claw device, used to make motion-picture film move, grew out of a sewing machine needle conceived by Singer in 1851. In the rooms given over to telephones and television, there is a reconstruction of the 1856 pantelegraph, the ancestor of the fax machine.

The history of trains begins with the first locomotive in Italy, used for the Naples-Portici line in 1839, and ends with 1970s models. A pavilion in Via Olona houses the air and sea transport section, featuring two historic pieces: the bridge of the transatlantic liner *Conte Biancamano* and a naval training ship.

The Leonardo da Vinci Gallery has fascinating wooden models of the machines and apparatus invented by the genius, shown together with his drawings. Some, like the rotating crane and the helical airscrew, which demonstrate principles of physics and applied mechanics, can be operated by the public.

San Vittore al Corpo ❽

Via San Vittore 25. **Map** 6 F1.
🅒 02-48 00 53 51. Ⓜ 2 Sant'-
Ambrogio. 🚌 50, 54, 58, 94.
◐ 7:30am–noon, 3:30–7pm. ✝
6pm pre-hols; 8:30, 10 & 11:15am;
12:15, 6 & 9 pm hols. 📷 (no flash).

THE ORIGINAL basilica on this site was founded in the 4th century, next to the mausoleum of Emperor Valentinian II, who died in 392. The church was rebuilt in the 11th and 12th centuries by Benedictine monks, who arrived here in 1010, and was again altered in 1560 by the Olivetans, who replaced the monks. The architect (either Alessi or Seregni) reversed the orientation and made it one of Milan's most sumptuous churches, with splendid late 16th-century paintings. The Baroque Arese Chapel (1668), designed by Gerolamo Quadrio, and the right-hand apse, with scenes from the life of St Gregory by Camillo Procaccini (1602), are of particular interest. Moncalvo frescoed the angel musicians on the cupola in 1619. The wooden choir stalls, with carvings of episodes from St Benedict's life, date from 1583; above them are three canvases on the same subject by Giovanni Ambrogio Figino. Last, the chapel of Sant'Antonio Abate was entirely frescoed in 1619 by Daniele Crespi.

Façade detail, San Vittore al Corpo

The façade of San Vittore al Corpo

Along the Naviglio Grande

Now one of the liveliest quarters in Milan, the Navigli formed the city's port district until the 19th century. Work on the Naviglio Grande canal began in 1177, followed by the Pavia, Bereguardo, Martesana and Paderno canals. A system of locks allowed boats to travel along the canals on different levels (Candoglia marble was taken to the Duomo in the 14th century in this way). Lodovico il Moro

One of the 12 locks

improved this network with the help of Leonardo da Vinci in the 15th century. Barges arrived laden with coal and salt and departed with handmade goods and textiles. Some sections of the canals, which once extended for 150 km (93 miles), were filled in during the 1930s and navigation ceased altogether in 1979. Thanks to the Navigli canals, in 1953 landlocked Milan was ranked the 13th port in Italy.

Typical houses
Along the Naviglio there are typical blocks of flats in "Milan yellow", built with running balconies around courtyards.

San Cristoforo al Naviglio
The church of the patron saint of boatmen is two buildings in one (12th and 14th century).

There are many antiques workshops and shops here.

The big barges have become nightclubs.

On the towpaths, horses or oxen once pulled the barges.

The church of Santa Maria delle Grazie al Naviglio faces the water.

Mercatone dell'Antiquariato
On the last Sunday of the month, from September to June, 400 antique dealers take part in this lively market on the Naviglio Grande.

Vicolo dei Lavandai
On the towpath you can still see the old washing troughs, sheltered by wooden roofs, where women washed clothes in the canal water.

Sant'Eustorgio ❾

Piazza Sant'Eustorgio 1. **Map** 7 B3.
📞 02-58 10 15 83. 🚃 3, 9, 15, 29,
30. 🚋 59. ⏰ 7:30am–noon, 3:30–
6:30pm. ✝ 5pm pre-hols; 9:30, 11am,
12:30, 5pm hols; 5pm Jul, Aug.

IN THE 11TH CENTURY work
began on building a basilica
over one founded by St
Eustorgius in the 4th century,
to house the relics of the
Magi. Frederick Barbarossa
destroyed it in 1162 and it was
rebuilt in 1190, with the city's
tallest bell tower, the first to
carry a clock, in 1306. At this
point the main body of the
present-day church was built:
a three-aisle nave with cross
vaulting supported by round
arches. On the left-hand side
of the façade, which was rebuilt in 1865, is a small pulpit
(1597) which replaced the
wooden one reputedly used
by St Peter Martyr in the 13th
century. On the right-hand
side you can see chapels built
in different styles dating from
the 13th–15th centuries.

Beyond the apse is the Portinari chapel (1462). In the 19th
century, Baroque elements
were removed from inside and
the original frescoes revealed.
The impressive effect is due to
the slight outward inclination
of the pillars, which have
elegantly sculpted 12th-cen-
tury capitals at the top.

The most interesting art is in
the chapels on the right. The
Brivio chapel houses Tom-
maso Cazzaniga's tomb of
Giovanni Stefano Brivio

THE RELICS OF THE MAGI

Emperor Costante donated the relics in around 315 and they
were taken to Milan by Bishop Eustorgius. Legend has it that

the sarcophagus was so heavy the cart
had to stop at the city gates, where the
original Sant'Eustorgio basilica was
founded and the Apostle Barnabas
baptised the first Milanese Christians.
Barbarossa transferred the relics to
Cologne in 1164. Some were returned
in 1903, an event still celebrated at
Epiphany with a procession.

**Tabernacle with
the relics of the Magi**

(1486). The middle bas-relief
depicts the *Adoration of the
Magi*, and the altarpiece is a
triptych by Bergognone. The
next chapel has Pietro Torelli's
tomb. In the Baroque Crotta-
Caimi chapel is a fine sarcophagus by Protaso Caimi, the
15th-century Campionese
sculptor, and a *St Ambrose on
Horseback*. The fourth chapel,
built by the
Visconti, has
beautiful 14th-
century frescoes:
on the vault are
the Evangelists;
below left, a
delicate *St
George and
the Dragon*, in
the style of
Giovannino de' Grassi; right,
the *Triumph of St Thomas*,
perhaps by Giovanni da
Milano. On the walls are the
sarcophagus of Stefano
Visconti, by Giovanni di Balduccio, and a 13th-century
Crucifix. The Torriani chapel –
the last to be linked to the
aisle by a single vault – is

frescoed with symbols of the
Evangelists, perhaps by Michelino da Besozzo. In the south
transept is the large late-
Roman sarcophagus that once
housed the relics of the Magi,
and on the altar is a Campionese school marble triptych of
the journey of the Magi (1347).
The Magi are also the subject
of the fresco on the left,
attributed to Luini.
The high altar
houses the remains
of St Eustorgius
and bears a
marble altar-front
depicting the
Passion
of Christ, an
unfinished
work by
various artists, including
Matteo da Campione.

Behind the altar are the
remains of the 4th-century
apse and a passageway
leading to the Portinari chapel,
commissioned by banker
Pigello Portinari as his tomb,
and to house the body of St
Peter Martyr. Its marvellous
architecture, the first example
of a 15th-century central-plan
church in Milan, exemplifies
the clarity of Bramante's vision
and features typical Lombard
decoration attributed to Vincenzo Foppa, including
masterful frescoes of the
miracles of St Peter and the
life of the Virgin Mary. On the
right-hand lunette, the saint
subdues the Devil in the guise
of Mary. Under the dome,
below dancing angels, is the
tomb of St Peter Martyr (1339)
by Giovanni di Balduccio,
held up by the eight Virtues
and showing scenes of his
ministry. The small chapel
on the left has a silver urn
containing the saint's skull.

**Sculpture on the façade
of Sant'Eustorgio**

The Neo-Romanesque façade of Sant'Eustorgio, built in 1865

The Sanctuary of Santa Maria dei Miracoli and San Celso

Santa Maria presso San Celso ⑩

Corso Italia 37. **Map** 7 C3.
📞 02-58 31 31 87. 🚋 15.
🚌 65, 94. ⏰ 8:30am–noon,
4–5:30pm. ✝ 6:30pm pre-hols;
9:30, 11am, 6, 7pm hols.
San Celso ask sacristan.

SAN CELSO was founded in the 11th century over a church built by St Ambrose in the 4th century to mark the spot where he had found the remains of the martyrs Celso and Nazaro. In 1493 construction began on a sanctuary dedicated to Santa Maria dei Miracoli, designed by Gian Giacomo Dolcebuono and subsequently by Vincenzo Seregni and Alessi. The late 16th-century façade is enlivened by sculptures by Stoldo Lorenzi and Annibale Fontana. The late Renaissance interior has a pavement by Martino Bassi and was frescoed by Cerano and Procaccini. There are major works of art in the various chapels: a painting (1606) by Procaccini; the *Holy Family with St Jerome* altarpiece (1548) by Paris Bordone; Antonio Campi's *Resurrection* (1560); *Baptism of Jesus* by Gaudenzio Ferrari; Moretto da Brescia's *Conversion of St Paul* (1539–40); *Martyrdom of St Catherine* by Cerano (1603); an altarpiece by Bergognone.

Under the cupola with terracotta Evangelists by De Fondutis and paintings by Appiani (1795) is the high altar (16th century) in semi-precious stones. The wooden choir is from 1570. Statues by Fontana and Lorenzi adorn the pillars. On the Altar of the Madonna is Fontana's *Our Lady of the Assumption*. Below, a 4th-century fresco lies under two embossed silver doors. By the right-hand transept is the entrance to **San Celso**, with 11th–15th-century frescoes and columns with carved capitals.

San Paolo Converso ⑪

Piazza Sant'Eufemia. **Map** 7 C2.
🚋 15. 🚌 65, 94.
⏰ for exhibitions only.

THIS CHURCH was founded in 1549 for the Angeliche di San Paolo convent and is attributed to Domenico Giunti, while the façade was designed by Cerano in 1611. Now deconsecrated, the church has a front section for the public and another one to the rear, facing the opposite direction, reserved for the nuns. The interior was frescoed in the late 1500s by Giulio and Antonio Campi: in the presbytery are episodes from the life of St Paul, the Ascension of Christ and the Assumption of Mary, framed in an architectural setting with bold foreshortening.

At the end of Corso di Porta Romana is Piazza Missori, with the remains of San Giovanni in Conca (11th cen-tury), once a Visconti mausoleum. The façade was remade for the Waldensian church in Via Francesco Sforza.

Sant'Alessandro ⑫

Piazza Sant'Alessandro. **Map** 7 C2.
📞 02-86 45 30 65. Ⓜ 1 Missori.
🚋 4, 12, 15, 24. 🚌 65.
⏰ 7:30am–noon, 4–7pm.
✝ 6:30pm pre-hols; 8am (winter),
10:30am (winter), noon, 6:30pm hols.

LORENZO BINAGO built this church in 1601 for the Barnabiti family. The interior has lavish Baroque furnishings and decoration; the frescoes were painted by Moncalvo and by Daniele Crespi. In the presbytery is the *Life of St Alexander* by Filippo Abbiati and Federico Bianchi. The high altar (1741) is decorated with semi-precious stones.

Next to the church are the Scuole Arcimbolde, schools for the poor founded in 1609 by the Barnabiti family, where the poet Giuseppe Parini studied. Opposite is Palazzo Trivulzio, rebuilt by Ruggeri in 1713, with the family coat of arms on the middle window. This family founded the Biblioteca Trivulziana, the library now in the Castello Sforzesco. Nearby Via Palla leads to the Tempio Civico di San Sebastiano, begun by Pellegrino Tibaldi in 1577 and completed in the 1700s. Its round interior has works by Legnanino, Montalto and Federico Bianchi.

The cupola and bell tower of Sant'Alessandro, seen from Corso di Porta Romana

SOUTHEAST MILAN

THE AREA BETWEEN Corso Monforte and Corso di Porta Romana was a typical suburb up to the early 19th century, characterized by aristocratic residences, monasteries and more modest houses typical of the artisans' and commercial districts of Milan. Development of the area began in the 17th century with the construction of Palazzo Durini, one of the most important civic buildings of its time. At the end of the 18th century Corso di Porta Romana and the adjacent streets were changed in keeping with the vast street network renewal plans encouraged by Maria

A statue in the Guastalla gardens

Theresa of Austria. When the empress ordered the suppression of many monasteries, the land where they had stood was purchased by rich nobles. Other areas became available when the Spanish ramparts were demolished. The old atmosphere of Southeast Milan survives above all around the Ca' Granda (now the University), which for almost 500 years was the city hospital, and in the first stretch of Corso di Porta Romana. However, the only vestige of the Verziere, the old vegetable market in Largo Augusto, is the place-name.

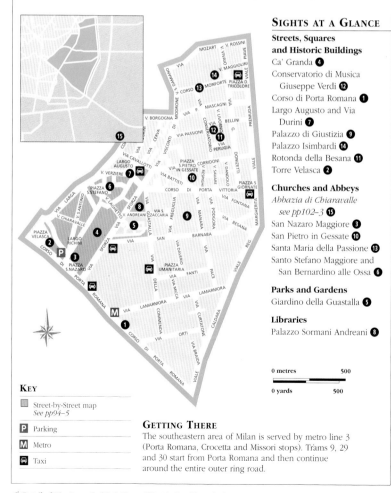

SIGHTS AT A GLANCE

Streets, Squares and Historic Buildings
Ca' Granda **4**
Conservatorio di Musica
   Giuseppe Verdi **12**
Corso di Porta Romana **1**
Largo Augusto and Via
   Durini **7**
Palazzo di Giustizia **9**
Palazzo Isimbardi **14**
Rotonda della Besana **11**
Torre Velasca **2**

Churches and Abbeys
Abbazia di Chiaravalle
   see pp102–3 **15**
San Nazaro Maggiore **3**
San Pietro in Gessate **10**
Santa Maria della Passione **13**
Santo Stefano Maggiore and
   San Bernardino alle Ossa **6**

Parks and Gardens
Giardino della Guastalla **5**

Libraries
Palazzo Sormani Andreani **8**

KEY

⬜ Street-by-Street map
   See pp94–5

🅿 Parking

Ⓜ Metro

🚕 Taxi

0 metres   500
0 yards   500

GETTING THERE
The southeastern area of Milan is served by metro line 3 (Porta Romana, Crocetta and Missori stops). Trams 9, 29 and 30 start from Porta Romana and then continue around the entire outer ring road.

◁ **Detail of *The Legend of St Anthony Abbot*, in San Pietro in Gessate**

Street-by-Street: San Nazaro to Largo Augusto

THERE ARE MANY interesting old buildings in this area, which includes the university quarter, with cafés and specialist bookshops, as well as crafts shops on Via Festa del Perdono. Architectural styles range from the 4th-century San Nazaro, founded by St Ambrose, to the Ca' Granda, the old hospital, a marvellous sight when viewed from Largo Richini because of its sheer size and the beauty of its 15th-century arcade. More changes of style come with the palazzi in Corso di Porta Romana and Via Sant'Antonio, and the modern Torre Velasca. The quarter's hospital tradition can be seen in the votive columns at the crossroads, where mass for the sick was celebrated, and the San Bernardino alle Ossa chapel, decorated with the bones of those who died in the the hospital.

Sant'Antonio Abat
was rebuilt in 1582. It houses paintings by Bernardino Campi, Moncalvo and Ludovico Carracci and is a kind of gallery of early 17th-century painting in Milan.

Torre Velasca
The symbol of modern Milan was built in 1956–8. The tower, 106 m (348 ft) high, houses both offices and flats and is often compared to medieval towers because of the shape of the upper section ❷

Duomo →

Corso di Porta Romana
Palazzi with magnificent gardens line this avenue. It follows the route of the ancient Roman road which led from Porta Romana all the way to Rome ❶

KEY

– – – – – Suggested route

★ San Nazaro Maggiore
One of four basilicas founded by Sant'Ambrogio, this church still has some of the original 4th-century masonry. It is preceded by the Trivulzio Chapel, the only Milanese architectural work by Bramantino (1512–50). The view of the back of the church is very striking ❸

STAR SIGHTS

★ San Nazaro Maggiore

★ Ca' Granda

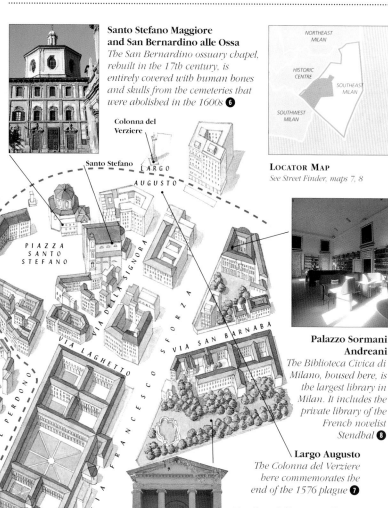

**Santo Stefano Maggiore
and San Bernardino alle Ossa**
*The San Bernardino ossuary chapel,
rebuilt in the 17th century, is
entirely covered with human bones
and skulls from the cemeteries that
were abolished in the 1600s* 6

LOCATOR MAP
See Street Finder, maps 7, 8

**Palazzo Sormani
Andreani**
*The Biblioteca Civica di
Milano, housed here, is
the largest library in
Milan. It includes the
private library of the
French novelist
Stendhal* 8

Largo Augusto
*The Colonna del Verziere
here commemorates the
end of the 1576 plague* 7

Giardino della Guastalla
*Milan's oldest public garden was
laid out in 1555. There are several
monuments, including a small
Neo-Classical temple designed
by Luigi Cagnola* 5

★ Ca' Granda
*This was the old city
hospital, also known as
Ospedale Maggiore. It was
built in 1456 to bring all the
small hospitals of the city
together on a single site. It
was in use until 1939.
Today it is home to Milan's
state university* 4

0 metres 300
0 yards 300

Entrance to the Teatro Carcano, in Corso di Porta Romana

Corso di Porta Romana ❶

Map 7 C2. Ⓜ 3 Missori. 🚊 4, 12, 15, 24, 27. 🚌 65, 94.

THIS AVENUE WAS laid out over a porticoed stretch of the ancient Roman road outside the city walls (2nd–3rd century AD) that led to Rome. It ran from Porta Romana – then just beyond present-day Piazza Missori – to a triumphal arch (near the widening in the road known as Crocetta), transformed by Barbarossa into a fortified gate in the walls in 1162. The new gate (1171), further back, was demolished in 1793.

The Corso is lined with many noble palazzi. The 17th-century Palazzo Acerbi at No. 3; Palazzo Annoni at No. 6, designed by Francesco Maria Richini (1631), famous for its art collection which includes works by Rubens and Van Dyck; Palazzo Mellerio at No. 13 and Casa Bettoni (1865) at No. 20, with statues of Bersaglieri flanking the door. Via Santa Sofia crosses the Corso, and over the Naviglio canal close to the Crocetta, whose name derives from a votive cross set there during the 1576 plague.

Opposite is the Teatro Carcano (1803), where the great Italian actress Eleonora Duse performed. The Corso ends at the Porta Romana (in Piazzale Medaglie d'Oro), built in 1598. To the right you can see a fragment of the Spanish walls built by Ferrante Gonzaga (1545); they ran for 11,216 m (37,000 ft) and were demolished in 1889

Torre Velasca ❷

Piazza Velasca 5. **Map** 7 C2. Ⓜ 3 Missori. 🚊 4, 12, 15, 24, 27. 🚌 65, 94.

THIS TOWER, built in the late 1950s by architects Belgioioso, Nathan Rogers and Peressutti, is one of the best-known monuments in modern-day Milan. The overhang of the upper part of the building and its red colour are reminiscent of Italian medieval towers, but the shape actually grew out of the need to create more office space in a limited area.

Cappella Trivulzio, in San Nazaro Maggiore (16th century)

San Nazaro Maggiore ❸

Piazza San Nazaro. **Map** 8 D2. 📞 02-58 30 77 19. Ⓜ 3 Missori. 🚊 4, 12, 15, 24, 27. 🚌 65, 94. 🕐 7:30am–12:15pm, 3:15–6:30pm. ⛪ 6pm pre-hols; 8:30, 10, 11:30am, 6pm hols. 🏛 📷 ♿

THE ORIGINAL basilica was built by Sant'Ambrogio in AD 382–6 to house the remains of the Apostles Andrew, John and Thomas, which is why it was known as the *Basilica Apostolorum*. It was dedicated to San Nazaro when his remains – found by Sant'Ambrogio near the basilica – were buried here in 396. The church was built outside the walls in an Early Christian burial ground – as can be seen by the sarcophagi outside and the epitaph in the right-hand transept – and looked onto an ancient Roman porticoed street. It was rebuilt after a fire in 1075 reusing much original material.

The church is preceded by the octagonal Trivulzio Chapel, begun in Renaissance style in 1512 by Bramantino and continued by Cristoforo Lombardo. It houses the tomb of Gian Giacomo Trivulzio and his family.

The nave of the church has a cross vault. Either side of the entrance you will see the remains of the Romanesque doorway covered by the Trivulzio Chapel. On the walls, among fresco fragments, are parts of the original masonry. In the crossing, the dome is supported by the 4th-century piers; two altars in the choir contain the remains of the Apostles and San Nazaro. Left of the altar is the small cruciform chapel of San Lino, with traces of 10th–15th-century frescoes. In the transepts are a fine *Last Supper* by Bernardino Lanino (right) and *Passion of Jesus* by Luini (left). The Chapel of St Catherine (1540) has Lanino's *Martyrdom of St Catherine* and a 16th-century stained glass window depicting the *Life of St Catherine*.

The remains of San Nazaro, found by Sant'Ambrogio in AD 396

Ca' Granda ❹

THE "CASA GRANDE", or Ospedale Maggiore, was built for Francesco Sforza from 1456 on with the aim of uniting the city's 30 hospitals. The "large house" was designed by Filarete, who built only part of it, and was finished in stages in the 17th and 18th centuries. In 1939 the hospital moved to a new site, and since 1952 the Ca' Granda has housed the liberal arts faculties of the Università Statale, Milan's

17th-century window

university. The hospital was modern for its time: there were separate wings for men and women – each with a central infirmary – and a large courtyard between them.

VISITORS' CHECKLIST

Via Festa del Perdono 5. **Map** 8
D2. 📞 02-583 51. Ⓜ 1, 3
Duomo, 3 Missori. 🚋 12, 23,
27. 🚌 54, 60, 65. ◗ 7:30am–
7:30pm Mon–Fri; 8am–noon Sat
(first 3 weeks of Aug: 7:30am–
3:30pm Mon–Fri). ● Sun &
hols (open in morning pre-hols).
♿ ∅ **Chiesa dell'Annunciata**
📞 02-58 30 74 65. ◗ 8am–
7pm (when University is open).

The church of the Annunciata (17th-century) contains a 1639 canvas by Guercino.

★ Fifteenth-century Façade
The brick façade has round arches and is richly decorated. There were workshops and warehouses at ground level.

The Neo-Classical Macchio Wing, seat of the Faculty of Letters, Philosophy and Jurisprudence, housed the benefactors' art gallery, with portraits by leading artists.

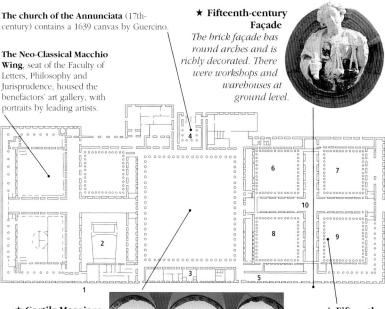

★ Cortile Maggiore
Francesco Maria Richini designed the courtyard with a Renaissance arcade and Baroque loggia, adding busts in yellow-pink-grey stone.

★ Fifteenth-century Courtyards
These housed the women's bathrooms, the ice-house and the woodshed. The Spezieria is the oldest courtyard.

KEY

- ☐ 15th-century section
- ☐ 17th-century section
- ☐ 18th–19th-century section
- **1** Entrance to the Faculties of Liberal Arts, Philosophy and Jurisprudence

2 Aula Magna
3 Courtyard entrance
4 Chiesa dell'Annunciata
5 Porticoes, 15th-century wing
6–9 Courtyards, 15th-century wing
10 Crociera, formerly the infirmary

STAR FEATURES

★ Fifteenth-century Façade

★ Cortile Maggiore

★ Fifteenth-century Courtyards

The fish pond in the Giardino della Guastalla, near Via Sforza

Giardino della Guastalla **5**

Via Francesco Sforza, Via San
Barnaba, Via Guastalla. **Map** 8 DE2.
🚋 12, 23, 27. 🚌 37, 60, 73, 77,
84, 94. ⬤ 8am–5pm.

THIS GARDEN WAS laid out in
1555 by Countess Ludo-
vica Torelli della Guastalla,
next to the college of the
same name for the daugh-
ters of impoverished
aristocrats. The garden
is Milan's oldest. In
the early 1600s it
was transformed
into an Italian-
style garden, and a
goldfish pond on
two communicating
terraces was added.
There is also a 17th-
century shrine
representing Mary
Magdalen attended
by angels and a Neo-
Classical temple
designed by Luigi
Cagnola. In 1939
the garden was
separated from the
adjacent Sormani
park and opened to
the public. At the
Via Guastalla exit (No. 19)
you can visit the Synagogue,
designed by Luca Beltrami
(1890–92) and, at the corner
of Via San Barnaba, the
church of Santi Barnaba e
Paolo, which is part of the
nearby Chierici Regolari di
San Paolo college. It is a
prototype of 16th-century
Lombard churches, founded
in 1558 and then modified by
Galeazzo Alessi. Inside are
paintings by Aurelio Luini,
son of Bernardino, Camillo
Procaccini and Moncalvo.

**Statue on the façade
of San Bernardino
alle Ossa**

Santo Stefano Maggiore and San Bernardino alle Ossa **6**

Piazza Santo Stefano. **Map** 8 D1.
Ⓜ 1, 3 Duomo. 🚋 12, 23, 27.
🚌 54, 60, 65. **Santo Stefano –
Archivio Storico Diocesano
(Historic Archive)** 📞 02-76 00 62
22. ⬤ 9:15am–12:15pm Mon–Fri
(entrance: Via della Signora 1).
San Bernardino alle Ossa
📞 02-76 02 37 35. ⬤ 8am–
2pm (noon Sun). ✝ 8:30am
Mon–Fri; 11am hols. 🚫 ♿

SANTO STEFANO
dates back to
the 5th century.
It was rebuilt in
1075 after being
destroyed by a fire
and was again rebuilt
in its present form in
1584 by Giuseppe
Meda. The Baroque
bell tower was built
in 1643–74 by Carlo
Buzzi: the pilaster
at the base is all
that remains of the
quadriporticus that
once faced the
medieval basilica.
The church is now used as
the Diocesan Archive. Next
door are San Bernardino alle
Ossa, originally medieval but
since rebuilt many times, and
the ossuary chapel (with a
concave façade) built in 1210
and altered in 1695. The latter
is small and entirely covered
with human bones and skulls.
The dim light and dark walls
make a striking contrast to the
bright colours of the fresco
on the vault by Sebastiano
Ricci (1695): *The Triumph
of Souls among Angels.*

Largo Augusto and Via Durini **7**

Map 8 DE1. Ⓜ 1, 3 Duomo. 🚋 12,
23, 27, 37. 🚌 54, 60, 65, 73, 84, 94.

SINCE 1580 THE Verziere
Column, commissioned
by San Carlo Borromeo to
celebrate the end of the 1576
plague, has stood in the
middle of Largo Augusto.
This is one of the few votive
columns to survive the late
18th century. Many were lost
after the suppression of the
monastic orders that owned
them, or sacrificed to make
room for new building
projects. This square marks
the beginning of Via Durini,
which is dominated by the
concave façade of Santa Maria
della Sanità (1708). No. 20 is
Casa Toscanini, the great conductor's house, and No. 24 is
Palazzo Durini, built in 1648
by Francesco Maria Richini.
On adjacent Corso Europa is
16th-century Palazzo Litta
Modignani, where a Roman
mosaic was found. Palazzo
Litta was altered in the 1700s.

Palazzo Sormani Andreani **8**

Corso di Porta Vittoria 6. **Map** 8 E1.
📞 02-78 22 19 📠 02-76 00 65 88.
🚋 12, 23, 27. 🚌 54, 60, 65, 73,
84, 94. ⬤ 9am–7:30pm Mon–Sat.
⬤ hols, Aug.

THE PALAZZO, constructed
in the 18th century, was
enlarged in 1736 by Francesco
Croce, who made it into one
of the most lavish residences

**Façade of Palazzo Sormani,
the Municipal Library since 1956**

of the time. Croce also designed the characteristic late Baroque curved façade. Reconstructed after World War II, the palazzo became the home of the Municipal (or Sormani Andreani) Library, the largest in Milan. It has over 580,000 works, including Stendhal's private library, a newspaper library with about 19,500 Italian and foreign publications, and a record and CD collection. A catalogue of all the Milan libraries is also here, as is the regional periodicals catalogue.

The Neo-Classical back opens onto a garden, part of the larger original one, which is used for small exhibitions. Nearby, at No. 2 Via Visconti di Modrone, is one of Milan's excellent traditional *pasticcerie*, the Taveggia pastry shop *(see p179)*.

Palazzo di Giustizia ❾

Corso di Porta Vittoria. **Map** 8 E1. 🚃 12, 23, 27. 🚋 37, 60, 73, 77, 84.

THE CENTRE of attention in the early 1990s because of the Mani Pulite (clean hands) corruption inquests and trials which changed much of the face of Italian politics, the Milan Law Courts were designed in typical Fascist style (1932–40) by Marcello Piacentini. The building also houses the Notarial Acts Archive, formerly in the Palazzo della Ragione *(see p54)*. The Palazzo has 1,200 rooms and 65 law courts with works by contemporary artists, including Mario Sironi's fresco in the Assize Court.

The Palazzo di Giustizia (1932–40), a typical example of Fascist architecture

Detail from *The Legend of the Virgin*, San Pietro in Gessate

San Pietro in Gessate ❿

Piazza San Pietro in Gessate. **Map** 8 E1. 📞 02-545 01 45. 🚃 12, 23, 27. 🚋 37, 60, 77, 84. 🕐 7:30am–6pm. ✝ 8am Mon–Fri; 7pm pre-hols; 9am, 12:15 & 7pm hols.

THIS CHURCH was built in 1447–75 by the Solari school and financed by the Florentine banker Pigello Portinari, whose emblem is on the outer wall of the apse. In the middle of the façade, rebuilt in 1912, is a portal with an effigy of St Peter, which was added in the 1600s. The Gothic interior has a three-aisle nave with ribbed vaulting and pointed arches and has preserved some original painting. The church was damaged during World War II, in particular the right-hand chapels, where there are traces of

frescoes by Antonio Campi, Moncalvo and Bergognone (whose *Funeral of St Martin* is in the fifth chapel). The third and fifth chapels on the left have fine frescoes by Montorfano: *Life of St John the Baptist* (1484) and *The Legend of St Anthony Abbot*. The eight choir stalls were rebuilt with the remains of the 1640 ones by Carlo Garavaglia, damaged in 1943 and partly used as firewood during the war. The left-hand transept (or Cappella Grifi) has frescoes of the *Life of Sant'Ambrogio* (1490) commissioned by the Sforza senator Ambrogio Grifi from Bernardino Butinone and Bernardino Zenale. In the lunettes under the vault, next to *Sant'Ambrogio on Horseback*, you can see the figure of a hanged man whose rope "drops" into the scene below, down to the hangman. These recently restored frescoes were discovered in 1862 under the plaster put on the walls during the plague to disinfect the church.

The arcade in the Rotonda della Besana

Rotonda della Besana ⓫

Via San Barnaba, corner of Via Besana. **Map** 8 F2. 🚋 9, 29, 30. 🚌 77, 84. ⃞ *for temporary exhibitions or summer cultural events only.*

THE ROTONDA was the cemetery of the nearby Ca' Granda Hospital designed in 1695 by Francesco Raffagno next to the Spanish walls, on present-day Viale Regina Margherita. The dead (about 150,000) were buried in the crypts under the arcades. When it was closed in 1783, viceroy Eugène de Beauharnais tried to change it into the Pantheon of the Regno Italico (1809), but the project fell through and the round brick building first housed patients with infectious diseases and then, up to 1940, was the hospital laundry. It is now used for temporary exhibitions and as an outdoor cinema in summer.

In the middle is the deconsecrated San Michele ai Nuovi Sepolcri, built in 1713. It has a Greek cross plan with a central altar, visible from all sides. The small skulls sculpted on the capitals are a reminder of the original function of this complex.

On Via San Barnaba is Santa Maria della Pace, designed by Pietro Antonio Solari in 1466, the property of the Order of Knights of the Holy Sepulchre. In 1805 the church was suppressed and the paintings removed (some are now in the Brera), but some 17th-century frescoes by Tanzio da Varallo remain.

The nearby monastery is the home of the Società Umanitaria, founded in 1893 to educate and aid the poor. It has a library devoted to labour problems. The only remaining part of the monastery is the refectory, with a *Crucifixion* by Marco d'Oggiono. Returning to Corso di Porta Vittoria, you come to Piazza Cinque Giornate, with a monument by Giuseppe Grandi (1895) commemorating the anti-Austrian insurrection of 1848 (*see p22*). The female figures symbolize the Five Days, whose dead are buried in the crypt below.

Conservatorio di Musica Giuseppe Verdi ⓬

Via Conservatorio 12. **Map** 8 E1. 📞 02-762 11 01. 🚋 54, 61, 77. ⃞ *for concerts only.*

MILAN'S CONSERVATORY was founded by Viceroy Eugène de Beauharnais in 1808 in a monastery. Important musicians and composers have studied here – but the young Verdi was refused admission. There is a chamber music hall and a large auditorium for symphonic music. The library boasts over 35,000 books and 460,000 pieces of written music, scores, etc., including works by Mozart, Rossini, Donizetti, Bellini and Verdi, as well as a small museum of precious stringed instruments.

Santa Maria della Passione ⓭

Via Bellini 2. **Map** 8 EF4. 📞 02-76 02 13 70. 🚋 54, 61, 77. 🚌 94. ⃞ 7am–noon, 3–6:15pm daily. ✝ 7:15, 8:15 am, 5:30pm Mon–Fri; 5:30pm pre-hols; 10, 11am, 5:30pm hols. 📷
Museum ⬤ *for restoration.*

THE SECOND LARGEST church in Milan, after the Duomo, was built under the patronage of the prelate Daniele Birago, who had donated the land to the Lateran Canons. Work began in 1486 to a design by Giovanni Battagio. Originally the church had a Greek cross plan but it was lengthened with a nave and six semi-circular chapels on each side in 1573 by Martino Bassi. The façade of the church – and the nearby convent, now the home of the Conservatory – was added in 1692 by Giuseppe Rusnati, who kept it low so that visitors could appreciate the majestic octagonal covering of the dome designed by Cristoforo Lombardo (1530). To enhance this view and link the church with the Naviglio, Abbot Gadio had the Via della Passione laid out in front of the entrance in 1540. The interior, with a frescoed barrel vault, is very atmospheric. Fourteen early 17th-century portraits of the saints of the Lateran Order, attributed to Daniele Crespi and his school, are on the piers. In the right-hand chapels, two works worth seeing are *Christ at the Pillar*

The Giuseppe Verdi Conservatory, housed in a former monastery

The octagonal dome of Santa Maria della Passione (17th century)

by Giulio Cesare Procaccini, on the altar of the third chapel, and the *Madonna di Caravaggio*, a fresco attributed to Bramantino, in the sixth chapel. The presbytery still has its original Greek cross structure. The paintings hanging from the piers, mostly the work of Crespi, narrate the Passion: don't miss *Christ Nailed to the Cross*. Behind the Baroque high altar is a wooden choir (16th century) with mother of pearl inlay. Either side of the choir are two 16th–17th-century organs, still used for concerts. The doors of the left one have scenes from the Passion painted by Crespi.

There are remarkable Cinquecento paintings in the transepts: the right-hand one has a *Deposition* altarpiece by Bernardino Luini (1510–15) with the *Legend of the Cross* in the predella; and on the altar of the left-hand one is Gaudenzio Ferrari's *Last Supper* (1543), with a *Crucifixion* by Giulio Campi (1560) alongside.

The chapels on the left-hand side of the nave contain fine works by Camillo Procaccini and Duchino and the first chapel is noteworthy because of the impressive realism of Crespi's *St Charles Fasting*. The organ recess to the right leads to the Museum, founded in the old

Santa Maria della Passione: one of the saints of the Lateran Order

monastery in 1972. It consists of four sections. The Old Sacristy has 17th-century Lombard paintings and ten 18th-century wooden panels with scenes from the Bible.

The 15th-century Chapter House was designed and painted by Bergognone: saints and doctors are in a false peristyle. On the right-hand wall is Christ with the Apostles. The Gallery has works by Crespi, Procaccini and Nuvolone; the Sala degli Arredi has 17th-century furniture and a vault frescoed by Giulio Campi (1558). In Via Bellini you can see the left side of the church and the dome. At No. 11 is the Art Nouveau Casa Campanini (1904), with wrought iron work by Alessandro Mazzucotelli.

Palazzo Isimbardi ⑭

Corso Monforte 35. **Map** 4 E5.
📞 02-77 40 29 73 or 02-77 40 24 16 (Lombardy Province PR Office). Ⓜ 1 San Babila. 🚋 9, 23, 29, 30. 🚌 54, 61, 94. 🄾 apply to APT.

THE SEAT OF the Milan provincial government since 1935, this palazzo dates from the 15th century but was enlarged by the noble families who lived in it, among whom were the Isimbardi, who purchased it in 1775. The 18th-century façade on Corso

Monforte leads to the porticoed court of honour (16th century), which still has its original herringbone pattern paving. The garden behind this boasts an admirable Neo-Classical façade designed by Giacomo Tazzini (1826).

The palazzo was recently opened to the public and features many interestingly decorated rooms and fine works of art, such as the wooden 17th-century globe by Giovanni Jacopo de Rossi. The most important room is the Giunta (Council Chamber), which in 1954 became the home of Tiepolo's masterful *Triumph of Doge Morosini*, which came from Palazzo Morosini in Venice. The Sala dell'Antegiunta has a lovely 18th-century Murano glass chandelier, while the Sala degli Affreschi boasts 17th-century frescoes taken from the villa of Cardinal Monti at Vaprio d'Adda. The Studio del Presidente is decorated with a Neo-Classical ceiling, partly in fine gold. In 1940 the Province of Milan enlarged the palazzo. The new façade on Via Vivaio was decorated with bas reliefs sculpted by Salvatore Saponaro depicting the activities of the Milanese. At No. 31 Corso Monforte is the Palazzo della Prefettura, rebuilt in its present state in 1782. It has frescoes by Andrea Appiani. It is not open to the public.

The 18th-century façade of Palazzo Isimbardi, in Corso Monforte

The Abbey of Chiaravalle ⑮

FRENCH CISTERCIAN MONKS began constructing this church in 1150–60 and it was dedicated to the Virgin Mary in 1221. The complex is a combination of French Gothic and Lombard Romanesque, resulting in a delightful example of Cistercian architecture. The bell tower was added in 1349. The entrance is in the 16th-century tower flanked by two small churches. In 1798 Napoleon suppressed the monastic order, the monks were forced to leave and the abbey deteriorated so much that in 1858 Bramante's 15th-century cloister was demolished to make room for a railway line. Restored and given back to the monks, the abbey has regained its former splendour and is again an oasis of peace.

★ **Frescoes**
The 14th-century frescoes on the dome narrate The Legend of the Virgin. *Those in the transept (above), represent among other things the genealogical tree of the Benedictine monks.*

★ **Wooden Choir**
The 44 stalls have carvings of the Life of St Bernard *by Carlo Garavaglia (1645), who according to legend took refuge in the abbey to expiate the murder of his brother.*

The interior had no paintings because this would have distracted the monks from their prayers. The 17th-century frescoes tell the story of the order.

Entrance

The top of the façade, made of brick, is what remains of the original. The porch was added in 162... The 16th-century main portal has figures of Cistercian saints including St Bernard holding the church in his hand.

★ **Bell Tower** *(ciribiciaccola)*
Eighty small marble columns adorn the bell tower designed by Francesco Pecorari in 1349. Called ciribiciaccola *(clever contraption) by the Milanese, its bells accompanied the farmers' and monks' working day. The tower bell rope still hangs in the church.*

VISITORS' CHECKLIST

Via Sant'Arialdo 102, Chiaravalle Milanese. 02-57 40 34 04. 3 Corvetto. 77. 9–11:30am, 3–5:30pm Mon–Sat; 3–4:30pm Sun. 8, 10 (Gregorian chant), 11:30am, 5, 6pm hols; 8am Mon–Fri. (no flash).

The many windows (double, triple and quadruple lancet) lend movement to the tower structure.

Madonna della Buonanotte
Painted in 1512 by Bernardino Luini at the top of the steps leading to the dormitory, this picture is known as the Madonna della Buonanotte *because she "said goodnight" to the monks going to bed.*

The chapter house, designed in the late 15th century by Bramante, has three graffiti from that period depicting Santa Maria delle Grazie, the Duomo and Castello Sforzesco.

Refectory

★ **Cloister**
Rebuilt in 1952 by using the one surviving side as a model, the cloister has a plaque commemorating the founding of the church, next to which is a stork, the symbol of Chiaravalle.

STAR FEATURES

★ **Wooden Choir**

★ **Cloister**

★ **Bell Tower** *(ciribiciaccola)*

★ **Frescoes**

31/12/01   10:52

www.waterstones.co.uk

CHANGE		.10
Cash		.60

| TOTAL | | .50 |
| NEWSPAPER | 1 | .50 |

212 CASH-1   1458 0394 003

www.waterstones.co.uk
Fax No: 0131 226 4689
Tel No: 0131 226 2666
VAT NO: 710631184
EH2 4HD
EDINBURGH
128 Princes Street
WATERSTONE'S BOOKSELLERS

WATERSTONE'S BOOKSELLERS
128 Princes Street
EDINBURGH
EH2 4AD
VAT NO: 710631184
Tel No: 0131 226 2666
Fax No: 0131 226 4689
www.waterstones.co.uk

212 CASH 1   1459 0394 003

EYEWITNESS TRAV   1   9.99
              TOTAL   9.99

          ALLOWANCE   3.00-
              TOTAL   6.99

WATERSTONE'S VO   1   1.00
WATERSTONE'S VO   1   1.00
WATERSTONE'S VO   1   1.00
              TOTAL   9.99

Book Token   10.00
          CHANGE   .01

        www.waterstones.co.uk

                  31/12/01   10:58

NORTHEAST MILAN

ELEGANT VIA MANZONI is the heart of a vast area stretching from the Brera quarter to Via Montenapoleone and Corso Venezia. Brera is known for its characteristic winding streets, some of which still have their 18th-century paving. The fashion district around Via Montenapoleone is the domain of the designer shops. Starting from Piazza San Babila and continuing

Logo of the Museo Bagatti Valsecchi

through Corso Venezia, with its many aristocratic palazzi, you will come to the Giardini Pubblici and the Villa Reale, home of the Modern Art Gallery. The area extending beyond the ramparts, which was undeveloped up to the early 19th century, includes the Cimitero Monumentale, the Stazione Centrale (main railway station) and the Pirelli building, Milan's tallest.

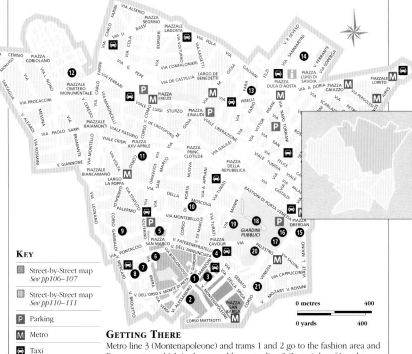

KEY

- 🟦 Street-by-Street map *See pp106–107*
- 🟦 Street-by-Street map *See pp110–111*
- **P** Parking
- **M** Metro
- 🚕 Taxi

GETTING THERE

Metro line 3 (Montenapoleone) and trams 1 and 2 go to the fashion area and Brera quarter, which is also served by metro line 2 (Lanza), bus 61 and trams 3, 4, 12, 14 and 27. The Cimitero Monumentale is served by trams 3, 4, 12, 14, 29, 30 and 33, while metro lines 2 and 3 stop at the Stazione Centrale.

SIGHTS AT A GLANCE

Streets and Squares
Archi di Porta Nuova ④
Bastioni di Porta Venezia ⑮
Corso Venezia, *see pp122–3* ㉑
Via Manzoni ①

Historic Buildings
Palazzo Cusani ⑦
Palazzo Dugnani ⑲
Pirelli Building ⑬
Stazione Centrale ⑭

Museums and Galleries
Museo Bagatti Valsecchi ③
Museo di Storia Naturale ⑰
Museo Poldi Pezzoli ②
Pinacoteca di Brera see pp114–17 ⑥
Planetarium ⑯
Villa Reale and Galleria d'Arte Moderna ⑳

Gardens and Cemeteries
Cimitero Monumentale ⑫
Giardini Pubblici ⑱

Churches
San Marco ⑤
San Simpliciano ⑨
Sant'Angelo ⑩
Santa Maria del Carmine ⑧
Santa Maria Incoronata ⑪

Street-by-Street: the Fashion District

Versace logo

VIA MONTENAPOLEONE represents the elegant heart of Milan and is one of the four sides of the so-called *quadrilatero* or fashion district (the other three sides are Via Manzoni, Via Sant'Andrea and Via della Spiga). When strolling through this district, besides the shops of some of the top Italian and international fashion designers, you will see grand Neo-Classical aristocratic residences such as Palazzo Melzi di Cusano, at No. 18 Via Montenapoleone, built in 1830. Via Bigli, on the other hand, is lined with 16th- and 17th-century palazzi with porticoed courtyards.

Archi di Porta Nuova
This city gate, once part of the medieval walls, is decorated with copies of 1st-century AD Roman tombstones. Left, a stele representing a family ❹

VALENTINO

Via Manzoni
This broad street is lined with aristocratic palazzi ❶

Grand Hotel et de Milan

Under the Portico del Lattèe (milkman's arcade) is the wall of the demolished church of San Donnino alla Mazza.

★ **Museo Poldi Pezzoli**
The Portrait of a Young Lady *(15th century), attributed to Antonio Pollaiolo, is the symbol of this museum created by Gian Giacomo Poldi Pezzoli. Besides paintings by Mantegna, Piero della Francesca and Bellini, it has rugs, armour and precious ceramics* ❷

STAR SIGHTS

★ **Museo Poldi Pezzoli**

★ **Museo Bagatti Valsecchi**

0 metres   50
0 yards   50

★ Museo Bagatti Valsecchi
This Neo-Renaissance palazzo was built as the family residence by the Bagatti Valsecchi brothers. It still has 16 rooms with their original 19th-century furnishings and many works of art belonging to the owners, who were art collectors ❸

LOCATOR MAP
See Street Finder, map 4

GIORGIO ARMANI

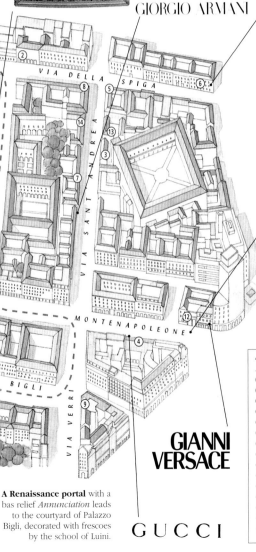

Via Montenapoleone follows the course of the ancient Roman walls. It gets its name from a bank that once stood here called "Monte Napoleone". Designer shops line the street.

KEY

━ ━ ━ ━ Suggested route

A Renaissance portal with a bas relief *Annunciation* leads to the courtyard of Palazzo Bigli, decorated with frescoes by the school of Luini.

GIANNI VERSACE

GUCCI

TOP FASHION DESIGNERS

① **Byblos** Via della Spiga 42.
② **Cerruti 1881** Via della Spiga 20.
③ **Chanel** Via Sant'Andrea 10a.
④ **Etro** Via Montenapoleone 5.
⑤ **Fendi** Via Sant'Andrea 16.
⑥ **Genny** Via della Spiga 4.
⑦ **Gianfranco Ferrè** Via Sant'Andrea 15.
⑧ **Hermès** Via Sant'Andrea 21.
⑨ **Jil Sander** Via P Verri 6.
⑩ **Krizia** Via della Spiga 23.
⑪ **Laura Biagiotti** Via Borgospesso 19.
⑫ **Mila Schön** Via Montenapoleone 2.
⑬ **Moschino** Via Sant'Andrea 12.
⑭ **Prada** Via Sant'Andrea 21.
⑮ **Romeo Gigli** Via della Spiga 30.

The inner garden of a palazzo in Via Manzoni

Via Manzoni ❶

Map 3 C4. **M** 1 Duomo, 3 Montenapoleone. 🚋 1, 2. 🚌 61, 94. Palazzi not open for visits.

ONCE KNOWN AS "Corsia del Giardino" (Garden Lane) because of its many parks, this street acquired its present name in 1865, when the great Italian novelist Manzoni died. Its aristocratic appearance is created by the patrician palazzi and Teatro alla Scala (see pp52–3), which stimulated the opening of chic cafés attracting a smart clientele. At No. 6 is 19th-century Palazzo Brentani, decorated with medallions with busts of illustrious persons, and No. 10 is Palazzo Anguissola (1775–8), which now houses the historic archive of the Banca Commerciale Italiana. No. 12, another 19th-century building, is the home of the famous Museo Poldi Pezzoli, and No. 29 is the Grand Hotel et de Milan (1865), where Giuseppe Verdi died in 1901.

Near the end of Via Montenapoleone stands Aldo Rossi's monument to former Italian President Sandro Pertini (1990) and, next to this, Palazzo Gallarati Scotti (No. 30), built in the early 1700s. Opposite, Via Pisoni takes you to the remains of the 15th-century cloister of the Umiliate di Sant'Erasmo monastery, now part of a modern building. In the last stretch is 18th-century Palazzo Borromeo d'Adda, which was a haunt for literati and artists, including Stendhal.

Museo Poldi Pezzoli ❷

Via Manzoni 12. **Map** 4 D5. 🕻 02-79 48 89. **M** 3 Montenapoleone. 🚋 1, 2. 🚌 61, 94. ⏰ 10am–6pm Tue–Sun. ● 1 Jan, Easter, 1 May, 15 Aug, 25 Dec. 🏷️ 📷 (no flash). ♿ ground floor only. 🎫 Lecture hall, Library.

THIS PRIVATE MUSEUM was established by nobleman Gian Giacomo Poldi Pezzoli and opened to the public in 1881. The building, a singular example of a late 19th-century aristocratic Milanese residence, contains Poldi Pezzoli's fine collection of paintings, sculpture, armour, rugs, watches, glass and textiles. The ground floor houses arms and armour from ancient Roman times to the 18th century. The Salone dell'Affresco, named after The Apotheosis of Bartolomeo Colleoni frescoed by Carlo Innocenzo Carloni, boasts a Tabriz carpet with hunting scenes (Persia, 1522–3), made of wool and silver on silk. In the adjoining room is the museum's collection of textiles, including a 15th-century cope with Florentine embroidery representing The Coronation of the Virgin, after a drawing by Botticelli.

The staircase, decorated with landscapes by Magnasco, leads to the first floor. In the Salette dei Lombardi is 15th–16th-century Lombard painting. Don't miss the canvases by Bergognone, Luini, the Leonardo-esque painters, a Polyptych by Cristoforo Moretti, and Vincenzo Foppa's Portrait of Giovanni Francesco Brivio. The portraits of Martin Luther and his wife by Lucas Cranach (1529) are

Poldi Pezzoli Museum logo

in the Sala degli Stranieri. A display case with precious porcelain separates the next room from the Salone Dorato. Designed by Poldi Pezzoli and destroyed by bombs in 1943, this hall was restored in 1974 by Luigi Caccia Dominioni. On display are fine works such as St Nicholas of Tolentino by Piero della Francesca, Botticelli's Madonna and Child and Pietà, a Madonna and Child by Andrea Mantegna, Giovanni Bellini's Pietà and a Portrait of a Young Woman attributed to Antonio Pollaiolo. Three small rooms house the Visconti Venosta collection of portraits by Fra Galgario, including Gentleman with Tricorn, and interesting 16th–18th-century clocks. The Saletta dei Vetri Antichi di Murano has fine specimens of glasswork, and the Gabinetto Dantesco features two stained glass windows narrating episodes from Dante's life. The last rooms house a collection of small bronzes, paintings by Tiepolo, a Sacred Conversation by Lotto, and Giovanni Bellini's Crucifixion. Lastly, the Gabinetto degli Ori has a collection of precious ancient jewellery and goldsmithery.

Botticelli's Pietà (1495), Museo Poldi Pezzoli

A cradle from the Camera Rossa in the Museo Bagatti Valsecchi

Museo Bagatti Valsecchi ❸

Via Santo Spirito 10. **Map** 4 D4.
📞 02-76 00 61 32. Ⓜ 3 Monte-napoleone. 🚋 1, 2. ⏰ 10am–6pm Tue–Sun. 🚫 Mon, 1 Jan, Easter, 1 May, 15 Aug, 25 Dec. 🎫 ♿ ground floor only. 📷 by appt. 🚻

OPENED IN 1994 in the prestigious late 19th-century residence of the two Bagatti Valsecchi brothers, Fausto and Giuseppe, this fascinating museum is an important record of art collectors' taste in that period. The building was designed in Neo-Renaissance style, with an elegant façade and two well proportioned courtyards, and was furnished with works of art and imitation Renaissance furniture. It was seen as a private house and not a museum, and was furnished with every possible comfort. The rooms feature tapestries, ceramics, ivory work and arms, as well as important paintings such as the elegant *Santa*

Giustina by Giovanni Bellini (c.1475; kept in what was Giuseppe Bagatti Valsecchi's bedroom), Bernardo Zenale's panels and a *Polyptych* by Giampietrino. The library, with its valuable 15th-century parchments and a series of 16th–17th-century porcelain pharmacy vases, is also worth a look.

The intriguing Valtellinese bedroom has a magnificent 16th-century bed with Christ ascending Calvary and scenes from the Old Testament carved in the bedstead. The Sala della Stufa Valtellinese is also interesting, with its marvellous 16th-century wood panelling with an elegant sculpted frieze and a piece of furniture ingeniously concealing a piano. The Camera Rossa contains a delightful small collection of 15th–17th-century furniture for children that includes a high chair, a baby walker and a cradle. The dining room has a collection of kitchenware, tapestries and sideboards.

Archi di Porta Nuova ❹

Map 4 D4. Ⓜ 3 Montenapoleone. 🚋 1, 2. 🚌 61, 94.

THIS CITY GATE, restored in 1861, is one of two surviving ones forming part of the medieval wall system. Construction began in 1171, and the gate was probably modelled on the corresponding Porta Romana, some of whose building materials it used. The inner side on Via Manzoni is decorated with copies of 1st-century AD Roman tombstones, while the outside facing Piazza Cavour bears a tabernacle decorated with a *Madonna and Child with Saints Ambrose, Gervase and Protasius* (1330–39).

Facing the piazza is Palazzo dei Giornali (No. 2), built in 1942 as the main office of the newspaper *Il Popolo d'Italia* and decorated with bas reliefs by Mario Sironi. The square is framed by the Giardini Pubblici, in front of which is a monument to Cavour by Odoardo Tabacchi (1865).

The Porta Nuova Arches seen from Via Manzoni

MUSEUMS DEVOTED TO THE HISTORY OF MILAN

Several museums, collectively the Civiche Raccolte Storiche, are devoted to the history of Milan. Palazzo Morando Attendolo Bolognini (No. 6 Via Sant'Andrea) houses the Museo di Milano and the Museo di Storia Contemporanea. The former features documents and paintings about old Milan and its illustrious citizens, and the latter has mementoes from the period of the two world wars. The palazzo is also home to the Civico Museo Marinaro Ugo Mursia, a nautical museum. The Museo del Risorgimento in Palazzo Moriggia (No. 23 Via Borgonuovo) covers the history of the Italian unification movement, from the late 1700s to the annexation of Rome (1870).

Sign for the entrance to a chocolate factory, now in the Museo di Milano

Street-by-Street: The Brera Quarter

THE NAME OF MILAN'S traditional Bohemian quarter derives from the Germanic word *braida*, which denoted a grassy area. The presence of art students at the Accademia di Belle Arti and the world-famous Brera art gallery has contributed to the lively feel of this quarter, which is reinforced by the many cafés, restaurants, galleries, antique shops and nightclubs established here. In summer the narrow streets are enlivened even more by street stalls and fortune tellers. An antiques market is held on the third Saturday of each month in Via Brera.

The Indian Café is one of the most popular spots in the area.

The Museo Minguzzi has 100 pieces by the Bolognese sculptor.

The Naviglio della Martesana canal flowed from the Adda river and along present-day Via San Marco. It was used for transporting foodstuffs and building materials. At the end of the street is the Tombone di San Marco, a wooden canal lock that regulated the water flow.

★ **San Simpliciano**
This church was one of the four basilicas founded by Sant'Ambrogio and has preserved most of its original Early Christian architecture **9**

CAFÉ LIFE IN THE BRERA

Inside the Jamaica café, in Via Brera

The cafés and bars of the Brera quarter are lively and atmospheric. The Tombon de San Marc (Via San Marco) was once the haunt of the stevedores from the nearby Naviglio and now welcomes customers of all kinds. The famous Jamaica café (Via Brera) has jazz sessions on Mondays. Other atmospheric spots are the Louisiana Bistrò (Via Fiori Chiari), Sans Égal, in the pedestrian precinct of Via Fiori Chiari, the Indian Café (Corso Garibaldi) and the ethnic Soul to Soul (Via San Marco) *(see pp178–9, pp190–91)*.

| 0 metres | 100 |
| 0 yards | 100 |

STAR SIGHTS

★ **Pinacoteca di Brera**

★ **San Simpliciano**

★ **San Marco**

★ San Marco
The façade of this church, founded in 1254, was rebuilt in 1871 in Neo-Gothic style. The only remaining part of the original is the stone doorway, which has a relief of Christ between two saints and among symbols of the Evangelists **5**

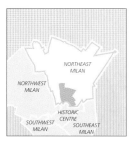

LOCATOR MAP
See Street Finder, maps 3, 4

★ Pinacoteca di Brera
The nucleus of one of Italy's top art galleries consists of works taken from churches that were suppressed in the late 1700s. The Brera boasts masterpieces by great artists such as Piero della Francesca, Mantegna, Raphael and Caravaggio **6**

The Civico Museo del Risorgimento, opened in 1896, is in Neo-Classical Palazzo Moriggia.

Palazzo Cusani
This building with a late Baroque façade (1719) is the headquarters of the Third Army Corps. On the first floor is the Officers' Club **7**

Santa Maria del Carmine
The 15th-century church was built with material taken from the nearby Castello Sforzesco when it was partly demolished **8**

- - - - Suggested route

The lunette over the entrance to San Marco

San Marco ❺

Piazza San Marco 2. **Map** 3 C4. 📞 02-29 00 25 98. 🚌 41, 43. ⏱ 7:30am –noon, 4–7:30pm. 🛐 7:45, 9:30am, 6:30pm Mon–Fri; 6:30pm pre-hols; 9:30, 11am, 12:15, 6:30pm hols.

THIS CHURCH WAS BEGUN in 1254 by the Augustine monk Lanfranco Settala. It was built on the site of an older church, dedicated by the Milanese to St Mark, patron saint of Venice, to thank the Venetians for help in the struggle against Emperor Frederick Barbarossa. In 1871 Carlo Maciachini built a new, Neo-Gothic façade around the Camionese school ogival portal and tabernacle.

The church has a Latin cross plan and nine patrician chapels, which were added to the right-hand aisle in the 14th–19th century. They contain 16th–17th-century paintings, including some by Paolo Lomazzo. In the right-hand transept is the *Foundation of the Augustine Order* by the Fiammenghini brothers, Settala's sarcophagus by Giovanni Balduccio (1317–49), and fragments of late Gothic frescoes found during the 1956 restoration. The presbytery is decorated with large canvases by Camillo Procaccini and Cerano depicting the Legend of St Augustine, and the *Genealogical Tree of the Order* by Genovesino (17th century), who also painted the *Angels' Backs* on the cupola. The left-hand transept leads to the Chapel of the Pietà, with *The Ascent to Calvary* by Ercole Procaccini. The left-hand aisle has canvases by Camillo and Giulio Cesare Procaccini and Palma

il Giovane, and a Leonardo-esque fresco found in 1975. From outside the Romanesque transept and the 13th-century bell tower are visible.

Pinacoteca di Brera ❻

See pp114–7.

Palazzo Cusani ❼

Via Brera 15. **Map** 3 C4. Ⓜ 2 Lanza. 🚋 3, 4, 12, 14. 🚌 61. ⏱ to the public.

ORIGINALLY BUILT in the 1500s, this palazzo was rebuilt in 1719 by Giovanni Ruggeri, who designed the late Baroque façade with its ornate windows and balconies, while the Neo-Classical façade facing the garden was designed by Piermarini. Tradition has it that the Cusani brothers ordered twin entrances so that each could have independent yet equal access. In the drawing room is an allegorical Tiepolo-like fresco (1740). The palazzo was the seat of the Ministry of War in the 19th century.

Santa Maria del Carmine ❽

Piazza del Carmine 2. **Map** 3 B4. 📞 02-86 46 33 65. 🚋 1, 3, 4, 12, 14, 27. 🚌 61. ⏱ 7:15–11:30am, 3:30–7pm. 🛐 6:30pm Mon–Fri; 6:30pm pre-hols; 9:45, 10:45 (English) & 11:45am, 4:45 (English) & 6:30pm hols.

SANTA MARIA DEL CARMINE was built in Gothic style in 1447 over a Romanesque church and was then rebuilt

in the Baroque period, while the present-day façade was designed by Carlo Maciachini in 1880. The spacious interior has a three-aisle nave covered by cross vaulting. The inclination of the first piers is due to the absence of a façade for a long period and the subsequent gradual settling of the building.

The right-hand transept contains part of the tomb of the Ducal Councillor Angelo Simonetta, above which are two paintings by Carlo Francesco Nuvolone and Fiammenghino; the opposite transept is decorated with a painting by Camillo Landriani.

The statues in the wooden choir (1579–85) are the original plaster models created for the spires of the Duomo by 19th-century artists. The Cappella del Rosario, built on the right of the choir (1673) by Gerolamo Quadrio, has marble dressing and is decorated with canvases by Camillo Procaccini depicting *The Legend of Mary*.

A statue in the choir

On the left-hand side of the church is the monastery cloister, with remains of noble tombs and ancient tombstones, and a Baroque sacristy, with furniture made by Quadrio in 1692.

Part of the Baroque sacristy, Santa Maria del Carmine

Angel Musicians by Aurelio Luini (16th century), in the church of San Simpliciano

San Simpliciano ⑨

Piazza San Simpliciano 7. **Map** 3 B4.
☎ 02-86 22 74. Ⓜ 2 Lanza.
🚋 3, 4, 12, 14. 🚌 43, 57, 70.
🕙 9:30–11:30am, 3–6pm (4–7pm Sun). ✝ 7:30am, 6pm Mon–Fri; 6pm pre-hols; 8, 10 & 11:30am, 6pm hols

THE CHURCH WAS founded by Sant'Ambrogio in the 4th century as the *Basilica Virginum* and completed in 401. It is preceded by a porch and once had open galleries on either side where penitents and new converts could take part in Mass. The façade, decorated with glazed plates, was added in 1870 by Maciachini, who retained the main portal. The capitals have 12th-century carvings of the processions of the Wise and Foolish Virgins. Fourteenth-century frescoes have been discovered in the first chapel on the right, and in the fourth is Enea Salmeggia's *Miracle of St Benedict* (1619). The apse is frescoed with the *Coronation of the Virgin* by Bergognone (1508). The Neo-Classical altar covers the wooden choir (1588), and on either side are two

organ pedestals frescoed by Aurelio Luini in the 1500s. The transept leads to the Early Christian Sacellum of San Simpliciano (closed), built to house the remains of San Simpliciano or of martyrs.

Sant'Angelo ⑩

Piazza Sant'Angelo 2. **Map** 4 D3.
☎ 02-65 45 51. 🚋 41, 43. 🚌 94.
🕙 6:30am–8pm. ✝ 7pm Mon–Fri; 7pm pre-hols; 9, 10 & 11 am, 12:15 & 7pm hols.

BUILT IN 1552 by Domenico Giunti to replace the older Franciscan church outside the Porta Nuova gate, which had been demolished to make room for the Spanish ramparts, Sant'Angelo is an important example of 16th-century Milanese architecture. The nave is separated from the presbytery by a triumphal arch with the *Assumption of Mary* by Legnanino (17th century). There are many 16th- and 17th-century paintings in the chapels. The first one on the right has canvases by Antonio Campi (1584) and a copy of the *Martyrdom of St Catherine of Alexandria* by

Gaudenzio Ferrari (the original is in the Brera); the second is Morazzone's *St Charles in Glory* and in the apse is Procaccini's *Legend of the Virgin*.

Santa Maria Incoronata ⑪

Corso Garibaldi 116. **Map** 3 C2.
☎ 02-65 48 55. Ⓜ 2 Garibaldi.
🚌 94. 🕙 6:15am–1:30pm, 4–7pm Mon–Sat; 8am–12:30pm, 4–7pm Sun. ✝ 7:30 & 9:30am, 4:30pm Mon–Sat; 8:30, 10 & 11:30am, 6:30pm hols.

THIS CHURCH consists of two buildings designed by Guiniforte Solari, which were merged in 1468. The left one was built for Francesco Sforza in 1451 and the other was built soon afterwards for his wife. The brick façade is double, as is the nave, which has two apses with 15th- and 17th-century frescoes. In the right-hand chapels are plaques in memory of Sforzesco court personages. The chapels opposite have frescoes by Montalto and Bernardino Zenale (the fresco in the first chapel is attributed to Zenale).

Lunette over one of the doors of San Simpliciano

SAN SIMPLICIANO, THE THREE MARTYRS AND THE CARROCCIO

St Ambrose asked the young Sisinius, Martirius and Alexander to go to Anaunia (today Val di Non) in northern Italy to spread Christianity. In 397 they were martyred and the bodies were given to Bishop Simpliciano, who buried them in the *Basilica Virginum*. According to legend, the martyrs were decisive in leading the Milanese to victory in the battle of Legnano against Barbarossa (1176). On that occasion three white doves flew out of the basilica and landed on the Carroccio (cart), the symbol of Milan, waiting to be blessed before the battle. On 29 May the city commemorates this event with a solemn ceremony.

Pinacoteca di Brera ❻

THE BRERA ART GALLERY holds one of Italy's most important art collections, featuring masterpieces by leading Italian artists from the 13th to the 20th century, including Raphael, Mantegna, Piero della Francesca and Caravaggio. The Pinacoteca is housed in the late 16th–early 17th-century palazzo built for the Jesuits in place of the Santa Maria di Brera Humiliati monastery. The Jesuits made this into a cultural centre by establishing a prestigious school, a library and the astronomical observatory – all activities supported by Empress Maria Theresa of Austria, who founded the Accademia di Belle Arti after the Jesuit order was suppressed (1773).

Portrait of Moïse Kisling
Amedeo Modigliani painted this work in 1915, reflecting his interest in African sculpture

Finding the Body of St Mark
The bold perspective and almost super-natural light in the room where the saint's body is found make this canvas (1562–6) one of Tintoretto's masterpieces.

KEY

- ☐ Jesi Collection (20th-century art)
- ☐ 13th–15th-century Italian painting
- ☐ 15th–16th-century Venetian painting
- ☐ 15th–16th-century Lombard painting
- ☐ 15th–16th-century Central Italian painting
- ☐ 17th–18th-century Italian and Flemish painting
- ☐ 18th–19th-century Italian painting

Twin staircases
lead to the entrance to the gallery on the first floor.

The Kiss
This canvas by Francesco Hayez (1859) is one of the most reproduced 19th-century Italian paintings – a patriotic and sentimental work epitomizing the optimism that prevailed after the unification of Italy.

★ **Dead Christ**
This masterpiece by Mantegna (c.1480) is striking for its intense light and bold fore-shortening. The work was among the artist's posses-sions at the time of his death.

VISITORS' CHECKLIST

Via Brera 28. **Map** 3 C4.
02-72 26 32 29. Info 02-199
199 100. 1, 3 Duomo, 2
Lanza. 1, 2, 3, 12, 14.
61. 9am–5:30pm Tue–Sat;
9am–12:30pm Sun, hols.
Mon, 25 Dec, 1 Jan. (no
flash).

This room has works by painters active in Lombardy from the late 15th to the mid-16th century, including Bergognone, Luini, Bramantino and Vincenzo Foppa.

★ **Montefeltro Altarpiece**
Piero della Francesca painted this great work in 1475 for Federico da Montefeltro, the Duke of Urbino, who is portrayed dressed in a Milanese suit of armour.

The courtyard with twin columns is the work of Richini (17th century).

GALLERY GUIDE
The Brera Gallery has 31 rooms, with works arranged in chronological order. The only exception is Room 1, where the Jesi Collection is on display. It includes 20th-century works which will be exhibited elsewhere in future. The paintings are also grouped together by schools of painting (Venetian, Tuscan, Lombard, etc.). The Sala della Passione on the ground floor is used for temporary exhibitions.

STAR EXHIBITS

★ **Dead Christ**

★ **The Marriage of the Virgin**

★ **Montefeltro Altarpiece**

Entrance

★ **The Marriage of the Virgin**
Raphael signed and dated (1504) his masterful altarpiece on the temple in the background. Some scholars say the young man breaking the staff is a self-portrait of the artist.

Exploring the Pinacoteca di Brera

THE ORIGINAL NUCLEUS of the Brera Gallery consisted mainly of plaster casts and drawings used as models for the art students of the Accademia di Belle Arti (founded in 1776). This collection was augmented with works from suppressed churches in Northern Italy and was officially opened in 1809, the paintings being arranged in rows on the wall, from floor to ceiling. The Pinacoteca became independent from the Accademia in 1882, and its fine collection further expanded through 19th- and 20th-century donations. The gallery has always suffered from lack of space, but there are plans to use the adjacent Palazzo Citterio.

Mantegna's masterpieces *Dead Christ* and *St Luke Altarpiece* (1453–4). Giovanni Bellini is represented by two Madonnas with Child and a *Pietà* (c.1470), and Carpaccio by *Legend of the Virgin*. There are portraits by Titian, Lotto and Tintoretto in room 7. *St Mark Preaching in Alexandria* (room 8) was painted for the Scuola Grande in St Mark's in Venice by Giovanni and Gentile Bellini.

The following room has works by Titian and Paolo Veronese, as well as the *Finding of the Body of St Mark*, which Tintoretto painted for Tommaso Rangone, who is portrayed as the kneeling man in the the middle of the scene.

The City Rises (c.1910) by Umberto Boccioni

JESI COLLECTION

THE 72 works donated by Emilio and Maria Jesi in 1976 and 1984 are at the beginning. The collection, mostly by Italian artists, covers the 1910–40 period. Key works include *Portrait of Moisè Kisling* by Modigliani, Umberto Boccioni's *Brawl in the Galleria* (1911) and *The City Rises* (a study for the canvas now in the New York MOMA), Carlo Carrà's *The Metaphysical Muse* (1917) and still lifes by Giorgio Morandi, as well as sculpture by Medardo Rosso, Arturo Martini and Marino Marini.

13TH–15TH-CENTURY ITALIAN PAINTING

THE SECTION given over to 13th–15th-century Italian art (rooms 2–4) includes frescoes from the Oratory at Mocchirolo, painted by an unknown Lombard master in around 1365–70. Among the gold-background works are the *Santa Maria della Celestia*

Polyptych by Lorenzo Veneziano (14th century), Ambrogio Lorenzetti's *Madonna and Child* and *Christ the Judge* by Giovanni da Milano. A fine example of the International Gothic style is the *Valle Romita Polyptych* by Gentile da Fabriano, flanked by Stefano da Verona's *Adoration of the Magi* (1435), in which the viola and carnation at the feet of Jesus symbolize his humility and the Passion.

15TH–16TH-CENTURY VENETIAN PAINTING

ROOMS 5 AND 6 feature works by 15th–16th-century artists active in the Veneto such as Giovanni d'Alemagna and Antonio Vivarini, who painted the *Praglia Polyptych* (1448). Room 6 also has

15TH–16TH-CENTURY LOMBARD PAINTING

A LARGE COLLECTION of 15th–16th-century Lombard paintings is exhibited in rooms 15, 18 and 19. The leading figure, Vincenzo Foppa, is represented by the *Polittico delle Grazie* (c.1483). An unknown master contributed the *Sforzesca Altarpiece* (1494), showing Lodovico il Moro and his family worshipping the Madonna. This room also has works by Bergognone, Gaudenzio Ferrari – an artist with a marked narrative vein, as can be seen in *Martyrdom of St Catherine* – and Bramantino's *Crucifixion*. Works influenced by Leonardo da Vinci include

Gentile da Fabriano's *Valle Romita Polyptych*

Supper at Emmaus, painted by Caravaggio in 1606

the small paintings for private chapels by De Predis and Luini *(Madonna del Roseto),* while the Cremona area is represented by names such as Boccaccino, Campi and Piazza.

15TH–16TH-CENTURY CENTRAL ITALIAN PAINTING

ROOMS 20–23 illustrate artistic movements in the regions of Emilia and Le Marche. The Ferrara school is represented by its leading artists, Cosmè Tura, Francesco del Cossa and Ercole de' Roberti (whose *Madonna and Child among Saints* was painted around 1480). Correggio's *Nativity* is a major Emilian school work, while painting in Le Marche is documented by the works of Carlo Crivelli, including his *Madonna della Candeletta* (1490–91), rich in symbols.

Room 24 houses the two best-known masterpieces in the Brera. Piero della Francesca's *Montefeltro Altarpiece* (c.1475), was commissioned by Federico da Montefeltro. The egg suspended from its shell is a symbol of the Creation and of the Immaculate Conception. Next is Raphael's splendid *Marriage of the Virgin (see p115).*

Christ at the Pillar is a rare painting by Bramante, while works by Bronzino and Genga represent Mannerism.

17TH–18TH-CENTURY ITALIAN AND FLEMISH PAINTING

ROOM 28 FEATURES works by the Bolognese school, founded by the Carracci, including Guido Reni and Guercino. The next room boasts a masterpiece by Caravaggio, *Supper at Emmaus* (1606), in which the appearance of Christ occurs in a setting illuminated only by the light emanating from Jesus's face. Lombard artists shown here are Cerano, Morazzone and Giulio Cesare Procaccini, who painted the *Martyrdom of Saints Rufina and Seconda* together. Baroque painting is represented by Pietro da Cortona and the still lifes of Baschenis. Among the non-Italian artists, don't miss Rubens (*Last Supper,* 1631–32), Van Dyck, Rembrandt (*Portrait of the Artist's Sister,* 1632), El Greco and Brueghel the Elder *(The Village).*

18TH–19TH-CENTURY ITALIAN PAINTING

THE FOLLOWING ROOMS cover various genres in 18th-century Italian art. Large-scale religious paintings are in room 34 with works by the Neapolitan Luca Giordano and two Venetians: Giovan Battista Tiepolo's *Madonna del Carmelo* (1721–7), intended to be viewed from the side, and Piazzetta's *Rebecca at the Well.*

Giacomo Ceruti (Il Pitochetto) represents "genre painting", which was popular in the 18th century. This is followed by Venetian *vedutismo,* views by Bernardo Bellotto, Guardi and Canaletto. The works of Bellotto and Canaletto are characterized by their bright light and precision of detail (the latter even used a camera obscura to help him render this "photographic" effect).

Portraiture is best exemplified by Fra Galgario (*Portrait of a Gentleman*).

Madonna della Candeletta by Crivelli

A representative 19th-century painting is Andrea Appian's Neo-Classical *Olympus,* while the Macchiaioli movement is on display with works by Silvestro Lega and Giovanni Fattori, among others. The Brera also has paintings by the leading exponent of Lombard Romanticism, Francesco Hayez: his famous *The Kiss* and several portraits. The gallery closes with Divisionist Giuseppe Pelizza da Volpedo's *The Flood* (1895–97), a hymn to the struggle of the working class, and an early version of his *Fourth Estate,* now on display at the Villa Reale *(see p121).*

Cimitero Monumentale  ⑫

Piazzale Cimitero Monumentale.
Map 3 A1. 🄲 02-659 99 38.
🚋 3, 4, 11, 12, 14, 29, 30, 33.
🚌 41, 51, 70, 94. 🅾
8:30am–5:15pm Tue–Sun;
8:30am–1pm hols. Free
map of the cemetery
available at the entrance.

EXTENDING OVER an area of 250,000 sq m (300,000 sq yds), the Cimitero Monumentale was begun by Carlo Maciachini in 1866. The eclectic taste of the time dictated the use of various styles for the cemetery, from mock-Lombard Romanesque to Neo-Gothic, with touches of Tuscan thrown in. The linchpin of the structure is the Famedio (*Famae Aedes*), or House of Fame, a sort of pantheon of illustrious Milanese and non-Milanese buried here. Author Alessandro Manzoni, Luca Beltrami, the architect who oversaw restoration of the Castello Sforzesco, the patriot Carlo Cattaneo and the Nobel Prize-winning poet Salvatore Quasimodo all have tombs in this cemetery. There are also busts of Garibaldi, Verdi and Cavour. The Romantic painter Hayez lies in the crypt. A visit to the Cimitero Monumentale, which is a kind of open-air museum of art from the late 19th century to the present, begins at the large square inside, which contains the tombs of important Milanese figures. Around the square are monumental shrines and the Civico Mausoleo Palanti, an enormous mausoleum with a crypt, used as an air raid shelter in 1943. Among its tombs are those of comic actor Walter Chiari and Hermann Einstein, Albert's father. On the terraces, to the left are the Elisi (sculpted by Francesco Penna, 1916) and Morgagni tombs, and an epigraph by Mussolini commemorating a disastrous aeroplane crash. In the central avenue are two tombs designed and sculpted by Enrico Butti: that of Isabella Casati, *Young Woman Enraptured by a Dream*, a typical Lombard realist work (1890), and the Besenzanica shrine with *Work* (1912). On your right, you will come to the monumental Toscanini tomb (Bistolfi, 1909–11), built for the conductor's son.

Among other monumental tombs for major figures in Milanese life are those of Carlo Erba, Bocconi, Campari and Falck. Many famous sculptors made pieces for this place: Leonardo Bistolfi, Giacomo Manzù, Odoardo Tabacchi, Adolfo Wildt and Lucio Fontana. The two enclosures beside the Famedio are for Jews and Catholics, with the remains of sculptor Medardo Rosso, publishers Arnoldo Mondadori and Ulrico Hoepli and Jules Richard, founder of the Richard-Ginori ceramics industry.

Sculpture by Fontana, Cimitero Monumentale

The Cimitero Monumentale, with tombs and shrines produced by famous sculptors

The Pirelli Building, symbol of Milan's postwar reconstruction

Pirelli Building ⑬

Piazzale Duca d'Aosta–Via Pirelli.
Map 4 E1. 🄼 2, 3 Centrale.
🚋 2, 5, 9, 33. 🚌 42, 60, 82.
🅾 to the public.

THE SYMBOL OF postwar reconstruction in Milan, the Pirelli Building, affectionately called "Pirellone" (big Pirelli) by the Milanese, was built in 1955–60. It was designed by a group of leading architects and engineers: Gio Ponti, Antonio Fornaroli, Alberto Rosselli, Giuseppe Valtolina, Egidio Dell'Orto, Pier Luigi Nervi and Arturo Danusso. At 127.10 m (417 ft) high, it was the largest reinforced concrete skyscraper in the world until the 1960s. The slender, elegant edifice occupies only 1,000 sq m (1,200 sq yds) and stands on the site where, in 1872, Giovan Battista Pirelli built his first tyre factory. The skyscraper was constructed as the Pirelli company's main offices. Among the many records established by the "Pirellone", was that it was the first building in Milan taller than the Madonnina on the Duomo (108.50 m, 356 ft). As a token of respect, a small statue of the Virgin Mary was placed on the Pirelli roof. Since 1979 the building has been the headquarters of the regional government of Lombardy. Next door is the luxurious Gallia Excelsior Hotel, opened in the 1930s.

The Stazione Centrale, with its spectacular iron and glass roof

Stazione Centrale ⑭

Piazzale Duca d'Aosta. **Map** 4 E1.
Ⓜ 2, 3 Centrale. 🚃 2, 5, 9, 33.
🚌 42, 53, 60, 82, 90, 91, 92.

Milan's main railway station is one of the largest and perhaps the most monumental in Europe. Ulisse Stacchini's project design was approved and ready in 1912, but construction work proved so slow that the building was not opened until 1931. The new railway station replaced one located in present-day Piazza della Repubblica.

The building is dressed in Aurisina stone, and was clearly inspired by the late Art Nouveau style in vogue in the early 20th century, in marked contrast with the austere 1930s architecture of the surrounding buildings.

The façade is 207 m (679 ft) wide and 36 m (118 ft) tall and is crowned by two winged horses. The large arcades link up with the Galleria dei Transiti, a gallery decorated with four medallions by Giannino Castiglioni representing Labour, Commerce, Science and Agriculture. In the large ticket office hall, flights of steps lead up to the huge departures and arrivals lobby, with tile panels representing the cities of Milan, Rome, Turin and Florence.

The massive building is a landmark in Milan and second only to the cathedral in size. There are numerous shops inside, and some are open 24 hours a day.

Bastioni di Porta Venezia ⑮

Map 4 E3. Ⓜ 1 Porta Venezia, 3 Repubblica. 🚃 1, 2, 9, 11, 29, 30.

What is today a major road was once part of the walls built to defend the city in 1549–61 by the Spanish governor Ferrante Gonzaga. In 1789 the walls became a tree-lined avenue for walking and coach parking. The Porta Venezia ramparts, flanked by the Giardini Pubblici, link Piazza della Repubblica and Piazza Oberdan. The former was laid out in 1931 when the 19th-century railway station was demolished and rebuilt 800 m (3,040 ft) away and greatly enlarged to cope with increasing traffic resulting from the opening of the St Gotthard (1882) and Simplon (1906) passes through the Alps.

Not far from the piazza, in Via Turati, is the Palazzo della Permanente, designed by Luca Beltrami in 1885 as the home of the Permanent Fine Arts Exhibition and now used for temporary exhibitions.

Piazza Oberdan is dominated by Porta Venezia, the city gate rebuilt in 1828 on the site of the Spanish gate of the same name and used as a customs toll station. The two buildings are decorated with statues and reliefs concerning the history of Milan. Porta Venezia separates Corso Venezia and Corso Buenos Aires, a major commercial thoroughfare.

In 1488–1513, Lazzaro Palazzi chose a site beyond the gate to build the lazzaretto, a hospital for plague victims commissioned by Lodovico il Moro. The few remains from the 1880 demolition can be seen in Via San Gregorio. A slight detour from Piazza Oberdan towards Viale Piave will take you past some interesting Art Nouveau style buildings: Casa Galimberti, designed by Giovan Battista Bossi in 1903–4, decorated with wrought iron and panels of ceramic tiles, and the Hotel Diana Majestic.

Plaque commemorating the lazzaretto

Casa Galimberti, decorated with wrought iron and tile panels

Planetarium ⓰

Corso Venezia 57. **Map** 4 E4. 02-
29 53 11 81. 1 Porta Venezia–
Palestro. 9, 29, 30. According
to programme.

DONATED TO THE CITY by the
publisher Ulrico Hoepli,
the Planetarium was built in
1930 in Classical style by
Piero Portaluppi. The pro-
jection hall has a large hemi-
spherical dome (the technology was updated in 1955)
and 600 swivelling seats to
enable you to gaze at the
movements of the stars.
  The Planetarium offers
guided tours (including tours
for students of the subject)
and scientific or popular-level
lectures on astronomy.

Museo di Storia Naturale ⓱

Corso Venezia 55. **Map** 4 E4. 02-
78 13 12. 1 Porta Venezia–
Palestro. 9, 29, 30. 9am–6pm
Mon–Fri, 9:30am–6:30pm Sat, Sun,
hols. 1 Jan, Easter, 1 May, 15
Aug, 25 Dec. (tel. 02-78 35
28). Lecture hall, Library.

THE MUSEUM OF Natural
History was founded in
1838 with the donation of the
Giuseppe de Cristoforis and
Giorgio Jan collections. The
building was constructed in
Neo-Romanesque style and
with terracotta decoration in
1893 by Giovanni Ceruti. The
museum has a specialist
library holding over 30,000
volumes, including sections
on mineralogy and zoology.
On the ground floor are the
mineralogy and entomology

The Giardini Pubblici, a rare area of greenery in Milan

collections, and part of the
Museo Settala, which was
created by a canon named
Manfredo. It features scientific
instruments and natural
history specimens of varied
provenance. In the palae-
ontology halls there are
reconstructions of dinosaurs
such as the Triceratops and
a large Allosaurus skeleton.
The ground floor also has
displays of molluscs and
insects. The upper floor is
reserved for reptiles, ceta-
ceans and mammals. There
are also several reconstructions of animal habitats.

Giardini Pubblici ⓲

Corso Venezia, Via Palestro, Via Manin,
Bastioni di Porta Venezia. **Map** 4 E4.
1 Porta Venezia–Palestro, 3
Repubblica–Turati. 1, 9, 11, 29,
30. 94. 6:30am–sunset daily.

THE PUBLIC GARDENS extend
for about 160,000 sq m
(192,000 sq yds) and form the
largest city park in Milan.
They were designed by Pier-

marini in 1786 and enlarged
in 1857 by Giuseppe Balzaretto, who annexed Palazzo
Dugnani and its garden.
Further changes were made
by Emilio Alemagna after the
international exhibitions held
in the 1871–81 period.
  The Giardini Pubblici are
also home to the Padiglione
del Caffè (1863), which is
now a nursery school.

Palazzo Dugnani ⓳

Via Manin 2. **Map** 4 D3.
3 Turati. 1, 2. 61, 94.
Tiepolo rooms only.
Museo del Cinema 02-655 49
77. 3–6pm Tue–Fri.

PALAZZO DUGNANI was built
in the late 1600s and renovated a century later. Since
1846 it has belonged to Milan
city council. A monumental
staircase leads up to a magnificent two-storey salon with a
gallery for musicians. Here, in
1731, the great Giambattista
Tiepolo painted the frescoes
*The Allegory of the Dugnani
Family* and *The Legends of
Scipio and Massinissa*. Both
were damaged by the 1943
bombings and by the terrorist
bomb that exploded in Via
Palestro in 1993.
  The palazzo houses the
Museo del Cinema which
documents the evolution of
motion-picture cameras from
the 18th-century magic lan-
terns to those used by the
Lumière brothers, as well as
apparatus that became obsolete
when talking pictures were
invented. There are also movie
posters from 1905 to 1930.

Reconstruction of a dinosaur skeleton, Museo di Storia Naturale

Villa Reale and Galleria d'Arte Moderna ⑳

M ILAN'S MODERN ART GALLERY is housed in a Neo-Classical villa built by Leopold Pollack in 1790 for Count Ludovico Barbiano di Belgioioso. It was lived in by Napoleon in 1802 and later by Marshall Radetzky. The gallery is devoted to 19th-century art movements in Italy, from Hayez to Piccio, the Scapigliatura, the Divisionism and the Macchiaioli artists Fattori and Lega. The villa also houses the Grassi and Vismara collections of 19th- and 20th-century Italian and foreign artists (including Impressionists, Matisse, Picasso, Morandi) as well as the Marino Marini Museum.

VISITORS' CHECKLIST

Via Palestro 16. **Map** 4 E4.
☎ 02-76 00 28 19.
Ⓜ 1 Palestro. 🚊 1, 2. 🚌 61,
94. ⭘ 9am–5:30pm daily.
⬤ 1 Jan, Easter, 1 May, 15 Aug,
25 Dec. ♿ 🖭 Many rooms
closed for restoration.
**Giardini di Villa Reale (Villa
Gardens)** ⭘ 9am–noon,
2–4pm Nov–Feb; 9am–noon,
2–6pm Mar, Oct;
9am–noon, 2–7pm Apr–Sep.

KEY

☐	Cineteca Italiana
☐	Vismara Collection
☐	Modern Art Gallery
☐	Marino Marini Museum
☐	Grassi Collection

Grassi Collection
In 1956 Nedda Grassi donated this fine collection to the city in memory of her son Gino. It comprises rugs, Oriental objets d'art and 135 paintings, including foreign and Italian 19th- and 20th-century artists such as Van Gogh, Cézanne, Corot and Gauguin, Fattori, Lega, Balla, Boccioni and Morandi.

Antonio Canova's bronze of Napoleon and plaster sculpture of Hebe are displayed here.

Furnishings and frescoes
decorate the main floor; the top attraction is the dining room, with a *Parnassus* by Appiani.

This room is used for civil weddings.

STAR EXHIBIT

★ **Fourth Estate**

★ **Fourth Estate**
In this fine 1901 canvas, Quarto Stato, Giuseppe Pelizza da Volpedo expresses solidarity with the struggles and suffering of the lower classes.

Marino Marini Museum
This section opened in 1973. It holds paintings and sculptures donated by Marini himself, including portraits of people he admired, such as Arp, De Pisis, Carrà, Chagall and Stravinsky.

Corso Venezia ㉔

F ORMERLY CALLED CORSO DI PORTA ORIENTALE, this famous and popular street was named after the gate in the medieval walls corresponding to present-day Via Senato. The same name was given to the quarter, whose emblem is the lion on the column in front of the church of San Babila. Corso Venezia was lined with relatively few buildings and bordered by kitchen gardens and orchards until the mid-18th century, when the reforms carried out by Maria Theresa of Austria led to the construction of the numerous patrician *palazzi* that make this one of Milan's most elegant streets.

LOCATOR MAP
See Street Finder, map 4

Three inner courtyards lead to the garden.

On the balustrade are statues of the *Dei Consenti* (the 12 chief Roman gods) by Pompeo Marchesi and Grazioso Rusca.

Palazzo Rocca-Saporiti ①
Giovanni Perego designed this building in 1812 and it reflects the taste of the Napoleonic period. On the façade is a frieze with scenes of Milanese history.

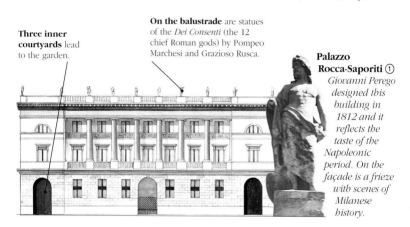

Palazzo Castiglioni ②
This palazzo was built by Giuseppe Somma-ruga in 1904. There were once two female nudes on the façade (later removed), hence its name Ca' di Ciapp (House of Buttocks).

On the first floor is a lovely three-flight staircase and the Sala dei Pavoni.

A loggia with Ionic columns emphasizes the central section.

The side facing Via San Damiano has retained its original 17th-century features.

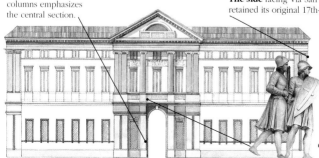

Palazzo Serbelloni ③
Completed in 1793 by Simone Cantoni, this palazzo played host to Napol-eon and Vittorio Emanuele.

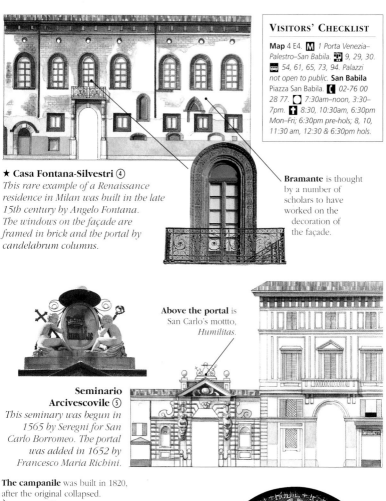

★ Casa Fontana-Silvestri ④
This rare example of a Renaissance
residence in Milan was built in the late
15th century by Angelo Fontana.
The windows on the façade are
framed in brick and the portal by
candelabrum columns.

Bramante is thought
by a number of
scholars to have
worked on the
decoration of
the façade.

Above the portal is
San Carlo's mottto,
Humilitas.

**Seminario
Arcivescovile ⑤**
This seminary was begun in
1565 by Seregni for San
Carlo Borromeo. The portal
was added in 1652 by
Francesco Maria Richini.

The campanile was built in 1820,
after the original collapsed.

**The present-day Neo-Romanesque
façade** was designed in 1906 by
Paolo Cesa Bianchi, who also built
the high altar.

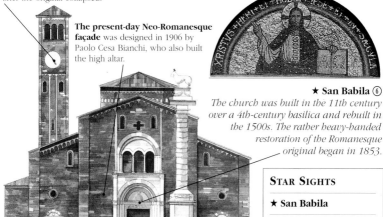

★ San Babila ⑥
The church was built in the 11th century
over a 4th-century basilica and rebuilt in
the 1500s. The rather heavy-handed
restoration of the Romanesque
original began in 1853.

STAR SIGHTS

★ San Babila

★ Casa
Fontana-Silvestri

THE LAKES OF
NORTHERN ITALY

INTRODUCING THE LAKES 126–127
THE LAKES AT A GLANCE 128–129
LAKE MAGGIORE 130–135
LAKE COMO 136–141
LAKE GARDA 142–149
THE SMALLER LAKES 150–151

THE LAKES OF NORTHERN ITALY

A PPRECIATED BY THE ANCIENT ROMANS *for their beautiful location and mild climate, the lakes of Northern Italy – most of which are in Lombardy – are deservedly renowned for the fascinating and unique combination of magnificent scenery and historic and artistic heritage that characterizes the lakeside towns.*

Besides Lake Maggiore, Lake Como and Lake Garda, there are smaller and less well-known bodies of water such as the lakes of Orta, Varese, Iseo and Idro. All these lovely lakes are the result of glaciation in the Pleistocene era, which enlarged clefts already in the terrain. The lake shores were inhabited during the prehistoric period – traces of ancient civilizations have been found almost everywhere – and for the most part were colonized by the Romans, as can be seen in the grid street plans of many towns and in the villas at Lake Garda. Churches, sanctuaries and castles were built here in the Middle Ages. In the winter the shores of the lakes can be battered by winds from Central Europe, but the climate remains quite mild thanks to the water. Typical Mediterranean vegetation can be seen every-where: vineyards, olive trees, oleanders and palm trees. The many splendid villa gardens along the lakes' shores enhance the environment, and nature reserves have been established to protect some stretches.

In the 18th century a visit to the lake region was one of the accepted stages on the Grand Tour, the trip to Europe considered essential for the education of young people of good birth. These shores were also favourites with writers, musicians and artists such as Goethe, Hesse, Klee, Toscanini, Hemingway, Stendhal, Byron and Nietzsche. The numerous vantage points, connected to the shore by funiculars, narrow-gauge trains and cable cars, offer truly spectacular views over the landscape.

The peaceful shores of Lake Como, southwest of Bellagio

◁ Torre di San Marco at Gardone Riviera, on the western shore of Lake Garda

Exploring the Lakes

THE LARGER LAKES offer the best facilities for visitors, with hotels, restaurants and cafés lining the lake front. The lake shores are dotted with pretty villages, castles (Sirmione sul Garda), villas and gardens such as Villa Taranto or the Vittoriale, the residence of the poet D'Annunzio at Lake Garda, as well as a number of small local museums. In summer, you may be able to participate in cultural events such as the famous Settimane Musicali di Stresa music festival at Lake Maggiore. Although the smaller lakes offer fewer facilities, they are very peaceful, unspoilt places.

Cannobio, Lake Maggiore

Bellinzona

Chiav

LAKE COMO

LAKE MAGGIORE

BELLAGIO

VERBANIA

STRESA

LECCO

COMO

LAGO DI VARESE

ARONA

LAGO D'ORTA

MILAN

GETTING THERE

The lakes of Northern Italy can be reached via Malpensa and Linate airports in Milan and Catullo airport in Verona. There are also good connections by motorway from Milan: the A8 autostrada goes to lakes Maggiore and Varese, the A9 to Lake Como, and the A4 to Iseo and Garda. Traffic on the major and minor roads is often heavy, so make allowances when planning. Boat services on the three major lakes are quite efficient; they go to the islands and are an enjoyable way of getting about.

0 kilometres   10

0 miles   10

THE LAKES

Lago d'Idro see p151
Lago d'Iseo see p151
Lago d'Orta see p150
Lago di Varese see p150–51
Lake Como see pp136–41
Lake Garda see pp142–9
Lake Maggiore see pp130–35

LOCATOR MAP

e Ossuccio bell tower on the island
Comacina, on Lake Como

Looking over Lago d'Iseo

N39

N42

N42

Serio

N42

A4

Oglio

N510

Mella

N510

N237

LAGO
D'ISEO

Pinzolo

N237

N572

SALÒ

SIRMIONE

A4

RIVA DEL GARDA ●

LAGO
D'IDRO

LAKE
GARDA

N45bis

N240

N45bis

N249

KEY

▭	Motorway
▭	Major road
▭	Minor road
▭	River
☀	Viewpoint

ardone Riviera, at Lake Garda, a charming town known mainly
r the Vittoriale degli Italiani, residence of the poet D'Annunzio

Lake Maggiore

WITH BORDERS IN PIEDMONT, LOMBARDY and the Ticino canton in Switzerland, Lake Maggiore, or Verbano, is the second largest lake in Italy (212 sq km, 82 sq miles) and has a maximum depth of 372 m (1,220 ft). For the most part it is fed and drained by the Ticino river, and is also fed by the Toce. The towns were embellished with churches and paintings from 1449 on, thanks to the wealthy

Villa statue, Isola Madre

Borromeo family, and with villas and gardens in the 18th–19th centuries. The opening of the Simplon pass and the introduction of ferry services (1826) helped trade to develop in the area.

★ **Isole Borromee**
Of the three islands, the best-known is Isola Bella, named after Isabella d'Adda, wife of Charles III Borromeo ❺

The two castles of Malpaga, built in the 13th–14th century opposite Cànnero Riviera, belonged to the Mazzardites, the pirates who raided the lake.

Magadino

Vira

Locarno

San Nazzaro

Ascona

Gerra–Gambarogno

Porto Ronco

Sant'Abbondio

Isola di Brissago

Brissago

Maccagno

Cannobio ❽

Cannero Riviera

Pieggio

Veltra

Ghiffa

Stresa
This old fishermen's village began to become a tourist attraction thanks to the descriptions of famous writers such as Stendhal, Byron and Dickens ❹

Intra

Pallanza

Isola Madre ❻

★ **Villa Taranto**
One of Italy's most well-known botanic gardens was founded here in 1931 by an Englishman called McEacharn in an area of about 16 ha (40 acres). Many examples of species of plants from all over the world, including Victoria amazonica, *are grown here.*

★ Santa Caterina del Sasso Ballaro

Perched on a rocky spur near Laveno, this monastery is one of the most enchanting sights on Lake Maggiore. It was built by a local merchant in the 12th century to fulfil a vow made when he was saved from a storm **⑪**

SIGHTS AT A GLANCE

Arona **②**
Baveno **⑥**
Cannobio **⑧**
Isole Borromee **⑤**
Laveno **⑩**
Lesa and Belgirate **③**
Luino **⑨**
Rocca di Angera **⑫**
Santa Caterina
del Sasso Ballaro **⑪**
Sesto Calende **①**
Stresa **④**
Verbania **⑦**

★ Rocca di Angera
The imposing medieval fortress of the Borromeo family has 14th- and 15th-century frescoes. It now houses the Doll Museum **⑫**

Arona
The huge 17th-century statue of San Carlo Borromeo was placed in Arona in honour of its illustrious citizen. A 35-m (115-ft) stairway leads to the top, where there is a fine panoramic view **②**

Sesto Calende
The town museum in Piazza Mazzini contains objects found in nearby Bronze Age sites.

Laveno

⑪

la Bella

Stresa

ore **③** 🛥
Belgirate

Lesa 🛥

Méina 🛥   **②** 🛥 Arona

⑫
Angera 🛥

KEY

= = = Ferry routes
🛥 Ferry service
🔆 Viewpoint

0 kilometres   2
0 miles   2

STAR SIGHTS

**★ Santa Caterina
del Sasso Ballaro**

★ Rocca di Angera

★ Villa Taranto

★ Isole Borromee

Sesto Calende ❶

Varese. 🏙 9,500. 🅸 APT Via
Carrobbio 2, Varese (0332-28 36 04).
🛋 antiques, 3rd Sat of month.

THE TOWN AT the southern
tip of Lake Maggiore
marks the end of two motor-
ways leading to the Verbano
region. The road to Arona
goes to **San Donato**, known
as "La Badia" or abbey, a 9th-
century basilica rebuilt in the
11th–12th century. The
capitals have sculpted figures
of animals and humans.
There are frescoes from the
15th and 16th centuries in the
nave and from the 18th
century in the crypt. South of
Sesto, near Golasecca, are
Iron Age tombs (9th–5th century BC), part of the civilization named after the place.
State road 33 to Arona will
take you to the **Lagoni di
Mercurago Regional Park**,
with varied bird species and
the remains of ancient villages.

🛐 San Donato
Via Abbazia 6. 🅲 0331-92 46 92.
🕐 8am–12 noon, 4–7pm daily.
**🏞 Lagoni di Mercurago
Regional Park**
Via Gattico 6, Mercurago.
🅲 0322-24 02 39.

Arona ❷

Novara. 🏙 16,000. 🅸 Piazzale
Duca d'Aosta (0322-24 36 01).
🛋 antiques, 3rd Sun of month.

ARONA ONCE OCCUPIED
an important trading
position between Milan
and the lake and mountain
regions of Northern Italy.
Because of its strategic

location, a Rocca or
fortress (the twin of
the one at Angera;
see p135), was built
here; it was enlarged
by the Borromeo and
dismantled by
Napoleon. Corso
Marconi has a view
of the Rocca at An-
gera, and leads to
Piazza del Popolo.
Here are the 15th-
century Casa del
Podestà, with an
arched portico, and
the 16th-century
Madonna di Piazza
church. Santi Martiri
has 15th-century
paintings by Bergogn-
one, and Santa Maria Nascente
has an altarpiece by Gau-
denzio Ferrari (1511).
     Just north of the centre is a
massive **statue of San Carlo**.
It was designed by Cerano in
1614 and finished in 1697. In
the church of San Carlo there
is a reconstruction of the
room where San Carlo was
born, which was taken from
the demolished Rocca.
     Villa Ponti is a mid-17th-
century villa with Baroque
and Art Deco decoration. It
stands in a garden with a
nympheum and a fountain.

🛐 Statue of San Carlo
Piazza San Carlo. 🅲 0322-24 96 69.
🕐 8:30 am–12:30pm, 2– 6:30pm
daily (5pm from 4 Oct) 22 Mar–10
Nov; 9am–12:30pm, 2–5pm Sat, Sun,
hols 11 Nov–21 Mar. 🖼 **San Carlo
and Birthplace of San Carlo**.
Collegio De Filippi. 🅸 Piazzale San
Carlo (0322-24 24 88).
🏛 Villa Ponti
Via San Carlo 57. 🅲 0322-444 22.
🕐 all year (by appt for small groups);
garden closed in winter. 🖼

The square in Arona with the huge statue of
San Carlo Borromeo

Lesa and Belgirate ❸

Lesa (Novara). 🏙 2,400. Belgirate
(Verbania). 🏙 500. 🅸 Via Principe
Tommaso 70, Stresa (0323-304 16).

LESA LIES ON A PARTICULARLY
charming stretch of the
lake between Arona and
Stresa, and has been a resort
for noble Lombard families
since the 18th century. The
**Museo Manzoniano di Villa
Stampa** has mementoes of
author Alessandro Manzoni,
who was a guest here. The
hamlet of Villa boasts the
Romanesque church of San
Sebastiano. Once past Lesa,
continue to Belgirate and its
charming historic centre,
whose houses have porticoes
and porches. This village also
commands a panoramic view
of the lake. It was a haunt of
philosopher Antonio Rosmini
and poet Guido Gozzano. On
the hills 4 km (2 miles) from
Belgirate is the 13th-century
Visconti di San Vito Castle,
decorated with frescoes of the
period. Nearby is the Romanesque church of San Michele,
with a leaning bell tower.

**🏛 Museo Manzoniano
di Villa Stampa**
Via alla Fontana, Lesa. 🅲 0322-764
21. 🕐 5–7pm Sat; 9:30am–noon Sun
Jul–Sep; also 10am–noon Thu, Aug.
**♠ Castello Visconti
di San Vito**
Via Visconti 1, Massino Visconti.
🅲 0331-25 63 37. 🕐 Aug:
10:30am–12:30pm, 3–7pm Sat, Sun
and week of 15 Aug. 🖼

Looking over the lakeside town of Arona

Stresa ❹

Verbania. 🏠 *4,800.* ℹ️ IAT
Via Canoniga 8 *(0323-301 50).*

THE ORIGINS OF MEDIEVAL Strixia, dating from before 1000, are partially hidden by the palazzi and villas built for the aristocracy in the late 19th–early 20th century, partly because of the opening of an electric rack-railway (the first in Italy), which goes to the top of Mount Mottarone. The town is now a centre for conferences and tour groups, attracted by the easy access to the Borromean islands. On the lakefront are 19th-century villas, Sant'-Ambrogio (18th century) and the **Villa Ducale** (1770), with mementoes of 19th-century philosopher Antonio Rosmini, who died here (the villa is now the Rosmini Study Centre). Mount Mottarone (1,491 m, 4,890 ft), a ski resort, has a view from the Alps to the plain.

🏛 Villa Ducale
Centro di Studi Rosminiani
Corso Umberto I 15. 📞 *0323-300 91.* ⬤ *closed to the public.*

ENVIRONS
🌳 **Parco di Villa Pallavicino**
State road 33. 📞 *0323-324 07.* ⬤ *9am–6pm daily Mar–Oct.* 🅿️ ♿
🚻 🍴
This villa near Stresa is famous for its gardens. The luxuriant English garden has centuries-old plants as well as exotic creatures such as llamas and pelicans.

The garden of the 18th-century palazzo on Isola Madre

Isole Borromee ❺

Verbania. ⛴ *from Arona, Laveno, Stresa, Baveno, Pallanza.* To Isola Madre: *tel. 0323-312 61; to Isola Bella: tel. 0323-305 56 Apr–Oct.* ⬤ *9am–noon, 1:30–5:30pm daily 27 Mar–24 Oct.* ⬤ *Oct–Mar.* 🎫 🎦 *by appt.* 🍴

THESE THREE ISLANDS, which can be reached easily from Stresa, became famous thanks to the Borromeo family, who built elegant palazzi and magnificent gardens there. The loveliest is **Isola Bella**, an old fishing village transformed from 1632 to 1671 by the Borromeo family into a lovely complex consisting of a Baroque palazzo and a terraced Italian-style garden with rare plants. Inside are a music room (where Mussolini met British and French officials in 1935), the Sala di Napoleone (where Napoleon stayed in

A fountain at Villa Pallavicino

1797), a ballroom, throne room and bedroom with 17th-century decoration and furnishings and paintings by Carracci, Cerano and Tiepolo. The six grottoes are decorated with shells and pebbles.
   Isola Madre, the largest island, boasts an 18th-century villa with a garden where white peacocks roam freely; it has rare plants as well as azaleas, rhododendrons, magnolias and camellias. The villa has period furnishings and a collection of 18th- and 19th-century puppet theatres.
   Tiny **Isola dei Pescatori**, once the leading fishing village, has retained its quaint atmosphere and architecture.

Baveno ❻

Verbania. 🏠 *4,500.* ℹ️ IAT Piazza Dante Alighieri 14 *(0323-92 46 32).*

MADE FAMOUS by its pink granite quarries, which among other things supplied the stone for the Galleria in Milan *(see p50)*, Baveno became a fashionable resort in the mid-19th century, entertaining guests such as Queen Victoria, who stayed in the Villa Clara (now Villa Branca) in 1879. A major attraction is Santi Gervasio e Protasio, with its 12th-century façade and 5th-century octagonal baptistery with Renaissance frescoes. Going towards Verbania, take the turn-off for San Giovanni at Montorfano, one of the loveliest churches in the area.

The garden at Villa Pallavicino, the home of many species of animals

Verbania ❼

🏠 *31,000.* **ℹ️ IAT** *Corso Zanitello 6-8 (0323-50 32 49).* 🛍️ *antiques, 3 Jul–4 Sep: from 5pm on Fri.*

Pallanza and Intra were merged in 1939 to create the town of Verbania (capital of the Verbano-Cusio-Ossola province established in 1992). The former, facing the Borromeo gulf, is the seat of the municipal government and has retained its medieval aspect and atmosphere. The latter dominates the promontory of Castagnola and has a decidedly Baroque and Neo-Classical flavour. Intra, the most important port of call on the lake and one of its major industrial centres, was the regional leader in textile manufacturing in the 18th century. Pallanza was the only town in Lake Maggiore not under Borromeo dominion, and it has some of the most important monuments. These include Romanesque Santo Stefano, the parish church of San Leonardo and 18th-century Palazzo Dugnani, home to the **Museo del Paesaggio**, which has on exhibit 16th–20th-century landscape paintings, sculpture by Arturo Martini and Giulio Branca and a plaster cast gallery. Isolino di San Giovanni was a favourite refuge of Arturo Toscanini. In the environs is 16th-century Madonna di

Effigy of McEacharn, who created the Villa Taranto gardens

Campagna, with a small Romanesque campanile and frescoes by Gerolamo Lanino and Camillo Procaccini (16th–17th centuries).

🏛️ Museo del Paesaggio

Via Ruga 44.
📞 *0323-50 24 18.*
🕐 *10am–noon, 3–6pm Tue–Sun Apr–Oct.*

ENVIRONS
🌿 Giardini di Villa Taranto

Via Rossano 22, Pallanza. 📞 *0323-55 66 67.* 🕐 *8:30am–7:30pm daily Apr–Oct.* 🅿️ 🚫 ♿ 🚻
In 1931 a British captain named McEacharn created one of the outstanding botanic gardens in Europe on the Castagnola promontory, using the lake water for irrigation. He is buried in the small park church. McEacharn exploited the valley terrain, creating terraced gardens, a winter garden and a marsh garden among small falls and water lily ponds. He donated the Villa Taranto garden to the Italian state and it was opened to the public in 1952. It has a range of exotic plants, including *Victoria amazonica* in the glasshouses. Azaleas, dahlias and rhododendrons (over 300 varieties) look wonderful in full flower.

Cannobio ❽

Verbania. 🏠 *5,300.* **ℹ️ IAT** *Viale Vittorio Veneto 4 (0323-713 93).*

This pleasant tourist resort is the last Italian town on the Piedmontese side of the lake. It still retains its old medieval character, exemplified in the Palazzo della Ragione or Palazzo Parrasio, the town hall with a 12th-century Commune Tower. The Santuario della Pietà, which was rebuilt by San Carlo Borromeo in 1583, contains a fine altarpiece by Gaudenzio Ferrari.

The Orrido di Sant'Anna, in Val Cannobina

In nearby Val Cannobina, the Orrido di Sant'Anna is worth a visit. This deep gorge was carved out of the rock by the Cannobino river.

Luino ❾

Varese. 🏠 *15,300.* **ℹ️ APT** *Via Chiara 1 (0332-53 00 19).*

Luino, which occupies a cove on the eastern side of the lake, is a town dating from ancient Roman times. Its name may have derived from the Luina torrent or perhaps from the local term *luina* (landslide). In the Middle Ages it was contested by the leading Como and Milanese families and became famous when Garibaldi landed there in 1848 with a group of volunteers and routed an entire Austrian detachment.

The large railway station (1882) shows how important the town was when it linked Italy with Central Europe, a position that declined when railway traffic shifted to Chiasso. Luino's market was founded by an edict of Charles V in 1541 and is still a tourist attraction. San Pietro in Campagna has frescoes by Bernardino Luini and a lovely Romanesque bell tower; the oratory of the Chiesa del Carmine dates back to 1477. A must is a visit to the town's symbol, the 17th-century oratory of San Giuseppe.

Laveno ❿

Varese. 🚶 *8,800.*
🛈 **APT** Piazza Italia 1
(0332-666 66).

**The natural harbour of Laveno,
once an Austrian naval base**

THE NAME OF this town goes back to Titus Labienus, the Roman general who was Caesar's legate in Cisalpine Gaul. Laveno was important strategically because of its port, the only natural harbour on Lake Maggiore. During their period of rule, the Austrians moored the gunboats controlling the lake here. Today the town is the main ferry point to the Piedmontese shores. The Ferrovie Nord railway linked Laveno to Varese and Milan, fostering commercial development, especially in the field of ceramics with the founding of well-known Società Ceramica Italiana Richard-Ginori, in 1856. In the town centre, the garden in the Villa Frua (18th century) is worth visiting.

A cable car goes up to Sasso del Ferro, at 1,062 m (3,483 ft), behind Laveno, with fine views of the lake, Monte Mottarone and Monte Rosa.

Santa Caterina del Sasso Ballaro ⓫

📞 *0332-64 71 72.* ⏰ *8:30am–noon,
2–5pm Sat, Sun, 17 Oct–Easter.*
✝ *4:30pm hols.* ⬛

TO GET TO THIS small monastery – one of the most enchanting in Northern Italy – perched on a steep rock 18 m (59 ft) above the lake, you can either climb the steps near Leggiuno or take the boat and enjoy the lovely views. The place was founded in the mid-12th century by a local merchant. The Dominicans arrived in 1230 and after numerous changes in fortune have since returned here. Over the centuries the original building was enlarged and rebuilt, as can be seen by the different architectural styles. The chapter at the entrance has important 14th–15th-century frescoes, including a *Crucifixion with Armigers* (14th century). The 17th-century fresco in the second portico, only partly preserved, represents a *Dance of Death*. The frescoes inside the church were executed in the 16th century, and the *Madonna and Child with Saints* on the high altar dates from 1612. By the entrance porticoes there is a large wine press made in 1759.

**14th–15th-century frescoes,
Rocca di Angera**

Rocca di Angera ⓬

Fortress and museum Via Rocca,
Angera. 📞 *0331-93 13 00.* ⏰
*9:30am–12:30pm, 2–6pm (5pm Oct)
daily Apr–Oct.* 🎫 ♿ ⬛ 🔢

A MAJESTIC FORTRESS, probably built over the ruins of an ancient Roman fortification, the Rocca once belonged to the archbishops of Milan. In the 13th century it was taken over by the Visconti family and in 1449 was granted as a fief to the Borromeo family, who still own it. The Visconti building has single and double lancet windows and partly lies against the earlier castle tower. The frescoes in the halls are well worth a look, especially those in the Salone Gotico, with a cycle of the *Battles of Ottone Visconti against the Torriani* (14th century). The vaults in this hall are decorated with the Visconti coat of arms, while those in the other rooms have geometric patterns and signs of the Zodiac. The Borromeo wing has frescoes removed from Palazzo Borromeo in Milan in 1946, with *Aesop's Fables* by the school of Michelino da Besozzo (15th century). The Rocca is used for art shows and is also home to the **Museo della Bambola** (Doll Museum) in the Visconti wing, one of the best of its kind in Europe, created with the collection of Princess Bona Borromeo. Besides dolls and dolls' houses, it contains books, games and children's clothing.

Santa Caterina del Sasso Ballaro, built on a cliff overlooking the lake

Lake Como

Decoration in Villa d'Este, at Cernobbio

THE LAKE, ALSO KNOWN AS LARIO, is the third largest in Italy and the deepest (410 m, 1,345 ft). It is shaped like a sprawling upside-down Y, with the arms of Como, Lecco and Colico. The Como shore is the most developed, with restaurants and hotels and a scenic road that follows the ancient Strada Regina, lined with elegant villas and aristocratic gardens. The Lecco area has more stark scenery and small coves. The lake is known for sudden gusts of wind that make navigation difficult. You may spot the typical "Lucia" boats, named after the heroine in Manzoni's *The Betrothed*, which was set here.

★ **Bellagio**

Its position at the junction of the arms of the lake and the spectacular view from the Spartivento point make this one of the most popular spots on Lake Como ⑫

★ **Como**

Construction of Como's Duomo began in 1396 and ended in 1740 with the huge dome. Next to it is the elegant 13th-century Broletto, the old town hall ❶

The bell tower on Santa Maria Maddalena at Ossuccio is one of the symbols of the lake.

Menaggio

Cadena

Isola Comacina

Tremezzo ❺

Colonno   Lenno ❹   Campo ❸

Argegno   Lake Como

Lezzeno

STAR SIGHTS
★ Bellagio
★ Como
★ Tremezzo

Nesso

Careno

Torriggia

Carate

Ùrio

Moltrasio

Pognana Lario

Torno ⑬

Faggeto Lario

Cernobbio ❷

Belvio

Tavernola

0 kilometres   5

0 miles

❶ Brunate

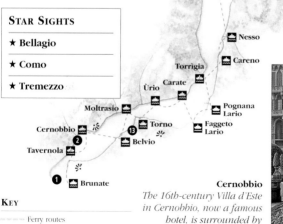

Cernobbio

The 16th-century Villa d'Este in Cernobbio, now a famous hotel, is surrounded by beautiful landscaped gardens with many fountains ❷

KEY

--- Ferry routes

📷 Ferry service

🔆 Viewpoint

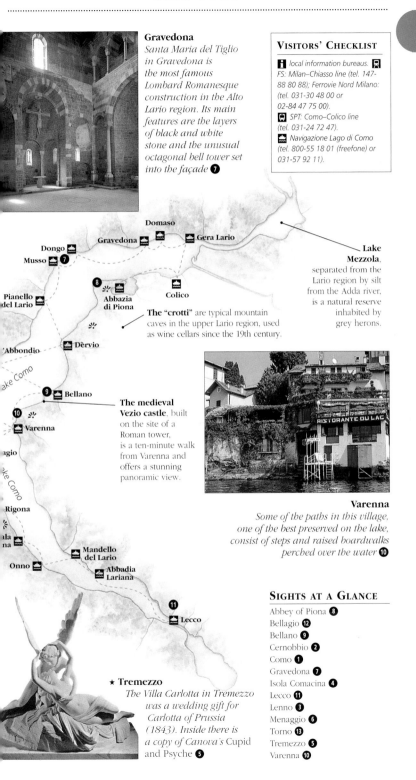

Gravedona

Santa Maria del Tiglio in Gravedona is the most famous Lombard Romanesque construction in the Alto Lario region. Its main features are the layers of black and white stone and the unusual octagonal bell tower set into the façade **7**

VISITORS' CHECKLIST

local information bureaus.
FS: Milan–Chiasso line (tel. 147-88 80 88); Ferrovie Nord Milano:
(tel. 031-30 48 00 or 02-84 47 75 00).
SPT: Como–Colico line
(tel. 031-24 72 47).
Navigazione Lago di Como
(tel. 800-55 18 01 (freefone) or 031-57 92 11).

Lake Mezzola, separated from the Lario region by silt from the Adda river, is a natural reserve inhabited by grey herons.

The **"crotti"** are typical mountain caves in the upper Lario region, used as wine cellars since the 19th century.

The medieval Vezio castle, built on the site of a Roman tower, is a ten-minute walk from Varenna and offers a stunning panoramic view.

Varenna

Some of the paths in this village, one of the best preserved on the lake, consist of steps and raised boardwalks perched over the water **10**

★ Tremezzo

The Villa Carlotta in Tremezzo was a wedding gift for Carlotta of Prussia (1843). Inside there is a copy of Canova's Cupid and Psyche **5**

SIGHTS AT A GLANCE

Abbey of Piona **8**
Bellagio **12**
Bellano **9**
Cernobbio **2**
Como **1**
Gravedona **7**
Isola Comacina **4**
Lecco **11**
Lenno **3**
Menaggio **6**
Torno **13**
Tremezzo **5**
Varenna **10**

Como **❶**

🏛 *86,000.* **🛈 APT** Piazza Cavour 18 *(031-26 97 12).*

Piazza del Duomo in Como, the birthplace of Pliny the Elder

COMUM WAS founded by the Romans in 196 BC and in the 12th century fought against Milan as an ally of Barbarossa, who built the medieval walls. In 1335 Como came under Visconti rule and in 1451 under Sforza rule. The town shared Milan's fate under Spanish and Austrian domination, becoming part of the Kingdom of Italy in 1859.

Como's many Romanesque churches include the 12th-century San Fedele and the jewel of the Comacine masters, 11th-century Lombard–Romanesque Sant'Abbondio.

The **Duomo**, begun in 1396, is dominated by Filippo Juvarra's Baroque dome. The sculpture on the Gothic façade and the Porta della Rana door were executed by Tommaso and Jacopo Rodari (c.1500). The nave and side altars are decorated with 16th-century tapestries and canvases by Ferrari and Luini. Next to the Duomo is the Romanesque-Gothic Broletto (1215).

The **Tempio Voltiano** (1927) contains relics of Alessandro Volta, the great physicist from Como, who gave his name to "voltage".

The Casa del Fascio (1936) is a good example of Italian Rationalist architecture. **Villa Olmo** was designed in 1797 by Simone Cantoni: it has frescoed rooms and a park, open to the public. A funicular goes up to Brunate.

🏛 Duomo
Piazza Duomo. **[** *031-26 52 44.* **]**
◷ *7am–noon, 3–7pm daily.*
🏛 Tempio Voltiano
Viale Marconi. **[** *031-57 47 05.* **]** **◷**
10am–noon, 3–6pm Tue–Sun Apr–Sep;
10am–noon, 2–4pm Oct–Mar. **●**
Mon. 🎟
🏛 Villa Olmo
Via Cantoni 1. **[** *031-25 24 43.* **]** **◷**
9am–noon, 3–6pm. **●** *hols.* 🎟 🚫

Cernobbio **❷**

Como. 🏛 *7,200.* **🛈** Via Regina 33b *(031-51 01 98).*

CERNOBBIO marks the beginning of the series of splendid villas surrounded by parks that have made the western side of the lake famous. **Villa d'Este**, built by Pellegrino Tibaldi in 1570 for the Gallio family, became a luxury hotel in 1873, frequented by princes and actors. The rooms have period furnishings and are used for conferences. The villa stands in an Italianate garden with a nympheum. 18th-century **Villa Erba** (now an exhibition centre) is known for its interior (visits by request): the Salone da Ballo, chapel and Sala delle Nozze, decorated by Giocondo Albertolli, are lovely.

🏨 Hotel Villa d'Este
Via Regina 40. **[** *031-34 81.* **]**
🏛 Villa Erba
Via Regina 2. **[** *031-34 91.* **]**
◷ *2–6pm Sat, 10am–6pm Sun May–Oct.* **●** *Nov–Apr.*

Lenno **❸**

Como. 🏛 *1,600.* **🛈 APT** Piazza Cavour 18, Como *(031-26 97 12).*

THIS TOWN IS FAMOUS for the **Villa del Balbianello**, built by Cardinal Durini in the 17th century onto a 16th-century building attributed to Pellegrini. The magnificent garden

The Villa d'Este in Cernobbio, once host to the Duke of Windsor and Mrs Simpson

---

FROM MULBERRY TO SILK

Como produces about 80 per cent of Europe's silk. Silk worms were imported in the 14th century and production thrived **Cocoons** in the 17th century with the large-scale cultivation of mulberries, the worms' food. Silk thread was woven and sent on the "silk route" in Austria and Bavaria. Competition from Chinese silk now forces Como to concentrate on quality silk, as shown in the Museo della Seta (Silk Museum) in Como.

with candelabrum plane trees has a loggia with a view of Isola Comacina on one side and the Tremezzina bay on the other. Access to the villa is by boat from Sala Comacina.

Also worth a visit are the octagonal baptistery and church of Santo Stefano, built in the 11th century over a Roman building and decorated with frescoes by Luini. Just above the town is the Cistercian abbey of Acquafredda, rebuilt in the 17th century, with frescoes by Fiammenghino. At nearby Giulino di Mezzegra, the Fascist dictator Benito Mussolini and his mistress Claretta Petacci were executed on 28 April 1945, following their capture on the previous day.

🏛 **Villa del Balbianello**
Balbianello. 📞 *0344-561 10 (FAI)*.
Garden 🕐 *10am–12:30pm, 3:30–6:30pm Tue, Thu–Sun Apr–Oct.*
Villa 🕐 *by booking only.*

Isola Comacina ❹

Como. 🚻 **APT** *Piazza Cavour 18, Como (031-26 97 12).* 🚢 *(as far as Sala Comacina, then by boat)*

T HE ONLY ISLAND on Lake Como has been inhabited since Roman times. It was fortified by the Byzantines and enjoyed a period of splendour in the Middle Ages. The people of Como conquered the fortress in 1169 and destroyed the seven churches on the island. The ruins, together with those of a mosaic-decorated baptistery,

Villa Carlotta, built in the 18th century by Marchese Giorgio Clerici

were found after World War II and are now being studied. Sala Comacina, where boats depart for the island, has an 18th-century church with a fresco by Carlo Carloni, and the villa of Cesare Beccaria, where Manzoni was a guest.

Tremezzo ❺

Como. 🏘 *1,300.* 🚻 **APT** *Piazza Cavour 18, Como (031-26 97 12).*

T HIS LAKESIDE town is a major tourist resort and its main claim to fame is the 18th-century **Villa Carlotta**. The residence, surrounded by a terraced garden with landscaped staircases, was converted in the 19th century into a Neo-Classical villa. It houses paintings by Hayez, furniture by Maggiolini and sculpture pieces by Canova, including a copy of *Cupid and Psyche* and *Terpsichore*.

Among the many rooms decorated with stuccowork is one with Appiani's frescoes taken from the Palazzo Reale in Milan. The villa is also famous for its garden.

🏛 **Villa Carlotta**
Via Regina 2b. 📞 *0344-404 05.* 🕐 *9–11:30am, 2–4:30pm daily 15 Mar–31 Oct; 9am–6pm daily Apr–Sep.*

Menaggio ❻

Como. 🏘 *3,200.* 🚻 **APT** *Piazza Garibaldi 4 (0344-329 24).*

T HE NAME MENAGGIO supposedly derives from two Indo-European words: *men* (mountain) and *uigg* (water), referring to the mouth of the Sanagra river on which the town lies. Menaggio is the leading commercial centre in the upper Lario region and a popular tourist resort as well. It is dominated by the ruins of the castle and has preserved some of its medieval layout. Sights worth visiting are the parish church of Santo Stefano – whose Baroque architecture conceals its Romanesque origin – and 17th-century San Carlo, with a good painting by Giuseppe Vermiglio (1625). The lakeside promenade, with its arcaded houses and villas, is a must. Past Menaggio, at Loveno, is the Neo-Classical Milyus-Vigoni villa with family portraits by Francesco Hayez. Around it is a lovely park, designed by Balzaretto in 1840, with many rare trees.

Menaggio, a lakeside town especially popular with British visitors

Gravedona 7

Como. 🏛 *2,800*. 🛈 **Pro Loco**
Piazza Cavour 7 *(0344-896 37)*.

A FORTIFIED TOWN of some
importance in ancient
Roman times, Gravedona was
destroyed by the people of
Como in the 13th century
because it was allied with
Milan. It later became capital
of the small Tre Pievi republic. The town then declined
and was ceded to Cardinal
Tolomeo Gallio, who in 1583
asked Tibaldi to build Palazzo
Gallio. Gravedona is known
for the church of **Santa Maria
del Tiglio** (12th century). The
aisled nave with tall galleries
houses a 12th-century wooden
Crucifix, a floor mosaic dating
from the 6th century and
various 12th–14th-century
frescoes. Santi Gusmeo e Matteo was frescoed by Fiam-
menghino, while Santa Maria
delle Grazie (1467) contains
16th-century frescoes. Nearby
Dongo is an ancient village
known for the Falck steel-
works, which was responsible
for building the metal parts of
the *Italia* and *Norge* airships.
Above Gravedona, at Peglio,
is the Sant'Eusebio complex,
with fine 17th-century
frescoes in the church. The
Spanish fort in the outskirts
was built in 1604 to guard
the Adda River plain.

Santa Maria del Tiglio
Via Bianchi 12. 📞 *0344-852 61*.
🕐 *9am–6pm daily*.

**Palazzo Gallio, designed by architect
Pellegrino Tibaldi in 1583**

The Cluniac Piona abbey, founded in the 11th century

Abbey of Piona 8

Via Santa Maria di Piona 1, Colico.
📞 *0341-94 03 31*. 🕐 *8:30am–
12:30, 3:30–6:30pm daily*. 🛈

A PROMONTORY on the north-
eastern shore of the lake
conceals this extraordinary
abbey built by Cluniac monks
in the 11th century. The
exterior of Romanesque San
Nicolao is adorned with small
arches and pilasters. There are
13th-century frescoes in the
apse. The bell tower dates
from 1700 and the cloister
(1252–7) has sculpted capitals
with fantastic figures and
13th-century frescoes.

Bellano 9

Lecco 🏛 *3,400*. 🛈 **APT** Via Nazario
Sauro 6, Lecco *(0341-36 93 90)*.

I N THE MIDDLE AGES
Bellano was the
summer residence
of Milanese bishops
and it has preserved
its medieval charac-
ter. Among houses
with wrought-iron
coats of arms is
the church of Santi
Nazaro, Celso e
Giorgio, the work of
Campionese masters
(14th century). Santa
Marta houses a *Pietà*
executed in 1518.
However, the main
appeal of Bellano is
the Orrido, a deep
gorge created by the
Pioverna torrent.

🌊 Orrido
🕐 *9am–1pm, 2:30–7:30pm daily
May–Sep; 10am–1pm, 3–6:30pm
Thu, Sat, Sun Oct–Nov.* 🈲

Varenna 10

Lecco. 🏛 *800*. 🛈 **Pro Loco** Piazza
Venini 1 *(0341-83 03 67)*.

T HIS SPLENDID VILLAGE of
ancient Roman origin,
with a perfectly intact
medieval layout, was a haven
for the inhabitants of Isola
Comacina when the citizens
of Como burned the island
(1169). In the town centre,
14th-century San Giorgio
has an altarpiece by Pietro
Brentani (1467), while Santa
Marta houses the parish art
gallery. Varenna is famous
for **Villa Cipressi**, with its
terraced garden, and **Villa
Monastero**, built over a
Cistercian monastery. Now a
conference centre, the villa
has preserved some of its
original furnishings and has
an elegant garden. All around
the town were quarries for
black Varenna marble – used
for the flooring in the Milan
Duomo. Since 1921 Mandello
del Lario has been the home of
the **Moto Guzzi factory**, with
a Motorcycle Museum.

🏛 Villa Cipressi
Via IV Novembre 18. 📞 *0341-83 01
13*. 🕐 *(garden) 9am–7pm (6pm Mar–
Jun) daily Mar–Sep*. ● *Oct–Feb*. 🈲
🏛 Villa Monastero
Via Polvani 2. 📞 *0341-83 01 29*.
🕐 *(garden) 9am–7pm (6pm Mar–Jun)
daily Mar–Sep*. ● *Oct–Feb*. 🈲

🏛 Museo Moto Guzzi della Motocicletta

Via Parodi 57, Mandello del Lario.
📞 *0341-70 91 11.* ⏰ *3–4pm Mon–Fri.* ⬤ *hols.*

Lecco ⓫

👥 *46,000.* **ℹ️ APT** Via Nazario Sauro 6 *(0341-36 93 90).*

L ECCO LIES ON the southern tip of the arm of the lake of the same name. It was inhabited in prehistoric times and fortified in the 6th century AD. In the 1300s it was taken over by Azzone Visconti, who built the Ponte Vecchio.

Manzoni set his novel *I Promessi Sposi (The Betrothed)* here. Mementoes of his life can be found in his childhood home, the **Villa Manzoni** at Caleotto, which also houses the Galleria Comunale d'Arte. In the centre are the Teatro della Società (1844) and San Nicolò, whose baptistery chapel has 14th–15th-century frescoes. The **Museo di Storia Naturale** in the 18th-century **Palazzo Belgioioso** is also of interest. Sites described by Manzoni in his novel have been identified, including the castle of the Unnamed at Vercurago, and Lucia's home at Olate. Near Civate is Romanesque **San Pietro al Monte** (12th century), with 11th–12th-century frescoes and reliefs with scenes from the Passion. A turn-off on the road to Bellagio leads to the Madonna del Ghisallo sanctuary.

The Italian writer Manzoni, author of *The Betrothed*

A drawing room in Villa Serbelloni overlooking the lake

🏛 Palazzo Belgioioso and Museo di Storia Naturale

Corso Matteotti 32. 📞 *0341-48 12 48.* ⏰ *9:30am–2pm Tue–Sun.* 🖼 ♿

⛪ San Pietro al Monte

Civate. 📞 *0341-55 15 76.* ⏰ *9am–3pm Sun (booking necessary Mon–Fri).*

🏛 Villa Manzoni

Via Guanella 1. 📞 *0341-48 12 47.* ⏰ *9:30am–2pm Tue–Sun.* 🖼 ♿

Bellagio ⓬

Como. 👥 *3,050.* **ℹ️ IAT** Piazza della Chiesa 14 *(031-95 02 04).*

K NOWN SINCE antiquity for its fine climate and scenery, Bellagio still has its medieval layout, with stepped alleyways. It became the site of splendid noble villas in the 18th century and then became a famous resort town with numerous hotels in the 19th century. Among the attractive residences, the loveliest are **Villa Serbelloni** and **Villa Melzi d'Eril**. The former was set in the middle of a park with woods and rose gardens by the Serbelloni, and in 1870 became a hotel which numbered Churchill and Kennedy among its famous guests. The Neo-Classical Villa Melzi was built in 1810 by Giocondo Albertolli. The interior is not open to the

public, but the Museo Archeologico, the chapel and the gardens are. Near the town are the 18th-century Trivulzio and Trotti villas. Don't miss 12th-century San Giacomo, with its pulpit decorated with symbols of the Evangelists.

One of the statues at Villa Melzi d'Eril

🏛 Villa Serbelloni

Piazza Garibaldi *(book at IAT).* ⏰ *11am–4pm Tue–Sun Apr–Oct.* 🖼

🏛 Villa Melzi d'Eril

Lungolario Marconi. 📞 *031-95 03 18.* ⏰ *9am–6:30pm Apr–Oct.* 🖼

Torno ⓭

Como. 👥 *1,100.* **ℹ️ APT** Piazza Cavour 18, Como *(031-26 97 12).*

T HE VILLAGE OF TORNO boasts the churches of Santa Tecla, which has a beautiful marble portal dating from 1480, and the 14th-century San Giovanni, with its remarkable Renaissance door. However, Torno is known most of all for the Villa Pliniana, built in 1573 (and attributed to Tibaldi) for Count Anguissola, the governor of Como. The villa is surrounded by a park and stands right by the lake. The writers Foscolo, Stendhal and Byron, and composer Rossini were all guests here.

Lake Garda

Remains of mosaics in the Roman villa at Desenzano del Garda

ITALY'S LARGEST LAKE was created by glaciation. The scenery is varied, with steep, rugged cliffs at the northern end and softer hills southwards, where the basin widens and Mediterranean flora prevails. Over the centuries the praises of Lake Garda have been sung by such greats as Catullus, Dante and Goethe, and today it caters for luxury holidays and tour groups alike. Garda is an ideal spot for windsurfing and sailing, and it hosts famous regattas such as the Centomiglia.

★ Desenzano del Garda
This is one of the liveliest and most popular towns on Lake Garda. Above, one of the frescoes in the Roman villa, built in the 4th century and discovered in 1921 ❷

★ Gardone Riviera
Near this pleasant tourist resort is the Vittoriale degli Italiani, where the writer Gabriele D'Annunzio lived from 1921 to 1938. It embodies the decadence of which this poet and novelist was the last exponent ❺

Villa Bettoni at Bogliaco (1756) has elegant frescoed rooms with masterpieces by Reni and Canaletto, as well as a garden with a nympheum.

Bogli⟨a⟩

Toscolano Maderno ❻

Gardone Riviera

Fasano

San Michele
Salò ❹

Isola di Garda

Manerba ❸

❶ Sirmione

San Pietro in Mavino

Desenzano del Garda ❷

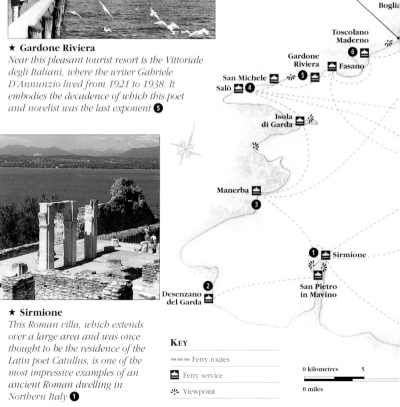

★ Sirmione
This Roman villa, which extends over a large area and was once thought to be the residence of the Latin poet Catullus, is one of the most impressive examples of an ancient Roman dwelling in Northern Italy ❶

KEY

- - - Ferry routes

⛴ Ferry service

☀ Viewpoint

0 kilometres   5

0 miles

VISITORS' CHECKLIST

🛈 Local information bureaus.
🚆 FS Milan–Venice line (147-88 80 88). 🚌 Azienda Provinciale Trasporti di Verona (045-800 41 29) or Società Italiana Autoservizi (02-86 46 48 54).
⛴ Navigazione Lago di Garda (800-55 18 01 freefone number).

Limone sul Garda
The abundance of citrus trees grown here is supposedly the reason why the locals have the longest life expectancy in Italy ⑪

⑧ 🚆 **Riva del Garda**

⑬ 🚆 **Torbole**

Limone 🚆 ⑦

At Torbole, now a surfers' paradise, Venetian ships – which defeated the Visconti in 1440 – were reassembled after being transported along the Val d'Adige.

Campione del Garda 🚆
Tignale 🚆

⑨ 🚆 **Malcèsine**

⑧
ano 🚆

🌤 **Isola di Trimelone**

🚆 **Brenzone**

🚆 **Castelletto di Brenzone**

🚆 **Pai**

Punta San Vigilio was named after the bishop from Trent who brought Christianity to the area in the 4th century.

🌤 **Torri del Benàco**

The Camaldolite Hermitage (16th century), which only recently allowed women visitors, has a splendid panoramic view.

ta San Vigilio
🚆 **Garda**
⑪ ●

🚆 **Bardolino**
⑫

🚆 **Lazise**

Gardaland
⑬

Torri del Benaco
The economy of this small town, which thanks to its strategic position controlled access to the upper lake region, is based on tourism and fishing. The townspeople have enjoyed special fishing privileges since the 1400s ⑩

SIGHTS AT A GLANCE

Bardolino and Lazise ⑫
Desenzano del Garda ②
Garda ⑪
Gardone Riviera ⑤
The Valtènesi and San Felice del Benaco ③
Limone sul Garda ⑦
Malcesine ⑨
Peschiera del Garda ⑬
Riva del Garda ⑧
Salò ④
Sirmione ①
Torri del Benaco ⑩
Toscolano Maderno ⑥

STAR SIGHTS

★ **Sirmione**

★ **Gardone Riviera**

★ **Desenzano del Garda**

Sirmione ❶

Brescia. 🏘 5,100.
ℹ️ Viale Marconi 2 (030-91 61 14).

ROMAN SIRMIO lay in the hinterland and only the villa quarter faced the lake. In the 13th century the Scaligeri lords of Verona turned it into a fortress to defend Lake Garda. In 1405 Sirmione was taken over by Venice, which then ruled until the 18th century. The main focus of the town is the **Rocca Scaligera**, a castle built by Mastino I della Scala (13th century), the inner basin of which served as shelter for the Veronese boats. Roman and medieval plaques are in the entrance arcade.

Fifteenth-century Santa Maria Maggiore, built over a pagan temple, has a Roman column in its porch, while the campanile was a Scaligera tower. The interior has 15th- and 16th-century frescoes and a 15th-century Madonna.

The famous **spas** use the water from the Boiola spring, known since 1546. San Pietro in Mavino, rebuilt in 1320, boasts fine 13th–16th-century frescoes. Sirmione is also famous for the so-called **Grotte di Catullo**, a huge Roman residence built in the 1st centuries BC–AD. The most evocative rooms are the Grotta del Cavallo, the Cryptoporticus and the pool. The Sala della Trifora del Paradiso and Sala dei Giganti overlook the lake. The Antiquarium has finds from the villa, including a mosaic of a seascape and a portrait of Catullus (1st century BC).

⛪ Rocca Scaligera
Piazza Castello. 📞 030-91 64 68.
🕐 8:30am–1:30pm Tue–Sun (until 6pm Sun from Apr). ⬤ hols. 🎫
Terme Catullo (Spa)
Piazza Castello 12.
📞 167-80 21 25.
🌿 Grotte di Catullo
Via Catullo 📞 030-91 61 57.
🕐 8:30am–7pm Tue–Sat; 9am–6pm Sun, hols Mar–14 Oct; 8:30am–4:30pm Tue–Sat; 9am–4:30pm Sun, hols 15 Oct–Feb. ⬤ Mon (Tue if Mon is hol). 🎫

***Christ Enthroned with Angels and Saints**, San Pietro in Mavino*

Desenzano del Garda ❷

Brescia. 🏘 21,000. ℹ️ Via Porto Vecchio 34 (030-914 15 10).
🏺 antiques, 1st Sun of month (except for Jan & Aug).

PROBABLY FOUNDED by the Romans on a site inhabited since prehistoric times, Desenzano was taken over by Venice in the 15th century, when it became the leading lakeside town. Since the 19th century it has been a tourist resort. The heart of the town centre is Piazza Malvezzi, home to an antiques market known for its silverware and prints. The 16th-century town hall and Provveditore Veneto buildings are also here. In the **Duomo** (16th century) is a fine *Last Supper* by Tiepolo. The **Museo Civico Archeo-logico**, in the cloister of Santa Maria de Senioribus, contains displays of Bronze Age finds and the oldest known wooden plough (2000 BC).

The **Villa Romana** was built in the 4th century AD and rediscovered in 1921. It had been covered by a landslide, which preserved some lovely mosaics with geometric motifs such as the *Good Shepherd* and *Psyche and Cupids*. Finds from the villa are in the Antiquarium.

⛪ Duomo
Piazza Duomo. 📞 030-914 18 49.
🕐 8–11:30am, 4–6:30pm daily.
🏛 Museo Civico Archeologico
Via Santa Maria. 📞 030-914 45 29 or 030-999 42 75. 🕐 3–7pm Tue, Fri–Sun, hols. ⬤ Mon, Wed, Thu.
🏛 Villa Romana
📞 030-914 35 47. 🕐 8:30am–7pm Mon–Fri; 9am–5:30pm hols Mar–14 Oct; 10am–4pm Mon–Fri; 9am–4:30pm hols 15 Oct–Feb. ⬤ Mon (Tue if Mon is hol). 🎫

The Valtènesi and San Felice del Benaco ❸

Brescia. 🏘 2,500.
ℹ️ Via Portovecchio 34, Desenzano del Garda (030-91 41 51 07).

THE AREA BETWEEN Desenzano and Salò, called Valtènesi, is rich in medieval churches and castles. At Padenghe, the Rocca (9th–10th century) is reached by a drawbridge. Nearby is 12th-century Sant'-Emiliano. The houses in Moniga del Garda are pro-tected by a 10th-century wall with turrets. Here stands Santa Maria della Neve, built in the 14th century. The Rocca di Manerba del Garda (8th century) lies on a headland

The Rocca Scaligera at Sirmione, with its tower and battlements

Cappella del Santissimo Sacramento, Salò Duomo (18th century)

over the lake where a castle once stood. The ruins have become part of a regional park. At Solarolo, the 15th-century Santissima Trinità has a fresco cycle with the *Last Judgment*, while prehistoric finds from this area are in the **Museo Archeologico della Valtènesi** at Montinelle. The bay between the Punta Belvedere and Punta San Fermo headlands is dominated by San Felice del Benaco. To the south is the Madonna del Carmine sanctuary (1452). In the town centre the parish church has a *Madonna and Saints* by Romanino. Opposite Punta San Fermo is Isola di Garda. Tradition has it that the Franciscans in the 13th-century monastery introduced citrus fruit cultivation to Lake Garda.

Museo Archeologico della Valtènesi
Piazzale Simonati, Montinelle.
0365-55 12 69. ☐ 7:30–9pm Tue–Sat; 10am–noon Sun summer. 2–4pm Sat; 10am–noon Sun winter.

The medieval church of San Pietro in Lucone

Salò ❹

Brescia. 10,200. Lungolago Zanardelli, Palazzo Municipale (0365-214 23).

A FORMER ROMAN town, in 1337 Salò became the seat of the Consiglio della Magnifica Patria, the governing body of 42 towns which met in the palazzo built by Sansovino in 1524 (now the Museo Archeologico). The late Gothic cathedral has a *Madonna and Saints* by Romanino (1529) and an altarpiece from 1476. Palazzo Fantoni is home to the Biblioteca dell'Ateneo di Salò and **Museo del Nastro Azzurro**, a military museum with items from 1796 to 1945. Palazzo Terzi-Martinengo at Barbarano was the seat of Mussolini's Salò puppet government.

Museo del Nastro Azzurro
Via Fantoni 49. 0365-216 03. ☐ 5–7pm Mon–Fri; 5–8pm Sat; 10am–1pm, 3–5pm hols, Jun–Aug, 3–5pm Sat in winter.

VINES, CHURCHES AND CASTLES
The Valtènesi area is known for its vineyards, where the rosé wine Chiaretto della Riviera del Garda is produced. A visit to the wineries here offers a chance to visit the inland region of this side of Lake Garda and also see the medieval fortresses of Soiano del Lago, Puegnago sul Garda and Polpenazze del Garda. In the cemetery of this last-mentioned village is the Romanesque church of San Pietro in Lucone, with its 15th-century frescoes depicting the lives of St Peter and the Apostles.

Gardone Riviera ❺

Brescia. 2,500. Corso Repubblica 39 (0365-203 47).

BOASTING THE HIGHEST winter temperatures in Northern Italy, Gardone Riviera became a fashionable tourist resort in the late 19th century because of its mild dry climate, which is beneficial for those suffering from lung ailments. Two celebrated villas are Villa Alba and Villa Fiordaliso.

Gardone is also famous for the **Vittoriale degli Italiani**, Gabriele D'Annunzio's residence, where the poet collected over 10,000 objects including works of art, books and mementoes, which he later donated to the state. In the garden are the Prioria, his residence, the Schifamondo with mementoes, the Auditorium and the Mausoleum. On display are objects related to his exploits during and after World War I, such as his motor boat and aeroplane.

Another attraction is the **Giardino Botanico Hruska**, a fine botanic garden with over 2,000 Alpine, Mediterranean and subtropical species of plants.

D'Annunzio, who lived out his days at the Vittoriale degli Italiani

Vittoriale degli Italiani
Gardone. 0365-201 30. ☐ 8:30am–8pm daily Apr–Sep; 9am–5pm Mon–Fri Oct–Mar. **House** ☐ 10am–6pm Tue–Sun Apr–Sep; 9am–5pm Tue–Sun Oct–Mar. ● Mon.

Giardino Botanico Hruska
Via Motta 2. 0365-203 47 (APT Gardone). ☐ 9am–6pm daily 15 Mar–15 Oct.

Canvas by Celesti in the Santi Pietro e Paolo parish church, Toscolano

Toscolano Maderno ❻

Brescia. 🏘 6,700. 🈺 Via Lungolago 18 (0365-64 13 30).

THIS TOWN IS MADE UP OF the two villages of Toscolano and Maderno. Sights of interest at Maderno are the Romanesque church of Sant'Andrea, with a panel by Paolo Veneziano, and the parish church of Sant'Ercolano, with paintings by Veronese and Andrea Celesti. Here the Gonzaga family built the Palazzina del Serraglio (17th century) for Vincenzo I's amorous assignations. Toscolano, ancient Benacum, was the largest town on Lake Garda in Roman times. At Santa Maria del Benaco, with 16th-century frescoes, archaeologists found Roman and Etruscan objects and the ruins of a mosaic-decorated villa (1st century AD). The parish church of Santi Pietro e Paolo has 22 canvases by Andrea Celesti. Gargnano boasts San Giacomo di Calino (11th–12th century) and San Francesco (1289), whose cloister has Venetian arches. Other sights are Villa Feltrinelli, Mussolini's residence during the Republic of Salò, and Villa Bettoni.

Limone sul Garda ❼

Brescia. 🏘 990. 🈺 Via Comboni 15 (0365-95 40 70).

KNOWN FOR ITS mild climate, Limone may have been named after the lemon tree terraces (no longer used) typical of this area. Or the name may derive from Limen (border), since the Austrian frontier was here until 1918. In the town centre are the 15th-century church of San Rocco and a parish church (1685), with canvases by Celesti. Near Tignale is the **Montecastello Sanctuary** (13th–14th century) with a Coronation of the Virgin (14th century) and medallions by the school of Palma il Giovane. Towards Tremosine is the Brasa river gorge, in a panoramic setting.

🔒 **Montecastello Sanctuary**
Via Chiesa, Tignale. ⭕ 9am–6pm daily mid-Mar–Oct. 🄲 0365-730 20.

Riva del Garda ❽

Trento. 🏘 13,500. 🈺 Giardini di Porta Orientale 8 (0464-55 44 44).

SITUATED AT A strategic point on the northern tip of the lake, in the Trentino region, Riva was under Austrian rule until 1918. The Rocca and Torre Apponale (13th century) were built to defend the town; an angel, the town symbol, stands on top of the tower. In the square opposite are Palazzo Pretorio (1370) and Palazzo del Provveditore (1482). The 12th-century Rocca is the home of the **Museo Civico**, with 14th–20th-century paintings. Santa Maria Assunta has two canvases by Piazzetta, while the octagonal, richly

frescoed Inviolata (1603) has works by Palma il Giovane (under restoration until 2001). The impressive waterfalls of the Varone river, above Riva, are 80 m (262 ft) high.

Nearby Torbole was described by Goethe in Italian Journey and is a popular spot for sailing.

🏛 **Museo Civico**
Piazza Battisti 3. 🄲 0464-57 38 69. ⭕ 9:30am–6pm Tue–Sun (5:30pm Oct–Mar; 10pm Jul, Aug).

Malcesine ❾

Verona. 🏘 3,500. 🈺 Via del Capitanato 6/8 (045-740 00 44).

Deposition (15th century), Malcesine parish church

ONE OF THE MOST fascinating towns along the lake shore, Malcesine stands on a stretch of impervious rock, hence the name mala silex, inaccessible rock. The 12th-century **Castello** was rebuilt by the Scaligeri of Verona in 1277. It houses the Museo di Storia Naturale del Garda e del Monte Baldo, the lake's natural history museum, which among other things shows how the Venetians transported ships to Torbole (1438–40). The parish church contains a 16th-century Deposition. Towering above Malcesine is Monte Baldo (2,218 m, 7,275 ft), accessible by cable car, with nature trails and stunning views.

The Legend of Maria (c.1614–20) by Martino Teofilo Polacco, in the Inviolata at Riva del Garda

The castle at Torri del Benaco, built in 1393

Castello Scaligero
Via Castello. ☎ 045-740 08 37.
◯ 9:30am–5pm Mon–Sun
15 Mar–15 Nov. ● 25, 28, 29 Dec,
3, 4 Jan.

Torri del Benaco ❿

Verona. 👥 2,500.
ℹ Via Don Gnochi 23 (045-627 03 84).

ROMAN CASTRUM TURRIUM was a major stop between Riva and Garda and has preserved the typical grid plan. Due to its strategic position, Torri was fortified and a castle was built; it is now a **museum**, with old farm tools and prehistoric finds. Santissima Trinità has some 15th-century frescoes.

🏛 Museo del Castello
Via Fratelli Lavanda. ☎ 045-629 61 11. ◯ 9:30am–12:30pm daily Apr–May & Oct; 9am–1pm, 4:30–7:30pm daily Jun–Sep.

Garda ⓫

Verona. 👥 3,500. ℹ Via Don Gnochi 23 (045-627 03 84).

BUILT AROUND A SMALL BAY, Garda was one of the major towns along the lake, controlling the southern basin. Its name, then given to the lake as well, comes from the German *Warten* (fortress), referring to the wall around the historic centre with its small port, accessible through the Torre dell'Orologio tower and gate. Among the historic buildings are the 15th-century Palazzo del Capitano, the Iosa, the dock of Palazzo Car-

lotti designed by Sanmicheli, and **Santa Maria Maggiore** (18th century) with a painting by Palma il Giovane and a 15th-century cloister. At the new port is Villa Albertini, with an English-style park, while at Punta San Vigilio is Villa Guarienti (1542), designed by Sanmicheli, where the WWF offers a tour of the Bronze Age rock engravings.

🔒 Santa Maria Maggiore
Piazzale Roma. ☎ 045-725 68 25.

Bardolino and Lazise ⓬

Verona. 👥 5,900. ℹ Piazzale Aldo Moro (045-721 00 78).
🛍 antiques, 3rd Sun of month.

THE CORNICELLO AND Mira-bello headlands enclosing Bardolino made it a natural harbour. Originally it was a prehistoric settlement and then became a Roman camp. The historic centre has two early medieval churches, San Zeno and San Severo. The first still has its 9th-century Carolingian cruciform structure. Romanesque San Severo was founded in the 9th century but rebuilt in the 12th. It has 12th–13th-century frescoes with battle scenes and episodes from the Bible. Don't miss the 10th-century crypt. Among the

civic buildings is the Loggia Rambaldi, in the Rambaldi family palazzo. Bardolino is also famous for its wine.

Lazise also boasted a prehistoric civilization. A castle was built in the 11th century and the lords of Verona erected the walls in the 1300s. The 16th-century Venetian Customs House is all that remains of the old harbour. Next to it is San Nicolò (12th century), with Giotto school frescoes. Near Colà a Spa was recently opened.

Terme di Villa Cedri
Piazza di Sopra 4, Località Colà di Lazise. ☎ 045-759 09 88.

Peschiera del Garda ⓭

Verona. 👥 8,700. ℹ Piazzale Betteloni 15 (045-755 03 81).

PESCHIERA HAS retained its military image more than any other town at Lake Garda. The old town lies on an island surrounded by a star-shaped wall – "a fortress beautiful and strong", says Dante. The walls were rein-forced by the Scaligeri of Verona, rebuilt for the new Venetian rulers by Sanmicheli in 1556, and completed with two forts by the Austrians two centuries later. Besides the frescoed 18th-century San Martino, there is the 16th-century Madonna del Frassino sanctuary, with a beautiful frescoed cloister.

San Zeno in Bardolino, crowned by a tower, containing traces of its original frescoes

Gardaland

The canoe safari, one of the many attractions

THIS THEME PARK was opened in 1975 and is one of the largest in Italy (500,000 sq m, 600,000 sq yds). The 38 attractions range from the rollercoaster to reconstructions of the pyramids and a jungle, the PalaBlù dolphin pool and the Village of the Elves, all ideal for families with children. The fun park facilities are good, with different kinds of refreshments, theme shops and souvenir photos. At busy times queues are kept informed about the length of the wait.

PalaBlù
Italy's largest dolphin pool: four dolphins perform acrobatic tricks in front of the crowd.

Space Vertigo
There's a bacteriological alarm in the space station – everyone must escape! The only hope is to jump into space at top speed from a 40-m (131-ft) high tower. Thrills galore for everyone.

Arab Souk

Top Spin

★ Cinema Dinamico
It looks like a normal movie theatre, but when the lights are off you are catapulted into a horror film or down a mountain on a kind of skateboard.

Monorail station

The floating tree trunks of the Colorado Boat confront the canyon rapids.

Magic Mountain
This super-fast rollercoaster is one of the most famous rides of all, with two hairpin bends and two death-defying spins. Only for the most intrepid of visitors.

The Valley of the Kings
Lovers of ancient Egypt can go into the temple of Abu Simbel, and discover the pharaohs' secrets among hieroglyphs, archaeologists and a mysterious green ray.

★ **Blue Tornado**
*Even more exciting than
the rollercoaster, this new
attraction (1998) offers
you the chance to
experience first-
hand the thrills of
piloting an
American
fighter
plane.*

★ **Jungle Rapids**
*Here you climb aboard a
rubber dinghy and are
taken over the rapids of
a canyon, past a
volcano, into the
heart of mysterious
and magical Southeast
Asia with its temples.*

Village of the Elves
*This attraction, like the
Ortobruco Tour and the Merry-
go-round, is for small children.*

Prezzemolo
*Gardaland's mascot, Prezzemolo
(Parsley) the dragon, is always
at the park entrance to welcome
all new visitors.*

0 metres   100
0 yards   100

STAR FEATURES

★ Blue Tornado

★ Jungle Rapids

★ Cinema Dinamico

The stepped Motta ascent, the setting for the Ortafiori festivities in April and May

Lago d'Orta

🅸 APTL Via Panoramica, Orta–San Giulio *(0322-90 56 14)*. **🚆** *FS Nova-ra-Domodossola line (147-88 80 88)*. **⛴** *Nav. Lago d'Orta (0322-84 48 62)*.

LAKE ORTA, or Cusio, is the westernmost lake in the lower Alps region, characterized by soft hills and scenery. Villages are dotted around the lake, along the shore or perched among green terracing. The Mottarone, a ski resort, and the other mountains surrounding the lake offer attractive hiking trails.

As far back as the 1700s, Orta was a tourist attraction and many villas were built in large parks. The chief town is Orta San Giulio, on a promontory in the middle of the lake. The village alleyways wind around Piazza Motta, on which lies the Palazzetto della Comunità (1582) and where the stepped Motta ascent begins. Opposite the square is the island of San Giulio, converted to Christianity by the Greek deacon Julius, who built the 4th-century **basilica**. The church was restored in the 11th–12th century and has a 12th-century Romanesque marble pulpit and

Figure on the pulpit, San Giulio

15th-century frescoes. Next door is the Palazzo del Vescovo (16th–18th century). Another sight is the **Sacro Monte**, a sanctuary built in 1591 on the rise above Orta. Dedicated to St Francis, it consists of 20 chapels with 17th–18th-century terracotta statues and frescoes. Opposite, perched over a steep quarry, is the Madonna del Sasso sanctuary (1748).

On the northern tip of the lake is Omegna, whose medieval quarter boasts the late Romanesque collegiate church of Sant'Ambrogio.

At Quarna there is the **Museo Etnografico e dello Strumento a Fiato**, with displays of wind instruments, made in this village for centuries. Other interesting villages are Vacciago di Ameno, with the Calderara Collection of contemporary art, featuring 327 international avant-garde works of the 1950s and 1960s; Gozzano, with the church of San Giuliano (18th century), Palazzo Vescovile and the seminary; and, lastly, Torre di Buccione. San Maurizio d'Opaglio has a curious attraction: a museum devoted to the production of taps.

🅰 Basilica di San Giulio
Isola di San Giulio.
APTL ring road, Orta San Giulio *(0322-90 56 14)*.
⬜ *9:30am–12:15pm, 2–6:45pm Tue–Sat; 9:30–10:45am, 2–6:45pm (5:45pm solar time) Sun, hols; 11am–12:15pm Mon.*

🅰 Sacro Monte
Via Sacro Monte. **☎** *0322-91 19 60*.
Chapels **⬜** *9:30am–6pm daily summer; 9:30am–5pm hols, 9:30am–4pm Mon–Fri winter.*

🏛 Museo Etnografico e dello Strumento Musicale a Fiato
Quarna Sotto. **☎** *0323-82 60 01*.
⬜ *10am–noon, 3–7pm Tue–Sun Jul–mid-Sep.* **⬤** *Mon.*

Lago di Varese

🅸 IAT Via Carrobbio 2, Varese *(0332-28 36 04)*. **🚆** *Ferrovie Nord Milano, Milan-Laveno line to Gavirate (02-84 47 75 00)*. **🚌** *Autolinee Varesine (0332-73 11 10)*.

THIS LAKE BASIN was created by glacial movement during the Quaternary era. It offers pleasant scenery, with rolling hills and the Campo dei Fiori massif. In prehistoric times it was inhabited by a prehistoric civilization, the important remains of which were found on the island of Isolino Virginia (which can be reached from Biandronno), where they are on display at the **Villa Ponti** museum.

Part of the lake shore is now protected as the Brabbia marsh nature reserve. Not far away, at Cazzago Brabbia, are ice-houses used to conserve fish in the 18th century. On the northern tip of the lake,

Fishing boats along the shores of the Lago di Varese

at Voltorre di Gavirate, the church of **San Michele** is worth a visit. It was part of a 12th-century Cluniac monastery and is now used for exhibitions. On the slopes of Campo dei Fiori you can see the lake of the **Sacro Monte** di Varese, a sanctuary made up of 14 17th-century chapels with frescoes and life-size statues narrating the Mysteries of the Rosary.

🏛 Villa Ponti
Isolino Virginia.
📞 0332-28 15 90 (Musei Civici di Varese) ⬤ 9:30am–12:30, 2–5pm Tue–Sun (5:30pm Sun). 📷

⛪ San Michele
Voltorre di Gavirate. 📞 0332-74 36 13. ⬤ during exhibitions.

⛪ Sacro Monte
Varese. 📞 0332-83 03 73. ⬤ Via Sacra always open.

Lago d'Iseo

ℹ IAT Lungolago Marconi 26, Iseo (030-98 13 61). 🚉 FS to Brescia, then Ferrovie Nord Milano (02-84 47 75 00). 🚌 SAB (035-28 9 0 11). ⛴ Navigazione Lago d'Iseo (035-97 14 83).

LAKE ISEO, ALSO KNOWN as Sebino, extends between the provinces of Bergamo and Brescia. It is the seventh largest lake in Italy and fourth in Lombardy, created by a glacier descending from the Val Camonica. The chief towns here are Iseo, Sarnico, Lovere and Pisogne. The historic centre of Iseo has retained its medieval character, with the church of

Sant'Andrea (1150), the Neo-Classical interior of which contains a painting by Hayez. Next to this is the tomb of the feudal landowner Giacomo Oldofredi and, on a hill at the entrance to the town, the Castello degli Oldofredi (both built in the 14th century), which in 1585 became a Capuchin monastery. At Provaglio d'Iseo there is the San Pietro in Lamosa Cluniac monastery, founded in 1030. Its 11th–12th-century Romanesque church has frescoes by the school of Romanino. Sarnico, at the southern end of the lake, was an important commercial and industrial town. Among the Art Nouveau houses built here by Giuseppe Sommaruga, is Villa Faccanoni (1912), one of the best examples of this style.

The road that follows the western side of the lake rounds the Corno headland, which has a fine views of Monte Isola, the largest lake island in Europe, with its typical villages, dominated by the Madonna della Ceriola sanctuary and the 15th-century Rocca Oldofredi. At the northern end of the lake is Lovere, which has medieval tower-houses.

On the lakeside is the **Galleria dell'Accademia Tadini**, featuring fine works of art ranging from the 14th to the 20th century, including Jacopo Bellini, Strozzi, Tiepolo, Hayez and Canova. The church of Santa Maria in Valvendra (1483) has paintings by Floriano Ferramola

The Piramidi di Zone pinnacles, some reaching 30 m (98 ft)

and Moretto and a 16th-century wooden altarpiece on the high altar. At Pisogne is Santa Maria della Neve (15th century), with scenes of the Passion frescoed by Romanino (1534). From here you can go to the Val Camonica rock engravings park. The lake is also famous for its lovely scenery, including the Piramidi di Zone, pinnacles protected from erosion by the rock massif above them, and the Torbiere d'Iseo, a marshy area with peat bogs which is now a nature reserve.

🏛 Galleria dell'Accademia Tadini
Via Tadini, Lovere.
📞 035-96 27 80. ⬤ 3–6pm Mon–Sat, 10am–12:30, 3–6pm Sun & hols mid-Apr–mid-Oct. 📷

Lago d'Idro

ℹ Pro Loco Via Trento 15, Idro (0365-832 24). 🚌 SIA (02-86 46 23 50).

THE HIGHEST LARGE LAKE in Lombardy (368 m, 1,207 ft above sea level) was turned into an artificial basin in 1932 to provide irrigation and hydroelectricity. It is dominated by the Rocca di Anfo, a fortress with a splendid panoramic view that was built over older fortifications by the Venetians in 1450, and then rebuilt many times. From here you can reach Bagolino, with its charming stone houses and San Rocco (1478), which contains a fresco cycle by Giovan Pietro da Cemmo.

Rocca Oldofredi, Monte Isola, the Martinengo residence since the 1500s

TRAVELLERS'
NEEDS

WHERE TO STAY 154-161

WHERE TO EAT 162-175

BARS AND CAFÉS 176-179

SHOPPING 180-187

ENTERTAINMENT 188-197

WHERE TO STAY

IT IS NOT EASY TO FIND atmospheric hotels or charming guesthouses in Milan because the city caters mostly to businessmen and women and the majority of hotels are therefore geared to their needs, with working facilities in the rooms and public areas. This type of accommodation comes in the medium–high price range and usually offers either private parking or nearby garage facilities. The four-star hotels not only have prestigious restaurants that are among the best in the city, but may also have lovely inner gardens not seen from the street. It is best to book accommodation well in advance, especially during the international fashion shows (held in March and October) and the many top trade fairs. At the lakes, on the other hand, the choice ranges from guesthouses to fascinating historic hotels, which have drawn visitors and celebrities from all over the world since the 19th century. The most luxurious are in charming 17th- and 18th-century villas, with flower-filled terraces, health clubs and heated pools. For more detailed information regarding accommodation in Milan and at the lakes, see pages 156–161.

Porter, Hotel Palace, Milan (see p159)

CHOOSING A HOTEL

THE ITALIAN FOR HOTEL is *albergo*. A *pensione* or *locanda* theoretically indicates a more modest guest-house, but in practice the distinctions are quite blurred.

Most of the hotels in Milan are concentrated in the Buenos Aires-Stazione Centrale area, near the Fiera and in the Città Studi district. The first group is situated for the most part in Piazza della Repub-blica and near the main railway station, which is practical for visitors on a short stay. Some of the more interesting hotels are the **Buenos Aires** *(see p158)*, the **Palace** *(see p159)* and the **Duca di**

Entrance to the Hotel Regency (see p157) in Milan

The foyer-lounge at the Four Seasons Hotel in Milan (see p159)

Milano *(see p159)* – both 5-star – and the **Principe di Savoia** *(see p159)*, in 1930s style. Around the Fiera, large hotels cater for business visitors. The **Regency** *(see p157)* is smaller, with a warm atmosphere. At Città Studi you can find clean, inexpensive 2-star hotels: two examples are the **Aspromonte** *(see p158)* and the **San Francisco** *(see p158)*.

In the historic centre a few charming, small hotels remain. The **Antica Locanda Solferino** *(see p158)* has a family atmosphere. The **Grand Hotel et de Milan** *(see p159)* and the **Four Seasons** *(see p159)* are both elegant, historic hotels.

At the lakes hotels are more geared to holidaymakers and families. Some of Italy's most famous luxury hotels are sited around the lake shores. The **Des Iles Borromées** *(see p160)* at Lake Maggiore was once a royal residence. Lake Como boasts famous luxury hotels such as the **Grand Hotel Villa d'Este** *(see p160)* at Cernobbio, and the **Grand Hotel Villa Serbelloni** *(see p160)* at Bellagio.

BOOKING

ACCOMMODATION can be booked by phoning or sending a fax. The hotel will probably ask for a credit card number in advance. Almost all Milanese hotels have e-mail facilities and some, usually the luxury ones, have websites where you can book directly online. Milan is a busy commercial city so it is best to book well in advance.

The Grand Hotel Villa Serbelloni *(see p160)* **at Lake Como**

GRADING

ALONG WITH the rest of Italy, hotels in Milan and at the lakes are classified by a star system, from one (the lowest) to five stars. It is best to avoid one-star hotels in Milan (unlike the rest of Italy) however.

Two-star hotels usually offer bed and breakfast, and rooms may not have private bathrooms. Three-star hotels offer en-suite bathrooms, TV and sometimes a mini-bar; room service is usually available.

Four-star hotels, besides the above facilities, usually provide a laundry service, services for business travellers and (in Milan) a shuttle service to and from the airports. Five-star hotels are luxurious and offer exclusive restaurants and facilities for conferences.

At the lakes, accommodation ranges from luxury hotels to family-run guesthouses. There are also inexpensive youth hostels and campsites with tents and caravans (RVs). Some have self-catering (efficiency) apartments.

PRICES

ACCOMMODATION in Milan is generally expensive. Because Milan is primarily a business destination, there is little seasonal variation in pricing, and tariffs may even increase when the fashion shows are held and when there are major events like the Furniture Fair at the Fiera. Some of the larger hotels may also require you to take half-board (map) during your stay.

At the lakes, prices vary according to the season: in spring and summer, the peak tourist seasons, prices are higher. August, the Italian holiday month, is the busiest time. Many hotels expect you to take full board, especially in the summer months. Some hotels close for part of the year, usually in winter.

By law, prices have to be displayed in every hotel bedroom. Beware of extras: mini-bar drinks will be expensive. A view and air conditioning will add to costs, and hotel phone charges are higher than standard rates. By law, the hotel must issue you with a receipt when you pay, and the receipt should be kept until you leave Italy.

Sign of the Garda & Suisse hotel *(see p161)*

CHILDREN

IN GENERAL, CHILDREN are welcomed everywhere in Italy, but hotels may not go out of their way to provide special facilities. Some of the cheaper hotels may not be able to provide cots. However, virtually all hotels, from the simplest to the most grand, will put a small bed or two into a double room for families travelling together. The price is usually an additional 30–40 per cent of the double room rate per bed. Hotels around the lakes tend to be better equipped for children than the business hotels of Milan. Babysitting services are offered by some large hotels at the lakes.

PETS

FOR THOSE TRAVELLING with their dog or other pet, some hotels actively welcome animals and provide special facilities for them, especially at the lakes. In Milan it is more difficult to find hotels and guesthouses that accept pets, but some of the larger hotels have rooms specially furnished for clients and can even offer dog-sitting services. However, if you mean to travel with pets it is always a good idea to check these details when booking.

Four poster bed in a room at the Villa Crespi *(see p161)*, **Lake Orta**

Choosing a Hotel

HOTELS IN MILAN are notoriously expensive, but they all – from two to five stars – offer good services and facilities for business travellers. Hotels around the lakes are more geared to holidays and some are set in their own park with a pool. All the hotels listed below offer rooms with private bath and telephone.

	CREDIT CARDS	TERRACE OR GARDEN	PARKING	BAR	RESTAURANT

MILAN

CITY CENTRE: *Gran Duca di York* ⓁⓁ
Via Moneta 1. **Map** 7 B1. 【 02-87 48 63. FAX 02-869 03 44.
A charming hotel in a historic building next to the Pinacoteca Ambrosiana.
Some rooms have a terrace. ● Aug, Christmas. TV 目 & 🏠 **Rooms:** 33

	■	●			

CITY CENTRE: *Sir Edward* ⓁⓁⓁ
Via Mazzini 4. **Map** 7 C1. 【 02-87 78 77. FAX 02-87 78 44.
Ⓦ www.infosquare.it/siredward @ siredw@infosquare.it
Almost in Piazza del Duomo, comfortable and inviting. TV 目 & **Rooms:** 39

	■				

CITY CENTRE: *Spadari al Duomo* ⓁⓁⓁⓁ
Via Spadari 11. **Map** 7 C1. 【 02-72 00 23 71. FAX 02-86 11 84.
Ⓦ www.spadarialduomo.com @ reservations@spadari.com
Situated opposite the Duomo, this hotel has designer furniture and works by
famous artists. Spacious rooms, some with a jacuzzi. TV 目 **Rooms:** 39

	■			●	■

CITY CENTRE: *De La Ville* ⓁⓁⓁⓁⓁ
Via Hoepli 6. **Map** 4 D5. 【 02-86 76 51. FAX 02-86 66 09.
Ⓦ www.senahotels.com @ delaville@tin.it
Between Piazza del Duomo and La Scala, with bright, well furnished rooms.
Pleasant bar with wood panelling. Impeccable service. TV 目 & **Rooms:** 109

	■		■	●	■

CITY CENTRE: *Grand Hotel Duomo* ⓁⓁⓁⓁⓁ
Via San Raffaele 1. **Map** 7 C1. 【 02-88 33. FAX 02-86 46 20 27.
Recently remodelled. Many rooms have a view of the Duomo spires.
Mini-suites on two levels. Panoramic roof garden. TV 目 & **Rooms:** 153

	■	●		●	■

NORTHWEST MILAN: *Antica Locanda dei Mercanti* ⓁⓁⓁ
Via San Tomaso 6. **Map** 3 B5. 【 02-805 40 80. FAX 02-805 40 90.
Ⓦ www.locanda.it @ locanda@locanda.it
Near Castello Sforzesco and the Duomo, this tiny hotel offers a welcoming atmosphere: books at the guests' disposal and wake-up service with a bell. **Rooms:** 14

	■				

NORTHWEST MILAN: *Europeo* ⓁⓁ
Via Canonica 38. **Map** 3 A3. 【 02-331 47 51. FAX 02-33 10 54 10.
@ milpeo.booking@tiscalinet.it An elegant hotel with extremely comfortable rooms.
One of the few in Milan with a pool. ● Aug. TV 目 ≋ **Rooms:** 45

	■	●			

NORTHWEST MILAN: *Johnny* ⓁⓁ
Via Prati 6. **Map** 2 D3. 【 02-34 18 12. FAX 02-33 61 05 21. @ johnny.hotel@tiscalinet.it
This small and comfortable family-run hotel offers good rates for long stays.
● Aug, Christmas. TV 🏠 **Rooms:** 31

			■	●	

NORTHWEST MILAN: *Lancaster* ⓁⓁ
Via Sangiorgio 16. **Map** 2 E3. 【 02-34 47 05. FAX 02-34 46 49. @ h.lancaster@tin.it
In a late 19th-century palazzo near the RAI and the Fiera, with comfortable
rooms. Efficient, courteous staff. ● Aug, Christmas. TV 目 🏠 **Rooms:** 30

	■				

NORTHWEST MILAN: *London* ⓁⓁ
Via Rovello 3. **Map** 3 B5. 【 02-72 02 01 66. FAX 02-805 70 37. @ hotellondon@traveleurope.it
A small hotel favoured by young American and British guests for its location
and reasonable rates. Spartan rooms. ● Aug, Christmas. TV 目 **Rooms:** 29

	■				

NORTHWEST MILAN: *Metro* ⓁⓁ
Corso Vercelli 61. **Map** 2 D5. 【 02-46 87 04. FAX 02-48 01 02 95.
In a recently remodelled building. Comfortable rooms. TV 目 & 🏠 **Rooms:** 37

	■		■		

NORTHWEST MILAN: *Montebianco* Ⓦ www.hotelmontebianco.com ⓁⓁ
Via Monterosa 90. **Map** 1 B3. 【 02-48 01 21 30. FAX 02-48 00 06 58.
A hotel managed with great courtesy and efficiency. Quite close to the Fiera.
Charming building with garden and spacious rooms. Book well in advance
when there are trade shows. TV 目 🏠 **Rooms:** 46

	■	●	■		

Price categories for a standard double room per night, with tax, breakfast and service included:
Ⓛ under L150,000
ⓁⓁ L150,000–250,000
ⓁⓁⓁ L250,000–350,000
ⓁⓁⓁⓁ L350,000–450,000
ⓁⓁⓁⓁⓁ over L450,000

CREDIT CARDS
The hotel accepts all major credit cards.
TERRACE OR GARDEN
Garden or terrace reserved for guests.
PARKING
Private parking on premises.
Hotels usually charge for parking facilities.
BAR
The hotel has a bar that is also open to non-residents.
RESTAURANT
The hotel has a good restaurant that is also open to non-residents.

	Credit Cards	Terrace or Garden	Parking	Bar	Restaurant
NORTHWEST MILAN: *Ariosto* ⓁⓁⓁ Via Ariosto 22. **Map** 2 E5. ☎ *02-481 78 44.* FAX *02-498 05 16.* W *www.hotelariosto.com* In an elegant quarter of Milan, this early 20th-century building has a grand staircase. Modern rooms. ● *Aug.* TV ▤ **Rooms:** *48*	■	●	■	●	
NORTHWEST MILAN: *Domenichino* ⓁⓁⓁ Via Domenichino 41–43. **Map** 1 B4. ☎ *02-48 00 96 92.* FAX *02-48 00 39 53.* W *www.hoteldomenichino.it* @ *hd@hoteldomenichino.it* On a quiet street near the Fiera, with comfortable, spacious rooms and some suites. ● *2 wk Aug, Christmas.* TV ▤ ♿ **Rooms:** *77*	■		■		
NORTHWEST MILAN: *King* ⓁⓁ Corso Magenta 19. **Map** 3 A5. ☎ *02-87 44 32.* FAX *02-89 01 07 98.* W *www.hotelking.com* In a lovely palazzo on Corso Magenta, conveniently located between the city centre and the Fiera. Comfortable rooms, courteous staff. TV ▤ **Rooms:** *48*	■		■		
NORTHWEST MILAN: *Palazzo delle Stelline* ⓁⓁⓁ Corso Magenta 61. **Map** 6 F1. ☎ *02-481 84 31.* FAX *02-48 19 42 81.* Located in a palazzo which is a congress centre. Modern and well equipped rooms. Close to the church with the *Last Supper.* ● *Aug.* TV ▤ ♿ **Rooms:** *105*	■	●	■		
NORTHWEST MILAN: *Marriott Grand* ⓁⓁⓁⓁ Via Washington 66. **Map** 3 C2. ☎ *02-485 21.* FAX *02-481 89 25.* W *www.marriott.com* @ *marriott@tin.it* Part of the hotel chain, offering luxurious, soundproofed rooms and one level for non-smokers. Large American breakfast. TV ▤ ♿ **Rooms:** *323*	■		■	●	■
NORTHWEST MILAN: *Regency* ⓁⓁⓁ Via Arimondi 12. **Map** 1 D1. ☎ *02-39 21 60 21.* FAX *02-39 21 77 34.* W *www.regencyhotel/milano.com* @ *regency@regency/milano.com* This late 19th-century patrician residence is now a charming hotel. Romantic attic rooms. ● *3 wk Aug, Christmas.* TV ▤ **Rooms:** *59*	■	●		●	
SOUTHWEST MILAN: *Ca' Bianca* ⓁⓁⓁ Via Lodovico il Moro 117. **Map** 5 A5. ☎ *02-89 12 81 11.* FAX *02-89 12 80 42.* A charming hotel in a characterful old house on the Naviglio. Comfortable, with balcony and terracotta floors. ● *Aug.* TV ▤ ♿ **Rooms:** *51*	■	●	■	●	■
SOUTHWEST MILAN: *Liberty* ⓁⓁ Viale Bligny 56. **Map** 8 D4. ☎ *02-58 31 85 62.* FAX *02-58 31 90 61.* Art Nouveau decor, in keeping with the style of this building. Modern furniture in the rooms and marble bathrooms. ● *Aug.* TV ▤ **Rooms:** *52*	■		■	●	
SOUTHWEST MILAN: *Regina* ⓁⓁⓁⓁ Via Cesare Correnti 13. **Map** 7 B2. ☎ *02-58 10 69 13.* FAX *02-58 10 70 33.* W *www.hotelregina.it* @ *info@hotelregina.it* In a converted 18th-century Milanese residence, with cosy, attractively furnished rooms. Near the Navigli canals. ● *Aug.* TV ▤ ♿ **Rooms:** *45*	■	●		●	
SOUTHWEST MILAN: *Zurigo* ⓁⓁⓁ Corso Italia 11/A. **Map** 7 C2. ☎ *02-72 02 22 60.* FAX *02-72 00 00 13.* W *www.brerahotels.com* An ecological hotel, serving organic breakfast. Bicycles for guests. Simple but comfortable rooms. TV ▤ ♿ **Rooms:** *41*	■		■	●	
SOUTHWEST MILAN: *Carrobbio* ⓁⓁⓁⓁ Via Medici 3. **Map** 7 B2. ☎ *02-89 01 07 40.* FAX *02-805 33 34.* W *www.traveleurope.it/hotelcarrobbio.htn* @ *hotelcarrobbio@traveleurope.it* A small, recently refurbished luxury hotel in a street in old Milan. Small, cosy, attractively furnished rooms. ● *Christmas.* TV ▤ **Rooms:** *43*	■				
SOUTHWEST MILAN: *Pierre* ⓁⓁⓁⓁ Via Edmondo De Amicis 32. **Map** 7 A2. ☎ *02-72 00 05 81.* FAX *02-805 21 57.* All the rooms are different: luxuriously furnished and with marble bathrooms. A hearty buffet breakfast is served. ● *Aug.* TV ▤ ♿ **Rooms:** *49*	■		■	●	■

	Credit Cards	Terrace or Garden	Parking	Bar	Restaurant
Price categories for a standard double room per night, with tax, breakfast and service included: Ⓛ under L150,000 ⓁⓁ L150,000–250,000 ⓁⓁⓁ L250,000–350,000 ⓁⓁⓁⓁ L350,000–450,000 ⓁⓁⓁⓁⓁ over L450,000	**CREDIT CARDS** The hotel accepts all major credit cards. **TERRACE OR GARDEN** Terrace or garden reserved for guests. **PARKING** Private parking on premises. Hotels usually charge for parking facilities. **BAR** The hotel has a bar that is also open to non-residents. **RESTAURANT** The hotel has a good restaurant that is also open to non-residents.				
SOUTHEAST MILAN: *Piacenza* ⓁⓁ Via Piacenza 4. **Map** 8 F4. **(** *02-545 50 41.* **FAX** *02-546 52 69.* **W** *www.hotelpiacenza.com* One of the few hotels in this area, Piacenza offers cosy, plainly furnished rooms and good amenities. Courteous staff. ● *Christmas.* **TV** ▤ **⌂ Rooms:** *24*	▦		▦		
NORTHEAST MILAN: *Aspromonte* Ⓛ Piazza Aspromonte 12/14. **Map** 4 F4. **(** *02-236 11 19.* **FAX** *02-236 76 21.* **W** *www.venere.it/milano/aspro* **@** *aspromonte@italyhotel.it* A small hotel offering quality at a reasonable price. The well-furnished rooms have every comfort. **TV** ▤ **⌂ Rooms:** *19*	▦	●	▦	●	
NORTHEAST MILAN: *Antica Locanda Solferino* ⓁⓁ Via Castelfidardo 2. **Map** 3 C3. **(** *02-657 01 29.* **FAX** *02-657 13 61.* A uniquely fascinating inn, frequented by artists and regulars. Book well in advance. ● *Aug.* **TV Rooms:** *11*	▦	●			▦
NORTHEAST MILAN: *Baviera* ⓁⓁⓁ Via P Castaldi 7. **Map** 4 E3. **(** *02-659 05 51.* **FAX** *02-29 00 32 81.* **W** *www.hotelbaviera.com* **@** *info@hotelbaviera.com* An impeccably run 3-star hotel near the main railway station. Well furnished rooms. Good value for money. **TV** ▤ **⌂ Rooms:** *75*	▦				
NORTHEAST MILAN: *San Francisco* ⓁⓁ Viale Lombardia 55. **Map** 4 F3. **(** *02-236 03 02.* **FAX** *02-26 68 03 77.* **W** *www.hotel-Sanfrancisco.it* A reasonably priced family-run hotel with simple rooms. Small garden with a pergola. Located in the Città Studi. **TV ⌂ Rooms:** *31*	▦		▦		
NORTHEAST MILAN: *Auriga* ⓁⓁⓁⓁ Via Pirelli 7. **Map** 4 E1. **(** *02-66 98 58 51.* **FAX** *02-66 98 06 98.* **W** *www.virtualia.it/auriga* **@** *hotelauriga@virtualia.it* Luxury rooms with amenities for businessmen. ● *Aug, Christmas.* **TV** ▤ **Rooms:** *52*	▦				
NORTHEAST MILAN: *Buenos Aires* ⓁⓁⓁ Corso Buenos Aires 26. **Map** 4 F3. **(** *02-29 40 01 69.* **FAX** *02-29 40 24 94.* **@** *info@hotelbuenosaires/milan.com* A small hotel in the heart of the Porta Venezia shopping district. Pleasant, soundproofed rooms with well-equipped bathrooms. **TV** ▤ **&** **⌂ Rooms:** *25*	▦		▦		
NORTHEAST MILAN: *Lombardia* ⓁⓁⓁ Viale Lombardia 74–76. **Map** 4 F3. **(** *02-289 25 15.* **FAX** *02-289 34 30.* **@** *hotelomb@tin.it* Recently renovated. Some rooms look over a small courtyard garden. Well cared for. Buffet breakfast. ● *Aug.* **TV** ▤ **⌂ Rooms:** *79*	▦	●			
NORTHEAST MILAN: *Cavour* ⓁⓁⓁ Via Fatebenefratelli 21. **Map** 3 C4. **(** *02-657 20 51.* **FAX** *02-659 22 63.* **W** *www.hotelcavour.it* Close to the Brera and the fashion quarter, this hotel has large, elegant rooms. Efficient, friendly service. **TV** ▤ **Rooms:** *113*	▦		▦	●	▦
NORTHEAST MILAN: *Manzoni* ⓁⓁⓁ Via S Spirito 20. **Map** 4 D4. **(** *02-76 00 57 00.* **FAX** *02-78 42 12.* **@** *hotel.manzoni@tin.it* An old-fashioned atmosphere, excellent and friendly service, in the heart of the fashion district. ● *Aug, Christmas, New Year.* **TV Rooms:** *52*	▦		▦	●	▦
NORTHEAST MILAN: *Ritter* ⓁⓁⓁ Corso Garibaldi 68. **Map** 3 B3. **(** *02-29 00 68 60.* **FAX** *02-657 15 12.* **@** *comfort@tiscalinet.it* High-level 3-star hotel tucked away in the Brera quarter. Terrace-solarium and small garden. Lavish buffet breakfast. **TV** ▤ **&** **⌂ Rooms:** *88*	▦	●	▦	●	▦
NORTHWEST MILAN: *Hermitage* ⓁⓁⓁⓁⓁ Via Messina 10. **Map** 3 A1. **(** *02-33 10 77 00.* **FAX** *02-33 10 73 99.* **W** *www.monrifhotels.it* **@** *hermitage.res@monrif.it* A classic hotel close to the RAI, with a garden and the well-known restaurant "Il Sambuco" (*see p171*). Bright, spacious rooms. ● *3 wk Aug.* **TV** ▤ **&** **⌂ Rooms:** *131*	▦	●	▦	●	▦

NORTHEAST MILAN: *Sanpi*   ⓁⓁⓁ
Via Lazzaro Palazzi 18/20. **Map** 4 E3. 📞 02-29 51 33 41. 🅵🅰🆇 02-29 40 24 51.
The rooms vary in size and have satellite and pay TV as well as a safe.
Garden and babysitting service. ● *3 wk Aug, Christmas and New Year.*
📺 🍽 ♿ **Rooms:** *71*

NORTHEAST MILAN: *Sheraton Diana Majestic*   ⓁⓁⓁⓁ
Viale Piave 42. **Map** 4 F4. 📞 02-205 81. 🅵🅰🆇 02-20 58 20 58. 🆆 www.sheraton.com
Art Nouveau-style hotel built in 1905 overlooking a large garden. Handsome
period furniture in the lounge, foyer and rooms. ● *Aug.* 📺 🍽 🛏 **Rooms:** *99*

NORTHEAST MILAN: *Four Seasons*   ⓁⓁⓁⓁ
Via Gesù 8. **Map** 4 D5. 📞 02-79 69 76. 🅵🅰🆇 02-77 08 50 00.
🆆 www.fourseasons.com 📧 milano@fourseasons.com
Milan's most exclusive hotel. Situated in the fashion district in a converted
monastery. Two good restaurants. 📺 🍽 ♿ 🛏 **Rooms:** *98*

NORTHEAST MILAN: *Grand Hotel et de Milan*   ⓁⓁⓁⓁ
Via Manzoni 29. **Map** 4 D4. 📞 02-72 31 41. 🅵🅰🆇 02-86 46 08 61.
🆆 www.grandhoteletdemilan.it 📧 infos@grandhoteletdemilan.it
Giuseppe Verdi died in this fascinating historic hotel boasting
fine 19th-century furniture. The lounge with fireplace and bar with Art
Nouveau skylights are impressive. Two restaurants. 📺 🍽 ♿ 🛏 **Rooms:** *95*

NORTHEAST MILAN: *Excelsior Hotel Gallia*   ⓁⓁⓁⓁ
Piazza Duca d'Aosta 9. **Map** 4 E1. 📞 02-678 51. 🅵🅰🆇 02-66 71 32 39.
🆆 www.excelsiorhotelgallia.it 📧 guest@excelsiorhotelgallia.it
For years the Gallia and the Principe di Savoia have been *the* hotels in Milan.
The foyer and public areas are still luxurious, with lovely large mirrors and
chandeliers. The royal suite is a real "museum". 📺 🍽 **Rooms:** *237*

NORTHEAST MILAN: *Palace*   ⓁⓁⓁⓁ
Piazza della Repubblica 20. **Map** 4 E3. 📞 02 633 61. 🅵🅰🆇 02-65 44 85. 🆆 www.weslen.com
A splendid foyer-lounge for special occasions. Spacious, luxuriously furnished
rooms with every comfort, some with Turkish bath. ● *Aug.* 📺 🍽 ♿ **Rooms:** *216*

NORTHEAST MILAN: *Principe di Savoia*   ⓁⓁⓁⓁ
Piazza della Repubblica 17. **Map** 4 D2. 📞 02-623 01. 🅵🅰🆇 02-659 58 38.
🆆 www.luxurycollection.com 📧 hotelprincipedisavoia@sheraton.com
A favourite with royalty and VIPs. A 1930s atmosphere. The white façade
is sumptuous. A myriad of services for guests. 📺 🍽 ♿ 🏊 **Rooms:** *299*

THE LAKES

LAKE MAGGIORE: *Villa Carlotta*   ⓁⓁⓁ
Belgirate. Via Sempione 121–125. 📞 0322-764 61. 🅵🅰🆇 0322-767 05.
🆆 www.bestwestern.it 📧 villacarlotta.no@bestwestern.it
In the middle of a large botanic garden. Large, well equipped rooms. The
restaurant is part of the "Buon Ricordo" chain. 📺 🍽 ♿ 🏊 🛏 **Rooms:** *129*

LAKE MAGGIORE: *Pironi*   ⓁⓁ
Cannobio. Via Marconi 35. 📞 0323-706 24. 🅵🅰🆇 0323-721 84. 📧 hotel.pironi@cannobio.net
Tastefullly furnished rooms in a converted 15th-century palazzo situated
among the quiet streets of Cannobio's historic centre. ● *Nov–Mar.* 📺 **Rooms:** *12*

LAKE MAGGIORE: *Villa Belvedere* 📧 hotel.villabelvedere@cannobio.net   ⓁⓁ
Cannobio. Via Casali Cuserina 2. 📞 0323-701 59. 🅵🅰🆇 0323-719 91.
A beautiful villa surrounded by a large park in a quiet position. Rooms have
a fine view of the lake and mountains. ● *mid-Oct–Mar.* 📺 🛏 🏊 **Rooms:** *18*

LAKE MAGGIORE: *Castello di Frino*   ⓁⓁ
Ghiffa. Via C Colombo 8. 📞 0323-591 81. 🅵🅰🆇 0323-597 83.
This small 16th-century castle in a panoramic position stands in a lovely park.
Frescoed rooms with period furniture. ● *mid-Oct–Feb.* ♿ 🛏 🏊 **Rooms:** *14*

LAKE MAGGIORE: *Park Hotel Paradiso*   ⓁⓁ
Ghiffa. Via Marconi 20. 📞 0323-595 48. 🅵🅰🆇 0323-595 48.
A delightful early 20th-century villa with a pool. Public areas with Art Nouveau
decor. Rooms overlook the lake. ● *Nov–mid-Mar.* 🛏 🏊 **Rooms:** *15*

LAKE MAGGIORE: *Verbano*   ⓁⓁ
Isola dei Pescatori. V Ugo Ara 2. 📞 0323-304 08. 🅵🅰🆇 0323-331 29. 📧 www.hotelverbano.it
This pretty red house is on the Isola dei Pescatori. The rooms have views
of Isola Bella and Palazzo Borromeo. ● *Jan, Feb.* ♿ 🛏 **Rooms:** *12*

Price categories for a standard double room per night, with tax, breakfast and service included:

Ⓛ under L150,000
ⓁⓁ L150,000–250,000
ⓁⓁⓁ L250,000–350,000
ⓁⓁⓁⓁ L350,000–450,000
ⓁⓁⓁⓁⓁ over L450,000

CREDIT CARDS
The hotel accepts all major credit cards.
TERRACE OR GARDEN
Garden or terrace reserved for guests.
PARKING
Private parking on premises.
Hotels usually charge for parking facilities.
BAR
The hotel has a bar that is also open to non-residents.
RESTAURANT
The hotel has a good restaurant that is also open to non-residents.

	Credit Cards	Terrace or Garden	Parking	Bar	Restaurant
LAKE MAGGIORE: *Villaminta* — ⓁⓁ	●	●	●		
LAKE MAGGIORE: *Des Iles Borromées* — ⓁⓁⓁⓁ	●	●	●	●	●
LAKE COMO: *Florence* — ⓁⓁⓁ	●	●		●	
LAKE COMO: *Grand Hotel Villa Serbelloni* — ⓁⓁⓁⓁⓁ	●	●	●	●	
LAKE COMO: *Grand Hotel Villa D'Este* — ⓁⓁⓁⓁ	●	●	●	●	
LAKE COMO: *Le Due Corti* — ⓁⓁⓁ	●	●		●	
LAKE COMO: *Terminus* — ⓁⓁⓁⓁ	●	●	●	●	●
LAKE COMO: *San Giorgio* — ⓁⓁ	●	●	●		
LAKE COMO: *Villa Flora* — Ⓛ	●	●	●		
LAKE COMO: *Du Lac* — ⓁⓁⓁ	●	●	●	●	
LAKE COMO: *Royal Victoria* — ⓁⓁ	●	●		●	●
LAKE GARDA: *Grand Hotel Fasano* — ⓁⓁⓁⓁ	●	●	●	●	

LAKE MAGGIORE: *Villaminta*   ⓁⓁ
Stresa. Via Sempione Nord 123. ☎ 0323-93 38 18. FAX 0323-93 39 55.
🌐 www.stresa.net/hotel/villaminta @ h.villaminta@stresa.net
North of Stresa is this beautiful villa in a park overflowing with flowers. The rooms have a superb view of the islands. ● Nov–Mar. TV 🏠 🏊 Rooms: 62

LAKE MAGGIORE: *Des Iles Borromées*   ⓁⓁⓁⓁ
Stresa. Lungolago Umberto I 67. ☎ 0323-93 89 38. FAX 0323-324 05.
🌐 www.stresa.net/hotel/borromees
A historic hotel on the Piedmontese side, once a favourite with royalty and now VIPs. Luxurious suites and public areas. ● Christmas TV 🍽 & 🏠 🏊 Rooms: 173

LAKE COMO: *Florence*   ⓁⓁⓁ
Bellagio. Piazza Mazzini 46. ☎ 031-95 03 42. FAX 031-95 17 22.
🌐 www.bellagio.co.nz @ hotflore@tin.it
A small lakefront hotel in two 19th-century houses. ● Nov–Mar. TV Rooms: 32

LAKE COMO: *Grand Hotel Villa Serbelloni*   ⓁⓁⓁⓁⓁ
Bellagio. Via Roma 1. ☎ 031-95 02 16. FAX 031-95 15 29.
🌐 www.villaserbelloni.it @ inforequest@villaserbelloni.it
A stupendous hotel for over a century. The monumental entrance stairway is crowned by a Murano glass chandelier. ● Nov–Mar. TV 🍽 & 🏠 🏊 Rooms: 85

LAKE COMO: *Grand Hotel Villa D'Este*   ⓁⓁⓁⓁ
Cernobbio. Via Regina 40. ☎ 031-34 81. FAX 031-34 88 44.
🌐 www.villadeste.it @ info@villadeste.it
This luxury hotel is world-famous. Set in a huge park, with magnificent rooms and an excellent restaurant. ● Jan–Feb. TV 🍽 & 🏊 Rooms: 166

LAKE COMO: *Le Due Corti*   ⓁⓁⓁ
Como. Piazza Vittoria 12/13. ☎ 031-32 81 11. FAX 031-32 88 00.
Once a 17th-century monastery, this hotel has rooms that overlook the two courtyards. Restaurant in the former stable. TV 🍽 🏠 🏊 Rooms: 64

LAKE COMO: *Terminus*   ⓁⓁⓁⓁ
Como. Lungo Lario Trieste 14. ☎ 031-32 91 11. FAX 031-30 25 50.
🌐 www.terminus.com @ larioterminus@galactica.it
This hotel has preserved its Art Nouveau-style atmosphere. TV 🍽 & Rooms: 38

LAKE COMO: *San Giorgio*   ⓁⓁ
Lenno. Via Regina 81. ☎ 0344-404 15. FAX 0344-415 91.
An early 20th-century building in a pleasant garden leading to the lake. Lovely views from rooms with a balcony. ● Mid-Oct–Mar. TV 🍽 Rooms: 26

LAKE COMO: *Villa Flora*   Ⓛ
Torno. Lungolago Castelli 7/11. ☎ 031-41 92 22. FAX 031-41 83 18.
Turn-of-the-century villa in a lovely garden. The public areas have period furniture. Large rooms, some with a terrace. ● Nov–mid-Mar. TV 🏊 Rooms: 20

LAKE COMO: *Du Lac*   ⓁⓁⓁ
Varenna. Via del Pristino 4. ☎ 0341-83 02 38. FAX 0341-83 10 81.
In a truly romantic position, a lovely 19th-century house on the lakefront. Some rooms have a breathtaking view. ● Mid-Dec & Feb. TV & 🏠 Rooms: 17

LAKE COMO: *Royal Victoria*   ⓁⓁ
Varenna. Piazza San Giorgio 5. ☎ 0341-81 51 11. FAX 0341-83 07 22.
🌐 www.royalvictoria.com @ hotelroyalvictoria@promo.it
A fine palazzo in the main square. The restaurant is excellent. TV 🏠 Rooms: 43

LAKE GARDA: *Grand Hotel Fasano*   ⓁⓁⓁⓁ
Fasano. Corso Zanardelli 190. ☎ 0365-29 02 20. FAX 0365-29 02 21.
🌐 www.grand-hotel-fasano.it @ info@grand-hotel-fasano.it
This 19th-century building was the hunting lodge of the Austrian imperial family. Luxuriously furnished. ● Nov–Mar. TV & 🏠 🏊 Rooms: 87

LAKE GARDA: *Villa del Sogno* ⓁⓁⓁ
Fasano. Via Zanardelli 107. (0365-29 01 81. FAX 0365-29 02 30.
W www.gardalake.it/villadelsogno @ villadelsogno@gardalake.it
A *fin de siècle* villa with one of the best views of the area. The rooms, some
with terraces, have Art Nouveau touches. ● Nov–Mar. TV 🍽 🖴 **Rooms:** 30

LAKE GARDA: *Garda & Suisse* ⓁⓁⓁ
Gardone. Via Zanardelli 126. (0365-29 04 85. FAX 0365-207 77.
Overlooking the lake and elegantly furnished, this hotel offers all the comforts
needed for a business trip. Fitness centre. ● Nov–Jan. TV 🍽 🚫 **Rooms:** 18

LAKE GARDA: *Villa Capri* ⓁⓁⓁ
Gardone. Corso Zanardelli 172. (0365-215 37. FAX 0365-227 20. W www.bagaglino.it
This 3-star family-run hotel is in a superb location. The "Villa Capri" annexe
has eight rooms with a view of the lake. ● Nov–Mar. TV 🍽 🚫 🖴 **Rooms:** 55

LAKE GARDA: *Grand Hotel* ⓁⓁⓁⓁ
Gardone. Corso Zanardelli 84. (0365-202 61. FAX 0365-226 95. W www.grandgardone.it
Impressive late 19th-century building dominating the Gardone lakeside. Winston
Churchill and D'Annunzio stayed here. ● Nov–Mar. TV 🍽 🚫 🖴 **Rooms:** 180

LAKE GARDA: *Villa Fiordaliso* ⓁⓁⓁⓁ
Gardone. Corso Zanardelli 132. (0365-201 58. FAX 0365-29 00 11.
W www.villafiordaliso.it @ info@villafiordaliso.it
A fascinating lakeside villa where D'Annunzio once lived. Magnificent
frescoed ceilings and Carrara marble in the lounges and in the suite
dedicated to Claretta Petacci. Gourmet restaurant. ● Christmas TV 🍽 **Rooms:** 7

LAKE GARDA: *Villa Giulia* ⓁⓁⓁ
Gargnano. Viale Rimembranza 20. (0365-710 22. FAX 0365-727 74.
W www.gardalake.it/hotel-villagiulia @ hvgiulia@gardanet.it
This splendid villa with a Neo-Gothic façade offering luxury and privacy.
Rooms overlook the lake or the park. ● Mid-Oct–Mar. TV 🏊 🖴 **Rooms:** 25

LAKE GARDA: *Du Lac et Du Parc* ⓁⓁⓁⓁ
Riva del Garda. Viale Rovereto 44. (0464-55 15 00. FAX 0464-55 52 00.
W www.garda.com/dulac @ hoteldulac@anthese.com
A large hotel in a spectacular, spacious park. The rooms are comfortable,
a good size and well equipped. ● Nov–Mar. TV 🍽 🚫 🏊 🖴 **Rooms:** 170

LAKE GARDA: *Laurin* ⓁⓁⓁ
Salò. Viale Landi 9. (0365-220 22. FAX 0365-223 82. W www.laurinsalo.com
@ laurinbs@tin.it Friezes, frescoes and cornices fill the walls and ceilings of this
1910 villa. Art Nouveau in the public areas and rooms. ● Mid-Dec–mid-Jan.
TV 🍽 🚫 🏊 🖴 **Rooms:** 37

LAKE GARDA: *Palace Hotel Villa Cortine* ⓁⓁⓁⓁⓁ
Sirmione. Via Grotte 6. (030-990 58 90. FAX 030-91 63 90. W www.villacortine.com
A luxurious Neo-Classical villa. Enormous rooms with period furniture, elegant
public areas and a park. Impeccable service. ● Nov–Mar. TV 🍽 🏊 🖴 **Rooms:** 49

LAGO D'ISEO: *L'Albereta* ⓁⓁⓁⓁ
Erbusco. Loc. Bellavista, Via V Emanuele 11. (030-776 05 50. FAX 030-776 05 73.
W www.terramoretti.it @ albereta@terramoretti.it
A masterpiece of the "maestro" Gualtiero Marchesi, who has created this *relais*
out of an old country mansion *(see also p175)*. TV 🍽 🏊 🖴 **Rooms:** 41

LAGO D'ISEO: *I Due Roccoli* ⓁⓁ
Iseo. Invino, Via Bonomelli. (030-982 29 77. FAX 030-982 29 80.
W www.idueroccoli.com @ relais@idueroccoli.com
This lovely rustic complex includes the residence, with elegant rooms, and a
farmhouse converted into a good restaurant. ● Nov–mid-Mar. TV 🏊 🖴 **Rooms:** 13

LAGO D'ORTA: *Hotel San Rocco* ⓁⓁⓁ
San Giulio. Via Gippini 11. (0322-91 19 77. FAX 0322-91 19 64.
W www.hotelsanrocco.it @ sanrocco@giacomini.com
A 17th-century convent, now a sophisticated hotel. The simply furnished rooms
overlook either a lake or a garden. Private boat for guests. TV 🚫 🖴 **Rooms:** 74

LAGO D'ORTA: *Villa Crespi* ⓁⓁⓁⓁ
San Giulio. Via Fava 8. (0322-91 19 02. FAX 0322-91 19 19.
W www.lagodortahotels.com @ villacrespi@tin.it
An incredible villa in Islamic style built in 1880. Rooms have precious textiles and
four poster beds. The restaurant is excellent. ● Jan–Feb. TV 🍽 🚫 🖴 **Rooms:** 14

WHERE TO EAT

ILAN IS A COSMOPOLITAN CITY and offers a wide range of restaurants in all price categories. As well as Milanese and Tuscan cooking (the latter has become a real speciality of the city), ethnic cuisine has recently come to the fore – from North African to Oriental and even South American, reflecting the city's multicultural character. The fish restaurants are excellent, offering skilfully prepared fish and seafood.

The Barchetta chef, Bellagio (see p173)

Restaurants are at their most crowded at the weekend, and it is often best to book in advance. Sunday brunch has become part and parcel of the Milanese life style, and a number of cafés offer this late morning meal. At the lakes there are restaurants with terraces overlooking the water, and cafés with tables outside. Menus are dominated by fish dishes and local specialities. For more detailed information, see the chart on pages 166–75, with a selection of 122 restaurants.

CHOOSING A RESTAURANT

IN MILAN the Brera and Navigli districts are filled with restaurants. Around the Brera the fashion crowd love **Briciola** *(see p170)*, while vegetarians head for **Le Stagioni dei Sapori** *(see p170)*. Near the Navigli is **Pizzeria Tradizionale** *(see p167)* where fans queue for a table. Near Porta Genova is **Osteria dei Binari** *(see p168)*, serving Lombard and Piedmontese dishes. The **Centro Ittico** *(see p171)* and **Malavoglia** *(see p171)*, near the fish market, have excellent fresh fish.

Classic restaurants in the centre include **Boeucc** *(see p166)* and **Al Girarrosto da Cesarina** *(see p171)*. Also popular are **Aimo e Nadia**

The Pizzeria Tradizionale sign, Milan (see p167)

(see p168), in the Bande Nere district, **L'Ami Berton** *(see p171)*, near the Città Studi, and **Alfredo Gran San Bernardo** *(see p167)*, near the Certosa.

Some of Italy's best restaurants are in beautiful locations near the lakes. At Lake Maggiore, **Il Sole di Ranco** *(see p172)* is one of Italy's finest. At Lake Como good places include **Il Griso** hotel restaurant *(see p173)* at Malgrate (Lecco), the **Barchetta** *(see p173)* at Bellagio and **Raimondi del Villa Flori**, a hotel restaurant near Como *(see p173)*. Lake Garda boasts excellent restaurants, such as **Villa Fiordaliso** *(see p174)*, at Gardone. At Erbusco (Lake Iseo), is **Gualtiero Marchesi** *(see p175)*, the restaurant of Italy's most famous chef.

The counter at the Briciola, in the Brera quarter of Milan (see p170)

To prevent disappointment, book a table ahead if there is a restaurant you are particularly keen on trying.

EATING HOURS

LUNCH is generally served between 1 and 2:30pm. Dinner is usually at about 8pm and goes on until about 11pm (or later in summer).

ETIQUETTE

THE MILANESE are very dress-conscious and smart dress will also ensure better service. Smoking is still popular in Italy and non-smoking areas in restaurants are rare.

TYPES OF RESTAURANTS

MILAN OFFERS an unusually wide range of types of cuisine for an Italian city. Alongside traditional Italian cooking you can also find Asian, North African and Mexican food of all kinds. Classic Milanese cooking survives in the traditional rest-

L'Ami Berton restaurant in the Città Studi area of Milan (see p171)

aurants of the centre. International cuisine is found in places frequented by business people. Italian regional cooking, from Tuscan to Piedmontese, Neapolitan and Sicilian, is increasingly popular in Milan.

There are several different types of restaurant. Traditionally, a *ristorante* is smarter and more expensive than an *osteria* or a *trattoria*, but the divisions are increasingly blurred. A pizzeria is usually an inexpensive place to eat and many serve pasta, meat and fish dishes as well as pizza. Those with wood-fired ovens *(forno a legna)* are the most highly rated. Milan's pizzerias tend to be more expensive than in the rest of Italy but the quality is excellent thanks to the many Neapolitan pizza chefs in the city. An *enoteca* or *vineria* is a place to taste wine and sample snacks.

Genuine small trattorias still abound as well as the increasingly rare *latterie* (dairies), which are small, crowded kitchens.

The Milan fish market is one of the best in Italy, and the city's excellent seafood restaurants guarantee superfresh fish.

At the lakes, much use is made of local fish such as carp, tench and shad, and you will also find regional specialities – in particular, Piedmontese, Valtellinese and Veneto cooking.

Gualtiero Marchesi's restaurant at Erbusco, Lake Iseo *(see p175)*

Raimondi del Villa Flori, Lake Como *(see p173)*

The wine cellar in the famous Il Sole di Ranco restaurant, Lake Maggiore *(see p172)*

READING THE MENU

A CLASSIC ITALIAN dinner begins with an *antipasto* or starter. The first course *(il primo)* is likely to be pasta or risotto but may be a hearty soup. The main course *(il secondo)* consists of meat or fish served with a side dish of vegetables *(contorno)*. Dessert *(il dessert)* follows and may consist of ice cream, fruit or pastries. Coffee *(il caffè)* comes next, and perhaps a digestif. A classic Milanese dinner might consist of *nervetti*, or *gnervitt (see p164)*, followed by *risotto alla milanese (see p164)*, and then a veal cutlet *(costoletta; see p165)*. Other typical dishes are *ossobuco (see p165)*, and *casoeûla (see p165)*.

Vegetarians will find that many pasta dishes are meat-free and that spring is a good time to try new young vegetables. Autumn is also good for non-meat eaters, as pumpkins, wild mushrooms and chestnuts start to appear on the menu. Cheeses are also a good option.

PAYING

M ENUS ARE USUALLY posted outside restaurants, with prices. An unavoidable extra is the cover charge *(coperto)*, which is charged per person. In general Milanese restaurants accept major credit cards, except for some of the smaller, family-run trattorias, where you will need cash. Commonly accepted cards include Visa and MasterCard. Even restaurants in the smaller villages around the lakes now increasingly accept credit cards. When paying for a meal (the Italian for the bill is *il conto*), it is normal to leave a small tip.

WHEELCHAIR ACCESS

U NFORTUNATELY, NOT ALL Milanese restaurants have facilities for the disabled. Wheelchair access may be even more of a problem at the lakes, with restaurants often sited at the top of long slopes or paths with steps. It is therefore advisable to telephone the restaurant beforehand for advice.

CHILDREN'S FACILITIES

L ESS EXPENSIVE PLACES such as trattorias and pizzerias are ideal for children. They may be less welcome in Milan's sophisticated restaurants. Restaurant owners at the lakes are more accustomed to families with children, and can often provide smaller portions if required.

What to Eat in Milan and at the Lakes

Lake Garda olive oil

CLASSIC MILANESE CUISINE boasts a long tradition, and dishes such as *costoletta* (breaded veal cutlet), *ossobuco* (veal shin with marrow) and risotto with saffron are well known in Italy and abroad. At the lakes, locally caught lake fish is widely used, especially whitefish, trout, pike and perch. At Lake Garda they produce good quality, light olive oil, and good wines such as Bardolino and Valpolicella (red) and Lugana, Bianco di Custoza and Soave (whites).

Gnervitt con Cipolle *is a Milanese antipasto consisting of calf cartilage with onions, oil and vinegar.*

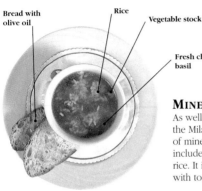

Bread with olive oil

Rice

Vegetable stock

Fresh chopped basil

MINESTRONE

As well as vegetables, the Milanese version of minestrone soup includes just-cooked rice. It is often served with toasted bread.

Agnolotti con Pesce Persico *consists of stuffed pasta parcels filled with perch, broccoli and parsley. It is a typical dish from Lake Maggiore and Lake Orta.*

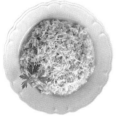

Risotto alla Milanese *is a traditional Milanese first course. The risotto is made yellow by the addition of saffron when the rice is almost done.*

Risotto Trota e Zucca *is a Lake Garda typical first course – risotto with pumpkin and trout, flavoured with chives and served with butter.*

Bigoli con le Aole *is a pasta dish. Thick spaghetti is served with aole or small freshwater fish. It is a traditional recipe from Lake Garda.*

Farfalle ai Funghi Porcini *is made with pasta butterflies and a sauce of fresh porcini mushrooms, parmesan and butter.*

Tinca Ripiena *is tench, stuffed with a mixture of breadcrumbs, parmesan cheese, bay leaf and parsley, and then baked.*

Rognone di Vitello Trifolato *is a Milanese dish of sliced veal kidneys, oil and garlic. It is served with hot polenta.*

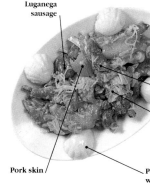

Luganega sausage

CASOEÛLA

This very rich Milanese dish is based on pork and cabbage and is often served with polenta made with maize flour.

Pork chop

Savoy cabbage

Pork skin

Polenta made with yellow flour

Costoletta alla Milanese *is an authentic Milanese veal cutlet of tender veal loin. The meat is covered with breadcrumbs and then lightly fried in butter.*

Ossobuco alla Milanese *is a cut of veal including the bone and its marrow. The meat is braised and served with risotto.*

Luccio alla Gardesana, *a Lake Garda speciality, is freshly caught pike served with vegetables, capers and olive oil.*

Coregone in Crosta *is a lake fish flavoured with aniseed, basil and lemon and cooked in a crusty casing of coarse salt.*

Pesce Persico Fritto, *a speciality from Lake Como, is prepared by flouring pieces of fresh perch and then lightly frying them in oil.*

Semifreddo al Limone *is a Garda dessert: ice cream cake made of lemon, cream and eggs. It is delicious with strawberry sauce.*

Panettone *is the classic Milanese Christmas cake. This dome-shaped sponge cake is made with flour, eggs, sugar, candied fruit and raisins.*

FRANCIACORTA WINES

Franciacorta is the area bordered by Lake Iseo, the outskirts of the town of Brescia, the beginning of the Po River valley and the Oglio River and is well known for its good wines. The red Terre di Franciacorta, aged for one or two years, is good with first courses and roast meat. The white Terre di Franciacorta has a minimum alcohol level of 11 per cent and goes well with fish dishes. Sparkling Franciacorta wine *(spumante)* makes a good aperitif and celebration wine.

Bottles of Franciacorta wines

Choosing a Restaurant

Ⓛ IKE ANY OTHER large city, Milan offers a wide range of restaurants and types of cuisine. Traditional Milanese cooking is slowly giving way to other Italian regional fare, ethnic cooking and the *nouvelle cuisine* of creative chefs. Around the Northern Italian lakes the local gastronomic tradition is much more deep-rooted.

	CREDIT CARDS	ATTENDED PARKING	FIXED-PRICE MENU	SEAFOOD RESTAURANT	TRADITIONAL CUISINE
MILAN					
CITY CENTRE: *Hostaria Borromei* ⓁⓁⓁ Via Borromei 4. **Map** 7 B1. [02-86 45 37 60. In the courtyard of a lovely palazzo in the old centre, a dozen tables with yellow linen tablecloths and soft candlelight. Lombard cuisine in a romantic setting. ● *Sat midday, Sun; Aug, Christmas.* 🔳	▦				▦
CITY CENTRE: *Serendib* ⓁⓁ Via Pontida 2. **Map** 3 B2. [02-659 21 39. Undoubtedly the best-run Sri Lankan restaurant in Milan. Excellent vegetables with curry or spicy coconut. ● *midday; Aug.*	▦				
CITY CENTRE: *Trattoria Milanese* ⓁⓁⓁ Via Santa Marta 11. **Map** 7 B1. [02-86 45 19 91. One of the few surviving trattorias in the heart of town, this place has been serving typical Milanese food since 1919. ● *Tue; Aug.*	▦				▦
CITY CENTRE: *Bistrot Duomo* ⓁⓁⓁ Via San Raffaele 2, La Rinascente. **Map** 7 C1. [02-87 71 20. The menu centres around meat dishes, including fine Milanese veal cutlets, but there is also excellent fish. Try the desserts. View of the spires on the Duomo. ● *Sun, Mon midday; Aug.*	▦				▦
CITY CENTRE: *Boeucc* ⓁⓁⓁⓁ Piazza Belgioioso 2. **Map** 4 D5. [02-76 02 02 24. Located in an old palazzo, a classic Belle Epoque restaurant: spacious rooms with crystal chandeliers and precious mirrors. Typical Milanese cuisine, with risotto and *ossobuco.* ● *Sat, Sun midday; Aug, Easter, Christmas.* 🍷 🍴	▦	●			▦
CITY CENTRE: *Marino alla Scala* ⓁⓁⓁⓁ Piazza della Scala 5. **Map** 3 C5. [02-80 68 82 01. In the Trussardi building with a great view of the Scala opera house. Well-prepared Lombard cooking. The novelty of this bright restaurant is that you can eat at any time of day. ● *Sun; 10–20 Aug, public holidays.*	▦				▦
CITY CENTRE: *Peck* ⓁⓁⓁ Via V Hugo 4. **Map** 7 C1. [02-87 67 74. One of the best restaurants in Milan, rich in gastronomic tradition. Only super-fresh, top-quality ingredients. ● *Sun; Jan, 1–20 Jul.* 🍷	▦		▦	●	▦
CITY CENTRE: *Biffi Scala & Toulà* ⓁⓁⓁⓁⓁ Piazza della Scala 2. **Map** 3 C5. [02-86 66 51. The proximity to the Scala and splendid dining room make for a truly special atmosphere. Milanese cooking featuring, among other things, fried rice and veal cutlets. ● *Sat midday, Sun; Aug; 1–7 Jan.* 🍴	▦				▦
CITY CENTRE: *Savini* ⓁⓁⓁⓁⓁ Galleria Vittorio Emanuele II. **Map** 8 D1. [02-72 00 34 33. One of Milan's historic restaurants, in business since 1867. Elegance and impeccable service. Classic Milanese cuisine. ● *Sat midday, Sun; Aug.* 🍷 🍴	▦		▦		▦
NORTHWEST MILAN: *Tagiura* ⓁⓁ Via Tagiura 5. **Map** 5 C2. [02-48 95 06 13. At first it looks like a bar, until you see three rooms behind the counter. Piacenza cuisine, with salami, cured meats and home-made pasta. Tables in the evening by reservation only. ● *Sun, Mon–Wed, Sat eve; Aug.* 🍷	▦				▦
NORTHWEST MILAN: *Leo* ⓁⓁⓁ Via Trivulzio 26. **Map** 1 B5. [02-40 07 14 45. Fresh fish cooked the old-fashioned way. An informal atmosphere and cordial service. The shellfish sauté is excellent; try the pennette with prawns, mixed fried fish and delicious grilled razor clams. Good value for money. ● *Sun, Mon; Aug.*				●	

| | | Price categories for a three-course meal for one, including drinks (except for wine), cover charge, service and taxes.
Ⓛ under L40,000
ⓁⓁ L40,000-60,000
ⓁⓁⓁ L60,000-80,000
ⓁⓁⓁⓁ L80,000-110,000
ⓁⓁⓁⓁⓁ over L110,000 | **CREDIT CARDS** Restaurant that accepts the major credit cards.
ATTENDED PARKING Parking under restaurant supervision.
FIXED-PRICE MENU Restaurant with a choice of two or three fixed-price menus, usually cheaper than eating à la carte.
SEAFOOD RESTAURANT Specializing in fish and seafood dishes.
TRADITIONAL CUISINE The cooking is based on typical regional fare. |

	CREDIT CARDS	ATTENDED PARKING	FIXED-PRICE MENU	SEAFOOD RESTAURANT	TRADITIONAL CUISINE
NORTHWEST MILAN: *Osteria della Cagnola* ⓁⓁⓁ Via D Cirillo 14. **Map** 2 F3. ☎ 02-331 94 28. Near RAI and the Fiera, this small, characteristic tavern offers some of the best examples of Milanese cooking. Besides the classic *gnervitt*, risotto and *ossobuco*, there is *baccalà* (salt cod). ● Sun; Aug.	■				■
NORTHWEST MILAN: *Quattro Mori* ⓁⓁⓁ Largo M Cairoli 1. **Map** 3 B5. ☎ 02-87 84 83. Facing Castello Sforzesco, this restaurant features excellent cooking, including fish dishes. Impeccable service. ● Sat midday, Sun; Aug, Christmas and New Year. 🔳	■			●	■
NORTHWEST MILAN: *Taverna della Trisa* ⓁⓁⓁ Via Ferruccio 1. **Map** 2 E2. ☎ 02-34 13 04. A Trentino restaurant with dark wood decor. The specialities are *speck* (smoked ham), *canederli* (dumplings) in broth and *finferli* mushrooms. Excellent Teroldego wine. Ask for a table on the veranda. ● Mon; Aug. 🍷🔳	■		●	■	
NORTHWEST MILAN: *Alfredo Gran San Bernardo* ⓁⓁⓁⓁ Via GA Borghese 14. **Map** 2 D1. ☎ 02-331 90 00. For years, a kind of temple of traditional Milanese cuisine. Among the best specialities are meatballs served as an antipasto, assorted risottos and a first-rate *cassoeûla*. ● Sun (also Sat Jun & Jul); Aug, Dec–Jan.	■				■
NORTHWEST MILAN: *Primo Novecento* ⓁⓁⓁⓁ Via Ruggero di Lauria 17. **Map** 2 D1. ☎ 02-33 61 16 43. Early 1900s decor and atmosphere. Good fried vegetables and fish, and octopus stewed in tomatoes. ● Sat midday, Sun; 3 wk Aug, 26 Dec–7 Jan. 🔳	■			●	
NORTHWEST MILAN: *Trattoria Franca* ⓁⓁⓁⓁ Viale Certosa 235. **Map** 2 D1. ☎ 02-38 00 62 38. A trattoria where great attention is paid to every detail. Many home-made products from the family farm. An example of how an unforgettable dinner can be achieved with home cooking. ● Sat, Sun; Aug, Christmas and New Year. 🍷	■				■
SOUTHWEST MILAN: *Al Pont de ferr'* ⓁⓁ Ripa di Porta Ticinese 55. **Map** 6 D4. ☎ 02-89 40 62 77. A tavern with varied wines, excellent cured meats, cheeses, flans and vegetable pies, soups and good first courses. ● Sun; Aug, Christmas and New Year. 🔳🍷	■				
SOUTHWEST MILAN: *Grand Hotel Pub* ⓁⓁ Via Ascanio Sforza 75. **Map** 7 A4. ☎ 02-89 51 15 86. A trattoria featuring fresh ingredients and traditional dishes. The gnocchi with smoked ricotta cheese are delicious. ● midday, Mon, Aug, New Year. 🔳🍷	■				
SOUTHWEST MILAN: *L'Angolo* ⓁⓁ Via Cola di Rienzo 48. **Map** 5 C3. ☎ 02-423 67 24. The fresh buffalo milk mozzarella that arrives daily from Campania is superb. Try the pizzas and fish dishes, too. ● Tues, Sun; 10–24 Aug.	■			●	
SOUTHWEST MILAN: *L'Oca Giuliva* ⓁⓁ Viale Bligny 29. **Map** 7 C4. ☎ 02-58 31 28 71. A lively place decorated with models of geese (*oca giuliva* means happy goose). Mediterranean food with Puglian touches. ● Mon; Aug, Christmas and New Year.	■				
SOUTHWEST MILAN: *Pace* ⓁⓁ Via G Washington 74. **Map** 5 C1. ☎ 02-46 85 67. This Tuscan trattoria offers good value for money. Try the antipasti, the fillet or sizeable *fiorentina* steak. ● Wed, Sat midday; Aug, Christmas.	■				
SOUTHWEST MILAN: *Pizzeria Tradizionale con cucina di pesce* ⓁⓁ Ripa di Porta Ticinese 7. **Map** 6 D4. ☎ 02-839 51 33. Besides the excellent pizza, prepared with quality ingredients, try the breaded fish and linguine with lobster. In the summer you can sit outside, near the Naviglio. Booking ahead is advisable. ● 10–20 Aug. 🔳	■			●	

Price categories for a three-course meal for one, including drinks (except for wine), cover charge, service and taxes.
Ⓛ under L40,000
ⓁⓁ L40,000-60,000
ⓁⓁⓁ L60,000-80,000
ⓁⓁⓁⓁ L80,000-110,000
ⓁⓁⓁⓁⓁ over L110,000

CREDIT CARDS
Restaurant that accepts the major credit cards.
ATTENDED PARKING
Parking under restaurant supervision.
FIXED-PRICE MENU
Restaurant with a choice of two or three fixed-price menus, usually cheaper than eating *à la carte.*
SEAFOOD RESTAURANT
Specializing in fish dishes.
TRADITIONAL CUISINE
The cooking is based on typical regional fare.

	CREDIT CARDS	ATTENDED PARKING	FIXED-PRICE MENU	SEAFOOD RESTAURANT	TRADITIONAL CUISINE
SOUTHWEST MILAN: *Shri Ganesh* ⓁⓁ Via Lombardini 8. **Map** 6 E4. ☎ 02-511 09 33. A pleasant setting in which to try the specialities of Indian cuisine. The chicken tandoori and lamb tikka are good, judiciously spiced. ● *midday; Tue, Aug.*	▪		▪		
SOUTHWEST MILAN: *Aurora* ⓁⓁⓁ Via Savona 23. **Map** 5 B3. ☎ 02-89 40 49 78. Antique furniture and classic Piedmontese cooking in this good trattoria. House specialities are boiled meat and dessert. ● *Mon midday.* ▮ ▦	▪				
SOUTHWEST MILAN: *Osteria del Binari* ⓁⓁⓁ Via Tortona 1. **Map** 6 D3. ☎ 02-89 40 94 28. Enjoy Lombard-Piedmontese dishes in a traditional house. Tempting antipasti, *ossobuco*, desserts galore. Piano bar in winter. ● *midday; Sun.* ▦	▪		▪		▪
SOUTHWEST MILAN: *Rifugio Pugliese* ⓁⓁⓁ Via Boni 16. **Map** 6 D2. ☎ 02-48 00 09 17. The menu in the shape of a mussel offers a range of Puglian specialities. The *burrata* (mozzarella) served with cherry tomatoes is excellent, as are the home-made *orecchiette* pasta with different sauces. ● *Sun; Aug.* ▦	▪				
SOUTHWEST MILAN: *Al Porto* ⓁⓁⓁⓁ Piazzale Generale Cantore. **Map** 6 F3. ☎ 02-89 40 74 25. A fish restaurant in a converted customs house, a favourite with celebrities. Well-prepared cuisine based on classic and traditional dishes. Good antipasti and a decent mixed grill. ● *Sun, Mon midday; Aug, Christmas, New Year.* ▮	▪			●	
SOUTHWEST MILAN: *L'Assassino* ⓁⓁⓁⓁ Via Amedei 8. **Map** 7 C2. ☎ 02-80 561 44. A traditional Tuscan trattoria. The spaghettini sautéed with fresh tomatoes and basil and the Chianina steak are very good. ● *Mon, Fri eve and Sat (in summer).*					
SOUTHWEST MILAN: *Osteria di Porta Cicca* ⓁⓁⓁⓁ Ripa di Porta Ticinese 51. **Map** 6 D4. ☎ 02-837 27 63. In the heart of the Navigli district is this pleasant, bright tavern. Imaginative, well-prepared cuisine. Good fish and meat dishes. ● *Sat midday, Sun.*	▪			●	
SOUTHWEST MILAN: *Aimo e Nadia* ⓁⓁⓁⓁⓁ Via Montecuccoli 6. **Map** 5 A1. ☎ 02-41 68 86. For years, one of the best restaurants in Milan. The Moroni family has kept up top standards with the utmost consistency. The dishes are the quintessence of simplicity and perfection. ● *Sat midday, Sun; Aug, New Year–6 Jan.* ▮ ▮	▪		▪		
SOUTHWEST MILAN: *La Scaletta* ⓁⓁⓁⓁⓁ Piazzale Stazione Porta Genova 3. **Map** 6 F3. ☎ 02-58 10 02 90. An elegant restaurant featuring creative cooking based on seasonal products. One of the best-known (and best) in town. ● *Sun, Mon midday; Aug.* ▮	▪				
SOUTHWEST MILAN: *L'Ulmet* ⓁⓁⓁⓁⓁ Via Olmetto 21, corner of Via Disciplini. **Map** 7 B2. ☎ 02-86 45 27 18. Antique furniture and a fireplace, a warm family atmosphere. Elegant Italian cuisine with some traditional regional dishes as well. The pastries and grappas are very good. ● *Sun, Mon midday; Aug, Christmas–6 Jan.* ▮ ▮	▪				
SOUTHWEST MILAN: *Sadler* ⓁⓁⓁⓁⓁ Via Conchetta, corner of Via Troilo 14. **Map** 7 A5. ☎ 02-58 10 44 51. One of the best places in town, with high-level creative cooking. The chef, who once worked at the famous Porta Cicca, is known for his extraordinary fish dishes and delectable desserts. ● *Sun midday; 9–31 Aug.* ▮ ▮ ▦	▪		▪	●	
SOUTHEAST MILAN: *Pizzeria napoletana La Taverna* Ⓛ Via Anzani 3. **Map** 8 F. ☎ 02-59 90 07 93. Typical Neapolitan pizzeria-friggitoria (with fried food). Melting, thin pizza cooked to perfection. Good Neapolitan dishes. ● *Mon; Aug.* ▦	▪				

SOUTHEAST MILAN: *Al Merluzzo Felice* ⑦⑦
Via Lazzaro Papi 6. **Map** 8 F4. 02-545 47 11.
Sicilian food including fish antipasti and numerous first courses. The
cannoli (pastry rolls) with ricotta are delicious. *Sun; 12 Aug–1 Sep.*

SOUTHEAST MILAN: *Cueva Maja* ⑦⑦
Viale Monte Nero 19. **Map** 8 E2. 02-55 18 57 40.
One of the best Mexican restaurants in town. Wide choice of cocktails.
Meat dishes with spicy sauces and melted cheese. *Mon; Aug.*

SOUTHEAST MILAN: *Dongiò* ⑦⑦
Via Corio 3. **Map** 8 F4. 02-551 13 72.
Home-made Calabrian-Piacentine dishes are featured in this trattoria. Try the
salami (especially the *coppa* – cured pork neck), the fresh pasta with hot chilli
and grilled caciocavallo cheese. *Sat midday, Sun; Aug, Christmas and New Year*

SOUTHEAST MILAN: *Taverna degli Amici* ⑦⑦
Via Spartaco 4. **Map** 8 F2. 02-55 19 40 05.
A small restaurant with wooden tables. Wide selection of Italian wines.
Popular for its meat dishes and mixed grills. *Sun; Aug.*

SOUTHEAST MILAN: *Trattoria dei Decemviri* ⑦⑦
Via dei Decemviri 14. **Map** 8 F1. 02-70 10 24 42.
Exceptionally fresh fish in a simple, informal setting. An excellent
Neapolitan *pastiera* tart. *Mon; Aug, Christmas–6 Jan.*

SOUTHEAST MILAN: *La Piola di Mariagrazia e Diego* ⑦⑦⑦
Via del Perugino 18. **Map** 8 F2. 02-55 19 59 45.
A fish-only trattoria run by a family from Foggia. Excellent raw fish
antipasti, unforgettable home-made pasta.The house desserts are good.
Sat midday, Sun; Aug, Christmas–6 Jan.

SOUTHEAST MILAN: *Masuelli San Marco* ⑦⑦⑦
Viale Umbria 80. **Map** 8 F3. 02-55 18 41 38.
A traditional Milanese trattoria with authentic home cooking. The dishes
vary according to the day. Excellent Piedmontese specialities, too.
Sun, Mon midday; 18 Aug–16 Sep, Christmas–6 Jan.

SOUTHEAST MILAN: *Trattoria del Pescatore* ⑦⑦⑦
Via Vannucci 5. **Map** 8 E4. 02-58 32 04 52.
The scent of delicious cooking comes from the inviting open kitchen.
Spaghetti with mullet roe and squid, lobster Catalan, excellent myrtle liqueur.
Book well in advance. *Sun; Aug, Christmas and New Year.*

SOUTHEAST MILAN: *Da Giacomo* ⑦⑦⑦⑦
Via Sottocorno 6. **Map** 4 F5. 02-76 02 33 13. W www.todine.net-dagiacomo
In an area with a large number of trattorias, Giacomo's stands out for
its fish dishes and delicious desserts. *Mon, Tue midday; Aug, Christmas–6 Jan.*

SOUTHEAST MILAN: *Mauro* ⑦⑦⑦⑦
Via Colonnetta 5. **Map** 8 E1. 02-546 13 80.
An elegant restaurant offering a range of fish specialities. Try the pappardelle
with prawns (shrimp) and curry and excellent baked turbot with potatoes.
Efficient, friendly service. *Sat midday, Mon; 2 wk mid-Aug, Christmas and New Year.*

SOUTHEAST MILAN: *Giannino* ⑦⑦⑦⑦⑦
Via Sciesa 8. **Map** 8 F1. 02-55 19 55 82.
This historic restaurant has a splendid copper hood in the open kitchen and a
lovely winter garden. The young chef Davide Oldani adds a dash of creativity
to classic dishes. *Sun; Mon midday, 2 wk mid-Aug.*

SOUTHEAST MILAN: *Porcao Churrascaria* ⑦⑦⑦
Via Abbadesse 30. **Map** 4 D. 02-688 38 83.
An authentic *churrascaria* (grill-room) in Milan. Brazilian dishes and
Brazilian waiters. Grilled meat of all kinds. *Sun; Aug.*

SOUTHEAST MILAN: *Yar* ⑦⑦⑦⑦
Via Mercalli 22. **Map** 7 C3. 02-58 30 52 34.
This combination restaurant-bistro offers top-quality Russian food in an elegant
setting. Various types of caviar, salmon and sturgeon. *Sun; Aug.*

NORTHEAST MILAN: *Massawa* ⑦
Via Sirtori 6. **Map** 4 F4. 02-29 40 69 10.
Eritrean cuisine. The main course is *zighinì*: sourdough bread
with meat and spicy vegetables and, on Friday, with fish. *Mon.*

Price categories for a three-course meal for one, including drinks (except for wine), cover charge, service and taxes. Ⓛ under L40,000 ⓁⓁ L40,000–60,000 ⓁⓁⓁ L60,000–80,000 ⓁⓁⓁⓁ L80,000–110,000 ⓁⓁⓁⓁⓁ over L110,000	**CREDIT CARDS** Restaurant that accepts the major credit cards. **ATTENDED PARKING** Parking under restaurant supervision. **FIXED-PRICE MENU** Restaurant with a choice of two or three fixed-price menus, usually cheaper than eating *à la carte*. **SEAFOOD RESTAURANT** Specializing in fish dishes. **TRADITIONAL CUISINE** The cooking is based on typical regional fare.	CREDIT CARDS	ATTENDED PARKING	FIXED-PRICE MENU	SEAFOOD RESTAURANT	TRADITIONAL CUISINE

NORTHEAST MILAN: *Vecchia Napoli* Ⓛ
Via Chavez 4. **Map** 4 F1. (02-261 90 56.
This authentic pizzeria has received prizes for the best pizza in Europe. Always very crowded but well worth your while. ● *Sun midday, Mon; Aug.*

	■				

NORTHEAST MILAN: *La Bitta* ⓁⓁ
Via del Carmine 3. **Map** 3 B4. (02-72 00 31 85.
An acclaimed trattoria offering mostly fish: from lightly fried crayfish with courgettes (zucchini) to a delicious fillet alla Voronov (with mustard, cream and brandy). Excellent value for money. ● *Sun, Sat midday; Aug.*

	■			●	

NORTHEAST MILAN: *Il ristorante il coriando* ⓁⓁ
Via dell'Orso 1. **Map** 3 C5. (02-869 32 73. Ⓦ www.ilcoriando.com
A pleasant restaurant offering fish dishes and typical Milanese cuisine.

	■		■		

NORTHEAST MILAN: *Il Doge di Amalfi* ⓁⓁ
Via Sangallo 41. **Map** 4 F5. (02-73 02 86.
This popular restaurant-pizzeria is next to the Ciak theatre. The pizza is excellent, as are the fish dishes. ● *Mon; Aug, Christmas–6 Jan.*

	■			●	

NORTHEAST MILAN: *Ostaria Vecju Friûl* ⓁⓁ
Via E De Marchi 5, corner of Via di Giustizia. **Map** 4 D4. (02-670 42 95.
A typical Friuli trattoria at the Naviglio della Martesana. Among the tempting antipasti are Suaris ham and salami. Try the ravioli, and then the classic *frico* (fried cheese pancake) with polenta. ● *midday, Sun; 1–25 Aug.* ▯

	■				

NORTHEAST MILAN: *Matarel* ⓁⓁⓁ
Corso Garibaldi 75. **Map** 3 B3. (02-65 42 04.
At the beginning of the Brera quarter is this classic Milanese restaurant: *gnervitt*, risotto and the *rostin negàa* (veal cutlet). ● *Tue, Wed midday; June–July.*

	■				■

NORTHEAST MILAN: *Gianni e Dorina – Il Pontremolese* ⓁⓁⓁ
Via G Pepe 38. **Map** 3 B1. (02-60 63 40.
The fascinating Isola quarter boasts this elegant (but relaxed) restaurant, where Dorina offers Tuscan fare from Lunigiana, using only the freshest top-quality ingredients. ● *Sat midday, Sun; Aug, Christmas.* ▯ ▦

	■	●			

NORTHEAST MILAN: *La Briciola* ⓁⓁⓁ
Via Marsala, at the corner of Via Solferino. **Map** 3 C3. (02-65 36 99.
Parisian bistro atmosphere in the heart of Brera with many plants and mirrors. Very popular with fashion and theatre people. Fried rice and browned *carpaccio* (thinly sliced veal with oil). ● *Sun, Mon; 26 Jul–26 Aug.* ▯

	■				

NORTHEAST MILAN: *Mykonos* ⓁⓁⓁ
Via Tofane 5. **Map** 4 F1. (02-261 02 09.
In a traditional house at the end of the Naviglio della Martesana is this classic Greek tavern. Book ahead. ● *midday; 10 days Aug.*

					■

NORTHEAST MILAN: *Piero e Pia* ⓁⓁ
Piazza Aspari 2. **Map** 4 F3. (02-71 85 41.
A pleasant setting for Piacenza specialities: *coppa* (cured pork neck), *pisarei e fasò* (peas and beans) and pork shank. ● *Sun; Aug, Christmas, New Year.* ▦

	■				

NORTHEAST MILAN: *Osteria Corte Regina* ⓁⓁⓁ
Via Rottole 60. **Map** 4 F1. (02-259 33 77.
Sophisticated cooking and elegant decor in an old farmstead on the north-eastern outskirts of Milan. Very good fish. ● *Sat midday, Sun; 2 wk mid-Aug.* ▦

	■	●		●	■

NORTHEAST MILAN: *Taiwan* ⓁⓁⓁ
Via Adda 10. **Map** 4 E2. (02-670 24 88.
Delicious Taiwanese cuisine. Among the specialities, steamed bread stuffed with crispy pork, giant crab with meat sauce, turbot stewed with mushrooms and bamboo. Book ahead for Chinese New Year.
● *Tue; 2 wk mid-Aug.*

	■			●	

NORTHEAST MILAN: *Al Girarrosto da Cesarina*   ⓁⓁⓁ
Corso Venezia 31. **Map** 5 E4. (02-76 00 04 81.
This very centrally located restaurant is ideal for business lunches.
Fish and meat with a Tuscan touch. ● *Sat, Sun midday; Aug, Christmas–6 Jan.*

NORTHEAST MILAN: *Centro Ittico*   ⓁⓁⓁⓁ
Via F Aporti 35. **Map** 4 F1. (02-26 14 37 74.
Near the fish market, with the freshest fish in town, cooked simply
and with skill. The raw shellfish is excellent. ● *Sun, Mon; Aug, Christmas–6 Jan.*

NORTHEAST MILAN: *Ilia*   ⓁⓁⓁⓁ
Via Lecco 1. **Map** 4 E3. (02-29 52 18 95.
This Tuscan trattoria is becoming one of the best in Milan. Delicious
deep-fried appetizers are served while you're waiting for the first course.
Traditional tripe and Florentine steaks. ● *Fri, Sat midday; Aug, Christmas–10 Jan.*

NORTHEAST MILAN: *Malavoglia*   ⓁⓁⓁ
Via Lecco 4. **Map** 4 E3. (02-29 53 13 87.
Sicilian fish specialities. Hot and cold seafood appetizers, pasta with sardines,
spaghetti with fish sauce as well as pasta alla Norma (with aubergines/
eggplant, tomatoes and ricotta). ● *midday, Mon; Aug, Christmas–6 Jan.*

NORTHEAST MILAN: *Valtellina*   ⓁⓁⓁ
Via Taverna 34. **Map** 8 F. (02-756 11 39.
This restaurant bases its menu on salame, meat and mushrooms. Excellent
antipasti and home-made appetizers in oil. ● *Mon; Aug, Christmas–6 Jan.*

NORTHEAST MILAN: *Joia*   ⓁⓁⓁⓁ
Via P Castaldi 18. **Map** 4 E3. (02-29 52 21 24.
First-class vegetarian food in an elegant setting. Creative dishes based on pasta,
vegetables and pulses (legumes). ● *Sat midday, Sun; Easter, Aug, Christmas–6 Jan.*

NORTHEAST MILAN: *La Terrazza di Via Palestro*   ⓁⓁⓁⓁ
Via Palestro 2. **Map** 4 E4. (02-76 00 22 77. Ⓦ *www.acenallaterrazza.it*
A fish restaurant famous for its "Mediterranean sushi". Creative Ligurian
cuisine, exemplified by the minestrone with pesto and scorpion-fish. View of
the Porta Venezia gardens. ● *Sun, Sat eve; 2 wk mid-Aug, Christmas–mid-Jan.*

NORTHEAST MILAN: *Ran*   ⓁⓁⓁ
Via Bordoni 8. **Map** 4 D1. (02-669 69 97. Ⓦ *www.ristoranteran.com*
The Japanese restaurant in Milan. The decor is simple and the chefs
are *sushi* masters. Try the "barchetta" mix: raw seabass, salmon and
octopus with rice and radish. The *tempura*, a delicate mixture of
deep-fried crayfish and vegetables, is superb. ● *Midday, Sun; 2 wk Aug.*

NORTHEAST MILAN: *Il Teatro dell'Hotel Four Seasons*   ⓁⓁⓁⓁⓁ
Via del Gesù 8. **Map** 4 D5. (02-77 08 14 35.
This restaurant reflects the aspirations of the best hotel in Milan, both in decor
and in the preparation and presentation of its dishes. Marvellous shellfish antipasti and risottos, splendid choice of desserts. ● *Midday, Sun; Aug, Dec.*

NORTHEAST MILAN: *L'Ami Berton*   ⓁⓁⓁⓁ
Via Nullo 14, corner of Via Goldoni. **Map** 4 E5. (02-70 12 34 76.
An elegant restaurant with a good selection of fish. In autumn, dishes often
feature mushrooms. The prawns marinated in onions and the sautéed mushrooms,
onions and potatoes are wonderful. ● *Sat midday, Sun; Aug,1st wk Jan.*

NORTHEAST MILAN: *Il Sambuco*   ⓁⓁⓁⓁ
Via Messina 10. **Map** 3 A2. (02-33 61 03 33.
The Hermitage hotel restaurant, which specializes in fish. The octopus
and squid stew and the potato, prawn and leek flan are very good, as is
the mixed fried fish. ● *Sat midday, Sun; 1–25 Aug, Christmas–New Year.*

THE LAKES

LAKE MAGGIORE: *Del Barcaiolo*   ⓁⓁⓁ
Arona. Piazza del Popolo 23. (0322-24 33 88.
Located in the 14th-century Palazzo del Podestà, with a lovely open kitchen.
Chargrilled meat and fish, and rustic antipasti. ● *Wed; 15 days Feb & Aug.*

LAKE MAGGIORE: *La Vecchia Arona*   ⓁⓁ
Arona. Lungolago Marconi 17. (0322-24 24 69.
This small, sophisticated restaurant offers great value for your money
with its tasting menu. A wide selection of French cheeses
and a matching wine cellar. ● *Fri; Jun, Nov.*

Price categories for a three-course meal for one, including drinks (except for wine), cover charge, service and taxes.
ⓛ under L40,000
ⓛⓛ L40,000-60,000
ⓛⓛⓛ L60,000-80,000
ⓛⓛⓛⓛ L80,000-110,000
ⓛⓛⓛⓛⓛ over L110,000

CREDIT CARDS
Restaurant that accepts the major credit cards.
ATTENDED PARKING
Parking under restaurant supervision.
FIXED-PRICE MENU
Restaurant with a choice of two or three fixed-price menus, usually cheaper than eating à la carte.
SEAFOOD RESTAURANT
Specializing in fish dishes.
TRADITIONAL CUISINE
The cooking is based on typical regional fare.

	CREDIT CARDS	ATTENDED PARKING	FIXED-PRICE MENU	SEAFOOD RESTAURANT	TRADITIONAL CUISINE

LAKE MAGGIORE: *Taverna del Pittore*   ⓛⓛⓛⓛ
Arona. Piazza del Popolo 39. ☎ *0322-24 33 66.*
A fine terrace overlooking the lake, elegant decor and beautifully cooked dishes. The fish – both from the lake and the sea – is good and painstakingly prepared. ● *Mon; Nov, Christmas.*
[CREDIT CARDS ■; SEAFOOD RESTAURANT ●]

LAKE MAGGIORE: *Del Lago*   ⓛⓛⓛⓛ
Cannobio. Carmine Inferiore, Via Nazionale 2. ☎ *0323-705 95.*
Probably one of the best restaurants in the area. The elegant cuisine is based on super-fresh fish from the sea. Well-stocked wine cellar, splendid view of the lake. ● *Tue, Wed midday; Nov–Feb.*
[CREDIT CARDS ■; ATTENDED PARKING ●; FIXED-PRICE MENU ■; SEAFOOD RESTAURANT ●; TRADITIONAL CUISINE ●]

LAKE MAGGIORE: *Piccolo Lago*   ⓛⓛⓛ
Fondotoce. Via Turati 87. ☎ *0323-58 67 92.*
A small inn overlooking the Mergozzo lake. Traditional local dishes, with some influence from the sea, which you can enjoy in summer along with the stunning views from the terrace. ● *Mon (Nov–May).*
[CREDIT CARDS ■; ATTENDED PARKING ●; SEAFOOD RESTAURANT ●; TRADITIONAL CUISINE ●]

LAKE MAGGIORE: *Il Porticciolo*   ⓛⓛⓛⓛ
Laveno. Via Fortino 40. ☎ *0332-66 72 57.*
A beautiful lakeside villa. The elegant restaurant offers creative cuisine characterized by the fresh home-made produce, such as the pasta, the bread and the desserts. ● *Tue, Jan–Feb.*
[CREDIT CARDS ■; ATTENDED PARKING ●; SEAFOOD RESTAURANT ●]

LAKE MAGGIORE: *L'Antico Maniero*   ⓛⓛⓛⓛ
Lesa. Via alla Campagna 1. ☎ *0332-74 11.*
This splendid restaurant is a converted 18th-century castle in the middle of an ancient park. Period consoles, mirrors and chandeliers make for an even more old-world atmosphere. Well-prepared dishes, with delicate combinations of fish and vegetables. ● *midday, Mon; Sun eve; 1–15 Jan, 1–15 Nov.*
[CREDIT CARDS ■; ATTENDED PARKING ●; SEAFOOD RESTAURANT ●]

LAKE MAGGIORE: *Milano*   ⓛⓛⓛⓛ
Pallanza. Corso Zanitello 2. ☎ *0323-55 68 16.*
A restaurant with a splendid veranda over the lake. The specialities are fish from the lake and exquisite desserts. ● *Tue; mid-Jan–mid-Feb, 1 wk Jun.*
[CREDIT CARDS ■; ATTENDED PARKING ●; SEAFOOD RESTAURANT ●; TRADITIONAL CUISINE ●]

LAKE MAGGIORE: *Il Torchio*   ⓛⓛ
Pallanza. Via Manzoni 20. ☎ *0323-50 33 52.*
Rustic but elegant, with a wooden beamed ceiling and attractively presented tables. The home-made ravioli and grilled fish are wonderful. ● *Mon.*
[CREDIT CARDS ■; SEAFOOD RESTAURANT ●; TRADITIONAL CUISINE ●]

LAKE MAGGIORE: *Il Sole di Ranco*   ⓛⓛⓛⓛⓛ
Ranco. Piazza Venezia 5. ☎ *0331-97 65 07.*
ⓦ *www.soleranco@relaischateaux.fr* @ *ivanett@tin.it*
One of the "Relais&Châteaux" chain, with a stupendous view. The Brovelli family has run this restaurant for five generations, making it one of the best in Italy. ● *Mon (except summer), Tue; Jan.*
[CREDIT CARDS ■; ATTENDED PARKING ●; SEAFOOD RESTAURANT ●; TRADITIONAL CUISINE ●]

LAKE MAGGIORE: *Da Mosé*   ⓛⓛⓛⓛ
Sesto Calende. Lisanza, Via Ponzello 14. ☎ *0331-97 72 10.*
A small villa in the middle of a pleasant garden on the road to Angera. Inviting, elegant decor and attentive staff. The selection of fish is good, the cheeses exceptional. ● *Mon–Tue, midday Wed–Fri; Jan, 7–21 Aug, Christmas–10 Jan.*
[CREDIT CARDS ■; ATTENDED PARKING ●; SEAFOOD RESTAURANT ●]

LAKE MAGGIORE: *Piemontese*   ⓛⓛⓛⓛ
Stresa. Via Mazzini 25. ☎ *0323-302 35.*
A restaurant with a long tradition in the heart of Stresa. Ingredients are chosen with care. The spaghetti with onions and chilli and pâté de foie gras with fondue are excellent. ● *Mon, Sun eve (Oct–May); Jan–Feb.*
[CREDIT CARDS ■; TRADITIONAL CUISINE ●]

LAKE COMO: *Silvio*   ⓛⓛ
Bellagio. Via Carcano 12. ☎ *031-95 03 22.*
This small hotel-restaurant is famous for its local cuisine at reasonable prices. *Lavarello* (a lake fish) is offered in a variety of ways. ● *6 Jan, Feb.*
[CREDIT CARDS ■; ATTENDED PARKING ●; SEAFOOD RESTAURANT ●; TRADITIONAL CUISINE ●]

LAKE COMO: *Barchetta* ⓁⓁⓁ **Bellagio.** Salita Mella 13. *031-95 13 89.* This romantic pergola with geraniums is in one of the most interesting parts of Bellagio. The chef Armando prepares local recipes with the utmost care, choosing exceptionally fresh ingredients. A wide range of lake fish and a highly tempting choice of cakes. *Tue (except summer); Nov–Feb.*	■			●	■
LAKE COMO: *Crotto dei Platani* ⓁⓁⓁ **Brienno.** Via Regina 73. *031-81 40 38.* *www.crottodeiplatani.it* Situated in a natural cave *(crotto)*, this restaurant features good local fare. Try the lake shad, prepared in different ways. *Tue, Wed midday (Nov), hols.*	■	●		●	■
LAKE COMO: *Musichiere* ⓁⓁⓁ **Cernobbio.** Via Cinque Giornate 32. *031-34 22 95.* *www.vademecumitalia.com/musichiere* The menu is based on healthy, hearty food with fresh ingredients. Try the gnocchi *alla Alessandro Volta* with tomatoes, onions, bacon and taleggio cheese, or the classic trout *alla Musichiere*, stuffed and oven-baked. *Sun (not summer); 1 wk Jan, 2 wk Aug.*	■			●	■
LAKE COMO: *Gatto Nero* ⓁⓁⓁ **Cernobbio.** Rovenna, Via Monte Santo 69. *031-51 20 42.* Just above Cernobbio, on the road to Monte Bisbino, is this pleasant place with a marvellous view of the lake. It features Lombard cuisine. The chopped kidneys cooked in brandy are especially good. *Mon, Tue midday.*	■			●	■
LAKE COMO: *Trattoria del Vapore* ⓁⓁⓁⓁ **Cernobbio.** Via Garibaldi 17. *031-51 03 08.* In the heart of town. A very pleasant trattoria with flavourful, well prepared local food. The risotto with perch and lake carp are very good. *Tue; Christmas– 25 Jan.*	■			●	■
LAKE COMO: *Locanda dell'Oca Bianca* ⓁⓁⓁ **Como.** Trecallo, Via Canturina 251. *031-52 56 05.* *www.ocabianca.it* In a carefully renovated farmhouse near Como, creative recipes are mixed with local dishes such as home-made pasta with vegetables and mountain pasture cheeses. *Mon; Jan, 1 wk mid-Aug.*	■	●		●	■
LAKE COMO: *Raimondi del Villa Flori* ⓁⓁⓁⓁ **Como.** Via per Cernobbio 12. *031-57 31 05.* A charming room with fine views of the lake and the park. Good, well prepared international cuisine. *Mon; Dec, Jan.*	■	●		●	
LAKE COMO: *Navedano* ⓁⓁⓁⓁⓁ **Como.** Camnago Volta, Via Pannilani. *031-30 80 80.* An elegant, well-kept restaurant featuring many fish dishes, such as the exquisite roast seabass with sautéed potatoes. *Tue; Aug, last 3 wk Jan.*	■	●		●	■
LAKE COMO: *Locanda dell'Isola* ⓁⓁⓁⓁ **Isola Comacina.** *0344-567 55.* What makes this place special is its location on an uninhabited island. A boat takes you to the restaurant pier from Sala Comacina. Only typical local dishes. *Tue (in spring); Nov–Mar.*			■	●	■
LAKE COMO: *Nicolin* ⓁⓁⓁ **Lecco.** Via Ponchielli 54. *0341-42 21 22.* A historic restaurant belonging to the Cattaneo family, run by father and son. The cooking ranges from classic Lombard dishes to the elegant creations of the son Giovanni. Try the soused (pickled) fish rolls. *Tue; Aug, 1st wk Jan.*	■	●		●	■
LAKE COMO: *Al Porticciolo 84* ⓁⓁⓁⓁ **Lecco.** Via Valsecchi 5. *0341-49 81 03.* Top-quality seafood. The hot and cold antipasti and home-made pasta dishes with shellfish sauce are delicious. *midday (except hols), Mon, Tue; Aug.*	■			●	
LAKE COMO: *Il Griso* ⓁⓁⓁⓁⓁ **Malgrate.** Via Provinciale 51. *0341-20 20 40.* Classic, elegant, famous: these adjectives perfectly describe a pillar of Lecco's gastronomic tradition. The best in international cuisine, with dishes including both meat and fish. The pâté de foie gras is delectable, and the prawns (shrimp) are extra-fresh. *15 days Dec–Jan.*	■	●		●	
LAKE COMO: *Il Ricciolo* ⓁⓁⓁ **Mandello.** Via Statale 165. *0341-73 25 46.* This small, intimate restaurant celebrates Lake Como cuisine. The speciality is *brodetto lariano* (fish soup), but tagliatelle with river crayfish and perch with lemon are good. *Sun eve, Mon; 2 wk Sep, Christmas–15 Jan.*	■	●		●	■

For key to symbols see back flap

	CREDIT CARDS	ATTENDED PARKING	FIXED-PRICE MENU	SEAFOOD RESTAURANT	TRADITIONAL CUISINE

Price categories for a three-course meal for one, including drinks (except for wine), cover charge, service and taxes.
Ⓛ under L40,000
ⓁⓁ L40,000–60,000
ⓁⓁⓁ L60,000–80,000
ⓁⓁⓁⓁ L80,000–110,000
ⓁⓁⓁⓁⓁ over L110,000

CREDIT CARDS
Restaurant that accepts the major credit cards.
ATTENDED PARKING
Parking under restaurant supervision.
FIXED-PRICE MENU
Restaurant with a choice of two or three fixed-price menus, usually cheaper than eating à la carte.
SEAFOOD RESTAURANT
Specializing in fish dishes.
TRADITIONAL CUISINE
The cooking is based on typical regional fare.

LAKE COMO: *Imperialino* ⓁⓁⓁⓁ
Moltrasio. Via Antica Regina 26. 𝄢 031-34 66 00.
One of the Imperiale Hotel restaurants, in a nice position over the lake. Local cuisine, with strong flavours. ● Mon (except summer); Jan–mid-Feb. 🔲

LAKE COMO: *La Tirlindana* ⓁⓁⓁ
Sala Comacina. Piazza Matteotti 5. 𝄢 0344-566 37.
Sit at tables in the lakeside square. Known for its delicious ravioli stuffed with lemon-flavoured cheese. ● Mon, Tues–Fri (Nov–Feb); 31 Oct–18 Nov. 🔲

LAKE COMO: *Vecchia Varenna* ⓁⓁ
Varenna. Contrada Scoscesa 10. 𝄢 0341-83 07 93.
In summer you eat on the splendid terrace facing the lake; in the winter in two cosy rooms. Typical valley and lake cuisine. Try the risotto finished with *scimudin* cheese. ● Mon; Jan. 🔲

LAKE GARDA: *Bagatta alla Lepre* ⓁⓁⓁⓁ
Desenzano. Via Bagatta 43. 𝄢 030-914 23 13.
Desenzano is generally a good place to eat out, and this relatively recent restaurant is especially recommended for its excellent fish, fine wine list and friendly staff. ● Tue. 🍷

LAKE GARDA: *Esplanade* ⓁⓁⓁⓁ
Desenzano. Via Lario 10. 𝄢 030-914 33 61.
A superb terrace over the lake and elegant decor. Fabulous cooking, with a range of combinations of lake, sea and land. Try the seafood terrine and pasta and risotto with spicy seafood sauce. ● Wed. 🍷🍽🔲

LAKE GARDA: *Cavallino* ⓁⓁⓁⓁ
Desenzano. Via Gherla 30, corner of Via Murachette. 𝄢 030-912 02 17.
A pleasant courtyard restaurant. Cavallino features fish, from the lake and the sea. The scallops and lobster are excellent, as is the pastry with Sauternes-flavoured zabaglione. ● Mon, Tue midday; Nov, 2nd wk Jan. 🍷🍽🔲

LAKE GARDA: *Locanda agli Angeli* ⓁⓁⓁ
Gardone. Piazza Garibaldi 2, road to Vittoriale. 𝄢 0365-208 32.
In the pedestrian-only alleys of upper Gardone, opposite the Vittoriale, is this small inn with good cooking. Try the delicious risotto with trout and pumpkin and the fragrant home-made breadsticks. ● Mon; Nov–Feb. 🍷

LAKE GARDA: *Villa Fiordaliso* ⓁⓁⓁⓁⓁ
Gardone. Corso Zanardelli 150. 𝄢 0365-201 58. ⓦ www.villafiordaliso.it
One of the elegant Relais&Chateaux chain, in a splendid converted villa overlooking the lake. This is one of the best restaurants in Italy, featuring creative, skilfully prepared and presented dishes. The *spaghetti chioggiotti* with shellfish are delectable. ● Mon; Tue midday; Nov–Feb. 🍷🍽🔲

LAKE GARDA: *Tortuga* ⓁⓁⓁⓁ
Gargnano. Via XXIV Maggio 5. 𝄢 0365-712 51.
This small, elegant restaurant is a firm fixture on the Lake Garda gastronomic scene. The food is based on fresh local products such as exquisite lake fish with oil and Garda capers. ● Mon eve (except summer), Tue; mid-Jan–Feb. 🍷🍽

LAKE GARDA: *Capriccio* ⓁⓁⓁⓁ
Manerba. Montinelle, Piazza San Bernardo 6. 𝄢 0365-55 11 24.
On a hill, with the terrace offering a breathtaking view. Seafood is the main-stay here, especially molluscs and crustaceans. The raw vegetable and seafood salad with Garda olive oil is superb. ● Tue (except summer); Jan, Feb. 🍷🍽🔲

LAKE GARDA: *Trattoria al Combattente* ⓁⓁ
Peschiera del Garda. San Benedetto, Via Sabino 29. 𝄢 045-755 32 27.
This pleasant trattoria between Peschiera and Sirmione serves only dishes based on fish caught in Lake Garda. Its forte is the mixed hot and cold antipasti. ● Mon. 🔲

LAKE GARDA: *Restel de Fer*   ⓁⓁ
Riva del Garda. Via Restel de Fer 10. [0464-55 34 81.
w www.restel-de-fer.de @ resteldef@tin.it
A simple place where you can enjoy the specialities of upper Lake Garda. The
dishes include medieval recipes. Excellent olive oil. ● *midday, Tue, Nov–Jan.*

LAKE GARDA: *Locanda San Vigilio*   ⓁⓁⓁⓁ
San Vigilio. Punta San Vigilio. [045-725 66 88.
This small, enchanting inn in a fascinating part of Lake Garda has
seven rooms for those who want to linger in this paradise. Ask for a table
in the loggia facing the lake, where you can enjoy the view and a fine
risotto with radicchio, after sampling the fine buffet. ● *Nov–Feb.*

LAKE GARDA: *La Rucola*   ⓁⓁⓁⓁ
Sirmione. Via Strentelle 3. [030-91 63 26.
An elegant restaurant in the historic centre, with brick walls and soft lighting.
The risotto with leeks and salame and the pike fillet with pancetta and
cabbage are good. Two tasting menus. ● *Thu, Fri midday; Jan–mid-Feb.*

LAKE GARDA: *Vecchia Lugana*   ⓁⓁⓁⓁ
Sirmione. Lugana, Piazzale Vecchia Lugana 1. [030-91 90 12.
This restaurant is near the Sirmione peninsula, and has offered top-level
cuisine for years. The mixed fish grill is famous for the abundance
and quality of the fish. ● *Mon, Tue; Jan–mid-Feb.*

LAKE GARDA: *Osteria dell'Orologio*   ⓁⓁ
Salò. Via Butturini 26. [0365-29 01 58.
A pleasant two-storey place in the historic centre of Salò, like an old-fashioned
wine bar with a kitchen, serving local wines and a few excellent dishes,
including home-made pappardelle with partridge. ● *Wed; mid-Jun–mid-July.*

LAKE GARDA: *Antica Trattoria Alle Rose*   ⓁⓁⓁ
Salò. Via Gasparo da Salò 33. [0365-432 20.
Recently restored, Gianni Briarava's restaurant, a milestone in lower Lake
Garda gastronomy, is now open. ● *Wed; Nov.*

LAKE GARDA: *Aurora*   ⓁⓁ
Soiano del Lago. Via Ciucani 1. [0365-67 41 01.
Simple, savoury cooking at this friendly country restaurant. The ravioli
with *bagos* cheese and stewed whitefish are very good. ● *Wed.*

LAGO D'ISEO: *Mongolfiera dei Sodi*   ⓁⓁⓁ
Erbusco. Via Olina 18. [0322-902 59.
The three rooms have antique furniture and a fireplace. The quality cuisine
is Tuscan-Lombard. Try the house Florentine steak. ● *Tues.*

LAGO D'ISEO: *Gualtiero Marchesi*   ⓁⓁⓁⓁ
Erbusco. Via Vittorio Emanuele 11. [030-776 05 62.
Italy's most famous chef, Gualtiero Marchesi, presides over this restaurant in a
splendid Relais, on a winery estate in Franciacorta. Unique class and atmosphere. The risotto with saffron is exceptional. ● *10 Jan–20 Feb.*

LAGO D'ISEO: *Osteria Il Volto*   ⓁⓁ
Iseo. Via Mirolte 33. [030-98 14 62.
This restaurant offers good value for money. The marinated fish
is good and the fillet of perch with herbs is delicious.
Franciacorta wines. ● *Wed; Thu midday; Jan, Jul.*

LAGO D'ISEO: *Al Desco*   ⓁⓁⓁ
Sarnico. Piazza XX Settembre 19. [035-91 07 40.
Signora Nadia's fish courses go beyond all expectations: the freshest of
ingredients, careful preparation and magnificent flavour. The meticulously
shelled fried prawns are exceptional. ● *Mon; Tue midday; Jan.*

LAGO D'ORTA: *Taverna Antico Agnello*   ⓁⓁⓁ
Orta San Giulio. Via Olina 18. [0322-902 59.
A rustic atmosphere in a 17th-century house. Among the specials: breast of
duck Tartar and lasagnette with goat's milk cheese. ● *Tue; mid-Dec–mid-Feb.*

LAGO D'ORTA: *Al Sorriso*   ⓁⓁⓁⓁ
Soriso. Via Roma 18. [0322-98 32 28.
One of Italy's top restaurants. The delights of Luisa Valazza's cooking attract
clients from all over the world. Every ingredient, from the oil to the lamb, is
guaranteed genuine and home-produced. The cheese trolley and wine list
alone deserve an award. ● *Mon, Tue midday; Aug; Christmas–mid-Jan.*

BARS AND CAFÉS

Logo of Bar Jamaica (see p179)

IN GENERAL, MILANESE bars and cafés are places to go for lunch or an aperitif. Breakfast for most Milanese office workers tends to consist of a cappuccino with a croissant, usually consumed at the bar counter. In the Brera quarter, cafés are lively and full of atmosphere. In the early evening they are popular places to relax in with colleagues and friends. Fashions come and go and a café that is "in" one month may be suddenly empty a few months later. To counteract such swings, many Milanese bars have initiated a "happy hour", when drinks are cheaper. Cafés are usually more crowded during the lunch break, when office workers stop for a quick salad or quiche. As well as cafés, Milan also has excellent cake shops or *pasticcerie*, where you can sample pastries and cakes. For a more formal afternoon tea there are tea rooms (*sala da thè*), which are also packed at lunchtime. Many are historic places with period furniture. At the lakes, some of the more enterprising bars and cafés offer entertainment in the evening, either with a piano bar area or a small band.

WHERE TO LOOK

IN MILAN, THERE ARE plenty of places to choose from, whether you are going out for an aperitif or to eat snacks, and the choice will vary from area to area. In the atmospheric Brera quarter the bars usually have tables outside in summer. These places are popular with the fashion set and art students. **Jamaica** (*see p179*) is one established institution, an ideal place for a cocktail before dinner as well as for a chicken salad for lunch or an after-dinner drink. **Sans Égal** (*see p179*) is equally popular; on Sunday afternoons they show football (soccer) live on television, and in the evening the place is filled with young rock music buffs.

Around the Navigli, which is a pedestrian precinct from 8pm on, all the bars and cafés have tables set out outside in summer, and it is possible to forget that Milan is a bustling commercial city altogether.

The Conca del Naviglio area is always busy. There are numerous places to try such as the **Caffè della Pusterla** (*see p179*), located in the renovated medieval walls of the city, the **Tribeca** (*see p178*), which is a good place to try for Sunday brunch, and the **Colonial Fashion Café** (*see p178*), which is deservedly famous for its aperitifs.

In the Ticinese quarter **Coquetel** (*see p178*) is a popular place, especially during happy hour, when the young Milanese get together for an early evening drink.

For those with a sweet tooth who like croissants and

Sans Égal business card (*see p179*)

pastries for breakfast, the place to go is **Angela** (*see p178*), near the Fiera, or **Sissi** (*see p178*), where you can enjoy cream pastries. If you like brunch, a habit that is increasingly popular in Milan, you can choose from among **Atlantique** (*see p178*), a favourite with VIPs, **Speak Easy** (*see p178*), which also serves good salads, and the **Orient Express** (*see p178*), with its appealingly old-fashioned look.

HISTORIC CAFÉS AND BARS

SOME OF MILAN'S most frequented cafés and pastry shops have a long tradition, and are housed in old palazzi with fine interiors. One interesting historic pasticceria is **Sant'Ambroeus** (*see p179*), famous for its traditional panettone. Another ornate setting for breakfast and an aperitif is **Taveggia** (*see p179*), which has been a favourite with the Milanese since 1910. Don't miss **Zucca**

Watching life go by at a café in Piazza del Duomo

in **Galleria** *(see p179)*, (formerly Camparino), a historic, old-fashioned bar and the place where the world-famous Campari drink was invented. Another must is **Cova** *(see p179)*, a café-pastry shop in Via Montenapoleone in business since 1817. In the heart of the fashion district, it is perfect for a cup of mid-afternoon hot chocolate or an evening aperitif. Lastly, the **Bar Magenta** *(see p178)* has been popular year in and year out and is now an evening haunt for the young Milanese crowd.

The historic Cova pastry shop in Via Montenapoleone *(see p179)*

WHAT TO ORDER

A VAST SELECTION of beers, wines, aperitifs, excellent cocktails and non-alcoholic drinks are served in Milanese bars. A wide range of international beers is available as well as the Italian brands Peroni and Moretti. The current fashion is for Latin-American cocktails, which are gradually replacing classics like the Alexander and Bloody Mary. Almost every bar produces its own house aperitif.

A tray of savouries
served with aperitifs

Italy is a wine-producing country and the regions of Piedmont, Lombardy and the Veneto all have extensive areas under vine. Piedmont is best known for its red wines, Barolo and Barbaresco, and the more affordable Barbera and Dolcetto. Good reds are also made in Franciacorta in Lombardy, in the Valtellina and near Verona where Bardolino and Valpolicella are made. White wines from these regions include Gavi, Soave, Bianco di Custoza and Lugana, and there are some very good sparkling wines.

Most bars provide snacks to go with early evening drinks. These may be very simple, such as crisps and peanuts, or may be more elaborate.

For generous snacks, try **Honky Tonks** *(see p178)*, where they serve Ascoli olives and pasta salad, as well as the classic *pinzimoni* dips with raw vegetables and canapés, during happy hour.

USEFUL HINTS

I T IS BEST TO GET AROUND by public transport as parking is notoriously difficult in Milan and popular bars are likely to be surrounded by scooters, motorbikes and cars. Most bars and cafés operate two price tariffs, with higher prices charged for sitting down at a table. Ordering and consuming at the bar counter is the most economical option, but you may prefer to linger and "people-watch".

Many bars operate a "happy hour" from 6:30 to 9:30pm, when drinks such as cocktails are sold at half-price, and as a result these places become extremely crowded. At bars attracting younger people the music is likely to be very loud, so if peace and quiet are needed, "happy hour" may not suit.

BARS IN HOTELS

U NLIKE THE OTHER BARS in town, those in the large hotels are mostly used as venues for business rendez-vous. They are ideal for this purpose, splendidly furnished, and usually quiet. The discretion and privacy creates ideal conditions for discussing business matters.

Among the most distinguished are the bar in the **Hotel Palace** *(see p159)*, with a fountain in the middle, and the Foyer, the bar in the **Hotel Four Seasons** *(see p159)*. The latter is decorated with theatre set designs. Additional charm is provided by an antique fireplace, re-creating the plush atmosphere of old Milanese palazzi.

Interior of one of Milan's chic restaurants

HAPPY HOUR

Colonial Fashion Café

Via De Amicis 12. **Map** 7 A2.
02-89 42 04 01.
8am–2am.

Fitted out with furniture and objects from all over the world, many reminiscent of the colonial style, this café is very popular for its aperitifs and also offers a wide range of delicious snacks.

Coquetel

Via Vetere 14. **Map** 7 B3.
02-836 06 88.
8am–2am.

For years this establishment has been popular with young Milanese. It is especially busy in the summer, when people stroll around the grassy stretches of the adjacent Piazza della Vetra, and drop in for a beer and a chat. The cocktails are very good. Happy hour is from 6:30 to 8:30pm.

Honky Tonks

Via Fratelli Induno, corner of Via Lomazzo. **Map** 2 F1.
02-345 25 62.
6pm–2am.   Sun.

This establishment in a converted garage is famous for the variety and sheer quantity of the snacks offered during happy hour. The counter is laden with heaps of Ascoli olives, croquettes, stuffed focaccia (flat bread) and cured meats of every kind. A good choice of traditional and Caribbean cocktails.

Magenta

Via Carducci 13. **Map** 3 A5 & 7 A1.
02-805 38 08.
8am–3am.   Mon.

This historic café is always in fashion, ideal for a light lunch snack or a beer in the evening. Try an aperitif at the counter with delicious savouries and *bruschetta*. The place has a good atmosphere, and the regulars are smart young Milanese, as well as students from the Università Cattolica and the San Carlo secondary school, both of which are nearby.

Makia-Corso

Sempione 28.
02-33 60 40 12.   12 noon–2am.

This chic cocktail bar-restaurant offers tasty Italian/European dishes at lunch, dinner and Sunday brunch as well as a great selection of snacks served on the original American 1930s bar at cocktail hour.

BRUNCH

Atlantique

Viale Umbria 42. **Map** 8 F4.
02-55 19 39 06.
atlantique@iol.it
 www.paginegialle.it/atlantique
11am–3am.   Mon.

This establishment boasts original, extravagant decor, including a famously huge chandelier. The Sunday brunch attracts many young locals. Atlantique is also a disco and a restaurant.

Orient Express

Via Fiori Chiari 8. **Map** 3 C4.
02-805 62 27.
8am–2am.   Sun eve.

The decor, atmosphere and service are all reminiscent of the good old days, when the famous Orient Express was in its heyday. Bar, restaurant and Sunday brunch.

Speak Easy

Via Castelfidardo 7. **Map** 3 C2.
02-65 36 45.   12 noon–3pm, 7pm–3am Mon–Sat (12 noon–5pm Sun).

"Eat as much as you like" is the motto in this place in the Brera quarter, which offers a tantalizing, varied buffet and fresh salads.

Tribeca

Via Conca del Naviglio 22. **Map** 7 A2.
02-89 42 03 96.
7pm–2am.   Wed.

The owners, including TV host Simona Ventura and star goalkeeper Gianluca Pagliuca, were inspired by the style of the famous New York district, after which their establishment was named. The buffet, with hot and cold dishes, is exceptional. Also on offer, quality *à la carte*.

BREAKFAST

Angela

Via Ruggero di Lauria 15. **Map** 2 D1.
02-34 28 59.   8am–7:30pm (8.30–1.30pm, 3–7pm Sat, Sun).   Mon.

This small pastry shop near the Fiera has a counter where you can pause and enjoy breakfast. Go for the pastries with custard or whipped cream, the warm puff pastry with ricotta cheese and the fresh croissants with hot custard.

Cafeàus

Ripa di Porta Ticinese 27. **Map** 6 D4.
02-89 42 93 56.
7:30am–8:30pm.   Tue.

This charming tearoom is on two floors. Breakfast here on delectable cakes and tarts. The tartlets and biscuits are very tasty. You can also have a lunch-time snack choosing from one of the many quiches they offer.

Leonarduzzi

Via Aurelio Saffi 7. **Map** 2 F5.
02-439 03 02.
7:15am–10pm.   Mon.

This ice cream parlour and pastry shop is famous for its crème patissière. The pastry rolls and cream puffs are delicious. Try the home-made yogurt or vanilla ice cream.

Marchesi

Via Santa Maria alla Porta 13.
Map 7 B1.   02-87 67 30.
7:30am–8pm (8:30am–1pm Sun).
Mon.

This historic pastry shop, in the centre between Via Meravigli and Piazza Cordusio, offers croissants, savouries, salads, a vast assortment of cakes and delicious tartlets.

San Carlo

Via Bandello 21, corner of Corso Magenta. **Map** 6 E1.   02-49 82 030.   6:30am–10:30pm.   Mon.

A stone's throw from Santa Maria delle Grazie, this pastry shop features delicious chocolate-based delicacies and irresistible cream-filled pastries.

Sissi

Piazza Risorgimento 20. **Map** 4 F5 & 8 F1.   02-76 01 46 64.
7am–8pm.   Mon.

A small pastry shop featuring a host of tempting morsels, including custard-filled croissants or raw ham savouries. The pretty courtyard with its pergola is ideal for Sunday afternoon tea.

SNACKS

Coin – The Globe

Piazza Cinque Giornate 1a.
Coin department store, 8th floor.
02-55 18 19 69.
1:30pm–2am.   Sun.

This restaurant, bar and food market, on the top floor of the Coin department store, is similar to those in Harrod's or Macy's. The restaurant offers light lunches and traditional dinners, both high quality. The bar offers fine aperitifs, and you will find delectable delicatessen specialities in the food market.

De Santis

Corso Magenta 9. **Map** 3 A5 & 6 F1.
 02-87 59 68. 11am–3pm, 8pm–1am. Sun.

This compact place specializes in filled rolls. On the walls are banknotes from all over the world and signed photographs of celebrities who have enjoyed choosing from 150 types of sandwich, made with fresh, tasty ingredients.

El Tombon de San Marc

Via San Marco 20. **Map** 3 C3.
02-659 95 07. 12:30–2pm, 5pm–2am. Sun.

A historic establishment that has resisted passing fashions since the 1930s. A warm, intimate atmosphere. Sandwiches and salads as well as excellent soups and various hot and cold dishes.

Latteria di Via Unione

Via dell'Unione 6. **Map** 7 C1.
02-87 44 01.
noon–3:30pm. Sun.

This dairy in the heart of town offers good vegetarian dishes. Get there early, because it is small and usually quite crowded.

Luini

Via Santa Radegonda 16. **Map** 7 C1.
02-86 46 19 17. 8am–2pm, 5–8pm. Sun, Mon pm.

For over 30 years this baker's has featured Puglian *panzerotti* (ravioli) filled with tomatoes and mozzarella.

Salumeria Armandola

Via della Spiga 50. **Map** 4 D4.
02-76 02 16 57.
8am–7pm. Sun.

People drop in here for a quick bite at the counter. The chef's specialities include baked pasta, roasted meat and a range of vegetable and side dishes.

 BARS AND CAFÉS

Biffi

Corso Magenta 87. **Map** 3 A5 & 6 F1.
02-48 00 67 02.
7:30am–8pm. Mon.

On a corner of Piazzale Baracca is this historic bar-pastry shop that dates from the end of the 19th century. Biffi is famous for its milk rolls with cured ham or butter and anchovies. The home-made *panettone*, made every year, is one of the best in Milan.

Caffè della Pusterla

Via De Amicis 24. **Map** 7 A2.
 02-89 40 21 46.
7am–1:30am. Sun.

This charming café is located in the former Pusterla, or minor gate, in Milan's medieval walls. A wide range of cocktails and a fine wine list too. The savouries served with the aperitifs are also very good.

Cova

Via Montenapoleone 8. **Map** 4 D5.
02-76 00 05 78.
8am–8:30pm. Sun.

Founded in 1817, this elegant pastry shop is right in the heart of the fashion district and is an ideal place for a pause during your shopping spree. Cova is well-known for its chocolates and stuffed panettone.

Jamaica

Via Brera 32. **Map** 3 C4.
02-87 67 23.
9am–2am.

This historic Milanese café is the haunt of artists and intellectuals, who flock to this fascinating corner of the Brera quarter. Busy at all hours. Drinks as well as good huge salads.

Sant'Ambroeus

Corso Matteotti 7. **Map** 4 D5.
02-76 00 05 40.
7:45am–8:15pm. Mon.

The atmosphere in what is probably Milan's most elegant pastry shop is plush, with sumptuous window displays and slick service. The tarts, pralines and cakes are famous. There is a lovely tearoom inside and tables outside under the arcade opposite.

Sans Égal

Vicolo Fiori 2. **Map** 3 4B.
02-869 30 96.
10am–3pm. Mon.

In an alley in the Brera quarter, this multi-faceted establishment is a sports pub on Sunday, a small lunch-time restaurant during the week, a drinks bar in the evening and a music pub at night.

Taveggia

Via Visconti di Modrone 2. **Map** 8 E1.
 02-76 02 12 57.
7:30am–8:30pm. Mon.

Another historic Milanese pastry shop, inaugurated in 1910. Great rice pudding, many different types of croissants and various delicacies. Taveggia is also popular for its aperitifs.

Victoria Café

Via Clerici 1. **Map** 3 C5.
02-805 35 98.
5pm–3am.

Behind Piazza della Scala is this Parisian-style *fin de siècle* café with red lamps on the tables, lace curtains and red leather seats. Popular for aperitifs and after dinner.

Zucca in Galleria

Piazza del Duomo 21. **Map** 7 C1.
02-86 46 44 35.
7:30am–8:30pm. Mon.

This famous bar (formerly Camparino) in the Galleria has period decor and tables outside. The world-famous Campari drink was created here in the late 1800s.

 **LAKE BARS & CAFÉS**

Matella (Lake Maggiore)

Via Ruga 1, Pallanza.
0323-50 19 88.
7:30am–midnight. Tue; mid-Oct–mid-Nov.

Bar-pasticceria shop in the 19th-century arcades of Palazzo Municipale featuring *amaretti* (macaroons). Nice tables for a drink outside.

Mimosa (Lake Garda)

Via RV Cornicello 1, Bardolino.
045-621 24 72. 8am–2am.

The barman at Mimosa is a true cocktail "magician". There is also a garden where you can listen to the music from the piano bar while sipping your drink or enjoying good home-made ice cream.

Monti (Lake Como)

Piazza Cavour 21, Como.
031-30 11 65.
7am–1am. Tue.

Bar-pastry shop in lovely Piazza Cavour, with tables outside and a view of the lake. Perfect for sipping tea and tasting pastries in tranquil surroundings.

Vassalli (Lake Garda)

Via San Carlo 84, Salò.
0365-207 52.
8am–10pm. Tue.

This historic bar-pastry shop in Salò has been popular for over a century. The aperitifs and cocktails are good, but Vassalli is most well-known for its desserts, such as the exquisite bacetti di Salò chocolates and the lemon mousse.

For key to symbols *see p291*

SHOPS AND MARKETS

Whether buying or just looking, shopping is a real pleasure in Milan. As well as the window displays of the leading national and international fashion designers – whose outlets are all within the area between Via Manzoni, Via Montenapoleone, Via della Spiga and Via Sant'Andrea, the so-called "quadrilateral" – you can find small shops and stores throughout the city. Shops are generally smart and stylish, especially in the city centre, as good design is highly regarded in Italy, and Milan is one of the most affluent cities. For those who are interested in interior design there is plenty of choice among the specialist shops, while lovers of antiques will love the Brera and Navigli quarters, where regular outdoor antique markets are held. Milan also has some excellent *pasticcerie*, where you can purchase authentic delicacies and traditional Milanese confectionery. At the lakes the choice is widest in the bigger towns, and includes clothes shops, craft shops and wine shops selling local produce.

Shopping in Milan

OPENING HOURS

Shops in Milan are usually open from 9:30am to 1pm and then from 3:30 to 7:30pm. However, many shops in the city centre and the department stores stay open all day, without a break, and major bookshops stay open until 11pm.

Shops are closed on Sunday and Monday mornings, except over Christmas, when they are usually open every day of the week. Food shops, on the other hand, close on Monday afternoon, with the exception of supermarkets.

During the summer holiday period, shops generally close for most of August, apart from the department stores which maintain their normal opening hours, even during this rather inactive month.

The Coin department store in Piazza Cinque Giornate

DEPARTMENT STORES

In common with other Italian towns, there are not many department stores in Milan. One of the most central is **La Rinascente**, which is open on Monday mornings and stays open until 10:00pm. Opposite the Duomo, it is perhaps the most prestigious department store in the city. Over eight floors everything from clothing, perfumes, toys and stationery is sold. The restaurant has a view of the Duomo and an exhibition space for art shows.

In Piazza Cinque Giornate there is the **Coin**, with quality products at medium-range prices, including clothes and household goods. **Upim**, in Piazza San Babila, is more downmarket and sells clothes and various articles at really low prices. Lastly, there is the **Centro Bonola**, a huge shopping centre that includes a huge Coop supermarket and an Upim department store, as well as 60 shops and numerous bars and cafés.

MARKETS

Italy's outdoor markets are always fun and Milan has some good specialist markets. The Mercatone dell'Antiquariato, held on the last Sunday of the month at the Alzaia Naviglio Grande, is an extensive antiques market with more than four hundred exhibitors offering antique objects and bric-a-brac. Every Saturday at the Darsena on Viale d'Annunzio there is the Fiera di Senigaglia, where you can find almost anything, from clothing to records and ethnic handicrafts.

The Mercato dell'Antiquariato in the Brera area, between Via Fiori Chiari and Via Madonnina, is also worth a visit. Every third Saturday of

Window shopping in fashionable Via Montenapoleone

The Fiera di Senigaglia along the Darsena

the month antiques, books, postcards and jewellery go on sale here. Lastly, don't miss the Mercato del Sabato on Viale Papiniano, which offers, among other things, clothes worn by models during the fashion shows.

FOOD SHOPS

GOURMETS WILL appreciate the well-stocked Milanese delicatessens and food shops. Perhaps the most famous is **Peck**, which since 1883 has been synonymous with fine food and delicacies. It is a large firm with 150 employees, and the shops are known for the high quality of the produce and the delicious recipes. Besides the main delicatessen in Via Spadari, selling hams, salami and cheeses of all kinds, there is also a popular Peck *rosticceria* in Via Cantù where you can buy the best ready-made dishes in Milan.

Corso Vittorio Emanuele, a popular street for shopping

Another top-quality establishment is **Il Salumaio** on Via Montenapoleone, which is both a delicatessen and a restaurant offering international, impeccably prepared and presented dishes. One of Italy's most famous chefs, **Gualtiero Marchesi**, now has an outlet where you can purchase his latest selections.

For those who love tea and infusions, **Gourmet House** is a paradise: 120 types of tea, high-quality blends, and everything you need to serve them in the best traditional manner.

Garbagnati is the best-known baker in town, and is especially known for panettone. Garbagnati have been making this traditional Milanese cake with a natural leavening process since 1937.

Go to **Fabbrica di Marroni Giovanni Galli** for sweet things; this shop has made the best marrons glacés in Milan since 1898. Equally famous is **L'Angolo di Marco**, in the Brera quarter, a delightful *pasticceria* (pastry shop) offering delectable treats of all kinds. At **Ranieri** they make a panettone with pineapple, and sweets and pastries with fresh fruit. Last but not least, **Marchesi** is the best place to go for meltingly good chocolates, both milk and dark.

SALES

SHOPS IN MILAN hold sales *(saldi)* twice a year: in early July and then in January, immediately after Epiphany. Discounts may even be as much as 70 per cent, but be wary, and check goods carefully before you buy, if the discount looks over-generous. Shopowners may use the sales as an excuse to get rid of old leftover stock or defective clothing.

Clothing and Accessories

THE CLOTHES SHOPS OF MILAN are known all over the world because of their associations with famous Italian fashion designers. The city centre fashion district is stormed each year by Italians and foreigners alike in search of the latest top fashion items. However, Milan is not just about expensively priced goods, and the true secret of pleasurable shopping can lie in discovering the less well-known shops which offer good prices and still work to high standards of quality.

CLASSIC CLOTHING

WOMEN IN SEARCH OF impeccable classic clothing for themselves and their children should seek out the **Pupi Solari** shop, which also makes wedding dresses to order. Lovers of colourful sports clothes, on the other hand, will be more than satisfied at **Urrah**. Elegant children's apparel and shoes can be found at **Gusella**, while **Host** features men's sports and informal clothes. Elegant, stylish clothes for men can be found at **Bardelli** or **Gemelli**, and **Brigatti** and **Ravizza** are ideal shops for those who prefer classic wear with a casual touch. **Ermenegildo Zegna** is the place to go for stylish men's classic clothing made of the best quality fabrics. **Boggi** offers both classic and sports clothes at reasonable prices. Lastly, the recently renovated **Neglia** has two floors filled with fashionable menswear, from clothing to accessories.

DESIGNER WEAR

ALMOST ALL THE SHOPS that feature the latest in top designer clothes are in or near the city centre *(see pp106–7)*. **Hugo Boss** is a recently opened shop of some size, selling elegant clothes for men. **Giò Moretti**, an institution in Via della Spiga, features articles by the top names as well as pieces by up-and-coming fashion designers. **Marisa** is a shop specializing in Italian and foreign designers and there is always something new and interesting, while

Banner has clothes for the young and sophisticated. **Biffi** is famous for its wide-ranging selection of top designer clothes.

Among non-Italian fashion designers there is **Calvin Klein**, who is growing more and more popular, and **Jil Sander**. **Guess**, the well-known New York designer, offers the latest lines.

The diffusion lines of the most famous designers can be found in the fashion district, where the main names have their own branches, from **Miu Miu** to **Gieffeffe**,

D&G and **Emporio Armani**. Lastly, **Antonio Fusco** attracts an enthusiastic clientele.

ACCESSORIES

FOR GOOD QUALITY sports shoes there is **Tod's**. Less well-known but equally good is the **Stivaleria Savoia**, which features classic styles that can also be made to measure. **Guido Pasquali** is proud of his stylish traditional and modern shoes.

Ferragamo, the Italian designer known all over the world for his top fashion styles, offers elegant classic shoes. More bizarre and unconventional articles can be found at **La Vetrina**, while **Camper** features original shoes known for their fine workmanship. **Garlando** offers a vast range of styles and colours that aim at the young people's market.

Crocodile, ostrich and leather handbags can be found at **Colombo**, while **Valextra** features high-quality

SIZE CHART

Children's clothing

Italian	2–3	4–5	6–7	8–9	10–11	12	14	14+ (age)
British	2–3	4–5	6–7	8–9	10–11	12	14	14+ (age)
American	2–3	4–5	6–6X	7–8	10	12	14	16 (size)

Children's shoes

Italian	24	25½	27	28	29	30	32	33	34
British	7½	8	9	10	11	12	13	1	2
American	7½	8½	9½	10½	11½	12½	13½	1½	2½

Women's dresses, coats and skirts

Italian	38	40	42	44	46	48	50	52
British	6	8	10	12	14	16	18	20
American	4	6	8	10	12	14	16	18

Women's blouses and sweaters

Italian	40	42	44	46	48	50	52
British	30	32	34	36	38	40	42
American	6	8	10	12	14	16	18

Women's shoes

Italian	36	37	38	39	40	41
British	3	4	5	6	7	8
American	5	6	7	8	9	10

Men's clothing

Italian	44	46	48	50	52	54	56	58
British	34	36	38	40	42	44	46	48
American	34	36	38	40	42	44	46	48

Men's shirts

Italian	36	38	39	41	42	43	44	45
British	14	15	15½	16	16½	17	17½	18
American	14	15	15½	16	16½	17	17½	18

Men's shoes

Italian	40	41	42	43	44	45	46
British	7	7½	8	9	10	11	12
American	7½	8	8½	9½	10½	11	11½

suitcases and briefcases. For something original head for the **Atelier Anne Backhaus**, where they make handbags and accessories using different materials.

The **Mandarina Duck** shops have stylish sports bags, luggage, casual handbags and knapsacks. **Borsalino** is the place to go for top-quality classic hats. **Giusy Bresciani** has more original designs, as well as gloves and other highly stylish accessories. **Cappelleria Melegari** deal in hats imported from all over the world and they can

do hat alterations in their workshop if a customer requires. A wide range of ties and knitwear can be found at **Fedeli** and at **Oxford**, where you can also find good ranges of men's shirts.

JEWELLERY

E LEGANT, CLASSIC JEWELLERY is featured at **Calderoni**, which has designed jewels for smart Milanese women since 1840, and **Cusi**, which has been in business since 1885. **Faraone** is known for high class jewellery, while Mario

Buccellati has gold and silver pieces of elegant workmanship. Another historic shop is **Bulgari**, known for its beautiful jewellery and watches. **Merù** features original and modern handcrafted jewels. Jewellery dating from the 19th century to 1950 is to be found at **Mirella Denti**. For modern costume jewellery, you will find a good collection at **Donatella Pellini**, and **Sharra Pagano** also has a good choice of the latest costume jewellery and jewellery styles, made of original materials.

DIRECTORY

CLASSIC CLOTHING

Bardelli
Corso Magenta 13.
02-86 45 07 34.

Boggi
Via Durini 28.
02-76 00 55 82.

Brigatti
Corso Venezia 15.
02-76 00 02 73.

Ermenegildo Zegna
Via Verri 3.
02-76 00 64 37.

Gemelli
Corso Vercelli 16.
02-48 00 00 57.

Gusella
Corso V Emanuele II 37b.
02-79 65 33.

Host
Piazza Tommaseo 2.
02-43 60 85.

Neglia
Corso Venezia 2.
02-79 52 31.

Pupi Solari
Piazza Tommaseo 2.
02-46 33 25.
W www.paginegialle.it/pupisolari

Ravizza
Via Hoepli 3.
02-869 38 53.
W www.ravizza1871.com

Urrah
Via Solferino 3.
02-86 43 85.

DESIGNER WEAR

Antonio Fusco
Via Sant'Andrea 11.
02-76 00 29 57.

Banner
Via Sant'Andrea 8a.
02-76 00 43 61.
W bannermi.it.

Biffi
Corso Genova 6.
02-83 11 70 52.

Calvin Klein
Via Durini 14.
02-76 00 41 52.

D&G
Corso Venezia 7.
02-76 00 40 91.

Emporio Armani
Via Durini 24.
02-76 00 73 48.

Gieffeffe
Corso Venezia 2.
02-76 00 40 72.

Giò Moretti
Via della Spiga 4.
02-76 00 31 86.

Guess
Piazza San Babila 4b.
02-76 39 20 70.

Hugo Boss
Corso Matteotti 11.
02-76 39 46 67.

Jil Sander
Via P Verri 6.
02-777 29 91.

Marisa
Via Sant'Andrea 1.
02-76 00 14 16.

Miu Miu
Corso Venezia 3.
02-76 00 17 99.

ACCESSORIES

Atelier Anne Backhaus
Corso di Porta Vigentina 10.
02-58 30 27 93.

Borsalino
Corso V Emanuele II 5.
02-89 01 54 36.

Camper
Via Torino 15.
02-805 71 85.
W www.camper.es

Cappelleria Melegari
Via Paolo Sarpi 19.
02-31 20 94.

Colombo
Via della Spiga 9.
02-76 02 35 87.

Fedeli
Via Montenapoleone 8.
02-76 02 33 92.

Ferragamo
Via Montenapoleone 3.
02-76 00 00 54
@ milanwstore@salvatoreferragamo.it

Garlando
Via Madonnina 2.
02-87 46 65.

Giusy Bresciani
Via Morone 8.
02-76 00 42 30.
@ 1stfloorgiusybres@aiol.it

Guido Pasquali
Via Sant'Andrea 1.
02-78 35 08.

La Vetrina
Via Statuto 4.
02-65 42 78.

Mandarina Duck
Corso Europa
02-78 22 10.

Oxford
Via Verri 2.
02-76 02 34 04.

Stivaleria Savoia
Via Petrarca 7.
02-46 34 24.

Tod's
Via della Spiga 22.
02-76 00 24 23.

Valextra
Piazza San Babila 1.
02-76 00 29 89.

JEWELLERY

Bulgari
Via della Spiga 6.
02-77 70 01.

Calderoni
Via Montenapoleone 23.
02-76 00 12 93.
W www.paginegialle.it/calderoni-oz

Cusi
Via Montenapoleone 21/a.
02-76 02 19 77.

Donatella Pellini
Via Santa Maria alla Porta 13.
02-72 01 05 69.

Faraone Tiffany
Via Montenapoleone 7a.
02-76 01 36 56.

Mario Buccellati
Via Montenapoleone 4.
02-78 09 03.
W www.paginegialle.it/buccellati

Merù
Via Solferino 3.
02-86 46 07 00.

Mirella Denti
Via Montenapoleone 29.
02-76 02 25 44.

Sharra Pagano
Corso Garibaldi 35.
02-29 51 41 73.

Design and Antiques

MILAN IS THE ACKNOWLEDGED CAPITAL of modern design and a paradise for enthusiasts, who can spend their free time browsing in the numerous shops and showrooms throughout the city. Every spring the Salone del Mobile, the famous Milan furniture fair, attracts all the top designers and trade buyers. During the fair, many of Milan's interior design shops extend their opening hours and put on various events for trade experts and visitors.

INTERIOR AND INDUSTRIAL DESIGN

AT **De Padova**, elegant, studiously avant-garde objects for the home, including furniture, are made of the finest materials. For stylish lighting there is **Artemide**, which is known for its superb modern designs, created by well-known names, and **Flos**, in Corso Monforte, which features sleek ultra-modern lighting of all kinds.

Fontana Arte is a kind of gallery and a leading light in the field of interior design. Founded in 1933, its displays include splendid lamps, mostly crystal.

Da Driade, located in the heart of the fashion district, features objects created in the last 30 years which have since become collectors' items. **Galleria Colombari**, on the other hand, offers modern antiques as well as contemporary design objects. **Spazio Cappellini** is a showroom for informal and elegant furniture, while **Zani & Zani** features interior design accessories, displayed in a chessboard pattern to show off the individual objects at their best. **Kartell** stocks various articles for the home and the office, while **Arform** specializes in Scandinavian design. **Venini** is an institution in the production of blown Venetian glass vases, while **Barovier & Toso** offer extremely high-quality chandeliers and vases, and **Cassina** features products by leading designers. **Eclectica** offers its customers individual and extravagant design articles

from the 1930s and 1940s, as well as imported and ethnic products and various handicrafts.

Koivu, in Corso Europa, specializes in designer furniture and interior design pieces of Scandinavian inspiration, mostly made of wood. Those who love stylish period furniture should stop by **L'Utile e il Dilettevole**, where 19th-century taste prevails, and **Dimorae**, where the furniture is beautifully displayed in welcoming settings.

San Patrignano Casa d'Arte stocks furniture, wallpaper, and genuinely handcrafted fabrics and embroidery for the modern home.

MEGASTORES

THE MEGASTORE, where you can purchase almost anything under the sun, from the tiniest household article to a large piece of furniture, is now becoming the rage in Milan as well as in other Italian cities. These large establishments *(empori)* are usually open late in the evening and on Sunday and are frequently able to offer their customers various additional services.

High Tech was one of the first to offer this new mode of shopping. Come here for exotic furniture, fabrics and wallpaper for the home, kitchenware, perfume and accessories imported from all over the world.

B612 is a large center dedicated entirely to travel and travelers, the only such center in Italy. Clothing and equipment are found in two big areas – the warm countries area and the cold

countries area. In addition, there is a bookshop, a library and a travel agency, as well as a cyberbar, where you can surf the net and have a coffee.

10 Corso Como is an unusual place featuring designer articles and objects from the Middle and Far East.

The ultramodern and unconventional **Moroni Gomma** offers boots, raincoats, kitchenware and interior design and household articles, all made of plastic or rubber *(gomma)*.

FABRICS AND LINEN FOR THE HOME

FOR ELEGANCE and high-class interior design, Milan cannot be beaten. There are many shops which specialize in fabrics and linen which can be made to order. **Etro**, in Via Pontaccio, is famous for its fabrics and stylish accessories. In the same street is **KA International**, a sales outlet for a Spanish chain of fabric shops, offering excellent value for money. Among the many other articles, **Lisa Corti** features original Indian cotton and cheesecloth fabrics with floral and stripe decorative patterns. **Mimma Gini** has characteristic fabrics from India, Japan and Indonesia; **Castellini & C** is known mostly for its linen articles. **Haas** is a historic shop that has sold high-quality fabrics and rugs since 1811.

Original and exclusive fabrics can be found at **Fede Cheti**. Among the shops featuring household linen, **Pratesi**, in the heart of the fashion district, is known for its classic and elegant ranges, while **Jesurum** is famous for its embroidered materials and fine lace cloth. **Zucchi** is a very well-known name in Italy for beautifully made fabrics. Bedlinen and table linen in modern and practical styles are featured at **Mirabello**. **Telerie Ghidoli** is an institution in Milan: five storeys entirely given over to linen at reasonable prices.

Since 1860 **Frette** has been a guarantee of high quality bedlinen, tablelinen and articles for the bathroom such as towels and bathrobes. They also offer delivery throughout the world as well as advice and help from an interior designer.

ANTIQUES

MILAN HAS NUMEROUS antique shops and workshops. Subert, in Via della Spiga, specializes in 18th-century furniture and scientific instruments. In the same street is **Mauro Brucoli**, where they specialize in 19th-century furniture

and objects as well as splendid jewellery dating from the same period. At Franco Sabatelli, which is also a furniture restorers, you can find picture frames of all periods, some even dating to the 16th century.

Lovers of 18th- and 19th-century British furniture must head for Old English Furniture, which also has a fine stock of medical and scientific instruments. If you prefer the unusual and even bizarre object, try **L'Oro dei Farlocchi**, a historic antique gallery in the Brera area.

Blanchaert & Arosio is one of Milan's best-known shops for antique glass, with Murano chandeliers and Venini vases. At **Antichità Caiati** you will find 17th- and 18th-century Italian paintings, and valuable canvases are also sold at **Antichità Gianetti**, as well as majolica, 18th-century Oriental screens and 16th–19th-century furniture. **Carlo Orsi** have exclusive antiques, including bronze sculpture, splendid paintings, fine furniture, ivory pieces and precious stones.

DIRECTORY

INTERIOR AND INDUSTRIAL DESIGN

Arform
Via della Moscova 22.
02-655 46 91.

Artemide
Corso Monforte 19.
02-76 00 69 30.

Barovier & Toso
Via Manzoni 40.
02-76 00 09 06.

Cassina
Via Durini 16.
02-76 02 07 58.

Da Driade
Via Manzoni 30.
02-76 02 30 98.

De Padova
Corso Venezia 14.
02-77 72 01.

Dimorae
Corso Magenta 69.
02-48 01 18 03.

Eclectica
Corso Garibaldi 3.
02-87 61 94.

Flos
Corso Monforte 7.
02-79 45 59.

Fontana Arte
Via Santa Margherita 4.
02-86 46 45 51.

Galleria Colombari
Via Solferino 37.
02-29 00 15 51.

Kartell
Via Turati, corner of Corso Porta 1.
02-659 79 16.

Koivu
Corso Europa 12.
02-76 02 08 21.

L'Utile e il Dilettevole
Via della Spiga 46.
02-76 00 84 20.

San Patrignano Casa d'Arte
Via Bigli 3.
02-76 01 40 29.

Spazio Cappellini
Via Statuto 12.
02-29 01 33 53.

Venini
Via Montenapoleone 9.
02-76 00 05 39.

Zani & Zani
Via San Damiano (corner of Corso Venezia).
02-79 80 96.

MEGASTORES

10 Corso Como
Corso Como 10.
02-29 00 26 74.

B612
Via Ludovico Muratori 13/13A.
02-54 12 12 70.

High Tech
Piazza XXV Aprile 12.
02-624 11 01.

Moroni Gomma
Corso Matteotti 14.

02-79 62 20.
Via Giusti 10.
02-33 10 65 65.

Mondadori Multicenter
Via Marghera 28.
02-48 04 71.

FABRICS AND LINEN FOR THE HOME

Etro
Via Montenapoleone 5
Via Bigli 2
02-76 00 54 50.
posta@etro.it

Fede Cheti
Via Manzoni 23.
02-86 46 40 05.

Frette
Via Montenapoleone 21.
02-76 00 37 91.
Via Manzoni 11.
02-86 44 33.
Corso Vercelli 23–25.
02-498 97 56.

Haas
Via Solferino 7.
02-805 79 26.

Jesurum
Via Verri 4.
02-76 01 50 45.
www.jesurum.it

KA International
Via Pontaccio 3.
02-86 45 12 44.

Lisa Corti
Via Conchetta 6.
02-58 10 00 31.

Mimma Gini
Via Santa Croce 21.

02-89 40 07 22.
02-89 42 21 47.

Mirabello
Via Montebello, corner of Via San Marco.
02-65 48 87.

Pratesi
Via Montenapoleone 27/e.
02-76 01 27 55.

Telerie Ghidoli
Piazza Fontana 1.
02-80 23 121

Zucchi
Via Ugo Foscolo 4.
02-89 01 14 14.

ANTIQUES

Antichità Caiati
Via del Gesù 17.
02-79 48 66.

Antichità Gianetti
Via Gesù 7.
02-76 00 83 62.

Blanchaert & Arosio
Via Nirone 19.
02-86 45 17 00.

Carlo Orsi
Via Bagutta 14.
02-76 00 22 14.

Mauro Brucoli
Via della Spiga 46.
02-76 02 37 67.

L'Oro dei Farlocchi
Via Madonnina opposite No. 5
02-86 05 89.

Books and Gifts

Milan is well supplied with good bookshops, many offering foreign-language publications as well as books in Italian. The larger bookstores in the centre are usually open late in the evening and also on Sunday. They have plenty of space where you can quietly browse through the books on display at your leisure. In addition there are plenty of small bookshops, many stocking rare or out-of-print books. Around the University there are many specialist bookshops. Music fans can head for the megastores and the many music shops in town, while the specialist gift article shops will help those interested in buying presents to take home.

BOOKSHOPS

The **Mondadori Multicenter** is centrally located, open every day until 11pm and on Sunday as well. It spreads out over two floors. On the ground floor, next to the newspapers and periodicals (including international ones), are the new releases, both fiction and non-fiction for visitors who read Italian. The mezzanine contains books of all kinds.

Computer buffs should head for the recently opened **Mondadori Informatica**, which is a paradise for people interested in IT.

Another large, well-stocked and very popular bookstore is **Rizzoli** in the Galleria Vittorio Emanuele, which has a fine arts section.

Feltrinelli has four bookshops in Milan, which are open every day including Sunday. The brand-new main bookshop in Piazza del Duomo, almost 500 sq m (5,380 sq ft) in size, has over 60,000 books and offers various services, such as wedding lists, to its customers.

Five-floor **Hoepli** is a serious bookstore steeped in tradition. It specializes particularly in scientific publications and subscriptions to foreign periodicals. The **American Bookstore** and **English Bookshop** specialize in English-language literature and the **Libreria Francese Ile de France** has a good selection of publications in French. For second-hand books, go to **Il Libraccio**, which has a number of branches. Besides school textbooks, it has various books, comic books and even CDs.

A small shop where opera fans can find interesting publications is **Il Trovatore**. Out-of-print editions, scores and libretti are offered together with valuable rarities such as facsimiles of scores by Donizetti or Verdi with the composers' signatures. This music store also provides a catalogue of its publications. **Books Import** specializes in art show catalogues and art history books, and books on architecture, design and photography, almost all of which are published abroad. Their section on hobbies is particularly good.

L'Archivolto, which specializes mostly in architecture and design, also has a section on antiques with books from the 1500s to the present. This shop also has modern design objects on display. The **Libreria della Triennale** also deals mainly in books on architecture and design, but has a well-stocked children's book section as well.

Art lovers will also enjoy the **Libreria Bocca**, in the Galleria Vittorio Emanuele. The **Libreria dei Ragazzi** is the only bookshop in town entirely given over to children's books, with games and educational books. The **Libreria del Mare**, as its name suggests, offers a wide range of prints and books on the sea (*il mare*), while the **Libreria Milanese** has books (including photographic ones), prints, posters and gadgets concerning Milan. **Milano Libri**, always up with the latest trends, has a section on high fashion and another on photography. **Luoghi e Libri** specializes in travel books, novels and non-fiction, and the **Libreria Magenta** offers a good range of foreign newspapers and periodicals. Comic-book fans should visit **La Borsa del Fumetto**, which also has rare and old editions.

Besides travel guides, the **Libreria dell'Automobile** has handbooks and illustrated books on cars and motorcycles. **Libreria dello Sport** features books and videos on all sports, and **Libreria dello Spettacolo** specializes in theatre and biographies of famous actors and actresses.

MUSIC, CDS & RECORDS

Music lovers will revel in the **Virgin Megastore**, which stocks a huge quantity of compact discs, music cassettes and video cassettes, as well as books, periodicals and gadgets concerning music. This store also sells tickets to concerts.

Another good music shop is the **Ricordi Media Store**, which has parts and scores as well as books on composers and their works. It is open even on Sunday (until 8pm), offers discounts on items at least once a month and also has a ticket office for concerts. **Messaggerie Musicali**, on three floors, boasts a vast range of records, tapes and CDs as well as a well-stocked section with books on music in various foreign languages.

The **Bottega Discantica** is a paradise for lovers of opera and church and symphonic music. **Supporti Fonografici** is a shop with a British flavour: besides the latest trends in music, there are records that are almost impossible to find elsewhere and a wide range of Italian and foreign periodicals as well as rare music-themed T-shirts. **Buscemi Dischi** is one of the best-stocked and low-priced music shops and is especially recommended for jazz lovers.

Rasputin, in Piazza Cinque Giornate, specializes in rock music, particularly from American bands, and offers a good assortment of the latest chart releases at reasonable prices.

GIFTS

VISITORS IN SEARCH of gifts would do well to try **Fiorucci** to start with. This large and very centrally located store sells everything from clothing to costume jewellery, household goods, gadgets and fun items.

If circumstances call for a more sophisticated gift, head for **Albrizzi**, a famous book-binder's dealing in quality notebooks, albums and other handcrafted articles. Another good alternative in this field is **La Piccola Legatoria**, where visitors will find excellent handcrafted stationery, including writing paper and cardboard articles.

Smokers will love **Lorenzi** which, besides a vast assortment of knives, scissors and toilet and gift articles, has high-quality pipes and accessories for smokers. Again for

the smoker, **Savinelli** is an institution in Milan. Since 1876 it has sold pipes of all kinds, at all prices, up to unique and extremely expensive ones.

For toys or games, try the **Città del Sole**, which stocks Milan's largest assortment of traditional wooden toys, educational games and board games for both children and adults. **Movo**, in business since 1932, is the domain of model-making enthusiasts, while **Pergioco** specializes in video games and DVDs, as well as computer games.

DIRECTORY

BOOKSHOPS

American Bookstore
Via Camperio 16.
02-72 02 00 30.
www.paginegialle.it/Americabook

Books Import
Via Maiocchi 11.
02-29 40 04 78.

English Bookshop
Via Mascheroni 12.
02-469 44 68.
www.yesplease.it

Feltrinelli
Via Manzoni 12.
02-76 00 03 86.
Via Foscolo 1–3.
02-86 99 69 03.
Corso Buenos Aires 20.
02-29 53 17 90.
Via P Sarpi 15.
02-349 02 41.

Hoepli
Via Hoepli 5.
02-86 48 71.

Il Libraccio
Via Arconati 16.
02-55 19 08 97.
Via Corsico 9.
02-837 23 98.
Via Santatecla 5.
02-87 83 99.
Viale Vittorio Veneto 22.
02-655 51 87.
www.libraccio.it

Il Trovatore
Via Carlo Poerio 3.
02-76 00 16 56.

L'Archivolto
Via Marsala 2.
02-65 95 552.

La Borsa del Fumetto
Via Lecco 16.
02-29 51 38 83.

Libreria Bocca
Galleria Vittorio Emanuele II 12.
02-86 46 23 21.

Libreria dei Ragazzi
Via Unione 3.
02-72 00 41 66.
www.librariadeiragazzi.it

Libreria del Mare
Via Broletto 28.
02-86 46 44 26.
www.librariadelmare.it

Libreria dell'Automobile
Corso Venezia 43.
02-76 00 66 24.

Libreria della Triennale
Viale Alemagna 6.
02-72 02 35 50.

Libreria dello Spettacolo
Via Terraggio 11.
02-86 45 17 30.

Libreria dello Sport
Via Carducci 9.
02-805 53 55.
www.librariadellosport.it

Libreria Francese Ile de France
Via San Pietro all'Orto 10.
02-76 00 17 67.

Libreria Magenta
Corso Magenta 65.
02-481 61 50.

Libreria Milanese
Via Meravigli 18.
02-86 45 31 54.

Luoghi e Libri
Via Mameli 8.
02-738 83 70.
Corso di porta Ticinese 46
02-58 10 13 10.

Milano Libri
Via Verdi 2.
02-87 58 71.

Mondadori
Corso Vittorio Emanuele II 34.
02-76 00 58 33.

Mondadori Informatica
Via Berchet 2.
02-80 62 71.
Corso di Porta Vittoria.
02-55 19 22 10.

Rizzoli
Piazza Cavour
02-65 95 682.
Galleria Vittorio Emanuele II 79.
02-86 46 10 71.

MUSIC, CDs & RECORDS

Bottega Discantica
Via Nirone 5.
02-86 29 66.

Buscemi Dischi
Corso Magenta 31.
02-86 45 52 65.
www.paginegialle.it/buscemi

Messaggerie Musicali
Galleria del Corso 2.
02-76 05 54 31.

Rasputin
Piazza Cinque Giornate 10.
02-55 01 64 28.

Ricordi Media Store
Galleria Vittorio Emanuele II

02-86 46 02 72.

Supporti Fonografici
Corso di Porta Ticinese 100.
02-89 40 04 20.
www.supportifono.com

Virgin Megastore
Piazza del Duomo 8.
02-72 00 33 54.

GIFTS

Fiorucci
Galleria Passarella 1.
02-76 00 32 76.

BOOKBINDING

Albrizzi
Via Bagutta 8.
02-76 00 12 18.

La Piccola Legatoria
Via Palermo 11.
02-72 02 29 36.

ARTICLES FOR SMOKERS

Lorenzi
Via Montenapoleone 9.
02-76 02 05 93.
www.glorenzi.com

Savinelli
Via Orefici 2.
02-87 66 60.

TOYS AND GAMES

Città del Sole
Via Orefici 13.
02-86 46 16 83.
www.paginegialle.it/citta-oz

Movo
Piazzale Principessa Clotilde 8.
02-655 48 36.

Pergioco
Via San Prospero 1.
02-86 46 34 14.

ENTERTAINMENT IN MILAN

THE ENTERTAINMENT SCENE is lively in Milan and there is plenty of choice for those who love night life, given the hundreds of clubs that animate the Brera and Navigli quarters in particular. Pubs, discos and nightclubs with live music, as well as late-night bistros, are filled every evening with people who come from all corners of Italy. The theatres offer the public a rich and varied programme: La Scala represents the top in opera and ballet. Major music concerts are usually held in the Palavobis arena (formerly

Ronaldo, star player of the Inter club

PalaTrussardi) or at the Filaforum at Assago. Milan is equally generous to sports lovers. Every Sunday from September to May the San Siro stadium plays host to the matches of local football teams Inter and Milan. It also stages national and international championship matches. Sometimes matches are also scheduled during the week. Horse racing takes place all year round at the Ippodromo racecourse. Milan's many sports and leisure clubs cater to those who like to play as well as watch sports.

INFORMATION

IN ORDER TO FIND OUT the latest information on the many evening events in Milan, check the listings in *Vivi-Milano*, a Wednesday supplement to the newspaper *Corriere della Sera*. Every Thursday the daily paper *La Repubblica* publishes *Tutto Milano*, which is also full of useful information.

The APT tourist offices in Piazza del Duomo and the Stazione Centrale (main railway station) provide free copies of the brochure *Milano Mese*, with all the information you need concerning art shows, light and classical music concerts, jazz and other cultural events in town. You can also use the Internet and log on to the *Inmilano* website: (www.rcs.-it/quotidiani/inmilano/-

benven.htm) for information on Milanese nightlife, exhibitions, cultural events and other forms of entertainment.

BUYING TICKETS

TICKETS FOR THE THEATRE and various concerts can be purchased in specialist booking offices such as **Ricordi Box Office**, **La Prevendita**, at the Virgin Megastore, and at **Last Minute Tour** (inside the Fiorucci store) or **Ticket web** (telephone reservations and online www.ticketweb.it). **Prenoticket** accepts telephone reservations only, while for La Scala you have to go to the box office at the theatre or book through the theatre Internet website (http://lascala.milano.it).

Tickets for football (soccer) matches can be purchased directly from the stadium box

Alcatraz, one of the trendiest discos in Milan (see p191)

offices. Alternatively tickets for Inter matches can be bought from the Banca Popolare di Milano, Banca Briantea, Banca Agricola Milanese and Milano Ticket. Tickets for AC Milan matches are sold by Cariplo bank, various businesses (40 bars and shops) and Milan Point, whose listings are shown at the Milan Club.

Tickets for the annual Formula 1 Grand Prix, held in September at the Autodromo Nazionale in Monza, are sold at the **Automobile Club Milano**, **Acitour Lombardia** and **AC Promotion**. The Monza race track is usually open to visitors at weekends when there are no other events going on. Cars and motorbikes can be driven on the track when it is free. For more information, inquire at the **Autodromo Nazionale**.

The Last Minute Tour ticket office at Fiorucci

The Filaforum at Assago, a sports arena also used for concerts *(see p191)*

CHILDREN

FAMILIES visiting Milan with children should be warned that the city does not have extensive specialist entertainment available for them. However, some of the museums and galleries are quite child-friendly. To stimulate the young imagination and provide lots of interesting educational material, there are the Planetarium *(see p120)*, the Science and Technology Museum *(see p88)* or the Civic Aquarium *(see p68)*.

As far as shows and spectacles are concerned, the **Nuovo Arti** motion picture theatre shows children's films, and the **Teatro delle Marionette** is a children's puppet theatre.

If on the other hand you opt for pure entertainment, the amusement park at the **Idroscalo** is a good choice.

From June to September **Aquatica** is a popular place to take children: slides, pools and shows make this aquatic park a children's paradise that will entertain both youngsters and adults alike.

Children over the age of 12 who are keen on video games can try out one of the numerous amusement arcades in the city. One that comes strongly recommended is **Astragames**. This establishment is very centrally located, and its two floors are open all year round, from 10am to 1am.

A good place for entertaining smaller children only is the **Play Planet**, a recreation centre where they can let off steam and use up a lot of energy or become involved in some of the creative workshops on offer. Play Planet is open all year round and there are also two rooms where birthday parties can be held.

In sunny weather there are always local public parks to take children to. Except for the Parco Sempione, which is used mostly by adults for sports activities or to walk their dogs, the most suitable parks for children are the ones at Porta Venezia and Via Palestro, where theoretically no one is allowed to enter unless accompanied by a child.

Young tourists enjoying an ice cream

DIRECTORY

TICKET AGENCIES

AC Promotion
Piazza Eleonora Duse 1.
02-76 00 25 74.

Acitour Lombardia
Corso Venezia 43.
02-76 00 63 50.

Autodromo Nazionale
Parco di Monza.
039-248 21.

Automobile Club Milano
Corso Venezia 43.
02-774 51.

La Prevendita
Virgin Megastore,
Piazza Duomo 8.
02-72 00 33 70.

La Scala
02-86 07 75.

Last Minute Tour
At Fiorucci (no telephone reservations taken).

Ticket Web
Via Cappucini 11.
www.ticketweb.it

Prenoticket
02-542 71.

Ricordi Box Office
Galleria Vittorio Emanuele II.
02-869 06 83.

CHILDREN

Aquatica
Via G Airaghi 61.
02-48 20 01 34.
www.parcoaquatica.com

Astragames
Corso Vittorio Emanuele II 11.
02-79 50 01.

Idroscalo (Fun Park)
Via Rivoltana 64.
02-756 03 93.

Nuovo Arti
Via Mascagni 8.
02-76 02 00 48.

Play Planet
Via Veglia 59.
02-668 88 38.
www.play-planet.it

Teatro delle Marionette
Via degli Olivetani 3b.
02-469 44 40.

Nightlife

ONE OF THE CHARACTERISTICS that distinguishes Milan from other Italian cities is the way in which the city really comes alive at night. From Tuesday to Saturday the city's pubs, bars, cafés and discotheques are generally packed, though there are fewer Milanese and more people from outside the city on Saturdays. Monday and, to a certain extent, Sunday, are the quiet days, offering only rare occasions for entertainment. During the week clubs and discos organize theme evenings, and some of them operate a strict door policy. Places offering live music are also very popular; they often feature promising performers. The majority are located in the Navigli district.

DISCOS AND CLUBS

FOR THE ENERGETIC on the lookout for new trends in music and dance, Milan is a great place to be. The many discos and clubs in town offer different types of music; and are so popular that they attract young people from all over Italy. The scene is quite volatile and with rare exceptions – some places have become positive institutions – Milan discos change their name, management and style periodically. It is quite common for a wildly popular club to fall out of favour, only to return to popularity once again some time later.

Some places charge an entrance fee; others are free but you are obliged to pay for drinks. Prices vary quite a lot; the so-called drinkcard system, whereby you pay for your drinks at the entrance, is fairly common.

One disco that has adopted this method is **Alcatraz**, a former factory converted into a multi-purpose venue for concerts, fashion shows and even conventions. Friday is given over to 1970s–80s revival dance music.

Next door is **Zenith**, which is more formal. There is a restaurant and also a private club called **De Sade**. Another chic disco that is popular with the prosperous younger generation is **Beau Geste**, where a range of music is performed. **Jammin'**, near the Darsena, has live soul music on Thursday. Friday and Saturday are for students.

Currently drawing in the fashion crowd is **Hollywood**. This is the place to go if you fancy celebrity spotting. The **Magazzini Generali**, which is also used for concerts and exhibitions, attracts a mixed crowd. The week opens on Wednesday and themed evenings include new musical trends and popular DJs. Friday is usually international night, with the latest music from around the world. Saturdays focus on the best of new dance, rock and contemporary pop music.

The **Shocking Club** is crowded every night from Monday to Saturday, and has become a Milanese institution. There is a strict door policy. A trendy multi-purpose disco is the **Café Atlantique**, which is a café, bar, restaurant and disco in one. **Rolling Stone** is a historic address where rock music reigns supreme. Thanks to its size, concerts are often held here.

The **Old Fashion**, inside the Triennale, is a disco with popular theme evenings. (The restaurant is also a big draw, especially for Sunday brunch.)

One of the largest discos in Milan is **Propaganda**. The place is also used for television programmes and music concerts.

For an alternative spot, try the **Rainbow**: it features rock and pop and on Friday and Saturday is mainly the haunt of teenagers. **Il Ragno d'Oro**, near the Spanish walls overlooking Porta Romana, is jam-packed in the summer.

NIGHTSPOTS WITH LIVE MUSIC

LISTENING TO LIVE MUSIC is a popular activity in the city and the choice of venues is wide. **Scimmie** is one of the city's historic nightspots. In the 1980s it was the place to go for live jazz, but recently has concentrated more on rock, blues and ethnic music. The place gets very crowded and it can be difficult to find a table unless you go early.

In the Navigli area, **Grilloparlante** is worth checking out for up-and-coming bands. **Il Capolinea** is another top spot for jazz. You can sit outside in the summer, and there is also a restaurant.

Nidaba is small, dark and smoky, but people still love the atmosphere and it's always full. Promising young music bands are encouraged to perform here.

Lastly, concerts of current music are held at the **Tunnel**, a converted warehouse under the Stazione Centrale (main railway station). Tunnel also functions as a cultural centre, hosting shows and exhibitions as well as book launches for new publications.

DISCOPUBS

FOR THOSE WHO WANT TO dance without going to a disco there are so-called discopubs. In the early evening, these places are ideal for a relaxing drink and quiet conversation. Later in the evening the atmosphere livens up considerably. **Loolapaloosa**, for example, is an Irish pub with a happy hour extending from 5 to 9pm. Late at night it transforms into a totally different creature: the volume is turned up and every available spot is used for dancing, including the tables and the counter.

The **Indian Café**, in the Brera area, has a happy hour from 6 to 8pm, and turns into a discopub in the evening. There are three floor levels and concerts are put on for very reasonable prices. Music tends to be rock-oriented.

Another discopub is in the heart of the Brera quarter. **Soul to Soul** is always packed, and is a good place to hear black music. You need a membership card.

A great place for followers of fashion is the **Grand Café Fashion**, which is popular with celebrities and models. Happy hour runs from 6:30 to 9:30pm, after which you can dance downstairs. The house aperitifs are excellent.

Stonehenge is a bar and disco on two floor levels, inspired by Celtic culture. It is popular for theme evenings, live music and Latin-American dance courses. Happy hour extends from 6 to 9pm.

LATIN-AMERICAN

LATIN-AMERICAN dance is increasingly popular in Milan. The place to go for uninhibited dancing is the **Tropicana**. It attracts mostly the over-thirty crowd and the best evenings to go are Thursday, Friday and Saturday.

If you find Cuban atmosphere intriguing and feel like trying out some Creole cuisine, the place to go is **Bodeguita del Medio**. Live music is on offer late at night and you can try salsa and merengue dancing.

A disco with Latin-American music only is **Coco Loco**, where entry is free but drinks are obligatory.

Sabor, on the other hand, alternates rock and blues evenings with nights entirely given over to Latin-American music. They also offer courses in salsa-merengue dancing, and anyone who wants to celebrate a special occasion can rent the club.

El Tropico Latino is a great place to try Mexican food while listening to music and sampling different types of tequila. Wednesday is the best evening to go.

MAJOR CONCERT VENUES

MILAN'S LARGEST CONCERTS are sometimes performed in places normally associated with football. The stadium San Siro (see *p194*) is sometimes used, but the usual venue is the **Filaforum**, an ultra-modern sports arena with a seating capacity of 12,000. Other venues are the **Palavobis**, the former Pala-Trussardi, which can hold 9,000 people, and the **Palalido**, with 5,000 seats. Although space is limited at the **Leoncavallo** social centre, interesting concerts are put on. In the summer, concerts are also held at the Idroscalo or under the Arco della Pace. Sponsored by the Milan city council, entry is free.

DIRECTORY

DISCOS AND CLUBS

Alcatraz
Via Valtellina 25.
(02-69 01 63 52.

Beau Geste
Piazza Velasca 4.
(02-805 77 72.

Café Atlantique
Viale Umbria 42.
(02-55 19 39 06.

Hollywood
Corso Como 15.
(02-659 89 96.

Il Ragno d'Oro
Piazza Medaglie d'Oro.
(02-55 19 50 09.

Jammin'
Piazza XXIV Maggio 8.
(02-58 10 27 66.

Magazzini Generali
Via Pietrasanta 14.
(02-55 21 13 13.

Old Fashion
Viale Alemagna 6.
(02-805 62 31.

Propaganda
Via Castelbarco 11.
(02-58 31 06 82.

Rainbow
Via Besenzanica 3.
(02-404 83 99.

Rolling Stone
Corso XXII Marzo 32.
(02-73 31 72.

Shocking Club
Piazza XXV Aprile 10.
(02-655 12 40.

Zenith – De Sade
Via Valtellina 21.
(02-688 88 98.

NIGHTSPOTS WITH LIVE MUSIC

Grilloparlante
Alzaia Naviglio Grande 36.
(02-89 40 93 21.

Il Capolinea
Via Lodovico il Moro 119.
(02-89 12 20 24.

Indian Café
Corso Garibaldi 97–99.
(02-29 00 03 90.

Nidaba
Via Gola 12.
(02-89 40 86 57.

Scimmie
Via A Sforza 49.
(02-89 40 28 74.

Tunnel
Via Sammartini 30.
(02-66 71 13 70.

DISCOPUBS

Grand Café Fashion
Via Vetere 6.
(02-89 40 29 97.

Loolapaloosa
Corso Como 15.
(02-655 56 93.

Soul to Soul
Via San Marco 33.
(02-29 00 63 50.

Stonehenge
Viale Pasubio 3.
(02-655 28 46.

LATIN-AMERICAN

Bodeguita del Medio
Viale Col di Lana 3.
(02-89 40 05 60.

Coco Loco
Via Corelli 62.
(02-756 12 26.

El Tropico Latino
Via Messina 1.
(02-34 28 49.

Sabor
Via Molino delle Armi 18.
(02-58 31 35 84.

Tropicana
Viale Bligny 52.
(02-58 31 82 32.

MAJOR CONCERT VENUES

Filaforum
Via Di Vittorio 6.
(02-48 85 71.

Leoncavallo
Via Watteau 7.
(02-26 14 02 87.

Palalido
Piazza Stuparich.
(02-39 26 61 00.

Palavobis
Via Elia 33.
(02-33 40 05 51.

Theatre and Cinema

THE THEATRE SEASON IN MILAN is undoubtedly one of the best and most varied in Italy. Visitors interested in a specific performance (especially if it is being put on in a well-known theatre such as the Scala or the Piccolo) should book well in advance, either directly through the theatre box office or by contacting one of the booking agencies in the city centre (see p189).

For those who prefer films to the stage, Milan has a great number of cinemas. A bonus is that new releases are shown in Milan ahead of most other Italian cities. Many of the cinemas are multiplexes with plenty of screens, and the majority are concentrated in the city centre. Foreign-language films are also screened.

THEATRES

IT WOULD BE A SHAME to leave Milan without having seen an opera at **La Scala** (see pp52–3). The season begins on 7 December, the feast day of Sant'Ambrogio, the city's patron saint. Lovers of ballet and classical music can also enjoy performances at the highest level from the theatre's ballet company and Filarmonica orchestra. It is important to book as far ahead of performances as possble, as, inevitably, there is much competition for seats at one of the world's most famous opera houses.

No less prestigious and world-famous is the **Piccolo Teatro**. Founded just after World War II by Giorgio Strehler as "an arts theatre for everyone", its productions are known for their excellence. The **Nuovo Piccolo Teatro**, opened in 1998, was dedicated to the maestro, who had planned a state-of-the-art theatre worthy of his company's quality productions for over 40 years. The new theatre, with a seating capacity of 974, hosts the major Piccolo Teatro productions.

The **Teatro Studio**, in the former Fossati theatre, was originally meant to be a rehearsal hall for the Piccolo Teatro, but later became an independent company. Though interesting from an architectural standpoint, it is not all that comfortable. The **Manzoni**, a traditional favourite with the Milanese, presents a very eclectic programme, ranging from musicals to drama and comedy, always with top-level directors and actors.

Another historic theatre is the **Carcano**, first opened in 1803. It was restructured in the 1980s and has a capacity of 990 people. Its repertoire is classical, and dance is sometimes offered as well. For comedy, head for the **Ciak**, which usually stars leading comic actors.

For lovers of experimental and avant-garde theatre there are the **Teatridithalia-Elfo** and **-Porta Romana** theatres, which are dedicated to performing original works that are always fascinating and may sometimes shock. The **Out Off** is also dedicated to avant-garde productions, but because of its limited seating capacity and location in the outskirts of town it is relatively unknown. Milanese experimental theatre is performed at the **CRT Teatro dell'Arte**, which recently increased its seating capacity to 800.

The **San Babila** theatre offers a programme of more traditional theatre. Here the fame of the directors and actors attracts a large number of spectators, so that getting hold of a ticket may be hard. The largest theatre in Milan is the **Smeraldo**, which can seat 2,100 people. Besides famous musicals, it plays host to dance performances, straight theatre and concerts. Recently associated with the Smeraldo theatre is the

Nazionale, which always features famous actors and has been concentrating more and more in recent years on dance and operettas.

The **Litta**, in Corso Magenta, is an elegant theatre which usually presents classic 20th-century plays. Another fascinating theatre is the **Teatro Franco Parenti**, which has a seating capacity of 500. The programme is quite varied, with particular attention being paid to new international works and music.

The small, intimate **Filodrammatici**, next to La Scala, presents a repertoire of classical works that also includes contemporary plays. The **Nuovo**, with its 1,020 seats, presents different kinds of theatrical productions, including musicals, comedies and dance, usually with famous actors.

CINEMAS

MOST OF THE LEADING cinemas in Milan are concentrated in the city centre, around Corso Vittorio Emanuele II. Most of these are multiplexes, which means there is plenty of choice. Ticket prices are reduced on Wednesday evening and in almost all cinemas on week-day afternoons as well. When popular new films are being shown there are always long queues, so go early.

Most non-Italian films are dubbed into Italian, without subtitles, so they will be difficult for anyone unfamiliar with the language. Visitors who want to see a film with the soundtrack in the original language (in lingua originale) can try the Anteo, **Arcobaleno**, **Centrale** or theatre 3 of the Odeon Cinema 5, where they have all-day showings of films in the original language.

The **San Lorenzo**, with 170 seats, promotes various cultural events and programmes, such as the African Cinema Festival. The **Auditorium San Fedele** is the home of three film clubs which offer different screening schedules and subject matter.

The **Odeon Cinema 5**, a multiplex, is the largest cinema in Milan, with ten theatres. On Corso Vittorio Emanuele II there are the **Pasquirolo**, with a seating capacity of 490, the **Mediolanum**, with 500 seats, the **Ambasciatori** with 734 seats.

In the Galleria del Corso are the **Mignon**, **Ariston** and **Corso**. Another popular venue is the **San Carlo** in Via Morozzo della Rocca. The **Anteo** has three theatres and also presents children's films.

The **Plinius**, in Viale Abruzzi, is a multiplex with five screens, while the **Colosseo**, in Viale Montenero, has three: the Visconti, Allen and Chaplin. The **President** cinema in Largo Augusto can seat 250 people and is very comfortable. On Corso Garibaldi the **Brera Multisala** has two theatres. The **Ducale**, in Piazza Napoli, is an old cinema which has been converted into a multiplex with four theatres.

A popular newcomer on the scene is the **Arcadia**, just outside Milan at Melzo. The six cinemas here include Energia, the biggest in Italy.

The renovated **Gloria** now has two theatres (Garbo and Marilyn), huge screens and a good audio system. The Nuovo Arti *(see p189)* in Via Mascagni is entirely given over to programmes of children's cinema.

Fans of arthouse films can head for the recently renovated **Ariosto**, the **Nuovo Corsica** or the **Sempione**. At the **De Amicis** cinema Milan city council organizes themed seasons of films, debates and film club showings.

Every year the Milan city council organizes cinema festivals, one of the best of which is the Panoramica di Venezia, held in September, when previews of the films competing in the Venice Film Festival are shown.

Many cinemas in Milan do provide wheelchair access, but it is always a good idea to telephone the box office beforehand for advice.

DIRECTORY

THEATRES

Carcano
Corso di Porta Romana 63.
02-55 18 13 77.

Ciak
Via Sangallo 33.
02-76 11 00 93.

CRT Teatro dell'Arte
Viale Alemagna 6.
02-86 19 01.

Filodrammatici
Via Filodrammatici 1.
02-869 36 59.

Litta
Corso Magenta 21.
02-86 45 45 45.

Manzoni
Via Manzoni 42.
02-76 02 05 43.

Nazionale
Piazza Piemonte 12.
02-48 00 77 00.

Nuovo
Piazza San Babila 37.
02-76 00 00 86.

Nuovo Piccolo Teatro
Largo Greppi.
02-72 33 32 22.

Out Off
Via Dupré 4.
02-39 26 22 82.

Piccolo Teatro
Via Rovello 2.
02-72 33 32 22.

San Babila
Piazza San Babila 2a.
02-76 00 29 85.

Smeraldo
Piazza XXV Aprile 10.
02-29 00 67 67.

Teatridithalia-Elfo
Via Ciro Menotti 11.
02-58 31 58 96.

Teatridithalia-Porta Romana
Corso di Porta Romana 124.
02-72 33 32 22.

Teatro alla Scala
Via Filodrammatici 2 (enrance from Piazza Scala).
02-72 00 37 44.

Teatro Franco Parenti
Via Pierlombardo 14.
02-545 71 74.

Teatro Studio
Via Rivoli 6.
02-72 33 32 22.

CINEMAS

Ambasciatori
Corso Vittorio Emanuele II 30.
02-76 00 33 06.

Anteo
Via Milazzo 9.
02-659 77 32.

Arcadia
Via Martiri della Libertà 5, Melzo.
02-954 16 41.

Arcobaleno
Viale Tunisia 11.
02-29 40 60 54.

Ariosto
Via Ariosto 16.
02-48 00 39 01.

Ariston
Galleria del Corso 1.
02-76 02 38 06.

Auditorium San Fedele
Via Hoepli 3b.
02-86 35 22 31.

Brera Multisala
Corso Garibaldi 99.
02-29 00 18 90.

Centrale
Via Torino 30.
02-87 48 26.

Colosseo
Viale Montenero 84.
02-59 90 13 61.

Corallo
Largo Corsia dei Servi.
02-76 02 07 21.

Corso
Galleria del Corso 1.
02-76 00 21 84.

De Amicis
Via Caminadella 15.
02-86 45 27 16.

Ducale
Piazza Napoli 27.
02-47 71 92 79.

Gloria
Corso Vercelli 18.
02-48 00 89 08.

Mignon
Galleria del Corso 4.
02-76 02 23 43.

Mediolanum
Corso Vittorio Emanuele II 24.
02-76 02 08 18.

Nuovo Corsica
Viale Corsica 68.
02-738 21 47.

Odeon Cinema 5
Via Santa Radegonda 8.
02-87 45 47.

Pasquirolo
Corsia dei Servi 11.
02-76 02 07 57.

Plinius
Viale Abruzzi 28–30.
02-29 53 11 03.

President
Largo Augusto 1.
02-76 02 21 90.

San Carlo
Via Morozzo della Rocca 12.
02-481 34 42.

San Lorenzo
Corso di Porta Ticinese 45.
02-58 11 31 61.

Sempione
Via Pacinotti 6.
02-39 21 04 83.

Sports and Outdoor Activities

PEOPLE VISITING MILAN ON BUSINESS may want to continue with a routine of practising a sport or exercising. If so, there are many facilities in the city, including health clubs and gymnasiums, that will suit the purpose. These centres often offer a range of activities under one roof so that you can make the most of your free time. Visitors preferring to spectate rather than participate can go and see the local football (soccer), basketball and hockey teams. All are in the first division and offer top-quality sport.

Sports Facilities

FOOTBALL (SOCCER) FANS should go to a match at the **Meazza** (or **San Siro**) **Stadium** (see p195) at least once in their lifetime. Called the "Scala of football", this stadium has a seating capacity of over 80,000. One particularly popular competition from both the sporting and the theatrical point of view is the local derby between the city's two teams, Inter and AC Milan. However, it is best to plan attendance in advance as tickets sell out fairly quickly.

For horse-racing fans there is the **Ippodromo**, where races are held all year long, except for December. Night races are held from June to September.

The Filaforum arena at Assago (see p191) is the home of the local basketball (Pallacanestro Olimpia) and volleyball (Gonzaga) teams. The arena also plays host to various tennis tournaments, first and foremost the Internazionale di Milano, which takes place in spring.

Ice hockey buffs can follow the matches of the Devils (the only remaining local team after the disbanding of Milano 24), who play at the **PalAgorà** arena.

Five-a-side Football

ONE OF THE MOST popular sports at the moment in Milan is five-a-side football (soccer). Anyone interested in playing should go to the **Centro Peppino Vismara**, where they play 11-, 7- and 5-a-side football. Another good leisure facility is the **Palauno**, where there are five pitches.

Golf

THERE ARE SEVERAL golf courses in the Milan area. The closest one to the city is **Le Rovedine Golf Club–Sporting Mirasole**, which is about 7 km (4 miles) from the city centre. There is also a restaurant for the use of players at the club.

Swimming

FOR A RELAXING SWIM, one good swimming pool is the **Piscina Solari**, which has five lanes. A good alternative is the **Piscina Giovanni da Procida**, which boasts a half-size Olympic pool with six lanes. There is also a gym at this site which is ideal for warming up.

The **Lido** is the city's most popular outdoor swimming pool. Visitors who are not daunted by large crowds and enjoy slides can come here to swim during the heat of the Milanese summer.

Skating

THOSE KEEN ON ROLLER skating will enjoy themselves at the multi-purpose **24 Sport Village**, which has rinks for roller skating, roller hockey and aerobic roller skating. They also offer facilities for many other sporting activities, including tennis, basketball, swimming and mountain biking. Ice-skaters can go to the **Palazzo del Ghiaccio**, which has an indoor rink where people can skate at their leisure from Tuesday to Saturday in the evening. It is also open in the afternoon at the weekends from 3 to 6pm.

The PalAgorà welcomes ice skaters from Wednesday to Saturday in the evening and also from 3 to 6pm at weekends. All the rinks have skates for rent. During the Christmas season an ice skating hire is usually set up in Piazza del Duomo enabling people to skate by starlight.

Squash

THIS SPORT IS IDEAL for fitness, and players are welcome at the **Squash Vico**. There are ten courts. Private and group lessons are available, and equipment can be hired. The centre is open every day, including the evening. However, to use these facilities visitors must buy a membership card, valid for two months.

Tennis

TENNIS PLAYERS CAN play in an ideal setting at the **Associazione Sporting Club Corvetto**. The Club does not operate a membership card scheme, and there are 13 indoor courts as well as a gymnasium, bar and restaurant and parking space reserved for customers.

The **Centro Sportivo Mario Saini** has 12 courts, either covered or open to the air, depending on the season. It is best to book ahead by telephone. Another place where it is possible to play in peace and quiet in a sporting club reserved exclusively for this sport, is the **Tennis Club 5 Pioppi**, in the Fiera district. There are four courts that can be used both in summer and winter.

Jogging

THE BEST AND healthiest place for running is the Monte Stella park (also known as the "Montagnetta"), near the San Siro Stadium. This large area of greenery is a good place to jog, following marked paths, or even for cycling around on mountain bikes. In the summer the park is often filled with numbers of apartment-dwelling Milanese, catching some sun.

DIRECTORY

SPORTS FACILITIES

Ippodromo
Via Piccolomini 2.
02-48 21 61.

PalAgorà
Via dei Ciclamini 23.
02-48 30 09 46.

**Meazza Stadium
(San Siro)**
Piazzale Axum.
02-48 70 71 23.

FOOTBALL

**Centro Peppino
Vismara**

Via dei Missaglia 117.
02-826 58 23.

Palauno
Largo Balessa 55.
02-423 53 15.

GOLF

**Le Rovedine
Golf Club–
Sporting Mirasole**
Via C Marx 16,
Noverasco di Opera.
02-57 60 64 05.

SWIMMING

Lido
Piazzale Lotto 15.
02-39 266100.

**Piscina Giovanni
da Procida**
Via Giovanni
da Procida 20.
02-33 10 49 70.

Piscina Solari
Via Montevideo 20.
02-469 52 78.

SKATING

**Palazzo
del Ghiaccio**
Via Piranesi 10.
02-739 81.

24 Sport Village
Via Assietta 19.
02-66 22 01 92.

SQUASH

Squash Vico
Via GB Vico 38.
02-48 01 08 90.

TENNIS

**Associazione Sport-
ing Club Corvetto**
Via Fabio Massimo 15/4.
02-53 14 36.

**Centro Sportivo
Mario Saini**
Via Corelli 136.
02-756 12 80.

**Tennis Club
5 Pioppi**
Via Marostica 4.
02-404 85 93.

SAN SIRO STADIUM

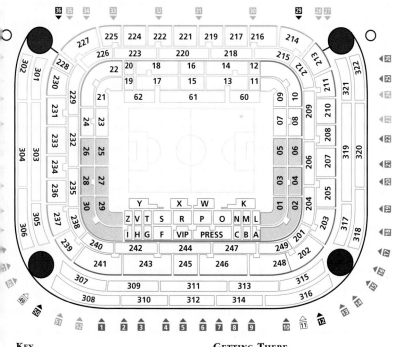

KEY

○ ticket office

1 stadium entrances

area for Milan guests

area for Inter guests

— block of seats

— block of seats

— block of seats

— block of seats

GETTING THERE

Avoid going by car, as parking space is very
hard to find. The best way to get there is to
take line 1 of the metro to the Lotto stop; from
there a shuttle bus goes to the stadium. At the
end of the match the No. 24 trams (under the
blue area) go to the city centre. Another option
is taking a taxi (from the Lotto metro as well).

ENTERTAINMENT AT THE LAKES

A T THE LAKES it is possible to devote a considerable amount of leisure time to entertainment and sport. At Lake Garda in particular, you will be able to practise any type of aquatic sport, have a go at trekking in the hinterland and dance the night away at the discos. Of the lakes, Garda also has the liveliest nightlife and is the most popular with young people. Lake Como, Lake Maggiore and the smaller lakes still offer a variety of opportunities for entertainment. In recent years the enterprising local APT

The logo of the Caneva aquatic amusement park

tourist offices, sponsored by the town administrations, have been quite successful in promoting initiatives aimed at making holidays more interesting for visitors. Outdoor markets, feasts, festivals and other events have therefore become more and more frequent. The lakes offer breathtaking scenery, an entertainment in itself and every year there are programmes of cultural events. In addition there are fine architectural and artistic works to be seen, lovely gardens to explore, and nature reserves to wander through.

SPORTS

I F KEEPING IN TOP PHYSICAL shape is a priority, there are plenty of activities that serve the purpose at the lakes. Lake Garda is the domain of windsurfing; Torbole and Riva in particular being the most popular places for surfers both in summer and winter. Sailing fans will enjoy the Centomiglia, an annual regatta organized by the Circolo Vela Gargnano sailing club and held on the second weekend of September. For a more relaxing time, there are also opportunities to go fishing.

In the Garda hinterland, hiking has become very popular, and touring the area on a mountain bike is the most recent vogue. More adventurous souls can take lessons in paragliding.

Lake Maggiore offers not only many aquatic sports but is quite popular with golf enthusiasts. There are state-of-the-art golf courses in lovely natural settings which are enjoyed by Italian and foreign golfers alike.

The hills and valleys around the lake are ideal places for horse riding, hiking, mountaineering, free climbing, hang-gliding and paragliding and, in the winter, when snow covers the high ground, skiing and snow-boarding.

The most popular sports at Lake Como are sailing and water skiing. Lessons are available from qualified instructors, whatever your age and experience.

Another enjoyable activity is canoeing. All the lakes have clubs where you can rent canoes and equipment.

A water skiing instructor and his pupil at Lake Como

For the more sedentary, there are many spas *(terme)* at the lakes or in the vicinity. These centres offer a variety of treatments.

OTHER ACTIVITIES

V ISITORS TO Lake Garda, especially families with children, might want to visit the Gardaland amusement park *(see pp148–9)*. It is recommended for children and adults alike, the ideal place to enjoy yourselves and even experience the occasional thrill. However, in peak season, be prepared for a very long wait at the most interesting attractions.

About 2 km (1 mile) from Gardaland is **Caneva**, the

A group of windsurfers in action at Lake Garda

Camels in the Natura Viva zoological park, at Bussolengo-Pastrengo near Lake Garda

largest water amusement park in Italy. Shows, water games and other displays, plus an area reserved for small children, make this a big aquatic attraction.

To take a closer look at some rare and endangered animal species, visit the **Parco Natura Viva**, a zoo located at Bussolengo-Pastrengo. A pleasant walk among ancient oak trees and plants takes visitors around the home of the 1,000 specimens in this lovely park. Cars are also allowed into the safari park, where a 6-km (4-mile) tour brings you into closer contact with some of the wild animals of the savannah.

Another popular place for lovers of interesting plants is the **Giardino Botanico della Fondazione André Heller** at Gardone Riviera: 1.5 ha (3.7 acres) of land with over 8,000 plants from every climatic zone in the world.

Logo of the Natura Viva zoological park

The **Parco Giardino Sigurtà** lies 8 km (5 miles) from Peschiera. This 50-ha (123-acre) garden is a temple to ecology.

At Lake Maggiore the Villa Pallavicino park *(see p133)* has a lovely 20-ha (49-acre) botanic garden with 40 different species of animals.

NIGHTLIFE

THE BEST AREA for night life is Lake Garda, which boasts internationally known nightspots. Desenzano, in particular, has a number of pubs and other spots for evening entertainment, while in the outskirts are some of the largest discotheques in Italy. The undisputed king is **Genux**, a gigantic and extremely popular place, especially in the summer. Another famous and very popular nightspot is **Fura**, a multimedia disco where theme evenings feature. On Friday there is funk, soul and "rare groove" music, while the other evening (and night) programmes are more unconventional.

At Lake Como the most popular disco is **Mascara,** where live music is played until midnight, after which there is dancing with a disc jockey. For live music, go to

L'Ultimo Caffè and **Skagen**. At Lake Maggiore, don't miss **La Rocchetta**, a disco situated in a splendid Art Nouveau villa with a view of the lake, and **Dancing Mirage**. At Verbania, go to **Tam Tam**, and **Byblos**, at Arizzano, is a lively spot.

DIRECTORY

ACTIVITIES

Caneva
Località Fossalta 1. Lazise.
045-759 06 33.

Giardino Botanico della Fondazione Andrè Heller
Via Roma. Gardone Riviera.
0336-41 08 77.

Parco Giardino Sigurtà
Valeggio sul Mincio.
045-637 10 33.
www.sigurta.it

Parco Natura Viva
Via Figara 40, Bussolengo-Pastrengo, Varenna.
045-717 00 52.
www.parconaturaviva.it

NIGHTLIFE

Byblos
Via Nuova Intra Premeno 6. Arizzano.
0323-533 03.

Dancing Mirage
Viale Baracca 16. Arona.
0322-443 31.

Fura
Via Lavagnone 13. Lonato.
030-913 06 52.

Genux
Via Fornace dei Gorghi 2. Lonato.
030-991 99 48.
www.genux.it

L'Ultimo Caffè
Via Giulini 3. Como.
031-27 30 98.

La Rocchetta
Via Verbano 1. Arona.
0322-480 51.

Mascara
Via Sant'Abbondio 7. Como.
031-26 83 56.

Skagen
Via P Paoli 80b. Como.
031-59 07 35.

Tam Tam
Piazza Flaim 16. Verbania.
0323-40 32 10.

One of the bars at the Genux discotheque at Lake Garda

SURVIVAL
GUIDE

PRACTICAL INFORMATION 200-205
TRAVEL INFORMATION 206-215

PRACTICAL INFORMATION

MILAN IS ONE of Italy's most efficient and business-like cities, with an excellent public transport network and good public services. In the capital of fashion, appearances do matter, and you are likely to receive better service and attention if you are smartly dressed. Milan has its share of petty crime, and it is advisable to take some basic precautions in order to enjoy your stay to the full. Keep bags and cameras close to you at all times, and take extra care travelling on public transport, where pickpockets

Logo of the City of Milan

may be operating. The public transport system is, however, the best way to get around the city. Walkers should stay alert in the chaotic traffic, and take particular care crossing streets. Tourist offices are the best places to go for practical information including maps. At the lakes, brochures are available from APT offices, with information on local festivals and other entertainment. Information can be obtained ahead of your visit from the Italian tourist office (ENIT) in the country of departure.

TOURIST INFORMATION

THE Italian tourist board, the Ente Nazionale Italiano per il Turismo (ENIT) has offices in many major capital cities including London, New York and Montreal, where maps and information on hotels, etc. are available. In Milan itself, the Informazione e Accoglienza Turistica (IAT) and Azienda di Promozione Turistica (APT) tourist offices provide detailed information about the city, including free lists of hotels and restaurants as well as information on cultural events.

At the lakes, look for APT offices or IAT offices in larger towns, or Pro Loco offices in smaller towns and villages (usually the town hall).

Logo of the APT in Milan

English is spoken and understood in most hotels and shops and frequently used on planes and tour buses. However, a few words of Italian will always be welcome.

PASSPORTS AND VISAS

EUROPEAN UNION nationals need a full passport to enter Italy, but can then stay as long as they like. Citizens of the US, Canada, Australia and New Zealand in possession of a full passport can stay in Italy for up to three months. For longer stays, special visas are needed from an Italian embassy.

All visitors must declare their presence to the police within eight days of arrival. If you are staying in a hotel, this will be done for you.

The *Milano Dove, Come, Quando* listings guide

USEFUL PUBLICATIONS

EVERY WEEK the daily newspapers *Corriere della Sera* and *La Repubblica* publish a special supplement (*Vivi-Milano* and *Tutto Milano* respectively) packed with up-to-date information about cultural activities in the city and the surroundings.

The Milan daily newspapers such as *Il Corriere* have local news sections, which also include theatre and music entertainment and venues and a cinema guide.

The APT office distributes free copies of *Milano Mese*, a brochure with listings of the various cultural events.

Another publication, *Milano Dove, Come, Quando* is a practical guide that will help you to get around the city. It is also obtainable from the Milan APT office.

The main APT tourist office in Milan (on the left)

People with access to the Internet will find a mass of information available on the web. One especially useful website is www.itwg.com.

MUSEUMS, MONUMENTS AND TOURS

Mᴵᴸᴬɴ's artistic and architectural masterpieces are housed in a variety of institutions, from art galleries and churches to palazzi and castles. In general, most state-owned museums are open from Tuesday to Sunday, churches are open daily. Privately owned museums will operate their own individual timetables.

Discounts are available for residents of the EU under 18 and over 60 in the majority of state-run places.

A good way of gaining an overview of the city is to travel on the **Tram Turistico**, a tour tram that departs from Piazza Castello. The tour lasts for about 1 hour 45 minutes, and audio tapes provide recorded descriptions of sights in Italian, English, French, German and Japanese.

Another tour is the **Giro della Città**, which begins at Piazza del Duomo in the

centre. This tour is available from Tuesday to Sunday and covers all the main monuments of Milan in approximately 3 hours.

In recent years the local administrations at the lakes have also been involved in a variety of cultural promotions. The Associazione Albergatori della Provincia di Varese (Varese hotel owners' association) has introduced a Welcome Card. Distributed free at hotels locally, it allows visitors to obtain a 10 per cent discount on the admission charge at many museums and sights in the area.

INFORMATION FOR STUDENTS

Tʜᴇ ᴄᴇɴᴛʀᴏ ᴛᴜʀɪsᴛɪᴄᴏ Studentesco (CTS) offers discount tickets to young people under 26, which can be used for travel not only in Milan, but in the rest of Italy and Europe as well.

As far as student accommodation is concerned, there is one youth hostel in Milan, the **Ostello della Gioventù P Rotta**. You need to present an annual membership card (which can be bought at the hostel itself).

Membership cards of the CTS, or Centro Turistico Studentesco

For more detailed information on youth hostels around the lakes, contact the Associazione Italiana Alberghi per la Gioventù (Italian Youth Hostelling Association).

ITALIAN TIME

Mᴵᴸᴬɴ ɪs ᴏɴᴇ ʜᴏᴜʀ ahead of Greenwich Mean Time. This means that London is one hour behind Italian time and New York and Los Angeles are 6 and 9 hours behind respectively, and Moscow is 2 hours ahead. Tokyo and Sydney are 8 and 9 hours ahead respectively.

DIRECTORY		

ITALIAN TOURIST BOARD OFFICES

ENIT UK
1 Princes Street, London
W1R 8AY.
(0207-408 1254.

ENIT US
499 Park Avenue, New York.
(212-843 6884.

TOURIST INFORMATION

APT Milan
Via Marconi 1.
(02-72 52 43 00.

Lake Maggiore
Ufficio Informazione di Varese
Via Carrobbio 2.
(0332-28 46 24.

IAT di Laveno
Palazzo Municipale.
(0332-66 66 66.

Lake Como
APT di Como
Piazza Cavour 17.
(031-33 00 111.

APT di Lecco
Via Nazario Sauro 6.
(0341-36 23 60.

Uff. Inf. di Cernobbio
Via Regina 33b.
(031-51 01 98.

Uff. Inf. di Bellagio
Piazza della Chiesa 14.
(031-95 02 04.

Uff. Inf. di Tremezzo
Via Regina 3.
(0344-404 93.

Uff. Inf. di Varenna
Piazza Venini 1.
(0341-83 03 67.

Lake Garda
IAT di Desenzano
Via Porto Vecchio 34.
(030-914 15 10.

IAT di Sirmione
Viale Marconi 8.
(030-91 61 14, 91 62 45.

IAT di Gardone
Corso Repubblica 35.
(0365-203 47.

IAT di Toscolano Maderno
Via Lungolago 18.
(0365-64 13 30.

IAT di Limone
Via Comboni 15.
(0365-95 40 70.

Lake Iseo
Cooptur Lago d'Iseo
Via Duomo 5.
(030-98 11 54.

IAT di Iseo
Via Marconi 2c.
(030-98 02 09.

TOURS OF MILAN

Giro della Città
Via Marconi 1.
(02-72 52 43 00.

Tram Turistico
Piazza Castello.
(02-805 53 23.

EMBASSIES AND CONSULATES

UK
Via San Paolo 7.
(02-72 30 01.

US
Via Principe Amedeo 2/10.
(02-29 03 51 41.

INFORMATION FOR STUDENTS

Ostello della Gioventù P Rotta
Viale Salmoiraghi 1.
(02-39 26 70 95.
 www.hostels-aig.org

Personal Security and Health

Italian pharmacy sign

IN MILAN, there is widespread petty crime, a problem common to all large cities. Stay wary and keep a close eye on your personal property such as bags or cameras, especially in the evening and, in some quarters, during the day as well. The towns and villages around the lakes are very safe areas however, and there should be no cause for concern. Should you fall ill during your stay, Italian pharmacists can advise on minor ailments.

HINTS FOR TRAVELLERS

IT IS NOT advisable to walk around alone in the evening in poorly lit streets far from the city centre. Unaccompanied women should take particular care.

Petty theft is a perennial problem, so keep a tight grip on your bag or case in crowded places, particularly in trams and on the metro. Pickpockets work their way around the public transport system and can operate un-noticed in crowds of people. Always keep handbags closed and do not carry haversacks (backpacks) or shoulder bags on your back. It is always best to keep valuables such as a wallet or mobile phone well out of sight.

When walking along the street, keep handbags on the inside, away from the road, to foil purse snatchers on scooters *(scippatori)*.

Visitors who are getting about by car should take all the usual precautions appropriate in a big city. Do not leave personal belongings or car radios visible inside the car, since they might attract potential thieves. It is best to try to leave your car in an attended parking space *(parcheggio custodito)*. Make sure you have adequate travel insurance before you leave.

HEALTH AND MEDICAL ASSISTANCE

THE CITY HAS state-of-the-art health facilities, should you become ill during your stay in Milan. All EU citizens should be armed with the E111 form, available from post offices, which entitles the holder to free emergency treatment and reciprocal health care in Italy. It is wise, however, for all visitors to have health insurance.

If the ailment is minor, go initially to a pharmacy *(farmacia)*.

A municipal policewoman directing traffic in Milan

Italian pharmacists are well trained to deal with routine problems. Each pharmacy can be identified by a neon green cross hung over the door. A list of pharmacies open at night *(servizio notturno)* and on public holidays will be on clear display. A useful chemist (drugstore) is the **Farmacia della Stazione Centrale**, at the main railway station, open 24 hours a day. If you need urgent medical assistance, call the **Emergenza Sanitaria/Ambulanze** (Health Emergencies/Ambulance), or go straight to the *Pronto Soccorso* (Casualty Department/Emergency Room) at the nearest hospital.

If you need a doctor at your hotel, call the **Guardia Medica** (Night Duty Physician). In the unlikely event of poisoning, contact the **Centro Antiveleni** (Poison Control Centre).

MOSQUITOES

IN SUMMER mosquitoes *(zanzare)*, which appear at the first sign of warm weather, can be a real pest. Despite the various anti-mosquito devices, such as citronella candles or electrical gadgets which burn insect-repellent tablets, it is difficult to fend them off altogether, especially when sitting at outdoor cafés (the Navigli quarter is fairly bad). People who are particularly allergic to mosquito bites should always apply insect repellent cream or spray.

Milanese police at a road block

Banking and Communications

MILAN HAS VERY GOOD PUBLIC SERVICES. There is a bank on almost every corner of the city and almost all have automatic cash dispensers. In general the post offices are well organized and run smoothly, despite the fact that the Italian postal system has a reputation for notoriously slow delivery. Public telephones can be operated by coins or phone cards, and are well maintained. Business visitors may find it useful to be able to hire a mobile phone. At the lakes there are fewer banks and post offices because of the small size of the towns and villages, but the service is good. Italy now has two currencies, the lira and the euro.

Telecom Italia phone cards, now collectors' items

USING TELEPHONES

TELECOM ITALIA runs the network of public telephones throughout Italy, including Milan and around the lakes. Milan is well supplied with telephone booths, which operate with telephone cards (*schede telefoniche*) (sold at tobacconists or newsstands) and coins. Public phones take coins of L100, L200 or L500 and cards are widely used. There are also public phones at Telecom offices. The largest branch is in Galleria Vittorio Emanuele II and it is open every day from 8am to 9:30pm. The Telecom bureau also offers a fax service.

The Telecom office in the Stazione Centrale (main station) is usually open from 8am to 8pm daily. From here you can telephone anywhere in the world. You can also receive faxes, and consult telephone directories for the whole of Italy, the rest of Europe and countries around the Mediterranean basin.

The cheapest phone rates are between 10pm and 8am Monday to Saturday, and all day on Sunday. It is convenient to make calls from your hotel room, but the charges will be much higher than at a public phone.

The area code (*prefisso*) for Milan is 02. The code should be included even when phoning within Milan. It is now necessary to dial numbers in full throughout Italy, even for local calls.

For information concerning international calls, dial 176; to make an international reverse charge (collect) call, the number to dial is 170.

New telecommunications companies such as Infostrada and Wind now compete with Telecom Italia, and telephone rates have become much more competitive.

Logo of
Telecom Italia

GSM mobile phones work in Italy (but make sure they are turned off on aeroplanes). It is possible to rent a mobile

DIAL THE RIGHT NUMBER

- Area code for calls to and within Milan: 02.
- Italian Directory Enquiries: 12.
- International Directory Enquiries: 176.
- Reverse charge international calls: 170.
- To call Great Britain from Italy, dial 0044, then the city area code deleting the first zero, and the number of the person you are calling.
- To call the US: 001.
- To call Ireland: 00353.
- To call Australia: 0061.
- To call Canada: 001.
- To call France: 0033.
- To call South Africa: 0027.

phone. These are available from three firms: TIM (Telecom Italia Mobile), Omnitel and Wind, all of which use the GSM network. Charges vary. A useful place if you need to hire a mobile phone is the **Eurochange Business Centre** at Malpensa airport.

Should you need access to the world wide web during your visit, Milan has a number of Internet cafés. Fees are normally charged per session.

The Telecom office in Galleria Vittorio Emanuele II

Main branch of the Credito Italiano, in Piazza Cordusio

BANKS

MILANESE BANKS are open from Monday to Friday from 8:30am to 1:30pm, and in the afternoon from 3 to 4pm – though this may vary by about a quarter of an hour from bank to bank. Almost all banks have cashpoint machines, or ATMs, which take all major credit cards as well, including American Express and Visa.

CURRENCY EXCHANGE

THERE ARE TWO CURRENCIES in use in Italy, the lira (plural lire) and the euro. Cash will be needed in smaller shops, in bars and for items like taxis, but it is better not to carry large amounts on you.

The safest way of carrying additional money is to buy travellers' cheques, which can be refunded if unused. It is wise to make a list of the cheque numbers separately, in case of theft.

It is a good idea to bring some lire with you, but it is possible to change money at the airports. At Linate, **Euro-change Linate**, at international arrivals, is open daily from 7am–midnight, and the office at international departures is open from 6am–10pm.

Both arrivals and departures at Malpensa have branches of **Eurochange Malpensa**, open daily from 7am–11pm. The **Banca Ponti** in Piazza del Duomo has an automatic exchange machine. **CIT** travel agents in the centre can also offer exchange facilities from Monday to Saturday.

Logo of cashpoint machines (bancomat)

CREDIT CARDS

BOTH IN MILAN and at the lakes, businesses accept major credit cards such as American Express, Visa, Diners Club International and MasterCard (Access).

Most banks have automatic cash dispensers (bancomat) where you can obtain money with credit cards or bank cards, using a pin number. In the event of the loss or theft of your credit card, you should immediately contact the numbers listed in the directory below.

POSTAL SERVICES

POST OFFICES in Milan are open from Monday to Friday from 8:00am to 2:00pm and on Saturday from 9:30am to 1:00pm. There are also thirteen post offices that have extended trading hours: weekdays from 8:00am to 7:00pm and on Saturday from 9:30am to 1:00pm. The **Ufficio Centrale** (central post office) is open all day and also has a poste restante (Fermo Posta) and express service (Postacelere).

At **Linate Airport Post Office** you can send parcels, letters and registered letters and there is a telegram office open from 8am to 2pm, including on Sunday.

This service is also offered at the **Ufficio Stazione Centrale** (main railway station) from Monday to Friday from 8:00am to 7pm and on Saturday from 9:30am to 1:00pm. Throughout Italy, stamps can be bought at post offices and also at tobacconists (tabaccai).

Stamps for normal post and revenue stamps

DIRECTORY	**Mondadori.** Via Marghera 28.	**Banca Ponti** Piazza Duomo 19.	**Diners Club International**
MOBILE HIRE	☎ 02-48 04 71.	☎ 02-72 27 71.	☎ 800-86 40 64.

MOBILE HIRE

Eurochange Business Centre
Malpensa airport.
☎ 02-58 58 10 74.

INTERNET CAFES

Hard Disk Café
Corso Sempione 44.
☎ 02-33 10 10 38.

Metaverse Internet Point
Via Plinio 48.
☎ 02-29 41 54 13.

CURRENCY EXCHANGE

Eurochange Linate
International arrivals ☎ 02-756 13 72. Int'l departures ☎ 02-702 00 69.

Eurochange Malpensa
International arrivals
☎ 02-58 58 35 76.
International departures
☎ 02-74 86 72 18.

CIT
Galleria Vittorio Emanuele II.
☎ 02-86 37 02 32.

CREDIT CARDS
(MISSING/STOLEN)

American Express
☎ 800-86 40 46.

Visa
☎ 800-87 72 32.

MasterCard
☎ 800-87 08 66.

POSTAL SERVICES

Ufficio Centrale
Via Cordusio 4.
☎ 02-72 48 21 26.
🖳 www.posta.it

Other Post Offices
☎ 02-717 847 (Linate).
☎ 02-67 39 51
Via Sammartini 2.
(Central Railway Station).

TRAVEL INFORMATION

TWO AIRPORTS link Milan with the rest of the world. Linate airport is only a few kilometres from the city centre and connects the capital of Lombardy with all the main Italian and European cities. It is conveniently located for European business travellers. Malpensa 2000 is an intercontinental airport about 50 km (30 miles) from Milan. There are car hire offices at both airports though it is often cheaper to book a fly-drive deal ahead rather than arrange hire on arrival. For those travelling by train, there are excellent train links between

An Alitalia airplane

Milan and other cities in Italy. The city is also well connected to the rest of Europe, with fast, easy routes to France and Switzerland, and to Austria and Germany via Verona. Visitors arriving by car will use the excellent road and motorway networks. Exits from the ringroad around Milan are clearly marked. However, these roads are always congested with traffic, so journey times can be slow. In the early morning, when commuters begin to make their way into the centre, getting into town may take twice as long as you expect.

ARRIVING BY AIR

VISITORS ARRIVING IN Milan by air will fly into either Linate or Malpensa 2000 airports. Milan is a major point of entry into Italy, along with Rome. Frequent direct flights from London to Milan are operated by British Airways and Alitalia, the Italian state airline. Alitalia offers the best choice of direct flights to the US, linking Milan with Boston, New York, Chicago, Miami and Los Angeles.

LINATE AIRPORT

THIS AIRPORT has always been popular with the Milanese because of its proximity to the city centre. However business has been scaled down as a result of the government's decision

to concentrate on the total renovation and enlargement of Malpensa airport. At present Linate handles the Milan–Rome flights of all carriers except Meridiana; two daily Alitalia and AirOne flights to Naples; two Alitalia flights to Sicily and Sardinia; three to five daily flights to London, Paris, Amsterdam, Madrid and Frankfurt.

The airport has Left Luggage facilities, car rental offices including Avis and Hertz, and plenty of car parking space.

In the future the majority of international flights will be handled at Malpensa.

How to Get to Milan
Getting from Linate to the centre of Milan is very straightforward. Visitors unfamiliar with the city and

**A view of the new
Malpensa 2000 airport**

burdened with a great deal of luggage would do best to take a taxi. Official taxis are white and line up at the taxi stand right in front of the airport exit. In general, the service is prompt.

An alternative is going by bus, which is perfectly comfortable and much cheaper: tickets cost only 1,500 lire and are sold at the vending machine near the bus stop.

There are two bus lines serving Linate airport. ATM bus number 73 passes at regular intervals from 5:30am to 0:20am and connects the airport with the city centre, going as far as Piazza San Babila. The STAM bus runs from 5:40am to 7pm every 20 minutes and from 7 to 9pm every 30 minutes, connecting Linate and the main station.

The Milan airport, Linate

The ring road *(tangenziale)* around Milan, often congested with traffic

MALPENSA 2000 AIRPORT

ONE OF EUROPE'S most modern airports, Malpensa 2000 opened in October 1998.

How to Get to Milan
In June 1999 a new railway line connecting Malpensa and the city centre came into operation. Trains to the airport depart from Piazza Cadorna every 30 minutes, at 10 and 40 minutes past the hour; those to Milan leave at 20 and 50 minutes past the hour.

Two efficient coach lines also offer a good airport service. The Malpensa Shuttle is scheduled as follows: Malpensa–Stazione Centrale every 20 minutes from 6:40am to 10pm and every 30 minutes from 10:30pm to 12:30am; Stazione Centrale–Malpensa every 20 minutes from 5:20am to 10pm; Malpensa–Linate every hour from 6:20am to 1:20am and Linate–Malpensa every hour from 4am to 11:30 pm. The Malpensa Express timetable is: Malpensa–Piazzale Cadorna every 30 minutes from 6:45am to 12:15am;

Cadorna–Malpensa every 30 minutes from 5:30am to 10:30 pm (every hour from 1 to 3pm). Tickets for Malpensa–Stazione Centrale and Malpensa–Cadorna cost 13,000 lire, and the Malpensa–Linate ticket is 18,000 lire. Tickets for children aged 2 to 12 are half-price. You can check in at the Air Terminal in the Milan Stazione Centrale.

ARRIVING BY CAR

VISITORS ARRIVING IN Milan from the *autostrada* (motorway) will approach the city via the ring roads, *tangenziale est* (east) and *tangenziale ovest* (west), which are often congested with heavy traffic. Approaching the centre, it is best to look for an official car park *(see p211)* and then use public transport. The alternative is to use the ATM parking areas *(see chart below)*, which are on the outskirts but are well served by the metro. These are open from 7am to 8pm, cost 1,000 lire for half a day and 2,000 for a whole day up to 8pm. On Sundays and public holidays (and after 8pm), ATM parking is free.

ARRIVING FROM	MOTORWAY EXITS	CAR PARK	NUMBER OF CARS	METRO AND BUS	DISTANCE FROM CITY CENTRE
Trieste Venice Verona Brescia	Cavenago/Cambiago	Gessate	500	M 2 (30/35 min.)	23 km
	Sesto San Giovanni/V.le Zara	Sesto Marelli	250	M 1 (20 min.)	8 km
	Tang. est/Cologno Monzese	Cologno Nord	500	M 2 (30 min.)	9 km
	Tang. est/Viale Palmanova	Cascina Gobba/ Crescenzago	800 600	M 2 (20 min.)	6 km
	Tang. est/Viale Forlanini	Forlanini	650	🚋 12 🚌 73	6 km
Turin Aosta Como Chiasso Varese Gravellona	Viale Certosa	Lampugnano	2,000	M 1 (20 min.)	5 km
	Pero	Molino Dorino	450	M 1 (25 min.)	8.5 km
	Tang. ovest/Milano Baggio	Bisceglie	900	M 1 (20/25 min.)	6 km
Ventimiglia Genoa	Viale Liguria/Centro Città/ Filaforum	Romolo/ Famagosta	250 560	M 2 (20 min.)	4–5 km
Naples Rome Florence Bologna	Milano/Piazzale Corvetto	Rogoredo/ San Donato	350 2,400	M 3 (20 min.)	5–7 km

An ETR departing from the Stazione Centrale in Milan

ARRIVING BY TRAIN

THE MAIN RAILWAY STATION in
Milan is the **Stazione
Centrale**, where all the major
domestic and international
trains arrive. Connections
with your destination in town
can be made by taxi, metro
(underground) lines 2 and 3
and many trams and buses,
all of which are just outside
the entrance. **Porta Garibaldi**, in the Centro Dire-
zionale area, and Milano
Lambrate (near Città Studi),
are much smaller railway
stations. Both can be reached
via metro line 2. Metro line 3
links the **Rogoredo** station,
near San Donato Milanese,
with central Milan.

A regional train service
connects the city with Como,
Varese and the Brianza
region, run by the Ferrovie
Nord Milano. Trains depart
from Piazzale Cadorna, where
metro lines 1 and 2 converge.

There is also the recently
opened Passante Ferroviario,
a suburban railway link
network that connects various
metro lines with the Porta
Garibaldi station, run by the
Ferrovie dello Stato (state
railway), and the Milano-
Bovisa station, run by
Ferrovie Nord.

A number of different types
of train operate on Italy's
railways. The fastest train
linking Milan and the main
national and international
cities is the **ETR Eurostar**,
which is first-class only. The
ticket price includes a supple-

ment and obligatory seat
reservation. Free drinks and
newspapers are provided.
Eurocity trains also offer
fast links between Milan and
major European cities such
as Paris and Barcelona.
Intercity trains link Milan
and the main cities within
Italy such as Florence
and Rome. On both
Eurocity and Intercity
services tickets
should be
booked ahead.
A supplement
is charged.

The other types
of train are slower, but the
fares are reasonable, and
calculated by the kilometre.
Espresso trains stop at main
stations, Diretto trains at most
stations, and the Locale stops
at every single station
on the route.

There are also trains with
sleeping cars for people travelling at night. A *cuccetta*

The new Ferrovie
dello Stato logo

(bunk bed) in a compartment
can be reserved. Compart-
ments hold 6 or 4 beds.
A more expensive but more
private alternative are the
Wagons-Lits carriages (*vagoni
letto*). Compartments have
washing facilities, and breakfast is provided. A first-class
ticket is obligatory for a one-
bed cabin.

Train tickets can be pur-
chased at railway stations or
in travel agencies. Tickets
must be validated before
departure, by date-stamping
them at the station. This is
done at small yellow stamp-
ing machines which are found
normally at the entrance to
each platform (*binario*).

Tickets are valid for two
months from the time of
purchase, but once date-
stamped, they are only good
for 24 hours. If you are
adversely affected by a railway strike, tickets for travel
should be stamped by a ticket
inspector or
cashier in order to
claim a refund.
Seats, *cuccette*
and sleeping car
bunks can be
booked at railway
stations or at any
travel agency with
terminals linked to
the stations. Reservations can
be made two months before
departure time. Should your
travel plans change and you
need to alter a ticket, there is
a charge. Cancellations cost
20 per cent of the price of the
ticket if you cancel 24 hours
before departure; after this
you will be charged 50 per
cent of the price.

The ticket counters at the Porta Garibaldi railway station

Coaches parked at Piazza Castello in Milan

SGEA, SIA and STIE cover many key destinations in Lombardy, including most of the major holiday centres around the lakes.

The main carrier for Southern Italy is **Marino Autolinee**, while for main destinations in Europe the principal firm is **Eurolines**.

Long-distance coaches are comfortable, with reclining seats, air conditioning, toilets and television. There are regular stops at motorway service stations.

Tickets for coach travel can be purchased directly at the Piazza Castello terminuses. Timetables and rates vary according to the length of the journey and the seasons. Reductions are sometimes available for small children and the elderly.

ARRIVING BY COACH

COACH TRAVEL is a common means of getting about in Italy. Coaches (in Italian, *pullman*) arriving in Milan end their journey at the coach terminus at Piazza Castello. The most important coach carrier connecting Milan with northern and central Italy is **Autostradale Viaggi**, with direct connections with the motorway.

DIRECTORY

AIRPORTS

Information Linate – Malpensa
☎ 02-74 85 22 00.
🖥 www.sea-aeroportimilano.it

Lost and Found
☎ 02-70 12 44 51
(7:30am–9pm).

Left Luggage
☎ 02-71 66 59.

First Aid
☎ 02-74 85 22 22.

Lost and Found
☎ 02-58 58 00 70 (T1).
☎ 02-74 85 42 15 (T2).

Left Luggage
☎ 02-58 58 02 98 (T1).
☎ 02-40 09 93 63.

First Aid
☎ 02-74 86 44 44 (T1).
☎ 02-74 85 44 44 (T2).

CONNECTIONS WITH MALPENSA

Malpensa Express
From Milan (Piazzale Cadorna).
☎ 02-27 76 31.

Malpensa Shuttle
From Milan (Stazione Centrale).
🖥 02-277 63.

Autolinea Linate – Malpensa
🖥 02-58 58 31 85.

AIRLINES

Aeroflot
☎ 02-66 98 69 85.

Air France
☎ 14 78 84 466.
☎ 02-76 07 323.

Air One
☎ 14 78 48 88 00.

Alitalia
☎ 147 86 56 43.
(all flights).
☎ 02-24 99 27 00.
🖥 www.alitalia.it

British Airways
☎ 02-72 41 61.
☎ 14 78 12 266.
🖥 www.britishairways.com/italy

Go
☎ 147-88 77 66.
🖥 www.go-fly.com

Iberia
☎ 02-88 99.

Japan Airlines
☎ 02-72 00 46 80.

Lufthansa
☎ 02-80 66 30 25.

Meridiana
☎ 02-58 41 71.

Qantas
☎ 02-86 45 01 68.

TWA
☎ 02-76 25 03 00.
☎ 80 08 41 843.

RAILWAY STATIONS

Stazione Centrale
☎ 147 88 80 88
(State Railway info).

☎ 02-67 07 09 58
(Reception Centre).

☎ 02-63 71 22 12
(Left Luggage).

☎ 02-669 45 25
(Railway Police).

Ferrovie Nord (Cadorna)
☎ 02-84 47 75 00.

Porta Garibaldi
☎ 02-655 20 78
(Information).

Rogoredo
☎ 02-569 33 55.

COACHES

Autostradale Viaggi
Piazza Castello 1.
☎ 02-80 11 61.

Eurolines
c/o Autostradale Viaggi
Piazza Castello 1.
☎ 02-72 00 13 04.
☎ Florence: 055-35 71 10 (main office).

Marino Autolinee
☎ 02-669 12 22.
☎ 02-236 37 31.

SGEA
Viale Bligny 8–12.
☎ 02-58 30 16 18.

SIA
Piazza Castello 1.
☎ 02-86 46 23 50.

STIE
Via Paleocapa 1.
☎ 02-86 45 06 29.

Getting Around Milan

Although there are some traffic-free areas in Milan, such as the Brera and the historic centre, where you can stroll in relative peace and quiet, the city is not really very pedestrian-friendly. Milanese traffic is always heavy and often chaotic. This, combined with the great difficulty in finding parking space, would discourage anybody from using a car in Milan. Double parking, collisions and traffic jams are

Ticket for a car park in Milan

everyday matters, to say the least. Public transport *(see p212)* and, for the brave, scooters, offer the best solution to the problem of getting around. The tram, bus and metro network is efficient and ticketing is straightforward, with a flat fare operating in the city centre. One-day tickets offer good value. Tickets should be bought in advance and should be date-stamped before use. Fines are imposed on anyone caught having a "free ride".

Walking in Milan

Some areas of Milan are very pleasant to walk around. Strolling around the fashion district, for example, window shopping, is always an enjoyable aspect of Milan. Another good area for people on foot is the Navigli quarter, which is a pedestrian zone after 8pm. However, oases like these are few and far between in Milan, and the pedestrians' lot is by no means an easy one.

The main problem is the heavy traffic. Drivers tend to treat the streets as race tracks, and even where people crossing the streets are using the zebra crossings, the road markings may be ignored by motorists. An additional problem is that the chronic lack of parking space means that cars are usually parked on the pavements (side-

Corso Buenos Aires on a weekday

walks), leaving pedestrians very little room to manoeuvre. This is a particular problem for those trying to get around with prams or pushchairs.

Driving around Milan

Visitors should try to avoid getting around Milan by car if possible. The heavy, chaotic traffic, motorists who sound their car horns for no apparent reason, one-way streets and no-entry areas are enough to turn a tour of the city into a nightmare. However, if you absolutely must use a car, it is possible to park (for a fee) without risking a fine.

The authorized ATM sales points, usually tobacconists, bars and newsstands, sell SostaMilano cards, which are pay-ahead car parking tickets. They are also sold by the ATM personnel near the official car parks. The price varies according to the length

of time: a 1-hour ticket costs 2,500 lire, the 2-hour one 5,000 lire. Both can be used from 8am to 8pm. In the evening from 8pm to midnight you can use the 2-hour ticket. Just scratch off the gilded part of the ticket so that the year, month, day, hour and minute of the beginning of your parking time is clearly visible and then place it either over the dashboard or on the rear-view mirror. SostaMilano cards are also used in those areas marked and bordered by blue lines. Areas with yellow lines are reserved for residents only. From 8am to 8pm parking is allowed for a maximum of two hours in the blue areas, and the price is 2,500 lire per hour. From 8pm to midnight there a single fee of 5,000 lire for four hours. An alternative is the garages *(autorimesse) (see p211)*.

Ask the staff at the car parks if you need help.

Looking down Corso Vittorio Emanuele to Piazza del Duomo

Motorbikes and scooters parked in Piazza Cordusio

SCOOTERS, MOPEDS AND BICYCLES

SCOOTERS AND MOPEDS (*moto*) are certainly a good means of getting around Milan. They are fast and agile, allowing you to avoid long queues and traffic jams.

Bicycles (*biciclette*) can also provide an alternative, pro-vided you are confident and keep your wits about you. The tram tracks can be a nuisance for bicycle wheels. A number of companies offer moped or bicycle hire (rent).

TAXIS

ONE OF THE MOST common means of transport used in Milan, particularly for business purposes, is the taxi. Official taxis are generally white, but you may see yellow ones or taxis with the livery of their sponsors. Taxi stands are located throughout the city; all taxis have telephones and the numbers are listed in the telephone directory. At the beginning of the ride the meter should read 6,000 lire, to which is added a supplement for holidays and night runs and for luggage. To call a taxi, ring the radio taxi service.

DIRECTORY

BICYCLES AND SCOOTERS FOR HIRE

AWS (*bicycles*)
Via Ponte Seveso 33.
02-67 07 21 45.
awssnc@tiscalinet.it

Bianco Blu (*scooters*)
Via del Ricordo 31.
02-26 30 81 58.
www.biancoblu.com

Orizzonte
Via Bertini 3a.
02-33 10 30 41.
www.comunic.it/orizzonte

RADIO TAXI

02-85 85 or 02-67 67 or 02-53 53.

CAR PARKS IN THE CITY CENTRE

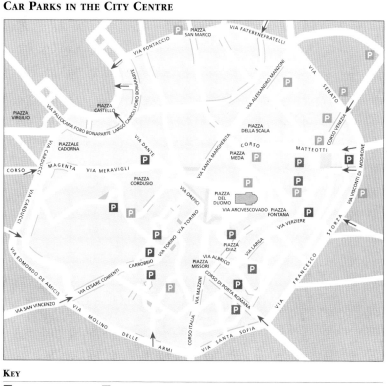

KEY

P Tariff A	P Free car park
P Tariff B	Pay car park

Resident parking — To city centre
Public transport park — City centre

Travelling by Public Transport

Logo of the Azienda Trasporti Municipali

To avoid stressful driving and parking problems, the best and least expensive way to get around town is to use public transport. Milan has a very efficient city transport system, run by the Azienda Trasporti Municipali (ATM), which comprises trams, buses, trolleybuses, and the three lines of the underground railway *(metropolitana)*.

TRAMS AND BUSES

TRAMS AND BUSES in Milan are all orange – except for the tourist trams *(see p201)*, which are green – and virtually serve the entire city. They are always extremely crowded, especially during rush hour, and generally pass by every ten minutes.

Bus and tram stops are easy to recognize. Each has a yellow sign displaying the route taken. Stops are often located on islands with seats for waiting passengers.

The yellow signs also have a timetable, but be careful to distinguish the summer *(estate)* from the winter *(inverno)* schedules, as they are posted side by side. Italian timetables always use the 24-hour clock, so that 20:00 hours is 8pm, for example.

The doors of trams and buses have signs indicating which to use to get on and off *(uscita* means exit), but they are often ignored, so don't be surprised if you see someone getting off where you are getting on, and vice versa.

Tickets should be bought before you get on, and your ticket should be date-stamped on the bus or tram. There is a small machine to validate *(convalidare)* your ticket; it is usually at the front, behind the driver, but on longer vehicles there are at least two, one in the front and the other at the back.

When you want to get off, press the red button to tell the driver you want to do so. A sign saying *"fermata prenotata"* will flash on and off until the next stop is reached.

Keep a close eye on your personal belongings, including your luggage, when travelling on public transport, particularly on a crowded bus or tram. Pickpockets may be on the lookout for handbags, mobile phones and wallets, and you must be wary.

THE METRO

AT PRESENT there are three underground railway (subway) lines: number 1 (red) was inaugurated in

An escalator at the exit of a Milan metro station

1964, while 2 (green) and 3 (yellow) are newer. Stations all have escalators (some have lifts/elevators for the disabled) and are usually located close to tram and bus stops. The trains run from about 6am to 12:30am and are often crowded. Once stamped, tickets can also be used for other means of public transport.

MILAN UNDERGROUND RAILWAY (METRO)

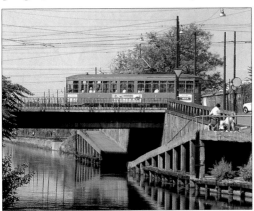

A tramcar going through the Navigli quarter

One of the Milan tourist trams *(see p201)*, painted green

PASSANTE FERROVIARIO

THIS TRAIN SERVICE links the northwest of Milan with the metro. The line goes from Porta Venezia to Bovisa, with intermediate stops at Piazza della Repubblica, Stazione Garibaldi and Via Lancetti.

TICKETS AND TIMETABLES

ALL TICKETS CAN be used for above-ground transport, the metro and the new Passante. Tickets cost 1,500 lire and are valid for 75 minutes on all lines. However, they cannot be used twice on the metro.

Tickets should be bought in advance as you cannot buy them on board. They are sold at newsstands, tobacconists and automatic vending machines, which operate with both coins and banknotes. The tourist tickets are good value. They cost 5,000 lire and are valid for 24 hours, or 9,000 lire (48 hours). Weekly and monthly passes *(abbonamenti)* are also available.

Milanese public transport, including the metro, usually operates from 6am to midnight, but some buses and trams stay in service until 1:30am. For detailed information, make enquiries at the ATM information bureaus.

DIRECTORY

ATM (Public Transport)
Linea Verde ATM
☎ 800-01 68 57.

Season Ticket Sales
Via Ricasoli 2.
🕐 8:45am–12:45pm, 2–3:45pm Mon–Fri.
Viale Stelvio 2.
🕐 8:30am–12:30pm, 2–4:15pm Mon–Fri.
Viale P Custodi 11. 🕐 8:30am–12:30pm, 2–4:15pm Mon–Fri.
You can purchase various passes at the Cadorna, Centrale FS, Duomo, Garibaldi FS, Loreto, Romolo and San Donato stations.

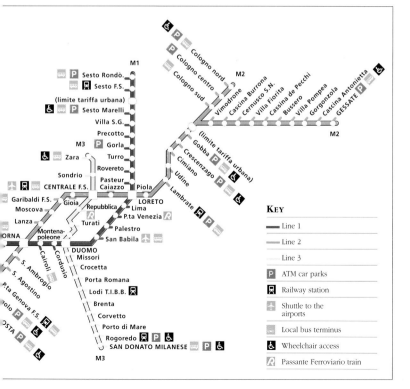

KEY

▬▬	Line 1
▬▬	Line 2
──	Line 3
🅿	ATM car parks
🚉	Railway station
✈	Shuttle to the airports
▦	Local bus terminus
♿	Wheelchair access
🚆	Passante Ferroviario train

Arriving at the Lakes

The funicular at Como in 1894

THE LAKES ARE EASILY ACCESSIBLE from Milan, both by car and by train. Visitors arriving by car will take the Autostrada dei Laghi motorway or the Valassina *superstrada*. There are good train links with all the lakes using either the Ferrovie dello Stato (FS) or the Ferrovie Nord (FNM) railways. Both offer decent services. Bus services link the various towns and villages around the lakes, or you may well prefer to use the ferries in order to avoid traffic jams on the crowded roads, especially at weekends.

A Ferrovie dello Stato regional train

LAKE MAGGIORE

TO GET TO LAKE Maggiore from Milan by car, take the A8 autostrada and then the exit for Sesto Calende. From here take the road to Angera to go to the Lombardy side of the lake, or the road to Arona to go to the Piedmontese side.

To get to the upper part of the lake, proceed northwards, turn off at Gravellona Toce and then follow the signs for Fondotoce and Verbania.

Should you decide to go to Lake Orta, take the Borgomanero turnoff and follow the signs for Gozzano-Orta San Giulio. The A8 autostrada is also the easiest way to get to Lake Varese from Milan: take the Varese exit and continue to Gavirate.

The lake is also accessible by train from the Porta Garibaldi railway station in Milan, where the local trains go as far as Luino, via Gallarate. Another rail company, the **Ferrovie Nord** railway operates from the station in Piazzale Cadorna. There are frequent daily train services to Laveno.

The most enjoyable way of travelling from one town to another on Lake Maggiore is to use the hydrofoils and ferries. The main towns are connected by the **Navigazione Lago Maggiore** service, which has a fleet of 30 vessels, including steamboats, motor boats and ferries. The timetables are posted at the local hotels, restaurants and all the ports, and are subject to seasonal changes.

If you are travelling to Lake Maggiore from outside Italy, the Malpensa 2000 airport (about 50 km, 30 miles from Milan) *(see p207)* is the closest to Lake Maggiore.

LAKE COMO

THE SHORTEST ROUTE from Milan to Lake Como by car is to take motorway *(autostrada)* A9, better known as Milano-Laghi, and exit at the Como Nord signs. To get to the western side of the lake, from Como take the statale 340 road, the ancient Via Regina, which goes as far as Sorico. If however you are headed for the other side, you have to go up the state road 583, which passes through Bellagio and goes as far as Lecco.

Traffic can be very heavy during the weekend, and as there is not much parking space around, the best solution may be to use a combination of car followed by one of the frequent hydrofoil or car ferry services. The hydrofoils are particularly frequent on the Como–Colico line, with intermediate stops, while the ferries stop only at Cadenabbia, Bellagio, Menaggio and Varenna. For detailed information, make enquiries at **Navigazione Lago di Como**.

The town of Como is also served by the Ferrovie dello Stato and Ferrovie Nord railways. The FS trains go to Como along the Milan–Chiasso line. The Nord trains leave from Piazzale Cadorna in Milan and arrive in the centre of town at Piazza Cavour. If you travel by air, the Malpensa 2000 airport is the closest one to Lake Como.

A ferry connecting the main towns around Lake Como

Lake Garda

VERONA IS THE NEAREST main town to the lake. It is on routes linking Milan with Venice, both road and rail. To reach Salò from the Milan–Venice A4 motorway, exit at the Brescia Centro signs and then go eastwards on the *tangenziale* (ring road) until you see signs for the Salò *superstrada* (highway). Alternatively you can exit at the Desenzano sign 118 km (73 miles) from Milan, cross the town and then go up the *statale* 572 road for 20 km (12 miles). A few kilometres past Salò is Gardone. Sirmione can be reached from Desenzano by following the southern side of Lake Garda for 9 km (6 miles), or by turning off the autostrada at the Sirmione-San Martino della Battaglia exit.

Navigarda tickets

To get to the Veneto side of the lake, take the A22 autostrada to Brennero and then exit at Affi.

To get to Lake Idro from Milan, take the A4 autostrada to Brescia Ovest and then proceed to Lumezzane.

Those coming from the east should take the state road that goes from Salò to Barghe, and then follow the signs for Madonna di Campiglio.

Lake Garda is also well served by trains. Desenzano del Garda and Peschiera del Garda are stops on the Milan–Venice line and coaches will take you onwards from these stations to Sirmione, Salò, Gardone and Limone. For more information, contact the **Azienda Provinciale Trasporti**.

A pleasant alternative is to travel on the lake: 21 boats offer continuous service on Lake Garda. The hydrofoils are the fastest means of crossing the lake and will save you time, while ferries go directly from Maderno to Torri del Benaco and back, for those who do not want to stop at every town on the route. Boat services are run by **Navigazione Lago di Garda (Navigarda)**.

The nearest airport is Catullo in Verona Villafranca. Other possibilities are Orio al Serio in Bergamo, Linate in Milan and Marco Polo in Venice.

Lake Iseo

THE EASIEST WAY to get to Lake Iseo by car is to take the A4 Milan–Venice motorway. Come off at the Ponte Oglio and Palazzolo exits to get to Rovato, Ospitaletto and Brescia Ovest exits to get to Iseo. If you go to the lake by train, the state railway takes you to Brescia, and from there you can go on the Ferrovie Nord Brescia-Iseo-Edolo line; passengers can take bicycles with them if required.

The best way to get to Sarnico and Lovere is to take a boat from Iseo.

Direzione Naviseo will provide information on timetabling. In the summer (from June to September) there is a train service to Sarnico on the Palazzolo-Paratico-Sarnico line, run by the Ferrovia del Basso Sebino, which operates in the Oglio River Regional Park in cooperation with the WWF and other environmental associations.

The Ferrovie Nord railway station in Piazzale Cadorna, Milan

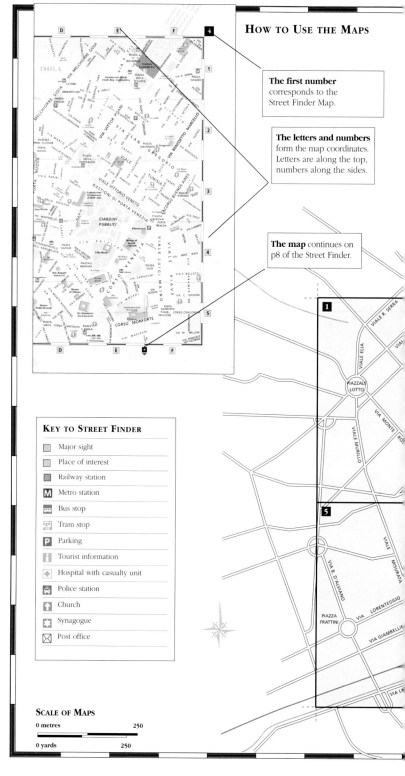

HOW TO USE THE MAPS

The first number
corresponds to the
Street Finder Map.

The letters and numbers
form the map coordinates.
Letters are along the top,
numbers along the sides.

The map continues on
p8 of the Street Finder.

KEY TO STREET FINDER

	Major sight
	Place of interest
	Railway station
M	Metro station
	Bus stop
	Tram stop
P	Parking
	Tourist information
	Hospital with casualty unit
	Police station
	Church
	Synagogue
	Post office

SCALE OF MAPS

0 metres	250
0 yards	250

MILAN STREET FINDER

ALL THE MAP REFERENCES in this guide, both in the *Milan Area by Area* and in the *Travellers' Needs* sections, refer to the maps in this *Street Finder*. The page grid superimposed on the *Area by Area* map below shows which parts of Milan are covered by maps in this section. Besides street names, the maps provide practical information, such as tram and bus stops, post offices, hospitals and police stations. The key on the opposite page shows the scale of the map and explains the symbols used. The main sights are shown in pink. On page 211 there is a map of the Milan metro system, including the Passante Ferroviario. Inside the back cover is a map showing the main stops on the Milan public transport network.

Street Finder Index

A

Abbiati Filippo (Via)	1 A4
Acquario	3 B4
Adda (Via)	4 D1
Adige (Via)	8 F4
Affari (Piazza degli)	7 B1
Africa (Largo)	1 C3
Agnello (Via)	8 D1
Agnesi Gaetana Maria (Via)	8 E4
Agudio Tommaso (Via)	2 E2
Alatri (Via)	1 B4
Albani Francesco (Via)	1 B2
Alberti Leon Battista (Via)	2 D1
Albertinelli (Via)	1 A3
Albertini Alfredo (Via)	2 F2
Alberto Mario (Via)	1 B4
Albricci Alberico (Via)	7 C2
Alcamo (Via)	1 A2
Alcuino (Via)	2 D2
Aleardi Aleardo (Via)	2 F1
	& 3 A2
Alemagna Emilio (Viale)	2 F3
Alessandria (Via)	6 F3
Alessi Galeazzo (Via)	7 A3
Alfieri Vittorio (Via)	3 A2
Algardi Alessandro (Via)	1 B1
Algarotti Francesco (Via)	4 D1
Allegranza Giuseppe (Via)	6 D2
Allori (Via)	1 A3
Altaguardia (Via)	8 E4
Altamura (Via)	1 A5
Altino (Via)	6 E2
Amedei (Via)	7 C2
Amendola–Fiera (metro station)	1 C4
Amendola Giovanni (Piazza)	1 C4
Amministrazione Provinciale	4 E5
Anco Marzio (Via)	6 F2
Anelli Luigi (Via)	8 D3
Anfiteatro (Via)	3 B3
Anfiteatro Romano	7 A2
Anfossi Augusto (Via)	8 F2
Angelicum	4 D3
Angioli (Via degli)	3 B4
Anguissola Sofonisba (Via)	5 A1
Annunciata (Via dell')	3 C4
Antonello da Messina (Via)	1 A5
Appiani Andrea (Via)	4 D3
Aquileia (Piazzale)	6 E1
Archimede (Via)	8 F1
Arco della Pace	2 F3
Arcole (Piazza)	6 F4
Arduino (Piazzale)	1 C3
Arena	3 A3
Arena (Via)	7 A2
Argelati (Piscina)	6 F4
Argelati Filippo (Via)	6 F4
Ariberto (Via)	6 F2
Ariosto Ludovico (Via)	2 E4
Arona (Via)	2 D1
Arzaga (Via)	5 A3
Asti (Via)	1 C5
Augusto (Largo)	8 D1
Aurispa Giovanni (Via)	7 B3
Ausonio (Via)	6 F2
	& 7 A2
Autari (Via)	6 E4
Avogadro (Via)	5 A5
Azario Pietro (Via)	6 F2
APT (Azienda di Promozione Turistica)	7 C1

B

Bach JS (Viale)	8 D4
Baiamonti Antonio (Piazza)	3 B2
Balbo Cesare (Via)	8 D4
Balestrieri Domenico (Via)	3 A3
Balilla (Via)	7 B4
Bandello Matteo (Via)	6 E1
Bande Nere (metro station)	5 A5
Baracca Francesco (Piazzale)	2 E5
Baracchini Flavio (Via)	7 C1
Baravalle Carlo (Via)	7 B4
Barbaro di San Giorgio Ramiro (Viale)	3 A3
Barbavara Francesco (Via)	6 F3
Barce (Via)	5 C3
Barinetti Giovanni Battista (Via)	2 E3
Barozzi Michele (Via)	4 E4
Barsanti Eugenio (Via)	6 E4
Bartolomeo d'Alviano (Via)	5 A2
Barzilai Salvatore (Via)	5 A3
Basiliche (Parco delle)	7 B3

Bassi Martino (Via)	1 A1
Battisti Cesare (Via)	8 E1
Bazzi Carlo (Via)	7 C5
Bazzi Giovanni Antonio (Piazza)	6 D2
Bazzoni Gian Battista (Via)	2 E5
Beatrice d'Este (Viale)	7 C4
Beauharnais (Viale)	3 A4
Beccaria Cesare (Piazza)	8 D1
Beccaria Cesare (Via)	8 D1
Beethoven Ludwig Van (Largo)	8 D5
Belfanti Serafino (Piazza)	6 F5
Belfiore (Via)	2 D5
Bellani Ettore (Via)	4 D1
Bellezza Giovanni (Via)	8 D4
Bellini Gentile (Via)	5 A4
Bellini Vincenzo (Via)	8 E1
Bellisario (Viale)	2 D4
Bellotti Felice (Via)	4 F4
Berengario (Viale)	1 C3
Bergamo (Via)	8 F2
Bergognone (Via)	6 E3
Bertacchi Giovanni (Via)	7 B4
Bertani Agostino (Via)	3 A3
Bertarelli Luigi Vittorio (Piazza)	7 C2
Bertieri Raffaello (Via)	5 B3
Bertini Giovanni Battista (Via)	2 F2
Bertinoro (Via)	1 A1
Besana Enrico (Via)	8 F2
Bettinelli Fratelli Angelo e Mario (Via)	7 A4
Bezzi Ergisto (Viale)	5 B1
Bianca di Savoia (Via)	7 C3
Biancamano (Piazzale)	3 B3
Bianca Maria (Viale)	8 F1
Biancardi G (Via)	1 B3
Bianchi Mosè (Via)	1 B3
Biancospini (Via dei)	5 A4
Bibbiena (Piazza)	7 B5
Bigli (Via)	4 D5
Bilbao (Piazza)	6 D5
Binda Ambrogio (Via)	5 C5
Biondi Ezio (Via)	2 D1
Bisleri (Via)	1 A5
Bixio Nino (Via)	4 F4
Bligny (Viale)	7 C4
Bobbio (Via)	6 F3
Boccaccio Giovanni (Via)	2 E5
Bocchetto (Via)	7 B1
Bocconi (Università Commerciale)	7 C4
Bocconi Ferdinando (Via)	7 C4
Boezio Severino (Viale)	2 D2
Boito Arrigo (Via)	3 C5
Bolivar Simone (Piazza)	5 C3
Boni Giacomo (Via)	6 D2
Bonnet Nino (Via)	3 B2
Bonzanni Aroldo (Via)	1 B4
Bordone Paris (Via)	1 B4
Bordoni Antonio (Via)	4 D1
Borelli Giovanni Alfonso (Via)	5 A2
Borgazzi (Via)	7 C3
Borghetto (Via)	4 F4
Borgogna (Via)	4 D5
Borgonuovo (Via)	3 C4
Borromeo (Piazza)	7 B1
Borromini Francesco (Via)	7 B5
Borsa	7 B1
Borsieri Pietro (Via)	3 C1
Borsi Giosuè (Via)	7 A5
Boschetti	4 E4
Boschetti (Via)	4 E4
Boscovich Ruggero (Via)	4 E2
Boselli Antonio (Via)	8 D5
Bossi (Via dei)	3 C5
Botta Carlo (Via)	8 F3
Braccio da Montone (Via)	3 A2
Bragadino Marco A (Via)	6 F2
Brahms Giovanni (Viale)	7 C5
Braida (Via della)	8 E3
Bramante Donato (Via)	3 A2
Breguzzo (Via)	1 A1
Brembo (Via)	8 F5
Brentonico (Via)	1 A1
Brera (Via)	3 C4
Brescia (Piazzale)	1 B4
Brin Benedetto (Via)	1 C3
Brioschi (Via)	7 B5
Brisa (Via)	7 B1
Broletto (Via)	3 B5
Brugnatelli Luigi (Via)	6 D5
Brunacci Vincenzo (Via)	7 A5
Brunelleschi Filippo (Via)	5 B5
Bruno Giordano (Via)	3 A2
Bruzzesi Giacinto (Via)	5 B4
Buenos Aires (Corso)	4 F3

Bugatti Gaspare (Via)	6 E3
Buonarroti (metro station)	1 C4
Buonarroti Michelangelo (Piazza)	1 C4
Buonarroti Michelangelo (Via)	1 C4
Buozzi Bruno (Piazza)	8 F4
Burchiello (Via del)	2 D5
Burigozzo Marco (Via)	7 B3
Burlamacchi Francesco (Via)	8 F4
Bussa Eugenio (Cavalcavia)	3 B1
Bussola Dionigi (Via)	6 D5
Byron (Viale)	3 A3

C

Caboto Sebastiano (Via)	6 D1
Caccialepori (Via)	1 A5
Cadamosto Alvise (Via)	4 F3
Cadorna (metro station)	3 A5
Cadorna Luigi (Piazzale)	3 A5
Cagnola Luigi (Via)	2 F3
Cagnoni (Via)	5 A1
Caiazzo (Piazza)	4 F1
Caiazzo (metro station)	4 F1
Caimi (Piscina)	8 F3
Caimi Giuseppe (Via)	7 B5
Cairoli (metro station)	3 B5
Cairoli Benedetto (Largo)	3 B5
Calabiana Arcivescovo (Via)	8 F5
Calatafimi (Via)	7 B3
Calco Tristano (Via)	6 F2
Caldara Emilio (Viale)	8 E2
California (Via)	6 D2
Calliano (Via)	1 A1
Camera del Lavoro	8 E1
Caminadella (Via)	7 A2
Campanini Alfredo (Via)	4 D1
Camperio Manfredo (Via)	3 B5
Campobasso (Via)	2 E1
Campo Lodigiano (Via)	7 B3
Camus Alberto (Largo)	2 D4
Caneva Generale Carlo (Piazzale)	2 D1
Canonica Luigi (Via)	2 F2
Canottieri Milano	5 B5
Canottieri Olona	5 C5
Canova Antonio (Via)	2 F3
Cantoni Giovanni (Via)	6 D1
Cantore Generale Antonio (Piazzale)	6 F3
Cantù Cesare (Via)	7 C1
Cappellini Alfredo (Via)	4 E2
Capponi Pier (Via)	2 D5
Cappuccini (Via)	4 E5
Cappuccio (Via)	7 A1
Caprera (Via)	6 D2
Caprilli (Via)	1 A2
Carabinieri d'Italia (Largo)	2 E4
Caradosso (Via)	2 F5
Caravaggio (Via del)	6 E2
Carcano Filippo (Via)	1 B3
Carceri Giudiziarie	6 E1
Carchidio (Via)	6 F4
Carducci Giosuè (Via)	3 A5
	& 7 A1
Carità (Strada della)	8 F4
Carlo Magno (Piazzale)	2 D2
Carmagnola Francesco Bussone Conte di (Via)	3 C1
Carmine (Via del)	3 B4
Carracci (Via dei)	1 B3
Carretto Aminto (Via)	4 E2
Carriera Rosalba (Via)	5 A4
Carrobbio (Largo)	7 B2
Carroccio (Via del)	7 A2
Cartesio (Via)	4 D2
Casale (Via)	6 F4
Casanova Luigi (Via)	4 E1
Casati Felice (Via)	4 E2
Cassala (Viale)	6 D5
Cassino (Via)	1 A1
Cassiodoro (Via)	2 D3
Castaldi (Via)	4 E3
Castaldi Panfilo (Via)	4 E3
Castelbarco Gian Carlo (Via)	7 C4
Castelfidardo (Via)	3 C2
Castello (Piazza)	3 A4
Castello Sforzesco	3 A4
Castelvetro Lodovico (Via)	2 E1
Castiglioni Cardinale (Via)	7 C5
Caterina da Forlì (Viale)	5 A2
Cavalcabò Pietro (Via)	5 C1
Cavalieri Bonaventura (Via)	4 D3
Cavalieri di Malta (Largo)	4 A3
Cavallotti Felice (Via)	8 D1
Cavenaghi Luigi (Via)	1 B4
Cavour Camillo Benso, Conte di (Piazza)	4 D4

Cecchi Antonio (Via)	5 C2
Cellini Benvenuto (Via)	8 F1
Cenacolo Vinciano	2 F5
Cenisio (Via)	2 E1
Centrale (Stazione FS)	4 E1
Centrale (metro station)	4 E1
Centro Direzionale	4 D1
Centro Sportivo Cappelli	7 C5
Cereso (Via)	6 E3
Ceresio (Via)	3 B1
Cernaia (Via)	3 C3
Cerva (Via)	8 E1
Cervantes Michele (Viale)	3 A3
Cesare da Sesto (Via)	6 F2
Cesariano Cesare (Via)	3 A3
Cézanne P (Via)	6 E5
Cherubini Francesco (Via)	2 D5
Chiesa Anglicana	3 C3
Chiesa Damiano (Piazzale)	2 D1
Chiesa Protestante	4 D3
Chiesa Russa Ortodossa	4 F3
Chieti (Via)	2 E1
Chiossetto (Via)	8 E1
Chiostri (Via dei)	3 B3
Chiusa (Via della)	7 B2
Chizzolini Gerolamo (Via)	2 E1
Cimabue (Via)	1 A1
Cimarosa Domenico (Via)	6 D1
Cimitero Monumentale	3 A1
Cimitero Monumentale (Piazzale)	3 A1
Cincinnato (Piazza)	4 E2
Cinque Giornate (Piazza)	8 F1
Ciovassso (Via)	3 C4
Circo (Via)	7 A1
Cirillo Domenico (Via)	2 F3
Città di Messico (Via)	1 B2
Claudiano (Via)	1 C3
Clefi (Via)	5 B1
Clerici (Via)	3 C5
Clusone (Via)	8 F2
Cola da Montano (Via)	3 B1
Cola di Rienzo (Via)	5 C3
Col del Rosso (Via)	7 B4
Col di Lana (Viale)	7 B4
Col Moschin (Via)	7 B4
Collecchio (Via)	1 A1
Colleoni Bartolomeo (Via)	1 C1
Colletta Pietro (Via)	8 F4
Colombo Cristoforo (Corso)	6 F3
Colonna Marco Antonio (Via)	1 C1
Colonna Vittoria (Via)	1 B5
Comerio Luca (Via)	2 E3
Comizi di Lione (Viale)	3 A3
Commenda (Via della)	8 E3
Como (Corso)	3 C2
Conca del Naviglio (Via)	7 A2
Conchetta (Via)	7 A5
Conciliazione (Piazza)	2 E5
Conciliazione (metro station)	2 E5
Conconi Luigi (Via)	1 B5
Concordia (Corso)	4 F5
Confalonieri Federico (Via)	3 C1
Coni Zugna (Viale)	6 E2
Conservatorio (Via)	8 E1
Conservatorio di Musica Giuseppe Verdi	8 F1
Consiglio di Zona 3	4 F2
Consiglio di Zona 5	7 B5
Copernico (Via)	4 E1
Coppi (Via)	1 A3
Corduslo (Piazza)	7 C1
Cordusio (metro station)	3 B5
Corio Bernardino (Via)	8 F4
Coriolano (Piazza)	3 A1
Corleone (Via)	2 D2
Cornalia Emilio (Via)	4 D1
Cornelio (Via)	5 C1
Coronelli (Via)	5 A4
Corpus Domini (Church)	2 F3
Correggio Antonio (Via)	1 B4
Correnti Cesare (Via)	7 A2
Corridoni Filippo (Via)	8 E1
Corsico (Via)	6 F3
Costanza (Via)	5 C2
Cozzi (Piscina)	4 E2
Crema (Via)	8 E4
Cremona Tranquillo (Via)	2 D4
Cremosano Marco (Via)	1 A2
Crespi Daniele (Via)	7 A2
Crispi Francesco (Via)	3 B2
Cristo Re (Church)	1 C2
Crivelli Carlo (Via)	8 D3
Crivellone Angelo Maria (Piazzale)	1 B4
Crocefisso (Via)	7 B2
Crocetta (Largo della)	8 D3
Crocetta (metro station)	8 D3

Crociate (Piazza delle) 3 B4
Crollalanza (Via dei) 6 E5
Cuneo (Via) 1 C5
Curie Pietro e Maria (Viale) 2 F4
Curio Dentato (Via) 5 A4
Curti Antonio (Via) 7 C5
Cusani (Via) 3 B5
Custodi Pietro (Via) 7 B4

D

D'Adda Carlo (Via) 6 D5
D'Annunzio Gabriele (Viale) 7 A3
D'Arezzo Guido (Via) 2 E5
D'Azeglio Massimo (Via) 3 B1
D'Oggiono Marco (Via) 7 A2
Da Cannobio Paolo (Via) 7 C1
Da Cazzaniga Tommaso (Via) 3 B3
Da Giussano Alberto (Via) 2 E5
Da Palestrina Pier Luigi (Via) 4 F1
Da Pisa Ugo (Via) 2 E3
Da Schio Almerico (Via) 5 A4
Da Volpedo Giuseppe Pellizza (Via) 1 B4
Dal Verme Jacopo (Via) 3 C1
Dandolo Enrico (Via) 8 F1
Dante (Via) 3 B5
Darsena 7 A3
Darwin Carlo Roberto (Via) 7 A5
Daverio Francesco (Via) 8 E2
De Agostini Giovanni (Piazzale) 6 D2
De Alessandri Giovanni (Via) 6 D1
De Amicis Edmondo (Via) 7 A2
De Angeli (metro station) 1 C5
De Angeli Ernesto (Piazza) 1 C5
De Castro Giovanni (Via) 2 D5
De Cristoforis Carlo (Via) 3 C2
De Gasperi Alcide (Viale) 1 A1
De Grassi Giovannino (Via) 6 F1
De Marchi Marco (Via) 4 D4
De Meis Angelo Camillo (Piazzale) 6 E1
De Taddei Marchese Malachia (Via) 5 C1
De Togni Aristide (Via) 6 F1
De Vincenti (Via) 1 A3
Del Fante Cosimo (Via) 7 B3
Del Piombo Sebastiano (Via) 1 B3
Della Robbia Luca (Via) 2 D4
Delleani L (Via) 1 B5
Desenzano (Via) 5 A1
Desiderio da Settignano (Via) 1 B3
Dezza Giuseppe (Via) 6 D1
Di Credi Lorenzo (Via) 1 B4
Diaz Armando (Piazza) 7 C1
Digione (Via) 5 C2
Diocleziano (Piazza) 2 E1
Disciplini (Via) 7 B2
Dolci Carlo (Via) 1 A4
Domenichino (Via) 1 B4
Domodossola (Largo) 2 D2
Domodossola (Via) 2 D2
Don Lorenzo Milani (Cavalcavia) 5 B5
Donati Mario (Via) 5 A3
Donizetti Gaetano (Via) 8 F1
Doria Andrea (Via) 4 F1
Duca d'Aosta (Piazza) 4 E1
Duccio di Boninsegna (Via) 2 D4
Dugnani Antonio (Via) 6 E2
Duilio (Via) 2 D2
Duomo 7 C1
Duomo (Piazza del) 7 C1
Duomo (metro station) 7 C1
Dürer A (Via) 1 A5
Durini (Via) 8 D1
Duse Eleonora (Piazza) 4 F4

E

Edison (Piazza) 2 B1
Egadi (Via) 6 D2
Eginardo (Viale) 1 A3
Einaudi Luigi (Piazza) 4 D1
Elba (Via) 6 D1
Elia Enrico (Viale) 1 A2
Elvezia (Via) 3 A3
Emanuele Filiberto (Via) 2 D1
Emiliani Gerolamo (Via) 8 F4
Eschilo (Via) 2 D3
Esposizione Permanente di Belle Arti 4 D3
Etiopia (Viale) 5 B2
Etna (Via) 6 D1

Eupili (Via) 2 E3
Euripide (Via) 2 D3
Europa (Corso) 8 D1
Ezio (Viale) 1 C4

F

Fanti Manfredo (Via) 8 E2
Faraday Michele (Via) 5 B5
Fara Generale Gustavo (Via) 4 D1
Faravelli Luigi Giuseppe (Via) 1 C1
Farini Carlo (Via) 3 B1
Faruffini Federico (Via) 1 B5
Fatebenefratelli (Via) 3 C4
Fatebenesorelle (Via) 3 C3
Favretto Giacomo (Via) 5 C2
Fedro (Via) 7 B5
Ferdinando di Savoia (Via) 4 D2
Ferrari Cardinale Andrea (Piazza) 8 D3
Ferrari Gaudenzio (Via) 7 A3
Ferrari Giuseppe (Via) 3 B1
Ferrario E (Via) 6 D1
Ferruccio Francesco (Via) 2 E2
Festa del Perdono (Via) 8 D1
Fezzan (Via) 5 B2
Fieno (Via) 7 C2
Fiera di Milano (Via) 1 C2
Filangeri Gaetano (Piazza) 6 F2
Filarete (Via) 2 E3
Filargo Pietro (Via) 6 D5
Filelfo Francesco (Via) 2 E2
Filippetti Angelo (Viale) 8 E4
Filzi Fabio (Via) 4 E1
Finocchiaro Aprile Camillo (Via) 4 E2
Fioravanti Aristotele (Via) 3 A2
Fiori Chiari (Via) 3 C4
Fiori Oscuri (Via) 3 C4
Firenze (Piazza) 2 D1
Fogazzaro Antonio (Via) 8 F2
Fontana (Piazza) 8 D1
Fontana (Via) 8 F1
Fontanesi Antonio (Via) 1 A3
Fonzaso (Via) 1 A5
Foppa Vincenzo (Via) 5 C2
Foppette (Via) 6 D4
Forcella Vincenzo (Via) 6 E3
Fornari Pasquale (Via) 5 A1
Foro Buonaparte 3 A4
Forze Armate (Via delle) 5 A1
Fra' Bartolomeo (Via) 5 C2
Fra' Galgario (Via) 5 A1
Franchetti Raimondo (Via) 1 B5
Frascati (Via) 1 A4
Frassinetti (Via) 1 A4
Frattini Pietro (Piazza) 5 A4
Freguglia Carlo (Via) 8 E1
Freud Sigmund (Piazza) 3 C1
Frisi Paolo (Via) 4 F3
Friuli (Via) 8 F4
Frua Giuseppe (Via) 5 B1
Fumagalli Angelo (Via) 6 F4
Fusaro (Via del) 5 C1
Fusetti Mario (Via) 7 A4

G

Gadda Carlo Emilio (Largo) 2 F2
Gadio Gerolamo Bartolomeo (Via) 3 A4
Galeazzo Gian (Viale) 7 B3
Galilei Galileo (Via) 4 D2
Galli Riccardo (Via) 1 A2
Galvani Luigi (Via) 4 D1
Gambara (Piazza) 5 A1
Gambara (metro station) 5 A1
Garian (Via) 5 C2
Garibaldi (metro station) 3 C1
Garibaldi Giuseppe (Corso) 3 B2
Gattamelata (Via) 1 C1
Gavirate (Largo) 1 A3
Gavirate (Via) 1 A3
Genova (Corso) 7 A2
Gentili Alberico (Via) 5 C1
Gentilino (Via) 7 B4
Gerusalemme (Piazza) 2 E1
Gessi Romolo (Via) 5 C2
Gesù (Via) 4 D5
Gherardini (Via) 2 F3
Ghiberti Lorenzo (Via) 1 B3
Ghirlandaio Domenico (Piazza) 1 B5
Ghisleri Arcangelo (Via) 6 F2
Giambellino (Largo) 5 A5
Giambellino (Via) 5 A4
Giambologna (Via) 7 B5
Giannone Pietro (Via) 3 A2
Giardini (Via dei) 4 D4

Giardini Pubblici 4 E4
Gigante (Via) 1 A4
Gignese (Via) 1 A3
Gignous Eugenio (Via) 1 B4
Gioberti Vincenzo (Via) 2 F5
Gioia (metro station) 4 D1
Gioia Flavio (Via) 1 C2
Gioia Melchiorre (Via) 3 C1
Giorgione (Via) 3 B2
Giorza Paolo (Via) 6 E4
Giotto (Via) 2 D5
Giovanni da Procida (Via) 2 D2
Giovanni XXIII (Via) 2 E3
Giovenale (Via) 7 B4
Giovine Italia (Piazza) 2 F5
Giovio Paolo (Via) 6 D1
Giuliano Savio (Via) 5 C2
Giusti Giuseppe (Via) 3 A2
Gnocchi VO (Via) 6 D3
Gobbi Ulisse (Via) 7 C4
Goethe (Via) 3 A3
Goito (Via) 3 C4
Gola Emilio (Via) 7 A4
Goldoni Carlo (Via) 4 F5
Gonzaga Maurizio (Via) 7 C1
Gorani (Via) 7 B1
Gorizia (Viale) 7 A3
Gracchi (Via dei) 5 B1
Gramsci Antonio (Piazza) 2 F2
Grancini Angelo Michele (Via) 2 D4
Grattacielo Pirelli (Sede Regione Lombardia) 4 E1
Grimani (Via dei) 5 C2
Griziotti Giacomo (Via) 2 D4
Grossi Tommaso (Via) 7 C1
Guastalla (Giardino) 8 D2
Guastalla (Via) 8 E1
Guercino (Via) 3 B2
Guerrazzi FD (Via) 2 E3
Guicciardini Francesco (Via) 4 F5
Guintellino (Via) 5 A5

H

Hoepli Ulrico (Via) 4 D5

I

Ibsen Enrico (Viale) 3 A4
Illica Luigi (Via) 3 A5
Immacolata Concezione (Church) 5 B1
Intendenza di Finanza 4 D3
Irnerio Carlo (Piazza) 5 C1
Isarco (Largo) 8 F5
Ischia (Via) 4 D1
Isola (Quartiere) 4 D1
Isonzo (Viale) 8 E5
Istituto delle Missioni Estere 1 B3
Istituto Ortopedico Gaetano Pini 8 D3
Istituto Sieroterapico Milanese 7 A5
Italia (Corso) 7 C2
Italico (Via 8 F3

J

Jacopo della Quercia (Via) 1 B3

K

Kramer Antonio (Via) 4 F4

L

La Foppa (Largo) 3 B3
Laghetto (Via) 8 D1
Lagrange Giuseppe L (Via) 7 A4
Lamarmora Alfonso (Via) 8 E2
Lambro (Via) 4 F4
Lambro Meridionale (Fiume) 6 D5
Lanino Bernardino (Via) 6 D2
Lanza (metro station) 3 B4
Lanza Giovanni (Via) 3 B4
Lanzone (Via) 7 A1
Larga (Via) 8 D1
Lattuada Serviliano (Via) 8 F3
Lauro (Via del) 3 B5
Laveno (Via) 1 A3
Lazio (Viale) 8 F3
Lazzaretto (Via) 4 E2
Lazzati Antonio (Via) 2 D1
Lecco (Via) 4 E3
Lega Lombarda (Piazza) 3 B3
Legnano (Via) 3 B3
Lentasio (Via) 7 C2
Leone XIII (Via) 2 D3
Leoni Pompeo (Via) 8 D5
Leopardi Giacomo (Via) 2 F5
& 3 A5

Lepetit Roberto (Via) 4 F1
Lesmi (Via) 7 A1
Letizia (Via) 6 E2
Leto Giunio Pomponio (Via) 5 C2
Liberazione (Viale della) 4 D2
Libia (Piazzale) 8 F3
Lido di Milano (Via) 1 A2
Liguria (Viale) 6 F5
Lincoln Abramo (Via) 8 F1
Linneo Carlo (Via) 2 E3
Lipari (Via) 6 D1
Litta Pompeo (Via) 8 F1
Livenza (Via) 8 E4
Livorno (Via) 4 E5
Lodi (Corso) 8 E4
Lodi Tibb (metro station) 8 F5
Lodovico il Moro (Via) 5 A5
Lomazzo Paolo (Via) 2 F1
Lombardini Elia (Via) 6 E4
Londonio Francesco (Via) 2 F2
Lorenteggio (Via) 5 A3
Lorenzini Giovanni (Via) 8 E5
Loria Moisè (Via) 6 D2
Losanna (Via) 2 E1
Lotto (metro station) 1 A1
Lotto Lorenzo (Piazzale) 1 A2
Lovanio (Via) 3 C3
Lovere (Via) 1 A1
Luini Bernardino (Via) 7 A1
Lusardi Aldo (Via) 7 C3

M

Macchi Mauro (Via) 4 F1
Machiavelli Niccolò (Via) 2 E3
Maddalena (Via) 7 C2
Madonnina (Via) 3 B4
Madre Cabrini (Via) 8 E3
Madruzzo Cristoforo (Via) 1 B2
Maffei Andrea (Via) 8 F2
Magenta (Corso) 3 A5
& 6 F1
Magenta (Porta) 2 E5
Maggi Carlo Maria (Via) 3 A3
Maggiolini Giuseppe e Carlo Francesco (Via) 4 F5
Magnasco Alessandro (Via) 1 B4
Magolfa (Via) 7 A4
Maino Giason del (Via) 1 A4
Majno Luigi (Viale) 4 F4
Malaga (Via) 6 D5
Malpighi Marcello (Via) 4 F3
Malta (Viale) 3 A3
Manara Luciano (Via) 8 E1
Mancini Lodovico (Via) 8 F1
Mangili Cesare (Via) 4 D3
Mangone Fabio (Via) 6 F2
Manin Daniele (Via) 4 D3
Mantegazza Laura (Via) 3 B5
Mantegna Andrea (Via) 2 E1
Mantova (Via) 8 F4
Manusardi (Corso) 7 A4
Manuzio Aldo (Via) 4 E2
Manzoni Alessandro (Casa del) 4 D5
Manzoni Alessandro (Via) 3 C4
Maratta (Via) 1 A4
Marcello Benedetto (Via) 4 F2
Marcona (Via) 8 F1
Marconi Guglielmo (Via) 7 C1
Marcora Giuseppe (Via) 4 D3
Marenco Romualdo (Via) 6 D1
Marengo (Piazzale) 3 B4
Margherita (Via) 1 C5
Mar Jonio (Via) 1 A3
Maroncelli Pietro (Via) 3 B1
Marostica (Via) 5 A1
Marradi G (Via) 7 A1
Marsala (Via) 3 C3
Martinitt (Via dei) 1 B5
Martiri Triestini (Via) 1 A4
Marussig Pietro (Via) 2 E1
Marziale (Via) 8 E1
Masaccio (Via) 1 B2
Mascagni Paolo (Via) 4 F4
Mascagni Pietro (Via) 4 E5
Mascheroni Lorenzo (Via) 2 E4
Massarenti Giuseppe (Via) 1 A4
Massaua (Via) 5 B2
Massena Andrea (Via) 2 E3
Mater Amabilis (Church) 1 C4
Matteotti Giacomo (Corso) 4 D5
Mauri Angelo (Via) 6 D1
Mayr Giovanni (Via) 4 F5
Mazzini Giuseppe (Via) 7 C1
Meda Filippo e Luigi (Piazza) 4 D5
Meda Giuseppe (Via) 7 A5
Medaglie d'Oro (Piazzale) 8 E4

Medici (Via) 7 B2
Medici Luigi (Largo) 2 F2
Melegnano (Via) 7 C3
Mellerio Giacomo (Via) 7 A1
Melloni Macedonio (Via) 4 F5
Meloria (Via) 1 B1
Melzi D'Eril Francesco (Via) 2 F3
Melzo (Via) 4 F3
Mentana (Piazza) 7 B1
Meravigli (Via) 3 B5
Mercalli Giuseppe (Via) 7 C3
Mercanti (Via dei) 7 C1
Mercato (Via) 3 B4
Messina (Via) 2 F1
                    & 3 A1
Metauro (Via) 5 B4
Micca Pietro (Via) 8 E2
Migliara Giovanni (Viale) 1 A3
Milazzo (Via) 3 C2
Milizie (Piazzale delle) 6 D4
Milton (Viale) 2 F4
Minghetti Marco (Via) 3 A5
Mirabello Carlo (Piazza) 3 C3
Missori (metro station) 7 C2
Missori Giuseppe (Piazza) 7 C1
Misurata (Viale) 5 C2
Modestino (Via) 6 F2
Modigliani Amedeo (Via) 6 D3
Mogadiscio (Via) 5 B2
Molière (Viale) 2 F4
Molino delle Armi (Via) 7 B2
Moncalvo (Via) 5 A1
Mondadori Arnoldo (Piazza) 7 C3
Moneta (Via) 7 B1
Monferrato (Via) 6 D1
Monforte (Corso) 4 E5
Monreale (Via) 1 A3
Monte Amiata (Via) 1 C3
Monte Asolone (Via) 2 F1
Montebello (Via) 4 C3
Monte Bianco (Via) 1 B3
Montecatini (Via) 6 D3
Monte Cervino (Via) 1 C3
Monte di Pietà (Via) 3 C5
Monte Falterona (Piazza) 1 A4
Monte Grappa (Viale) 3 C2
Monte Leone (Via) 1 C3
Montello (Viale) 3 B2
Montenapoleone
  (metro station) 4 D4
Montenapoleone (Via) 4 D5
Monte Nero (Via) 8 E2
Monte Rosa (Via) 1 B3
Monte Santo (Via) 4 D2
Montevideo (Via) 6 E2
Monti Vincenzo (Via) 2 E3
                    & 3 A5
Montorfano Donato (Via) 1 B4
Monviso (Via) 2 F1
Mora Gian Giacomo (Via) 7 A2
Morandi Rodolfo (Piazzale) 4 D4
Morazzone (Via) 2 F2
Morbelli Angelo (Via) 1 B4
Morigi (Via) 7 B1
Morimondo (Via) 5 B5
Morivione (Quartiere) 7 C5
Morone Gerolamo (Via) 3 C5
Moroni Giovanni Battista
  (Via) 5 A1
Morosini Emilio (Via) 8 F3
Morozzo della Rocca Enrico
  (Via) 6 F1
Mortara (Via) 6 F3
Moscati Pietro (Via) 2 F2
Moscova (metro station) 3 B3
Moscova (Via della) 3 B3
Motta Emilio (Via) 4 E5
Mozart (Via) 4 E5
Muratori Lodovico (Via) 8 F4
Murillo (Viale) 1 A3
Museo Archeologico 7 A1
Museo del Risorgimento 3 C5
Museo di Milano 4 D5
Museo di Storia Naturale 4 E4
Museo Nazionale della
  Scienza e della Tecnica 6 F1
Museo Poldi Pezzoli 4 D5
Mussi Giuseppe (Via) 2 E2

N

Nago (Via) 1 A1
Napoli (Piazza) 5 C3
Naviglio Grande 5 A4
Naviglio Grande (Alzaia) 5 A4
Naviglio Pavese 7 A4
Naviglio Pavese (Alzaia) 7 A4
Necchi Lodovico (Via) 6 F1
Negrelli (Piazzale) 5 A5
Negri Gaetano (Via) 7 B1
Neri Pompeo (Via) 5 B3
Niccolini GB (Via) 3 A2

Nievo Ippolito (Via) 2 D3
Nirone (Via) 7 A1
Novegno (Via) 1 C3
Novi (Via) 6 E3
Numa Pompilio (Via) 6 F2

O

Oberdan Guglielmo
  (Piazza) 4 F3
Oderzo (Via) 1 A1
Olivetani (Via degli) 6 E1
Olmetto (Via) 7 B2
Olona (Via) 6 F2
Omboni Giovanni (Via) 4 F3
Omenoni (Casa degli) 3 C5
Ore (Via delle) 8 D1
Orefici (Via) 7 C1
Organdino Giuseppe (Via) 5 C1
Oriani Alfredo (Via) 8 D3
Orobia (Via) 8 F5
Orseolo Pietro (Via) 6 F3
Orso (Via dell') 3 C5
Orti (Via) 8 E3
Orto Botanico 3 C4
Osoppo (Via) 1 A5
Ospedale 8 E2
Ospedale dei Bambini
  Vittore Buzzi 2 E1
Ospedale Fatebenefratelli 3 C2
Ospedale Maggiore di Milano
  (Policlinico) 8 D2
Ospedale Regina Elena 8 E2
Ospedale San Giuseppe 6 F1
Ottolini Giordano (Via) 7 B5

P

Pace (Via della) 8 E2
Pacioli Fra' Luca (Via) 6 F3
Pagano (metro station) 2 D5
Pagano Mario (Via) 2 E3
Pagliano Eleuterio (Via) 1 B3
Palazzetto dello Sport
  (Palalido) 1 A2
Palazzi Lazzaro (Via) 4 E3
Palazzo Archinto 8 E1
Palazzo Arcivescovile 8 D1
Palazzo Bagatti Valsecchi 4 D4
Palazzo Belgioioso 4 D5
Palazzo Borromeo 3 C4
Palazzo Clerici 3 C5
Palazzo Cusani 3 C4
Palazzo della Ragione 7 C1
Palazzo dell'Arte 3 A4
Palazzo delle Stelline 6 F1
Palazzo del Senato 4 E4
Palazzo di Brera 3 C4
Palazzo di Giustizia 8 E1
Palazzo Dugnani 4 D3
Palazzo Durini 8 E1
Palazzo Litta 3 A5
Palazzo Marino 3 C5
Palazzo Reale 7 C1
Palazzo Rocca Saporiti 4 E4
Palazzo Serbelloni 4 E5
Palazzo Sormani 8 D1
Palazzo Stanga 7 A1
Paleocapa Pietro (Via) 3 A5
Palermo (Via) 3 B3
Palestro (metro station) 4 E4
Palestro (Via) 4 D4
Palladio Andrea (Via) 8 E4
Pallavicino Giorgio (Via) 2 D4
Palma Jacopo (Via) 5 A1
Pandino (Via) 5 A5
Panizza Bartolomeo (Via) 6 E1
Panizzi (Via) 5 A3
Pantano (Via) 7 C2
Panzacchi (Via) 7 A1
Panzeri Pietro (Via) 7 A3
Panzini Alfredo (Via) 2 D4
Paoli Pasquale (Via) 6 F4
Papi Lazzaro (Via) 8 F4
Papiniano (Viale) 6 E1
Papini Giovanni (Via) 1 C1
Parini Giuseppe (Via) 4 D3
Parmigianino (Via) 1 B5
Paselli Ernesto (Via) 7 B5
Passeroni Gian Carlo (Via) 8 F4
Passione (Via) 8 E1
Passo Buole (Via) 8 F4
Pastorelli Giovanni (Via) 6 D5
Pastrengo (Via) 3 C1
Pasubio (Viale) 3 B2
Patellani Carlo (Via) 8 D4
Pattari (Via) 8 D1
Pavia (Via) 7 A5
Pecorari Francesco (Via) 7 C1
Pellegrini (Via dei) 8 D3
Pellico Silvio (Via) 3 C5
                    & 7 C1

Pepe Guglielmo (Via) 3 B1
Perosi (Via) 5 A3
Peschiera (Via) 2 F3
Pestalozzi Giovanni Enrico
  (Via) 5 C5
Pesto (Via) 5 C4
Petitti Carlo Ilarione (Via) 1 C1
Petrarca Francesco (Via) 2 E4
Petrella Enrico (Via) 4 F1
Piacenza (Via) 8 E4
Piatti (Via dei) 7 B2
Piave (Viale) 4 F4
Piccolo Teatro 3 B5
Pichi Mario (Via) 7 A4
Piemonte (Piazza) 1 C5
Pier della Francesca (Via) 2 D1
Pier Lombardo (Via) 8 F3
Piermarini Giuseppe
  Francesco (Via) 2 F3
Pietrasanta (Via) 8 D5
Pinacoteca Ambrosiana 7 B1
Pinacoteca di Brera 3 C4
Pinamonte da Vimercate
  (Via) 3 B2
Pini Gaetano (Via) 8 D3
Pio Albergo Trivulzio 5 B1
Pioppette (Via) 7 B2
Pirandello Luigi (Via) 6 D1
Pirelli Giovanni Battista
  (Via) 4 D1
Pisanello (Via) 1 A5
Pisani Vittor (Via) 4 E2
Planetario 4 E4
Plutarco (Via) 2 D3
Po (Piazza) 8 E1
Podgora (Via) 8 E1
Poggibonsi (Via) 1 A5
Pogliaghi (Via) 5 A5
Poldi Pezzoli (Via) 1 A3
Polibio (Via) 6 D1
Politecnico (Università) 6 D1
Poliziano Angelo (Via) 2 E1
Polo Marco (Via) 4 D2
Pompeo (Via) 2 D3
Pontaccio (Via) 3 B4
Ponte Vetero (Via) 3 B5
Ponti Andrea (Via) 6 D5
Pontida (Via) 3 B2
Porrone Bassano (Via) 3 C5
Porta Carlo (Via) 4 D4
Porta Garibaldi 3 C2
Porta Garibaldi
  (Stazione FS) 3 C1
Porta Genova 6 F3
Porta Genova (Stazione FS) 6 F3
Porta Genova
  (metro station) 6 F3
Porta Lodovica 7 C4
Porta Monforte 4 F5
Porta Nuova 4 D2
Porta Nuova (Archi di) 4 D4
Porta Nuova (Bastioni) 3 C2
Porta Nuova (Corso di) 3 C2
Porta Romana 8 E3
Porta Romana (Corso di) 7 C2
Porta Ticinese 7 B3
Porta Ticinese (Corso di) 7 B2
Porta Venezia 4 F4
Porta Venezia (Bastioni di) 4 E3
Porta Venezia
  (metro station) 4 E3
Porta Vercellina (Viale di) 6 E1
Porta Vigentina 8 D4
Porta Vigentina (Corso di) 8 D3
Porta Vittoria 8 F1
Porta Vittoria (Corso di) 8 E1
Porta Volta 3 B2
Porta Volta (Bastioni di) 3 B2
Poste e Telegrafi 4 F1
Poste Telegrafo e
  Telefoni 7 B1
Pozzi Antonia (Via) 1 B3
Pozzobonelli (Cascina) 4 F1
Praga Emilio e Marco
  (Via) 2 D3
Prati Giovanni (Via) 2 D3
Preda (Via) 7 B5
Prefettura 4 E5
Premuda (Viale) 8 F1
Presolana (Via) 8 F2
Previati Gaetano (Via) 1 B4
Primule (Via delle) 5 A4
Prina Giuseppe (Via) 2 F2
Principe Amedeo (Via) 4 D3
Principessa Clotilde
  (Piazzale) 4 D2
Procaccini Giulio C
  (Via) 2 E1
Procopio (Via) 5 C3
Properzio (Via) 8 F3
Provveditorato agli Studi 8 D5
Pucci Marcello (Via) 2 E3

Q

Quadrio Maurizio (Via) 3 B1
Quadronno (Via) 7 C3
Quarnero (Via) 5 C1
Quattro Novembre (Piazza) 4 E1
Questura 4 D4
Quinto Alpini (Largo) 2 E4

R

RAI (Radio Televisione
  Italiana) 2 E2
Randaccio Giovanni (Via) 2 E3
Ranzoni Daniele (Viale) 1 B5
Rasori Giovanni (Via) 2 E5
Rastrelli (Via) 7 C1
Ravizza (Parco) 8 D4
Ravizza Carlo (Via) 1 B4
Razza L (Via) 4 E2
Reale (Villa) 4 E4
Redaelli Piero (Via) 5 A3
Reggimento Cavalleria
  Savoia (Via) 2 E4
Reggio (Via) 8 E3
Regina Giovanna (Viale) 4 F3
Regina Margherita (Viale) 8 F1
Rembrandt (Via) 1 A5
Repubblica (Piazza della) 4 D2
Repubblica (metro station) 4 D3
Resistenza Partigiana
  (Piazza della) 7 A2
Respighi Ottorino (Via) 8 E1
Restelli Francesco (Viale) 4 D1
Revere Giuseppe (Via) 2 F4
Ricciarelli Daniele (Via) 1 A4
Richard (Viale) 5 B5
Richini Francesco (Largo) 8 D2
Ripa di Porta Ticinese 6 D4
Ripamonti Giuseppe (Via) 8 D4
Riva Rocci Scipione (Via) 5 B3
Riva Villasanta Alberto (Via) 2 E2
Romagnoli Ettore (Via) 5 B3
Romagnosi Gian Domenico
  (Via) 3 C5
Romana (Piazza) 3 C5
Romana (metro station) 8 E4
Romano Giulio (Via) 8 E4
Romolo (metro station) 6 E5
Romolo (Via) 6 E5
Roncaglia (Via) 5 C2
Ronchetti Anselmo (Via) 4 E5
Rondoni Pietro (Via) 5 A3
Rontgen Guglielmo (Via) 7 C4
Ronzoni Gaetano (Via) 7 A3
Rosales Gaspare (Via) 3 C2
Rosario (Piazza del) 6 E3
Rosmini Antonio (Via) 3 A2
Rossetti Dante Gabriel
  (Via) 2 D4
Rossini Gioacchino (Via) 4 F5
Rotonda della Besana 8 F2
Rotondi Giovanni (Via) 2 D3
Rovani Giuseppe (Via) 2 F5
Rovello (Via) 3 B5
Rubens Pier Paolo (Via) 1 A5
Ruffini Fratelli (Via) 2 F5
Rugabella (Via) 7 C2
Russi (Via) 1 A1

S

Sabbatini Leopoldo (Via) 7 C4
Sabotino (Viale) 8 E4
Sacchi Giuseppe (Via) 3 B5
Sacco Luigi (Via) 5 C1
Sacra Famiglia (Church) 1 C4
Sacro Volto (Church) 3 C1
Saffi Aurelio (Via) 2 F5
Salaino Andrea (Via) 6 E2
Sala Luigi (Via) 6 D5
Salasco (Via) 8 D4
Salmini Vittorio (Via) 8 E2
Salmoiraghi (Viale) 1 A1
Salutati Coluccio (Via) 6 D1
Salvini Tommaso (Via) 4 E4
Sambuco (Via) 7 B3
Sammartini Giovan Battista
  (Via) 4 E1
San Babila (Piazza) 4 D5
San Babila (metro station) 4 D5
San Barnaba (Via) 8 D2
San Benedetto (Church) 5 B2
San Bernardino alle Monache
  (Church) 7 A2
San Calimero (Church) 8 D3
San Calimero (Via) 8 D2
San Calocero (Via) 7 A2
San Camillo (Church) 4 E2
San Carlo (Church) 4 D5
San Carlo al Lazzaretto
  (Church) 4 F3

San Celso (Church) **7 C3**
San Cipriano (Church) **6 E5**
San Cristoforo (Church) **5 C5**
San Cristoforo (Quartiere) **5 C5**
San Cristoforo (Via) **5 C4**
San Damiano (Via) **4 E5**
San Fedele (Church) **3 C5**
San Fedele (Piazza) **3 C5**
San Fermo della Battaglia (Via) **3 C3**
San Francesco d'Assisi (Via) **7 C3**
San Gioachino (Piazza) **4 D2**
San Giorgio al Palazzo (Church) **7 B1**
San Giovanni di Dio (Via) **6 F1**
San Giovanni sul Muro (Via) **3 B5**
San Gottardo (Church) **8 D1**
San Gottardo (Corso) **7 A4**
San Gottardo al Corso (Church) **7 A4**
San Gregorio (Church) **4 F2**
San Gregorio (Via) **4 E2**
San Lorenzo Maggiore (Basilica) **7 B2**
San Luca (Via) **7 B3**
San Mansueto (Via) **8 D4**
San Marco (Church) **3 C4**
San Marco (Piazza) **3 C4**
San Marco (Via) **3 C3**
San Martino della Battaglia (Via) **7 C3**
San Maurilio (Via) **7 B1**
San Maurizio (Church) **7 A1**
San Michele del Carso (Viale) **6 E1**
San Nazaro Maggiore (Church) **8 D2**
San Nicolao (Via) **3 A5**
San Paolo (Via) **4 D5**
San Paolo Converso (Church) **7 C2**
San Pietro all'Orto (Via) **4 D5**
San Pietro dei Pellegrini (Church) **8 E3**
San Pietro in Gessate (Church) **8 E1**
San Pietro in Sala (Church) **2 D5**
San Pio V (Via) **7 A1**
San Primo (Via) **4 E4**
San Raffaele (Via) **7 C1**
San Rocco (Via) **8 E4**
San Satiro (Basilica) **7 C1**
San Sebastiano (Church) **7 B1**
San Senatore (Via) **7 C2**
San Sepolcro (Church) **7 B1**
San Sepolcro (Piazza) **7 B1**
San Simpliciano (Church) **3 B4**
San Simpliciano (Via) **3 B4**
San Siro (Ippodromo) **1 A2**
San Siro (Via) **1 C4**
San Sisto (Via) **7 B1**
San Tomaso (Via) **3 B5**
San Vincenzo (Via) **7 A2**
San Vincenzo in Prato **7 A2**
San Vito (Church) **5 B4**
San Vito (Via) **7 B2**
San Vittore (Via) **6 E1**
San Vittore al Corpo (Church) **6 F1**
Sangiorgio Abbondio (Via) **2 E3**
Sant'Agnese (Via) **7 A1**
Sant'Agostino (Church) **7 A1**
Sant'Agostino (Piazza) **6 F2**
Sant'Agostino (metro station) **6 F2**
Sant'Alessandro (Church) **7 C2**
Sant'Ambrogio (Basilica) **7 A1**
Sant'Ambrogio (Piazza) **7 A1**
Sant'Ambrogio (Pusterla di) **7 A1**
Sant'Ambrogio (metro station) **6 F1**
Sant'Andrea (Church) **8 E4**
Sant'Andrea (Via) **4 D5**
Sant'Angelo (Church) **4 D3**
Sant'Angelo (Piazza) **3 C3**
Sant'Anna (Church) **1 B2**
Sant'Antonio (Via) **8 D1**
Sant'Antonio di Padova (Church) **3 B1**
Sant'Eufemia (Church) **7 C2**
Sant'Eufemia (Via) **7 C2**
Sant'Eusebio (Via) **6 D1**
Sant'Eustorgio (Church) **7 B3**
Sant'Eustorgio (Piazza) **7 A3**
Sant'Ildefonso (Church) **1 C1**
Sant'Orsola (Via) **7 B1**
Santa Cecilia (Via) **4 E5**
Santa Croce (Via) **7 B3**
Santa Lucia (Via) **7 C3**
Santa Margherita (Via) **3 C5**
Santa Maria Addolorata (Church) **5 A2**
Santa Maria alla Porta (Via) **7 B1**
Santa Maria degli Angeli e San Francesco (Church) **1 A5**
Santa Maria dei Miracoli, (Santuario) **7 C3**
Santa Maria del Carmine (Church) **3 B4**
Santa Maria della Pace (Church) **8 E2**
Santa Maria della Passione (Church) **8 E1**
Santa Maria della Visitazione (Church) **7 C2**
Santa Maria delle Grazie (Church) **2 F5**
Santa Maria delle Grazie (Piazza) **2 F5**
Santa Maria delle Grazie al Naviglio (Church) **6 F4**
Santa Maria del Rosario (Church) **6 E3**
Santa Maria di Caravaggio (Church) **7 B5**
Santa Maria Fulcorina (Via) **7 B1**
Santa Maria Incoronata (Church) **3 C2**
Santa Maria Nascente (Church) **1 A1**
Santa Maria Segreta (Church) **2 E5**
Santa Maria Segreta (Via) **7 B1**
Santa Marta (Via) **7 B1**
Santa Sofia (Via) **7 C2**
Santa Teresa del Bambino Gesù (Church) **1 C1**
Santa Valeria (Via) **7 A1**
Santi Angeli Custodi (Church) **8 F4**
Santi Barnaba e Paolo (Church) **8 E2**
Santi Protaso e Gervaso (Church) **1 B4**
Santissima Trinità (Piazza) **3 A2**
Santo Spirito (Via) **4 D4**
Santo Stefano (Piazza) **8 D1**
Sanzio Raffaello (Via) **1 C5**
Sardegna (Via) **5 C1**
Sarfatti Roberto (Via) **7 C4**
Saronno (Via) **2 E2**
Sarpi Paolo (Via) **3 A2**
Sartirana (Via) **6 F3**
Sassetti Filippo (Via) **4 D1**
Savarè Manlio e Gioachino (Via) **8 E1**
Savona (Via) **5 B3**
Savonarola Fra' Gerolamo (Via) **2 D2**
Scala (Piazza della) **3 C5**
Scalabrini (Largo) **5 A4**
Scaldasole (Via) **7 A3**
Scarampo Lodovico (Viale) **1 B1**
Scarlatti Domenico (Via) **4 F1**
Scarpa Antonio (Via) **2 E5**
Schievano Enrico (Via) **6 E5**
Sciesa Amatore (Via) **8 F1**
Scoglio di Quarto (Via) **7 A4**
Scrosati (Via) **5 A3**
Sebenico (Via) **3 C1**
Segantini Giovanni (Via) **6 F4**
Segesta (Piazzale) **1 A3**
Sei Febbraio (Piazza) **2 D3**
Selinunte (Piazzale) **1 A4**
Seminario Arcivescovile (Ex) **4 D5**
Sempione (Corso) **2 D1**
Sempione (Parco) **3 A4**
Sempione (Piazza) **2 F3**
Sempione (Porta) **2 F3**
Senato (Via) **4 D4**
Seneca (Via) **8 F3**
Senofonte (Via) **2 D3**
Seprio (Via) **1 C5**
Serao Matilde (Via) **6 D1**
Serbelloni Gabrio (Via) **4 E4**
Serra Renato (Viale) **1 B1**
Servio Tullio (Via) **6 F2**
Sesto Calende (Via) **1 A1**
Settala Lodovico (Via) **4 E2**
Settembrini Luigi (Via) **4 F1**
Settimio Severo (Largo) **2 E5**
Settimo Ruggero (Via) **6 C1**
Sforza Cardinale Ascanio (Via) **7 A4**
Sforza Francesco (Via) **8 D2**
Shakespeare William (Viale) **3 A4**
Sicilia (Piazza) **5 C1**
Signora (Via della) **8 D1**
Signorelli Luca (Via) **2 F2**
Signorini Telemaco (Via) **1 C1**
Silva Guglielmo (Via) **1 B2**
Simonetta Cicco (Via) **7 A3**
Sinagoga (Synagogue) **8 E2**
Sirte (Via) **5 C3**
Sirtori Giuseppe (Via) **4 F3**
Soave Francesco (Via) **8 D5**
Società Umanitaria **8 E2**
Soderini (Via) **5 A3**
Sofocle (Via) **2 D4**
Solari (Parco) **6 E2**
Solari Andrea (Via) **6 D3**
Soldati Giacomo (Via) **2 F1**
Solferino (Via) **3 C2**
Soperga (Via) **4 F1**
Soresina Giovanni Battista (Via) **6 E1**
Sormani (Via dei) **6 D2**
Sottocorno Pasquale (Via) **4 F5**
Spadari (Via) **7 C1**
Spagnoletto Ribera Giuseppe (Via) **1 B4**
Spallanzani Lazzaro (Via) **4 F3**
Spartaco (Via) **8 F2**
Speri Tito (Via) **3 B2**
Spiga (Via della) **4 D4**
Spinola Ambrogio (Via) **1 C3**
Sraffa Angelo (Largo) **7 C4**
Stampa (Via) **7 B2**
Statuto (Via) **3 B3**
Stazione Ferrovie Nord (Milano) **3 A5**
Stazione Porta Genova (Piazzale) **6 F3**
Stelline (Via delle) **5 B1**
Stendhal (Via) **6 D2**
Stromboli (Via) **6 D2**
Strozzi Piero (Via) **5 A2**
Stuparich Carlo (Piazza) **1 A1**
Sturzo Luigi (Viale) **3 C1**
Svetonio (Via) **8 F3**

T

Tabacchi Odoardo (Via) **7 B5**
Tadino Alessandro (Via) **4 F2**
Tagiura (Via) **5 B2**
Tamburini Pietro (Via) **2 E4**
Tantardini A (Via) **7 B5**
Tarchetti (Via) **4 D3**
Tarquinio Prisco (Via) **6 F2**
Tarra Giulio (Via) **4 E1**
Tartaglia Nicolò (Via) **2 F1**
Tasso Torquato (Via) **2 E4**
Tazzoli Enrico (Via) **3 B1**
Teatro alla Scala **3 C5**
Teatro Carcano **8 D2**
Teatro Dal Verme **3 B5**
Teatro Fossati **3 B4**
Teatro Nazionale **1 C5**
Teatro Studio (Ex Fossati) **3 B4**
Telesio Bernardino (Via) **2 E4**
Tempesta Pietro (Via) **1 B3**
Tenaglia (Via) **3 B3**
Tenca Carlo (Via) **4 E2**
Teodorico (Viale) **1 C1**
Terraggio (Via) **7 A1**
Teuliè Pietro (Via) **7 C4**
Tibaldi (Viale) **7 B5**
Tintoretto Jacopo (Via) **1 C4**
Tiraboschi Gerolamo (Via) **8 F3**
Tito Lucrezio Caro (Piazza) **7 B4**
Tivoli (Via) **3 B4**
Tiziano (Via) **2 D4**
Tobruk (Via) **5 C3**
Tocqueville (Via di) **3 B2**
Tolstoi Leone (Via) **5 B3**
Tombone di San Marco **3 C2**
Tommaseo Nicolò (Piazza) **2 E5**
Toniolo G (Via) **7 C4**
Tonoli Rita (Via) **2 E3**
Torchio (Via del) **7 A2**
Torino (Via) **7 B1**
Torre Carlo (Via) **6 E5**
Torriani Napo (Via) **4 E1**
Torricelli E (Via) **7 A5**
Tortona (Via) **6 D3**
Toscana (Viale) **7 C5**
Tosi Arturo (Via) **6 E5**
Tosi Franco (Via) **6 D5**
Traiano Marco Ulpio (Via) **1 C1**
Tranchedini N (Via) **1 C2**
Trebazio (Via) **2 E2**
Trebbia (Via) **8 E4**
Trento (Piazza) **8 E5**
Treves Claudio (Largo) **3 C3**
Trezzo d'Adda (Via) **6 D3**
Tricolore (Piazza del) **4 F5**
Trieste (Via) **5 C1**
Tripoli (Piazzale) **5 B2**
Trivulzio AT (Via) **1 B5**
Troya Carlo (Via) **5 C4**
Tulipani (Via dei) **5 A4**
Tunisia (Viale) **4 E2**
Turati (metro station) **4 D3**
Turati Filippo (Via) **4 D3**
Türr Stefano (Piazzale) **1 C1**

U

Uccello Paolo (Via) **1 B2**
Uffici della Provincia **8 E1**
Ulpiano Domizio (Via) **5 C2**
Umanitaria (Piazza) **8 E2**
Unione (Via dell') **7 C1**
Università Cattolica **7 A1**
Università degli Studi di Milano (Ex Ospedale Maggiore) **8 D2**

V

Vacani (Via) **1 A3**
Vaina (Via) **8 E3**
Valenza (Via) **6 F4**
Val Lavizzana (Via) **5 A1**
Val Leventina (Via) **1 A5**
Valparaiso (Via) **6 E2**
Val Vigezzo (Via) **1 C1**
Vannucci Atto (Via) **8 D4**
Varazze (Via) **1 A4**
Varese (Via) **3 B2**
Vasari Giorgio (Via) **8 F3**
Vasto (Via) **3 B3**
Vecchio Politecnico (Via del) **4 D4**
Vegezio Flavio (Via) **1 C3**
Velasca (Torre) **7 C2**
Velasquez (Piazzale) **1 A5**
Venafro (Via Privata) **2 F2**
Venezia (Corso) **4 E4**
Veniero S (Via) **1 B2**
Venticinque Aprile (Piazza) **3 C2**
Ventimiglia (Via) **6 F3**
Ventiquattro Maggio (Piazza) **7 A3**
Venti Settembre (Via) **2 E5**
Vepra (Via) **6 D2**
Vercelli (Corso) **2 D5**
Verdi Giuseppe (Via) **3 C5**
Verga Andrea (Via) **6 D1**
Verga Giovanni (Via) **3 A2**
Verona (Via) **8 E4**
Veronese Paolo (Via) **2 D4**
Verri Pietro (Via) **4 D5**
Verziere (Via) **8 D1**
Vesio (Via) **1 A1**
Vespri Siciliani (Via) **5 B3**
Vespucci Amerigo (Via) **4 D2**
Vesuvio (Piazza) **6 D2**
Vetere (Via) **7 B3**
Vetra (Piazza della) **7 B2**
Vetta d'Italia (Via) **6 D2**
Vico Gian Battista (Via) **6 E1**
Viganò F (Via) **3 C2**
Vigevano (Via) **6 F3**
Vigliani PO (Viale) **1 B2**
Vigna (Via) **7 A1**
Vignola (Via) **8 D4**
Vignoli Tito (Via) **5 B3**
Vigoni Giuseppe (Via) **7 C3**
Vigorelli (Ex Velodromo) **2 D2**
Villoresi Eugenio (Via) **6 E4**
Virgilio (Piazza) **2 F5**
Visconti di Modrone (Via) **8 E1**
Visconti Venosta Emilio (Via) **8 F2**
Vitruvio (Via) **4 F2**
Vittadini Carlo (Via) **8 D4**
Vittorio Emanuele II (Corso) **8 D1**
Vittorio Emanuele II (Gall.) **7 C1**
Vittorio Veneto (Viale) **4 E3**
Vivaio (Via) **4 F5**
Viviani Vincenzo (Via) **4 D2**
Vodice (Via) **1 A3**
Voghera (Via) **6 E3**
Volta Alessandro (Via) **3 B2**
Volterra (Via) **5 C1**
Volturno (Via) **3 C1**

W

Wagner (metro station) **1 C5**
Wagner Riccardo (Piazza) **2 D5**
Washington Giorgio (Via) **5 C1**
Watt Giacomo (Via) **5 C5**
Winckelmann GG (Via) **5 B3**

Z

Zaccaria Sant'Antonio Maria (Via) **8 E2**
Zamenhof LL (Via) **7 B5**
Zandonai Riccardo (Largo) **2 D4**
Zanzur (Via) **5 C2**
Zarotto A (Via) **4 E3**
Zavattari Fratelli (Piazzale) **1 A3**
Zenale Bernardino (Via) **6 F1**
Zezon Achille (Via) **4 E1**
Zola Emilio (Viale) **2 F4** & **3 A4**
Zuara (Via) **5 B2**
Zuccaro (Via) **5 A4**

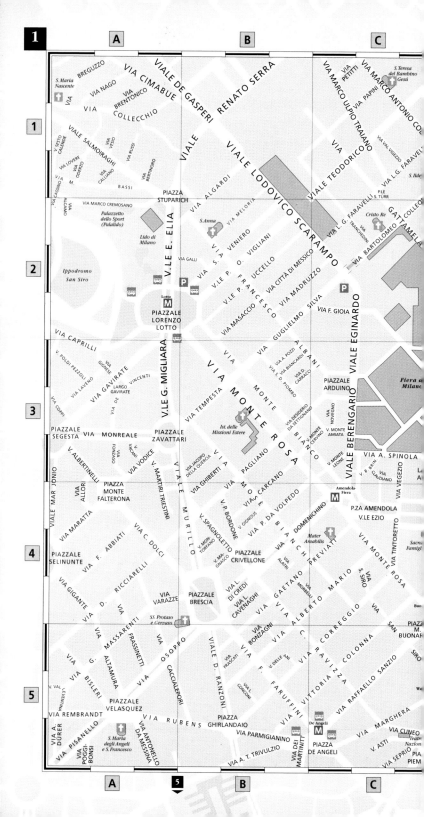

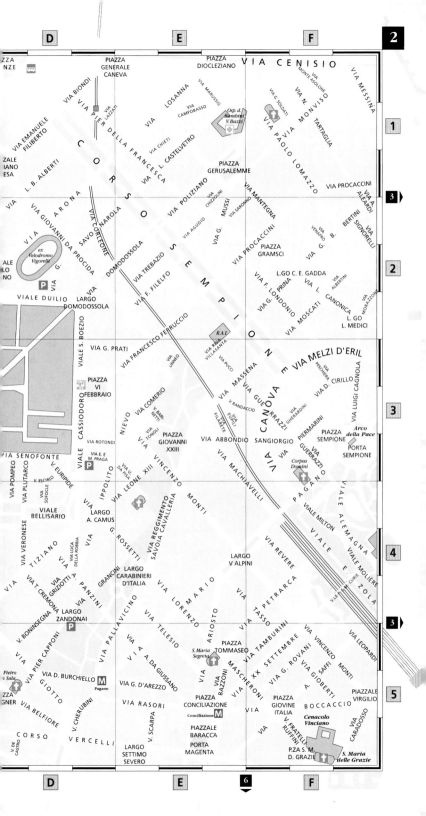

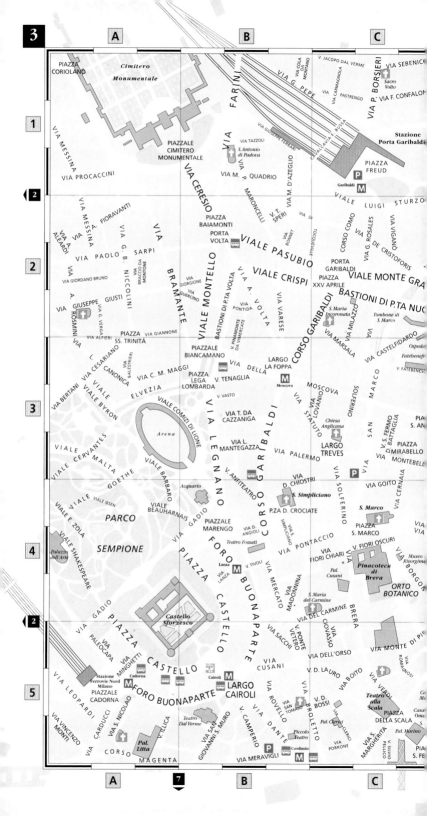

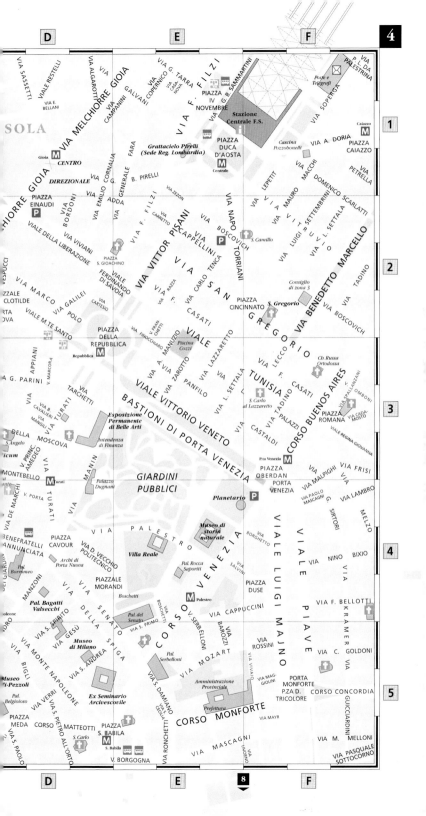

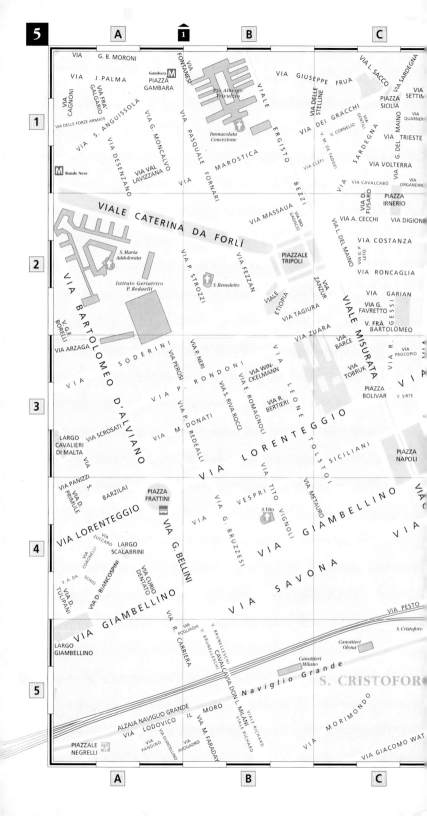

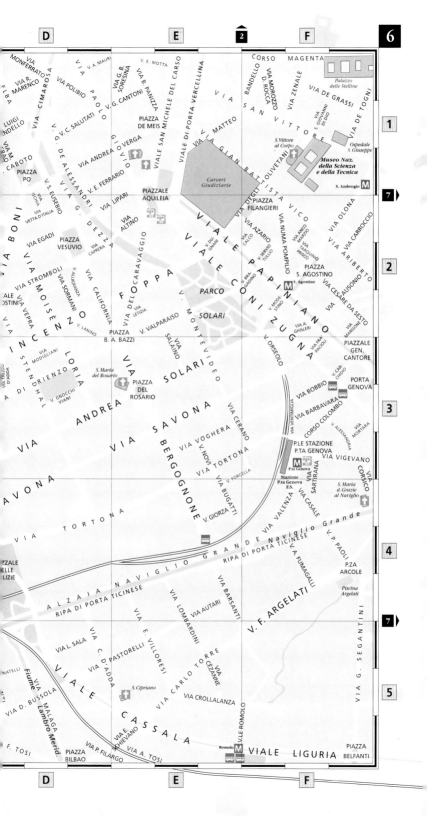

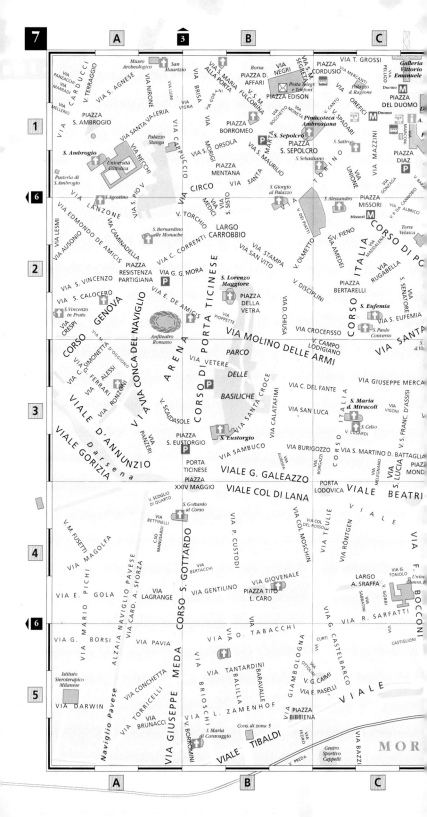

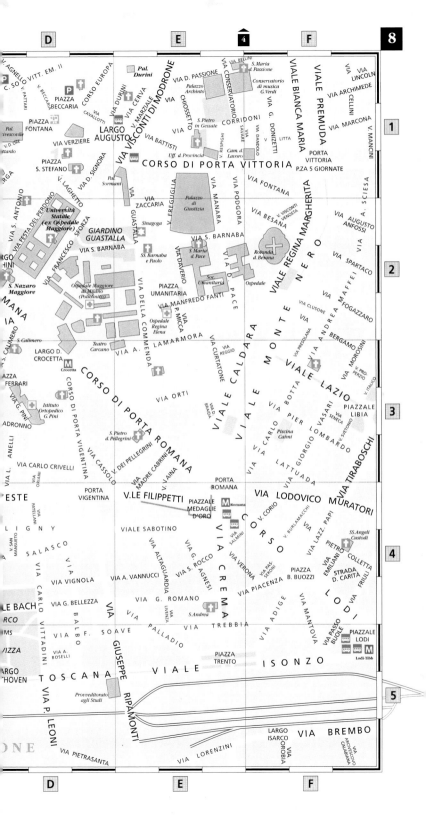

General Index

The numbers in **bold type**
refer to main entries.

A

Acquafredda Abbey 139
Abbiati, Filippo 91
    St Bernard 87
Abbondio, Antonio 32
Accademia del Disegno 56
Accademia di Belle Arti 110, 114, 116
Accademia Tadini 151
Achille Bertarelli Collection 66
Acquario Civico 63, **68**
Adaloaldo, king 83
Adda river 69, 110, 136, 137
Agilulf, king 16
Agostino di Duccio 66
    St Sigismund on a Journey 66
Alberico XII di Belgioioso d'Este 51
Albertolli, Giocondo 141
Alboin, king 16
Alemagna, Emilio 62, 68, 120
Alessi, Galeazzo 50, 98
Alighieri, Dante 142
    Divine Comedy 59
    Inferno 147
Alps 133
Ambrosian Republic 17, 19, 64
Angelica di San Paolo convent 91
Angera 132
Angilberto, archbishop 86
Anspert da Biassono, archbishop 55, 84, 86
Antelami, Benedetto 66
    Re Magi relief 66
Antonio da Saluzzo 46
Appiani, Andrea 59, 91, 101, 117, 121, 139, 141
    Olympus 117
    Parnassus 121
    Portrait of Napoleon 59
Archi di Porta Nuova 106, 109
Arcimboldi brothers 57
Arco della Pace 21, 61, 62, 68, 69, 139
Arena Civica 21, 62, 68
Areste, Bartolomeo 74
Arianteo 37
Ariberto d'Intimiano, bishop 16, 17, 48
Aristotle 57, 59
Armani, Giorgio 107
Arona 131, **132**
Arp, Hans 121
Assicurazioni Generali 75
Atellani residence 74
Anspert's Atrium (Sant'Ambrogio) 84, 86
Attila 16
Ausonius 55
Authari, king 16

B

Bagatti Valsecchi, Giuseppe 109
Bagolino 151
Bagutta-Pittori all'Aria Aperta 36
Baldo, Monte 146
Balduccio, Giovanni 112
Balla, Giacomo 54, 121
Balzaretto, Giuseppe 120, 139
Bambaia (Busti Agostino) 59, 67
Banca Commerciale Italiana 108
Banca dell'Agricoltura 45
Bar Jamaica 110
Bar Magenta 74
Barbarossa, Federick 16, 36, 90, 96, 112, 113, 138
Barbiano di Belgioioso, Ludovico 121
Bardolino **147**

Barnabas 90
Barnabiti family 91
Barzaghi, Francesco 68
Baschenis, Evaristo 59, 117
    Still Life with Musical Instruments 59
Basilica
    Sant'Ambrogio 12, 15, 27, 30, 78, **84–7**
    Sant'Eustorgio 30, 32, 39, 79, 82, **90**
    San Giuliano (Gozzano) 150
    San Giulio (Isola di San Giulio) 150
    San Lorenzo alle Colonne 12, 15, 27, 30, 32, 78, 79, **80–81**, 82
    Santa Maria Maggiore 43
    San Nazaro Maggiore 15, 1, 94, **96**
    San Simpliciano 15, 110; **113**
    Santa Tecla 43
Basilica Martyrum (Sant'Ambrogio) 84
Basilica Virginum (San Simpliciano) 113
Bassano, Jacopo 58
    Rest on the Flight into Egypt 58
Bassi, Martino 31, 50, 81, 91, 100
Battagio, Giovanni 100
Bava Beccaris, Fiorenzo 24
Baveno 133
Beatrice d'Este 71
Beccaria, Cesare 21, 29
    Essays on Crime and Punishment 21, 29
Bedoli, Mazzola Girolamo 59
    Annunciation 59
Belgioioso, Lodovico Barbiano di 96
Belgioioso Collection 67
Belgirate 132, 136
Bellagio 141
Bellano 140
Bellini, Gentile
    St Mark Preaching in Alexandria 116
Bellini, Giovanni 67, 106, 108, 151
    Crucifixion 108
    Pietà 34, 108, 116
    Madonna and Child 67
    Poet Laureate 67
    St Mark Preaching in Alexandria 116
    Santa Giustina 109
Bellini, Vincenzo 100
Bellotto, Bernardo 117
Beltrami, Luca 50, 62, 64, 65, 67, 75, 98, 103, 118, 119
    Assicurazioni Generali building 75
    Casa Dario 75
Bembo, Bonifacio 65, 67
    Resurrection 67
Benedictines 84, 85, 86, 88
Bergamo 151
Bergognone (Ambrogio da Fossano) 91, 99, 101, 108, 115, 116, 132
    Christ among the Doctors 87
    Risen Christ 87
    Funeral of St Martin 99
    Coronation of the Virgin 113
    Sacred Conversation 58
Bernardino da Siena 83
Bertini brothers 46, 49
Bertini, Giuseppe 59, 108
    Dantesque stained glass 59
Bianchi, Federico 91
    Life of St Alexander 91
Bianchi, Mosè 59
Biandronno 150
Biblioteca Ambrosiana 20, 28, **59**
Biblioteca Sormani Andreani 95, 99
Biblioteca Trivulziana 66, 91
Biffi, Giovanni Battista 21

Binago, Lorenzo 91
Bini, Giuseppe 46
Birago, Daniele 100
Bistolfi, Leonardo 118
BIT 36
Boccaccio, Giovanni 59, 67
Boccioni, Umberto 118, 121
    Unique Forms of Continuity in Space 54
    The City Rises 116
    Brawl in the Galleria 116
Bogliaco 142
Boiola 144
Bolli, Bartolomeo 74
Bombings (World War II) 24, 25, 43, 52, 55, 71, 72, 84, 98, 120
Bonino da Campione 66
    Mausoleum of Bernabò Visconti 66
Bordone, Paris 71
    Holy Family and St Jerome 91
    Holy Family with St Catherine 71
Borgia, Lucrezia 59
Borromeo, Bona 135
Borromeo, Federico 20, 34, 56, 58
Borromeo, San Carlo 20, 48, 49, 50, 56, 98, 123, 134
Borromeo family 130, 131, 132, 134, 135
Borsa Valori (Stock Exchange) 75
Bossi, Giovan Battista 119
Botticelli, Sandro 108
    Pietà 108
    Madonna and Child 108
    Madonna del Padiglione 56, 58
Bramante (Donato di Pascuccio di Antonio) 17, 30, 55, 64, 71, 78, 84, 87, 102, 114, 123
    Christ at the Pillar 117
Bramantino (Bartolomeo Suardi) 58, 64, 67, 94, 96
    Annunciation 75
    Crucifixion 116
    Deposition 67
    Madonna di Caravaggio 101
    Madonna of the Towers 58
Branca, Giulio 134
Brasa torrent 146
Brentani, Pietro 140
Brera, Mercato dell'Antiquariato 39
Brera, Pinacoteca *see* Pinacoteca
Brera quarter 12, 105, **110–11**
Bresci, Gaetano 24
Brescia 144, 151
Bril, Paul 59
Brivio, Giovanni Stefano (sarcophagus) 90
Broggi, Luigi 75
Broletto 82
Bronzino (Agnolo di Cosimo) 117
Brueghel, Jan the Elder 117
    The Village 117
Brueghel, Jan 59
    Mouse with Roses 59
    Allegories of Water and Fire 59
Brunate 138
Burgundians 16
Burri, Alberto 54
Buses 212
Butinone, Bernardino 71, 99
Butti, Enrico 118
Buzzi, Carlo 46, 98
Byron, George Gordon 127, 130
Byzantines 139

C

Ca' Granda (Ospedale Maggiore) 12, 17, 19, 27, 33, 93, 94, 95, **97**, 100
Caesar 135
Caffè Greco 29
Caffè Trianon 51
Cagnola, Luigi 55, 69, 95, 98

Caimi, Protaso 90
Cairo, Francesco 59
Calderara Collection of Contemporary
  Art (Vacciago di Ameno) 150
Campari, Davide 118
Campi, Antonio 99, 113
  Resurrection 91
Campi, Bernardino 67, 94
  Transfiguration 50
Campi, Giulio
  Crucifixion 101
Canale 5 25
Canaletto (Canal Giovanni Antonio)
  117, 142
Canons' bell tower (Sant'Ambrogio)
  84
Candoglia marble 46, 77, 89
Canella, Carlo
  Battle at Porta Tosa 22–3
Cannobino torrent 134
Cannobio **134**
Canonica, Luigi 68
Canova, Antonio 59, 121, 151
  Cupid and Psyche (copy) 137, 139
  Self-portrait 59
  Terpsichore 139
Cantoni, Simone 122, 138
Caravaggio (Michelangelo Merisi) 34,
  58, 111, 114, 117
  Basket of Fruit 57, 58
  Supper at Emmaus 117
Carloni, Carlo Innocenzo 139
  Apotheosis of Bartolomeo Colleoni
  108
Carlotta of Prussia 137
Carnevale Ambrosiano 36, 39
Carpaccio, Vittore 116
  Legend of the Virgin 116
Carrà, Carlo 54
  The Metaphysical Muse 116
Carracci, Agostino 117
Carracci, Annibale 117
Carracci, Ludovico 94, 117
Carroccio 17, 113
Casa Bettoni 96
Casa Campanini 101
Casa del Fascio 138
Casa Fontana-Silvestri 123
Casa Galimberti 32, 119
Casa di Lucia 141
Casa Manzoni **51**
Casa degli Omenoni 32, **51**
Casa del Podestà 132
Casa Toscanini 98
Casati, Isabella 118
Caselli Daziari 68, 69
Castles
  Castello di Cannero 127
  Castello dell'Innominato 141
  Castello degli Oldofredi 151
  Castello di Porta Giovia *see* Castello
    Sforzesco
  Castello Scaligero 147
  Castello Sforzesco 17, 19, 22, 27,
    32, 61, 62, 63, **64–7**, 70, 91, 103,
    118
  Castello di Vezio 137
  Castello Visconti di San Vito 132
  Malpaga castles 130
Castiglioni, Ermenegildo 118
Castiglioni, Giannino 119
Cattaneo, Carlo 21, 22, 118
Catullus 142
Cavour, Benso Camillo count of 109,
  118
Cazzaniga, Francesco 71
Cazzaniga, Tommaso 71, 90
Cecca 39
Celesti, Andrea 146
Celts 15
Centomiglia 142

Cerano, (Giovan Battista Crespi) 49,
  50, 67, 91, 112, 132, 133
  *Madonna Freeing Milan from
    the Plague* 71
  Martyrdom of St Catherine 91
  *Martyrdom of Saints Rufina and
    Seconda* 117
  Vision of St Ignatius 50
Cernobbio 136, **138**
Certosa di Garegnano **70**
Ceruti, Giovanni 120
Cesa Bianchi, Paolo 123
Cesare da Sesto 67
Cézanne, Paul 121
Chagall, Marc 121
Chapels
  Cappella di Sant'Antonio Abate 88
  Cappella di Sant'Aquilino 81
  Cappella Arese 88
  Cappella di San Bartolomeo 87
  Cappella di San Bernardino alle
    Ossa 94
  Cappella Brivio 90
  Cappella di Santa Caterina 96
  Cappella di Santa Corona 71
  Cappella Crotta-Caimi 90
  Cappella Ducale 65, 66
  Cappella di San Giorgio 87
  Cappella dei Grifo 99
  Cappella della Madonna delle
    Grazie 71
  Cappella di Mocchirolo 116
  Cappella Portinari 30, 90
  Cappella del Santissimo Sacramento
    87
  Cappella di San Sisto 80
  Cappella della Torre 71
  Cappella Torriani 90
  Cappella Trivulzio 31, 94, 96
  Ossuary chapel 98
Charles V 17, 20, 83, 134
Chiaravalle Abbey 12, 13, 27, **102–3**
Chiaravalle, Fiera 38
Chiaretto 145
Chiari, Walter 118
Chiasso 19
Chierici Regolari di San Paolo
  College 98
Chiostrino delle Rane 71
Churches
  Chiesa dell'Annunciata 97
  Chiesa del Carmine (Luino) 134
  Chiesa della Madonna di
    Campagna 134
  Chiesa della Madonna di Piazza
    (Arona) 132
  Inviolata (Riva del Garda) 146
  Sacro Monte (Varese) 151
  Sant'Abbondio (Como) 138
  Sant'Alessandro **91**
  Sant'Ambrogio (Stresa) 133
  Sant'Andrea (Iseo) 151
  Sant'Andrea (Maderno) 146
  Sant'Angelo **113**
  Sant'Antonio Abate 94
  San Babila 122, 123
  Santi Barnaba e Paolo 98
  San Bernardino alle Monache 78,
    83
  San Bernardino alle Ossa 95, **98**
  San Carlo (Menaggio) 139
  San Carlo al Corso 45, 51
  San Celso 91
  San Cristoforo al Naviglio 89
  San Donato (Sesto Calende) 132
  San Donnino alla Mazza 106
  Sant'Emiliano (Padenghe) 144
  Sant'Ercolano (Maderno) 146
  Sant'Eusebio (Gravedona) 140
  San Fedele (Como) 138
  San Fedele 31, 44, **50**

Churches (cont.)
  San Francesco (Gargnano) 146
  Santi Gervasio e Protasio
    (Baveno) 133
  San Giacomo (Bellagio) 141
  San Giacomo di Calino (Gargnano)
    146
  San Giorgio (Varenna) 140
  San Giorgio al Palazzo **55**
  San Giovanni (Torno) 140
  San Giovanni a Montorfano
    (Baveno) 133
  San Giovanni in Conca 91
  San Giuseppe (Luino) 134
  San Gottardo in Corte 19, **54**
  Santi Gusmeo e Matteo
    (Gravedona) 140
  San Leonardo (Pallanza) 134
  San Marco 19, 31, 111, **112**
  Santa Maria Assunta
    (Riva del Garda) 146
  Santa Maria del Benaco
    (Toscolano) 146
  Santa Maria di Brera 66
  Santa Maria del Carmine 111, **112**
  Santa Maria delle Grazie (Milan)
    12, 17, 19, 28, 30, 61, **71**, 72, 103
  Santa Maria delle Grazie
    (Gravedona) 140
  Santa Maria delle Grazie al Naviglio
    89
  Santa Maria Incoronata **113**
  Santa Maria Maddalena
    (Ossuccio) 136
  Santa Maria Maddalena al Cerchio
    78
  Santa Maria Maggiore (Garda) 147
  Santa Maria Maggiore (Sirmione) 144
  Santa Maria dei Miracoli 91
  Santa Maria Nascente (Arona) 132
  Santa Maria della Neve
    (Moniga del Garda) 144
  Santa Maria della Neve (Pisogne)
    151
  Santa Maria della Pace 100
  Santa Maria della Passione **100**
  Santa Maria della Sanità 98
  Santa Maria della Scala 50, 52
  Santa Maria de Senioribus
    (Desenzano del Garda) 144
  Santa Maria del Tiglio (Gravedona)
    137, 140
  Santa Maria in Valvendra (Lovere)
    151
  Santa Maria presso San Celso **91**
  Santa Maria presso San Satiro **55**
  Santa Marta (Bellano) 140
  Santa Marta (Varenna) 140
  San Martino (Peschiera del Garda)
    147
  San Maurizio **75**, 83
  San Michele (Belgirate) 132
  San Michele ai Nuovi Sepolcri 100
  Santi Nazaro, Celso e Giorgio
    (Bellano) 140
  San Nicolao (Colico) 140
  San Nicolò (Lazise) 147
  San Nicolò (Lecco) 141
  San Paolo Converso **91**
  San Pietro al Monte (Lecco) 141
  San Pietro in Campagna (Luino)
    134
  San Pietro in Gessate 19, **99**
  San Pietro in Lucone (Polpenazze
    del Garda) 145
  San Pietro in Mavino (Sirmione)
    144
  San Rocco (Bagolino) 151
  San Rocco (Limone sul Garda) 146
  San Satiro 55
  San Sebastiano (Villa) 132

Churches (cont.)
San Sepolcro **55**, 57, 58
San Severo (Bardolino) 147
San Sisto 79
Santo Stefano (Lenno) 139
Santo Stefano (Menaggio) 139
Santo Stefano (Pallanza) 134
Santo Stefano Maggiore 95, **98**
Santa Tecla (Torno) 141
Santissima Trinità (Solarolo) 145
Santissima Trinità (Torri del
Benaco) 147
San Vittore al Corpo **88**
San Zeno (Bardolino) 147
Churchill, Winston 141
Cimitero Monumentale 28, 105, **118**
Cinque Giornate di Milano 21, **22–3**
"ciribiciaccola" bell tower 103
Cisalpine Gaul 135
Cistercians 87
Civate 141
Civiche Raccolte d'Arte Antica 66
Civiche Raccolte Storiche 109
Civico Mausoleo Palanti 118
Claudius Marceluso 15
Cluniacs 151
Cnaes Cornelius Scipio 15
Coach service 209
Colico 136
Collegiata dei Santi Martiri 132
Comando del Terzo Corpo d'Armata
111
Como 136, **138**
Confalonieri, Federico 21
Congress of Vienna 21
Conservatorio di Musica Giuseppe
Verdi **100**
Constantine, emperor 15, 49, 80
Corot, Jean-Baptiste-Camille 121
Corrado II 17
Correggio (Antonio Allegri) 34,
51, 67, 117
*Madonna and Child with the
Young St John the Baptist* 34
Nativity 117
Portrait of Giulio Zandemaria 67
Corsia del Giardino 105, 108
Corso
Buenos Aires 119
Europa 98
Italia 77
Magenta 61, **74**, 83
Marconi 132
Matteotti 51
Monforte 93, 101
Porta Orientale 122
Porta Romana 20, 91, 93, 94, **96**
Porta Ticinese 77, 82
Porta Vittoria 100
San Gottardo 77
Sempione 62, **69**
Venezia 12, 21, 24, 32, 105,
119, **122–3**
Vittorio Emanuele II 20, 44, **51**
Corte Ducale 64, 66
Corteo dei Re Magi 39
Cortile della Rocchetta 64
Counter Reformation 20, 48, 44, 50,
56
Court of Assise 99
Cranach, Lucas 108
portraits of Martin Luther and his
wife 108
Credit cards 205
Credito Italiano 75
Crespi, Daniele 59, 88, 91, 100, 101
Christ Nailed to the Cross 101
St Charles Fasting 101
*Legend of the Foundation
of the Order* 70
Crivelli, Carlo

Madonna della Candeletta 117
Saints 67
Croce, Francesco 98
Currency exchange 205
Cusio 150
Custoza 23
Cybele 75

D

D'Alemagna, Giovanni 116
Praglia Polyptych 116
D'Annunzio, Gabriele 142, 145
Dacians 58
Danusso, Arturo 118
Darsena 89
De Chirico, Giorgio 54, 68
Mysterious Baths 68
De Cristoforis, Giuseppe 120
De Fedeli, Stefano 65, 67
Resurrection 67
De Foix, Gaston 59
De Fondutis, Agostino 55, 91
Deposition 55
*Flagellation of Christ with
Caiaphas and St Peter* 55
Christ Washing His Disciples' Feet
55
De Leyva, Marianna 50
De Pecis, Giovanni Edoardo 57, 59
De Pisis, Filippo 121
De Predis, Ambrogio 117
Profile of a Lady 58
De Rossi, Giovanni Jacopo 101
De' Grassi, Giovannino 90
De' Roberti, Ercole 117
Madonna and Child among Saints
117
Del Cossa, Francesco 117
Dell'Orto, Egidio 118
Della Guastalla, Torelli Ludovica 98
Della Scala, Mastino I 144
Della Scala, Regina 52
Della Torre *see* Torriani
Demìo, Giovanni 71
Crocifissione 71
De Pecis Collection 59
Derby 38
Desenzano del Garda 142, **144**
Desio 17
Di Balduccio, Giovanni 54
Diatreta Cup 75
Dickens, Charles 130
Diocesan Archive 98
Dominicans 135
Dominioni Caccia, Luigi 108
Dongo 140
Donizetti, Gaetano 100
Duchino, (Paolo Camillo Landriani)
101
Duomo (Como) 138
Duomo (Desenzano del Garda) 144
Duomo (Milan) 12, 13, 17, 19, 27, 29,
30, 31, 39, 45, **46–9**, 100, 103, 112,
140
Duomo (Salò) 145
Duse, Eleonora 96

E

Edict of Milan 15, 80
Einstein, Albert 118
Einstein, Hermann 118
El Greco 117
Emergencies 203
Entertainment at the Lakes **196–7**
Entertainment in Milan **188–9**
Night life **190–91**
Sports **194–5**
Theatre and cinema **192–3**
Erba, Carlo 118
Eruli 16

Estate all'Idroscalo 36
Estate all'Umanitaria 37
Etruscans 15
Eugenio di Beauharnais 100
Eustorgius, bishop 90

F

Falck 24, 140
Falck, Giorgio Enrico 118
Fattori, Giovanni 117, 121
Federico da Montefeltro 115
Ferdinand of Austria 54, 78
Ferdinand I 69
Ferramola, Floriano 151
Ferrari, Daniele 50
Ferrari, Gaudenzio 71, 132, 134, 138
Baptism of Jesus 91
Deposition 87
Martyrdom of St Catherine 116
*Martyrdom of St Catherine of
Alexandria* 113
Last Supper 101
*Virgin Mary with St Bartholomew
and St John the Baptist* 87
Ferrovie dello Stato 74, 208, 214,
215
Ferrovie Nord 135, 208, 214, 215
Festa del Naviglio 37
Festival Latino-Americano 37
Fiammenghino (Giovanni Battista
della Rovere) 112
Fiammenghino (Giovanni Muro della
Rovere) 112
Fiera degli *Oh bej Oh bej* 39, 78
Fiera dei Fiori 36
Fiera di Milano 24, **70**
Fiera di Senigallia 39
Figino, Ambrogio 67, 88
Filarete (Averulino Antonio) 17, 19,
64, 97
Filippino degli Organi 49
Florence 17
Fo, Dario 25
Fontana, Angelo 123
Fontana, Annibale 91
Fontana, Lucio 54, 118
Woman at the Mirror 35
Foppa, Vincenzo 67, 75, 83, 90, 108,
114
Polittico delle Grazie 116
Portrait of Francesco Brivio 108
Formula 1 Grand Prix, Monza 38
Fornaroli, Antonio 118
Foro Buonaparte 21, 63, 68
Foscolo, Ugo 141
Fotoshow 37
Four Seasons Fountain 70
Fra Galgario (Vittore Ghislandi) 59,
67, 108
Gentleman with Tricorn 108
Portrait of a Gentleman 117
France 20
Fracci, Carla 53
Franciscans 145
Francis I of Austria 69
Franks 16
Funi, Achille 54

G

Gadda, Carlo Emilio 28
L'Adalgisa 28
Gaffurio, Franchino 56
Galizia, Fede 67
Galleria Comunale d'Arte (Varenna)
141
Galleria d'Arte Moderna 35, 105, 121
Galleria del Sempione 62
Galleria Vittorio Emanuele II 24, 43,
44, **50**, 133
Gallia Excelsior Hotel 118
Gallio, Tolomeo 140

Garavaglia, Carlo 99, 102
Life of St Bernard 102
Garda **147**
Gardaland **148–9**
Gardone Riviera 142, **145**
Gargnano 146
Garibaldi, Giuseppe 51, 118, 134
Gauguin, Paul 121
Gemelli, Agostino 87
Genga, Girolamo 117
Genoa 10
Genovesino (Luigi Miradori) 112
Genealogical Tree of the Order 112
Group of Angels 112
Gentile da Fabriano
Valle Romita Polyptych 116
Ghirlandaio, Domenico
Adoration of the Child 58
Giacomo Della Torre (tomb) 71
Giampietrino (Giovanni Pedrini) 109
Polyptych 109
Giardini Pubblici 105, 109, 119, 120
Giardino Botanico Hruska 145
Giardino della Guastalla 95, 98
Giordano, Luca 117
Giorgione 58
Giotto 17
Giovan Pietro da Cemmo 151
Giovanni da Milano 90
Christ the Judge 116
Giovanni di Balduccio 66, 90
Giovanni di Balduccio, school of
*Madonna and Child with St
Ambrose Proferring the Model
of the City* 82
Giulino di Mezzegra 139
Giunti, Domenico 91, 113
Goethe, Johann Wolfang von 142, 146
Travels in Italy 146
Golasecca 132
Golden Altar (Sant'Ambrogio) 78, 85,
86, 87
Golfo Borromeo 133, 134, 135
Golfo della Tremezzina 139
Gonfalon of Milan 66
Gonzaga family 146
Gonzaga, Ferrante 96, 119
Gozzano 150
Gozzano, Guido 132
Grand Hotel et de Milan 24, 29, 108
Grand Tour 127
Grandi, Giuseppe 100
Grassi, Gino 121
Grassi, Nedda 121
Grassi, Paolo 28, 39
Grassi Collection 35, 121
Gravedona 137, **140**
Gratian 85
Grifo, Ambrogio 99
Grotte di Catullo 144
Guardi, Francesco 117
Gucci 107

Habsburg family 17, 20, 83, 134
Hayez, Francesco 59, 114, 117, 118,
121, 139, 151
The Kiss 114, 117
Matilda Juva Branca 35
Health and medical assistance **202–3**
Hemingway, Ernest 127
Henry II 58
Heraclitus 58
Hesse, Hermann 127
Hinterland of Milan 10
Historic Centre **42–59**
Area map 43
Street-by-Street map 44–5
Hoepli, Ulrico 120, 118
Holy Nail of the Cross 49
Honorius, Bishop 16

Hotel Diana Majestic 119
Hotels **154–61**
Huns 16

IBM 88
Ilias Picta 59
Indian Café 110
Inganni, Angelo 52
Inquisition 71
Inter (football club) 38, 70, 194
International Exposition 62
Intra 134
Isabella d'Adda 130
Iseo 151
Isola Bella 130, 133
Isola Comacina **139**, 140
Isola di Garda 145
Isola Madre 133
Isola dei Pescatori 133
Isola di San Giovanni 134
Isole Borromee 130, **133**
Isolino di San Giovanni 134
Isolino Virginia 150
Italian time 201

Jan, Giorgio 120
Jesi Collection 114, **116**
Jesuits 50, 114
Jubilee 48
Jucker Collection 54
Juvarra, Filippo 138

Kafka, Franz 146
Kennedy, John 141
Klee, Paul 35, 127
Knoller, Martin 51, 54, 74

Labò, Oreste 68
Lake Como 10, 127, **136–41**, 214
Lake Garda 10, 127, **142–9**, 215
Lake Idro 127, **151**
Lake Iseo 127, **151**, 215
Lake Maggiore 10, 69, 127, **130–35**,
214
Lake Mezzola 137
Lake Orta 127, **150**
Lake Varese 127, **150**
Lambrate, sarcophagus of 66
Landriani, Camillo 112
Lanino, Bernardo
Last Supper 96
Legend of St George 87
*Madonna and Child with the
Infant St John the Baptist* 87
Martyrdom of St Catherine 96
Lanino, Gerolamo 134
Largo Augusto 93, 98
Largo Carrobbio 79
Largo Gemelli 87
Largo Richini 94
Last Supper
see Leonardo da Vinci
Laveno 131, **135**
Lawrence, Bishop 80
Lazise 147
Lazzaretto 20
Lecco 136, **141**
Lega, Silvestro 117, 121
Leggiuno 135
Legnanino, Stefano Maria Legnani 91,
113
Assumption of Mary 113
Legnano, Battle of 16, 113
Lenno **138**
Leonardo da Vinci 17, 28, 34, 57, 64,
65, 66, 71, 72, 73, 74, 89, 116
Codex Atlanticus 28, 34, 51, 59

Last Supper 12, 17, 19, 27, 28, 30,
72–3, 74
Portrait of a Musician 56, 58
Leonardo da Vinci Gallery 88
Leoni, Leone 49, 50
Lesa **132**
Ligurians 15
Limone sul Garda 143, **146**
Linate airport 10, **206–7**
Lingeri, Pietro 69
Locati, Sebastiano 68
Loggia degli Osii 55
Loggia Rambaldi (Bardolino) 147
Lomazzo, Paolo 112
Lombard League 16, 17, 36
Lombardi, Franco 87
Conversion of St Augustine 87
Lombardo, Cristoforo 96, 100
Lombards 16
Lombardy 10, 16, 130
Lombardy regional government 118
Londonio, Francesco 59
Longo, Alfonso 21
Longoni, Emilio 59
Locked Out of School 59
Lorenzetti, Ambrogio 116
Madonna and Child 116
Lorenzi, Stoldo 91
Lost property 203
Lotto, Lorenzo 67, 108, 116
Sacred Conversation 108
Young Man 67
Loveno 139
Lovere 151
Louis XII 17
Luina torrent 134
Luini, Aurelio 98, 113
Luini, Bernardino 55, 66, 75, 90,
98, 108, 114, 117, 134, 138
Benedictory Christ 58
Deposition 101
*Holy Family with St Anne and the
Young St John the Baptist* 58
Madonna della Buonanotte 103
Madonna del Roseto 117
Passion of Jesus 96
Luino **134**

Maciachini, Carlo 112, 113, 118
Madonna del Carmine Sanctuary 145
Madonna della Ceriola Sanctuary 151
Madonna del Frassino Sanctuary 147
Madonna del Ghisallo Sanctuary 141
Madonna del Sasso Sanctuary 150
Madonnina 13, 46
Magatti, Pietro Antonio 59
Maggiolini, Giuseppe 54, 67, 139
Magnasco, Alessandro 59, 108
Malcesine **146**
Malpensa 2000 airport 10, **207**
Mandello del Lario 140
Manerba del Garda 144
Mangone, Fabio 58
"Mani Pulite" 99
Mantegazza, Antonio 67
Kneeling Apostles 67
Mantegna, Andrea 67, 106, 108, 111,
114, 115
Dead Christ 115, 116
Madonna and Child 108
Madonna in Glory with Saints 67
St Luke Altarpiece 116
Manzoni, Alessandro 24, 29, 38, 44,
50, 51, 108, 118, 132, 136, 139
The Betrothed 20, 29, 44, 50, 141
Manzoni, Piero 54
Manzù, Giacomo 118
Marco D'Oggiono 67, 100

Crucifixion 100
Maria Theresa of Austria 21, 93, 114, 122
Marinetti, Filippo Tommaso 24
Marini, Marino 116
Marino, Tommaso 50
Maroncelli, Piero 21
Martini, Arturo 54, 116, 134
Martini, Simone 59
Martin V, Pope 46
Matisse, Henri 121
Matteo da Campione 90
Maximian, emperor 15
Mazzardites 130
Mazzucotelli, Alessandro 101
McEacharn, Neil 130, 134
Meda, Giuseppe 49, 66, 98
Medical assistance 203
Medici, Gian Giacomo 49
Mediolanum 15
Menaggio **139**
Meneghin 39
Mengoni, Giuseppe 24, 44, 50
Mercato dell'Antiquariato 89
Merlo, Carlo Giuseppe 74
Metanopoli 25
Metropolitana (Milan underground railway) 212
Metternich 33
Mezzanotte, Paolo 75
Michelangelo Buonarroti 49, 58, 67
   Pietà 58
   Rondanini Pietà 65, 67
Michelino da Besozzo, school of 90
   Aesop's Fables 135
Michelozzi, Michelozzo di Bartolomeo 67
Midland 15
Milan football clubs 38, 70, 194
Milano Cortili Aperti 36
Milano d'Estate 37
Milano–Sanremo race 36
Modigliani, Amedeo 54, 114
   Portrait of Moisè Kisling 114, 116
MODIT–Milanovendemoda 36, 38
MOMA 116
Moncalvo, (Guglielmo Caccia) 88, 91, 94, 98, 99
Mondadori, Arnoldo 118
Monte Camerale di Santa Teresa 107
Monte Isola 151
Monte Rosa 135
Montecastello Sanctuary 46
Montinelle 145
Montorfano, Giovanni Donato da 71, 72
   Crucifixion 72
   Legend of St Anthony Abbot 99
   Life of St John the Baptist 99
Monza 16, 37
Morandi, Giorgio 54, 116, 121
Morazzone (Pier Francesco Mazzucchelli) 59, 67
   Adoration of the Magi 59
   Martyrdom of Saints Rufina and Seconda 117
   San Carlo in Glory 113
Moretti, Cristoforo 108
   Polyptych 108
Moretto (Alessandro Bonvicino) 59, 151
   Conversion of St Paul 91
   Martyrdom of St Peter of Verona 59
Moroni, Giovan Battista 59
   Portrait of Michel de l'Hospital 59
San Vittore Sacellum mosaics 78
Moto Guzzi factory 140
Mottarone, Monte 133, 135, 150
Mozart, Wolfgang Amadeus 54, 100

Museums
   Civico Museo Archeologico **74**
   Civico Museo d'Arte Contemporanea 35, 54
   Civici Musei del Castello Sforzesco 34, **66–7**
   Civico Museo Marinaro Ugo Mursia 109
   Civico Museo del Risorgimento 109, 111
   Museo dell'Abbigliamento Infantile 135
   Museo dell'Acquario 68
   Museo Archeologico (Salò) 145
   Museo Archeologico della Valtènesi (Montinelle) 145
   Museo Bagatti Valsecchi 35, 107, **109**
   Museo della Bambola 131
   Museo della Basilica di Sant'Ambrogio 87
   Museo del Castello di Torri del Benaco 147
   Museo delle Cere 119
   Museo del Cinema 120
   Museo Civico (Riva del Garda) 146
   Museo Civico Archeologico (Desenzano del Garda) 144
   Museo di Criminologia e delle Armi Antiche 86
   Museo del Duomo 35, 48, **49**
   Museo Etnografico e dello Strumento a Fiato 150
   Museo Francesco Messina 79, 82
   Museo di Milano 22, 109
   Museo Marino Marini 35, 121
   Museo Minguzzi 110
   Museo Moto Guzzi della Motocicletta 141
   Museo del Nastro Azzurro (Salò) 145
   Museo Nazionale della Scienza e della Tecnica 34, **88**
   Museo del Paesaggio 134
   Museo Poldi Pezzoli 35, 106, **108**
   Museo del Rubinetto (San Maurizio d'Opaglio) 150
   Museo Settala 57, 59, 120
   Museo di Storia Contemporanea 109
   Museo di Storia Naturale **120**
   Museo di Storia Naturale (Lecco) 141
   Museo di Storia Naturale del Garda e del Monte Baldo 146
   Museo Teatrale alla Scala 52
Museum opening hours **201**
Mussolini, Benito 24, 28, 118, 133, 139, 146
Muzio, Giovanni 51, 69, 78, 101, 109
Muzio, Lorenzo 51

N

Napoleon Bonaparte 21, 31, 33, 46, 59, 62, 68, 69, 74, 78, 102, 121, 122, 132
Napoleon III 68
Narses 16
National Centre for Manzoni Studies 51
National Exposition 68
Nava, Cesare 81
Navigli canals 16, 17, 46, 62, 74, 77, 96, 100
Naviglio della Martesana 110
Naviglio Grande 77, 89
Naviglio Pavese 77
Nervi, Pier Luigi 118
Nicola da Verdun 49
Nietzsche, Friedrich 127, 146
Niguarda 97

Northeast Milan **104–23**
   Area map 105
   Street-by-Street map 106–7, 110–11
Northwest Milan **60–75**
   Area map 61
   Street-by-Street map 62–3
Notarial Acts Archive 99
Nuvolone, Carlo Francesco 112
Nuvolone, Panfilo 101

O

Officers' Club (Palazzo Cusani) 111
Oggi Aperto 36
Olate 141
Oldofredi, Giacomo 151
Oldrado da Tresseno 54
Olivetans 88
Omegna 150
Omm de Preja 51
Order of the Knights of the Holy Sepulchre 100
Orrido di Bellano 140
Orrido di Sant'Anna 134
Orta-San Giulio 150
Orticola 37
Ospedale Maggiore *see* Ca' Granda
Ostrogoths 16

P

Padenghe 144
Padiglione del Caffè 120
Sforzesca Altarpiece 15, 116
Palazzetto della Comunità (Orta-San Giulio) 150
Palazzi, Lazzaro 119
Palazzina del Serraglio 146
Palazzo
   Acerbi 96
   Anguissola 108
   Annoni 96
   dell'Arte 63, 69
   Bigli 107
   Borromeo **55**, 135
   Borromeo d'Adda 108
   Brentani 108
   dei Capitani del Lago (Malcesine) 146
   del Capitano (Garda) 147
   Carlotti (Garda) 147
   Castiglioni 122
   Citterio 116
   del Comune (Desenzano del Garda) 144
   Cusani 111, **112**
   Dugnani **120**
   Dugnani (Pallanza) 134
   Durini 20, 93, 98
   Fantoni (Salò) 145
   Gallarati Scotti 108
   Gallio 140
   dei Giornali 109
   dei Giureconsulti 55
   di Giustizia **99**
   Isimbardi **101**
   Litta 60, **74**
   Litta Biumi 78, 83
   Litta Modignani 98
   Marino **50**
   Mellerio 96
   Melzi di Cusano 106
   Morando Attendolo Bolognini 109
   Moriggia 109
   Morosini 101
   dei Panigarola 55
   Parrasio *see* Palazzo della Ragione (Cannobio)
   della Permanente 119
   della Prefettura 101
   Pretorio (Riva del Garda) 146
   del Provveditore (Riva del Garda) 146

Palazzo (cont.)
del Provveditore Veneto
(Desenzano del Garda) 144
Radice Fossati 83
della Ragione 32, 43, 54, 99
della Ragione (Cannobio) 134
Reale 21, 35, **54**, 139
Rocca-Saporiti 122
delle Scuole Palatine 55
Serbelloni 33, 122
Sormani Andreani **98**
dello Sport 70
Stampa 83
delle Stelline 74
Terzi-Martinengo (Barbarano)
145
dei Tribunali 99
Trivulzio 91
Vescovile (Gozzano) 150
Pallanza 134
Palma il Giovane 112
Pandiani, Giovanni
The Soldier's Widow 23
Panoramica di Venezia 38
Parco delle Basiliche 82
Parco Dugnani 120
Parco Regionale dei Lagoni
di Mercurago 132
Parco Sempione 32, 62, **68**
Parco Sormani 98
Parini, Giuseppe 51, 91
Parking 207, 211
Pascal, Blaise 88
Pataria movement 16
Parabiago Patera 75
Pavia 16, 82
Pecorari, Francesco 54, 103
Pelizza da Volpedo 117, 121
The Flood 117
Fourth Estate 117, 121
Pellegrini (Pellegrino Tibaldi) 31, 46,
48, 50, 91, 132, 138, 139, 140, 141
Pellico, Silvio 21
Pellini, Eugenio 118
Penna, Francesco 118
Perego, Giovanni 122
Peressutti, Enrico 96
Permanent Fine Arts Exposition 119
Personal security **202**
Pertini, Sandro 108
Peschiera del Garda **147**
Petacci, Claretta 24, 139, 145
Peterzano, Simone 70
Petrarca, Francesco 59, 70
Piacentini, Marco 99
Piazza
Affari **75**
d'Armi 70
Beccaria 99
Belgioioso 29, **51**
Cavour 109
Giulio Cesare 70
Cinque Giornate 100
Cordusio **75**
del Duomo 43, 44, 50
Fontana 25, 45
del Liberty 45, **51**
Malvezzi (Desenzano del Garda)
144
Meda 44, 51
Mercanti **54**
Missori 91, 96
Motta (Orta-San Giulio) 150
Oberdan 119
del Popolo 92
della Repubblica 119
San Babila 51, 105
San Sepolcro 24, 28
Santo Stefano 29
della Scala 43, 50, 51
della Vetra 32, 79, **82**

Piazza, Callisto 75
Marriage at Cana 75, 87
Piazzale Loreto 24, 28
Piazzale Medaglie d'Oro 96
Piazzetta, Gian Battista 117, 146
Rebecca at the Well 117
Picasso, Pablo 35, 121
Piccio (Giovanni Carnovali) 121
Piccolo Teatro 28, 39, 61, 192
Piedmont 130
Piermarini, Giuseppe 21, 33, 45, 51,
52, 54, 112, 120
Piero della Francesca 106, 111, 114
Montefeltro Altarpiece 115, 117
San Nicola da Tolentino 108
Pietro da Cortona 117
Pinacoteca Ambrosiana 27, **56–9**
Pinacoteca di Brera 15, 27, 34, 100,
111, **114–17**
Pius IV, pope 48, 49
Piona Abbey **140**
Pioverna 140
Piramidi di Zone 151
Pirelli, Giovan Battista 118
Pirelli Building 25, 33, 105, **118**
Pisogne 151
Pitocchetto (Giacomo Ceruti) 117
Pittori sul Naviglio 36
Plague 20
Planetario **120**
Po river 69
Poldi Pezzoli, Gian Giacomo 106, 108
Pollack, Leopold 121
Pollaiolo, Il 106
Portrait of a Young Woman 108
Pomodoro, Arnaldo 45
Ponte Vecchio sull'Adda 141
Ponti, Gio 68, 118
Porta di Santo Spirito 64
Porta Nuova 82, 113
Porta Orientale *see* Porta Venezia
Porta Romana 20, 66, 96, 109
Porta Ticinese 77, 79, 82
Porta Tosa 22, 93
Porta Venezia 119
gardens 33
ramparts 70, 105, **119**
Porta Vercellina 74
Porta Vittorio 22
Porta, Carlo 29
Ninetta del Verzee 29
Portaluppi, Piero 74, 120
Portinari, Pigello 90, 99
Postal services 205
Preda, Carlo
Death of St Benedict 87
Premier league football 38
Premio Bagutta 38
Prina, Giuseppe 112
Procaccini, Giulio Cesare 112
Christ at the Pillar 101
Magdalen 59
*Martyrdom of Saints Rufina and
Seconda* 117
Procaccini, Camillo 49, 67, 88, 91, 98,
101, 112, 134
Procaccini, Ercole
Ascent to Calvary 112
Provaglio d'Iseo 151
Punta Belvedere 145
Punta di Cornicello 147
Punta del Corno 151
Punta di Mirabello 147
Punta San Fermo 145
Punta San Vigilio 147
Pusterla dei Fabbri 66
Pusterla di Sant'Ambrogio 86

Q
Quadrilateral fashion district 12, 105,
106–7

Quadrio, Gerolamo 88, 112
Quadroni di San Carlo 49
Quarna 150
Quasimodo, Salvatore 118

R
Radetzky, Joseph, Count von Radetz
21, 22, 23, 121
Raphael 34, 58, 111, 114
Cartoon for *The School of Athens* 57,
58
Marriage of the Virgin 115, 117
Raffagno, Francesco 100
RAI (Italian State TV) 69
Railway links 213
Rangone, Tommaso 116
Relics of the Magi 90
Rembrandt van Rijn
Portrait of the Artist's Sister 117
Reni, Guido 59, 117, 142
Penitent Magdalen 59
Republic of Salò 25, 145, 146
Ricci, Sebastiano 98
*The Triumph of Souls among
Angels* 98
Richard-Ginori 68, 118
Richard, Jules 118
Richini, Francesco Maria 31, 46, 50,
55, 74, 81, 96, 97, 98, 115, 123
Restaurants **162–75**
Choosing a restaurant 162
Franciacorta wines 165
Paying 163
Reading the menu 163
What to Eat **164–5**
Portrait of Maximin 74
Riva del Garda **146**
Rivellino di Porta Vercellina 64
Rocca d'Anfo 151
Rocca di Angera 131, 132, **135**
Rocca di Polpenazze del Garda 145
Rocca di Puegnago sul Garda 145
Rocca Scaligera 144
Rocca di Soiano del Lago 145
Rogers, Nathan 96
Roman circus 83
Roman columns 79, 80
Romanino (Gerolamo Romani) 67,
145, 151
Madonna and Saints 145
Romans 15, 83, 127, 138, 140, 144
Rome 10, 15, 16, 94
Roncaglia, Diet of 17
Rosmini, Antonio 132, 133
Rosselli, Alberto 118
Rossi, Aldo 108
Rossini, Gioacchino 100, 141
Rosso, Medardo 116, 118
Rothari's Edict 16
Rotonda della Besana 37, **100**
Rubens, Pieter Paul 96
Last Supper 117
Ruggeri, Giovanni 112
Rusnati, Giuseppe 100

S
Sacro Monte (Isola di San Giulio) 150
Sagra del Carroccio 36
Sagra di San Cristoforo 37
Sagra di San Giovanni 37
Sala Comacina 139
Sala degli Affreschi (Palazzo
Isimbardi) 101
Sala dell'Antegiunta (Palazzo
Isimbardi) 101
Sala delle Asse (Castello Sforzesco)
65, 66
Sala della Balla (Castello Sforzesco)
67
Sala delle Colombine (Castello
Sforzesco) 67

Sala dei Ducali (Castello Sforzesco) 66
Sala della Giunta (Palazzo Isimbardi) 101
Sala degli Scarlioni (Castello Sforzesco) 67
Sala Rossa (Palazzo Litta) 74
Sala Verde (Castello Sforzesco) 67
Salieri, Antonio 52
Salmeggia, Enea
Miracle of St Benedict 113
Salò 144, **145**
Salone degli Specchi (Palazzo Litta) 74
Salotto della Duchessa (Palazzo Litta) 74
Sanagra 139
Sant'Ambrogio 12, 15, 30, 31, 39, 48, 49, 52, 58, 66, 78, 84, 85, 87, 91, 94, 96, 99, 110, 113
San Carlo Borromeo (statue) 131
Santa Caterina del Sasso Ballaro 131, **135**
San Dionigi monastery 48
San Donato Milanese 25
San Felice del Benaco **144**, 145
San Giovanni alle Fonti baptistery 43, 49
Santa Maria Maddalena al Cerchio convent 83
San Michele cloister 151
San Maurizio d'Opaglio 150
San Pietro in Lamosa monastery 151
San Sigismondo oratory 87
San Siro stadium 68, **70**, 195
Santo Stefano baptistery 43
San Vittore in Ciel d'Oro Sacellum 85, 87
San Vittore monastery 88
Sangiorgio, Abbondio 69
Sanmicheli, Michele 147
Sansovino (Jacopo Tatti) 145
Santuario della Pietà 134
Saponaro, Salvatore 101
Sarnico 151
Sasso del Ferro 135
Savignano, Luciana 53
Savini 50
Savoy, House of
Carlo Alberto, king 22, 23
Eugenio 21
Vittorio Emanuele II, king 33, 50
Vittorio Emanuele III, king 54
Scala Ballet School 53
Scaligeri family 144, 146, 147
Schifamondo 145
Scrigno Passalacqua 67
Scrofa semilanuta 15
Scuole Arcimboldo 91
Sebino *see* Lake Iseo
Seminario Arcivescovile 123
Seregni, Vincenzo 70, 88, 123
Sestiga della Pace 69
Sesto Calende **132**
Settala, Lanfranco 112
Settala, Manfredo 59, 120
Settebello 88
Settimius Severus 62
Sforza family 12, **18–19**, 63, 68, 84, 138
Ascanio 19
Bianca Maria 19
Bona 19
Ercole Massimiliano 19
Francesco I 17, 18, 19, 64, 97, 113
Francesco II 19, 20
Galeazzo Maria 19, 54, 65, 66
Gian Galeazzo Maria 19
Muzio Attendolo 19
Lodovico il Moro 17, 18, 19, 20, 28, 64, 66, 71, 72, 74, 89, 116

Shops and Markets **180–81**
Antiques **184–5**
Books **186–7**
Clothing and accessories **182–3**
Design **184**
Fabrics 184
Food shops 181
Gifts 187
Jewellery 183
Markets 180
Music **186–7**
Opening hours 180
Sales 181
Silk production 138
Simonetta, Angelo 112
Simplon Pass 69, 130
Singer 88
Sinigaglia Collection 57
Sirmione 142, **144**
Sironi, Mario 54, 99, 109
SMAU 36, 38
Società Ceramica Italiana Richard-Ginori 135
Società Storica Lombarda 51
Società Umanitaria 100
Solari, Cristoforo 71, 91
Solari, Guiniforte 17, 71, 99, 113
Solari, Pietro Antonio 67, 83, 100
Madonna del Coazzone 67
Solarolo 145
Sommaruga, Giuseppe 122, 151
Sottocorno, Pasquale 23
Southeast Milan **92–103**
Area map 93
Street-by-Street map 94–5
Southwest Milan **76–91**
Area map 77
Street-by-Street map 78–9
St Ambrose *see* Sant'Ambrogio
St Augustine 31, 49, 55, 87
St Bartholomew 49
St Benedict 88
St Bernard 102
St Catherine of Alexandria 49
St Catherine of Siena 71
St Celso 91
St Eustorgius 90
St Gervase 87
St Gregory 88
St Helena 49
St John the Good 49
St Lazzaro (statue) 82
St Mark 31, 112
St Nazaro 96
St Peter Martyr 90
St Protasius 87
St Simpliciano 113
St Tecla 49
Stacchini, Ulisse 119
Stadio Civico Giuseppe Meazza *see* San Siro stadium
Stampa, Massimiliano 83
Stazione Centrale 33, 105, **119**
Stefano da Verona
Adoration of the Magi 116
Stendhal, Henri Marie Beyle 95, 108, 127, 130, 141, 146
Stilicho, Sarcophagus of 85, 86
Storer, Gian Cristoforo 80
Stramilano 36
Stravinsky, Igor 121
Strehler, Giorgio 28, 39, 192
Stresa 130, **133**

T
Tabacchi, Odoardo 109, 118
Tagliamento river 69
Tangenziale est 11, 207
Tangenziale ovest 11, 207
Tanzio da Varallo, (Antonio D'Errico) 100

Taurini, Giovanni 50
Taveggia 99
Taxis 211
Tazzini, Giacomo 101
Telecom Italia 204
Telemilano 25
Tempio Civico di San Sebastiano 91
Tempio della Vittoria 78
Tempio Voltiano 138
Terme di Catullo 144
Terme di Villa Cedri 147
Terragni, Giuseppe 69, 138
Theatres **192–3**
Teatro dell'Arte 69
Teatro Carcano 96
Teatro Lirico 28
Teatro Litta 74
Teatro alla Scala 12, 21, 25, 27, 44, **52–3**
Teatro della Società 141
Teatro Dal Verme 61
Theodolinda 16
Theodora 66
Theodoric 16
Ticino river 17, 69, 130
Tiepolo, Gian Battista 59, 87, 112, 120, 133, 144, 151
Allegory of the Dugnani Family 120
Madonna del Carmelo 117
Legend of Saints Vittore and Satiro 87
Legend of Scipio and Massinissa 120
Triumph of Doge Morosini 101
Last Supper 144
Tignale 146
Tintoretto (Robusti Jacopo) 49, 114, 116
The Finding of the Body of St Mark 114, 116
Christ among the Doctors 49
Titus Labienus 135
Titian (Tiziano Vecellio) 51, 58, 67, 91, 116
Adoration of the Magi 56, 58
Man in Armour 58
Toce river 130
Tombone di San Marco 110
Torbiere d'Iseo 151
Torbole 143, 146
Torelli, Pietro 90
Torno **141**
Torre di Ansperto 75
Torre di Buccione 150
Torre del Castellano 64
Torre del Comune 55
Torre del Filarete (Filarete's Tower) 65
Torre dei Gorani 83
Torre dell'Orologio 147
Torre del Parco 68
Torre di San Marco 126, 145
Torre Velasca 33, 94, **96**
Torri del Benaco 143, **147**
Torriani family 17, 18
Torriani, Napo 55
Toscanini, Arturo 25, 52, 127, 134
Toscolano Maderno **146**
Tourist information 200
Traballesi, Giuliano 54
Train services 208, 214
Trajan Column 58
Trams 212
Tramaglino, Renzo 20
Treaty of Constance 16
Treaty of Utrecht 21
Tremezzo 137, **139**
Tremosine 146
Triennale di Milano 63, **69**
Trivulzio, Gian Battista 46
Trivulzio, Gian Giacomo 96

Trivulzio Candelabrum 46, 49
Trivulzio Tapestries 64, 66, 67
Trotti, Giovanni Battista 67
Tura, Cosmè
Tuscany 17

U

Ucelli, Guido 88
Umiliate di Sant'Erasmo 108
Università Cattolica del Sacro Cuore
    78, 87

V

Vacciago di Ameno 150
Val Camonica 74, 151
Val Cannobina 134
Val di Non 113
Valentinian II 88
Valentino 106
Valtènesi **144**
Valtolina, Giuseppe 118
Van Dyck, Anthony 96, 117
Van Gogh, Vincent 121
Varenna 137, **140**
Varese 135
Varone river falls 146
Vasari, Giorgio 73
Vedova, Emilio 54
Venetians 147
Veneziano, Lorenzo
    *Santa Maria della Celestia
    Polyptych* 116
Venice 144, 146
Veneziano, Paolo 146
Verbania **134**
Vercurago 141
Verdi, Giuseppe 21, 29, 51, 100, 108,
    118
    Nabucco 29
Vermiglio, Giuseppe 139
Veronese 116, 146
Verri, Alessandro 21, 29
Verri, Pietro 29
Versace 106, 107
Verziere 93
Verziere Column 98
Vicolo dei Lavandai 89
Victoria amazonica 130, 134
Via
    Bellini 101
    Borgonuovo 109
    Brera 110
    Brisa **75**, 83
    Canova 69
    Cappuccio 83
    Carducci 74
    Carrobbio, Largo **82**
    Circo 78, **83**
    Dante 61, 63
    Della Passione 100

Via (cont.)
    Domodossola 70
    Durini 98
    Fatebenefratelli 25
    Festa del Perdono 94
    Francesco Sforza 91
    Guastalla 98
    Manzoni 52, 82, 105, 106, **108**,
        109
    Marino 50
    Medici 79, 82
    Melzi d'Eril 69
    Mercanti 55
    Molino delle Armi 82
    Montenapoleone 105, 106, 107,
        108
    Morigi 83
    Olona 88
    Palestro 120
    Palla 91
    Pisoni 108
    Regina Margherita 100
    Sant'Andrea 106, 109
    Sant'Antonio 94
    San Barnaba 98, 100
    San Gregorio 119
    San Marco 110
    Sant'Orsola 83
    San Paolo 51
    San Sisto 82
    Santa Sofia 96
    Senato 122
    Soncino 83
    Della Spiga 106
    Del Torchio 79, 82
    Torino 79, **82**, 83
    Turati 119
    Vigna 83
    Visconti di Modrone 99
    Vivaio 101
Viale Piave 119
Villa
    Alba 145
    Albertini 147
    del Balbianello 138, 139
    di Cesare Beccaria 139
    Bettoni 142
    Bettoni 146
    Carlotta 139
    Cipressi 140
    Ducale 133
    Erba 138
    d'Este 136, 138
    Faccanoni 151
    Feltrinelli 146
    Fiordaliso 145
    Frua 135
    Guarienti 147
    Henfrey (Branca) 133
    Manzoni 141

Villa (cont.)
    Melzi d'Eril 141
    Milyus-Vigoni 139
    Monastero 140
    Olmo 138
    Pallavicino 133
    Pliniana 141
    Ponti (Isolino Virginia) 150
    Ponti 132
    Reale 35, 37, 105, 117, **121**
    Romana 144
    Serbelloni 141
    Stampa 132
    Taranto 130, 134
    Trivulzio 141
    Trotti 141
Vincenzo I 146
Virgil 15
Visconti 12, 17, **18–**9, 31, 62, 63, 67,
    90, 91, 135, 138
    Andreotto 18
    Azzone 18, 54, 82, 141
    Bernabò 18, 52
    Bianca Maria 18
    Filippo Maria 18, 19, 64
    Galeazzo I 18
    Galeazzo II 18, 64
    Gian Galeazzo 17, 18, 46, 48,
        64
    Gian Maria 18
    Giovanni 18, 70
    Luchino 18
    Marco 18
    Matteo 18, 55
    Matteo II 18
    Obizzo 18
    Ottone 17
    Stefano 18, 90
    Tebaldo 18
    Umberto 18
Visconti Venosta Collection 108
Vismara Collection 35
Victoria of England, Queen 133
Vittoriale degli Italiani 142, 145
Vivarini, Antonio 116
    Praglia Polyptych 116
Volta, Alessandro 138
Voltorre di Gavirate 151
Volvinius 85

W

Wenceslaus 18
WWF 147
World War II 24, 25, 43, 52, 55, 68,
    70, 71, 72, 84, 98, 120

Z

Zenale, Bernardino 99, 109, 113
    Triptych 87
Zucca in Galleria 44, 79

Acknowledgments

DORLING KINDERSLEY WOULD LIKE to thank all the people, organizations and associations whose contributions and assistance have made the preparation of this book possible. Special thanks are due to the following organizations and individuals: APT di Como (Sig. Pisilli), Silvia Dell'Orso, Direzione Civiche Raccolte d'Arte del Castello Sforzesco (Walter Palmieri), Giorgio Facchetti, Diana Georgiacodis, Alberto Malesani (Gardaland), Enrico Pellegrini, chef of the *Locanda degli Angeli* (Gardone), Augusto Rizza, Silvia Scamperle, Carla Solari, Crisca Sommerhoff, Valentina Tralli.

FOR DORLING KINDERSLEY
Michelle Clark (Proofreader); Mary Sutherland (US Editor); Louise Bostock Lang (Senior Managing Editor); Annette Jacobs (Managing Art Editor); Vivien Crump (Editorial Director); Gillian Allan (Art Director); Douglas Amrine (Publisher).

PICTURE CREDITS
Key: t = top; tl = top left; tlc = top left centre; tc = top centre; trc = top right centre; tr = top right; cla = centre left above; ca = centre above; cra = centre right above; cl = centre left; c = centre; cr = centre right; clb = centre left below; crb = centre right below; cb = centre below; bl = bottom left; br = bottom right; b = bottom; bc = bottom centre; bcl = bottom centre left; bcr = bottom centre right; (d) = detail.

Every effort has been made to trace the copyright holders. The publisher apologizes for any unintentional omissions and would be pleased, in such cases, to add an acknowledgment in future editions.

All the photographs reproduced in this book are from the IMAGE BANK, Milan, except for the following:

APT DI COMO: 140tr, 140bl.

ARCHIVIO FOTOGRAFICO DEL TEATRO ALLA SCALA: 52bl, 53tl, 53br.

ARCHIVIO FOTOGRAFICO ELECTA: 56–57 (all the photographs), 58tr, 58tl, 58c, 58bl, 59tr, 59c, 64cr(d), 142tl, 142tr, 144cr, 145tl, 145cr.

ARCHIVIO FOTOGRAFICO STORICO ACHILLE BERTARELLI: 41tc, 153tc, 199tc.

SIMONETTA BENZI: 33cr (d), 36tl, 51tr, 51cl, 51cr, 68cr, 69cr, 74br, 75tr, 75cl, 78tr, 80br, 82tc, 85br, 87br, 88cr, 88br, 90c, 90bl, 97tl, 97cr, 97cb, 98cl, 100tl, 100br,

101br, 112tl, 113br, 122tr, 122cs, 122br, 123tr, 123cl, 123br, 188bl, 204c, 204br.

DISCOTECA GENUX: 196cb.

DORLING KINDERSLEY PHOTO LIBRARY: 164 (*Risotto alla milanese*), 165 (*Ossobuco alla milanese* and panettone), 189bl.

FABIO DE ANGELIS: 27tl, 27cl, 30br, 31tl, 31tr, 31bl, 32tl, 35br (d), 44tl, 45br, 49tl, 49c, 80tl, 80tr, 83tr, 83cr, 83bl, 84tl, 85tc, 85bl, 88tm, 90tc, 96c, 96br, 98br, 99tr, 100c, 102tr, 111br, 112cr, 112br, 119bl, 119cr, 145bl, 121tl, 177br, 180bl, 188cr, 203 (ambulance, fire brigade and police vans).

GIOVANNI FRANCESIO: 30bl.

GRAND HOTEL VILLA SERBELLONI (BELLAGIO): 141tr, 155tl.

HOTEL DU LAC (VARENNA): 137cr.

HOTEL FOUR SEASONS (MILAN): 154cr.

HOTEL REGENCY (MILAN): 154bl.

HOTEL VILLA CRESPI (ORTA SAN GIULIO): 155br.

KRIZIA: 36c.

MUSEO DEL RISORGIMENTO: 8–9c.

OMEGA FOTOCRONACHE: 24cl, 25bl, 28tr, 28cl, 28bl.

PASTICCERIA COVA (MILAN): 177tr.

LAURA RECORDATI: 30cl, 54tl, 55br, 78br, 91br, 96tl, 98tl, 101c.

RISTORANTE AMI BERTON (MILAN): 162bl.

RISTORANTE IL SOLE (RANCO): 163bl.

RISTORANTE L'ALBERETA (ERBUSCO): 163tl.

RISTORANTE LA BRICIOLA (MILAN): 162tl.

RISTORANTE PIERINO PENATI (VIGANÒ BRIANZA) 164 (*Gnervitt con cipolle* and *cotoletta alla milanese*).

RISTORANTE VILLA FLORI (COMO): 163tl.

AUGUSTO RIZZA: all the photographs on pages 164–5 except those from the Dorling Kindersley Picture Library.

MARCO SCAPAGNINI: 142cl, 154tc, 155cr, 162tc, 180tc.

VERSACE: 106tl.

DORLING KINDERSLEY SPECIAL EDITIONS

Dorling Kindersley books can be purchased in bulk quantities at discounted prices for use in promotions or as premiums. We are also able to offer special editions and personalized jackets, corporate imprints, and excerpts from all of our books, tailored specifically to meet your own needs.

To find out more, please contact: (in the United Kingdom) – SPECIAL SALES, DORLING KINDERSLEY LIMITED, 80 STRAND, LONDON WC2R 0RL

(in the United States) – SPECIAL MARKETS DEPARTMENT, DORLING KINDERSLEY PUBLISHING, INC., 95 MADISON AVENUE, NEW YORK, NY 10016.

Phrase Book

In Emergency

Help!	Aiuto!	eye-**yoo**-toh
Stop!	Fermate!	fair-**mah**-teh
Call a doctor.	Chiama un medico	kee-**ah**-mah oon **meh**-dee-koh
Call an ambulance.	Chiama un' ambulanza	kee-**ah**-mah oon am-boo-**lan**-tsa
Call the police.	Chiama la polizia	kee-**ah**-mah lah pol-ee-**tsee**-ah
Call the fire brigade.	Chiama i pompieri	kee-**ah**-mah ee pom-pee-**air**-ee
Where is the telephone?	Dov'è il telefono?	dov-**eh** eel teh-**leh**-foh-noh?
The nearest hospital?	L'ospedale più vicino?	loss-peh-**dah**-leh pee-**oo** vee-**chee**-noh?

Communication Essentials

Yes/No	Sì/No	see/ noh
Please	Per favore	pair fah-**vor**-eh
Thank you	Grazie	**grah**-tsee-eh
Excuse me	Mi scusi	mee **skoo**-zee
Hello	Buon giorno	bwon **jor**-noh
Goodbye	Arrivederci	ah-ree-veh-**dair**-chee
Good evening	Buona sera	**bwon**-ah **sair**-ah
morning	la mattina	lah mah-**tee**-nah
afternoon	il pomeriggio	eel poh-meh-**ree**-joh
evening	la sera	lah **sair**-ah
yesterday	ieri	ee-**air**-ee
today	oggi	**oh**-jee
tomorrow	domani	doh-**mah**-nee
here	qui	kwee
there	la	lah
What?	Quale?	**kwah**-leh?
When?	Quando?	**kwan**-doh?
Why?	Perchè?	pair-**keh**?
Where?	Dove?	**doh**-veh?

Useful Phrases

How are you?	Come sta?	**koh**-meh stah?
Very well, thank you.	Molto bene, grazie.	**moll**-toh **beh**-neh **grah**-tsee-eh
Pleased to meet you.	Piacere di conoscerla.	pee-ah-**chair**-eh dee coh-**noh**-shair-lah
See you later.	A più tardi.	ah pee-**oo** tar-dee
That's fine.	Va bene.	va **beh**-neh
Where is/are ...?	Dov'è/Dove sono ...?	dov-**eh**/doveh **soh**-noh?
How long does it take to get to ...?	Quanto tempo ci vuole per andare a ...?	**kwan**-toh **tem**-poh chee voo-**oh**-leh pair an-**dar**-eh ah ...?
How do I get to ...?	Come faccio per arrivare a ...?	koh-meh **fah**-choh pair arri-var-eh ah..?
Do you speak English?	Parla inglese?	**par**-lah een-**gleh**-zeh?
I don't understand.	Non capisco.	non ka-**pee**-skoh
Could you speak more slowly, please?	Può parlare più lentamente, per favore?	pwoh par-**lah**-reh pee-**oo** len-ta-**men**-teh pair fah-**vor**-eh?
I'm sorry.	Mi dispiace.	mee dee-spee-**ah**-cheh

Useful Words

big	grande	**gran**-deh
small	piccolo	**pee**-koh-loh
hot	caldo	**kal**-doh
cold	freddo	**fred**-doh
good	buono	**bwoh**-noh
bad	cattivo	kat-**tee**-voh
enough	basta	**bas**-tah
well	bene	**beh**-neh
open	aperto	ah-**pair**-toh
closed	chiuso	kee-**oo**-zoh
left	a sinistra	ah see-**nee**-strah
right	a destra	ah **dess**-trah
straight on	sempre dritto	**sem**-preh **dree**-toh
near	vicino	vee-**chee**-noh
far	lontano	lon-**tah**-noh
up	su	soo
down	giù	joo
early	presto	**press**-toh
late	tardi	**tar**-dee
entrance	entrata	en-**trah**-tah
exit	uscita	oo-**shee**-ta
toilet	il gabinetto	eel gah-bee-**net**-toh
free, unoccupied	libero	**lee**-bair-oh
free, no charge	gratuito	grah-**too**-ee-toh

Making a Telephone Call

I'd like to place a long-distance call.	Vorrei fare una interurbana.	vor-**ray far**-eh oona in-tair-oor-**bah**-nah
I'd like to make a reverse-charge call.	Vorrei fare una telefonata a carico del destinatario.	vor-**ray far**-eh oona teh-leh-fon-**ah**-tah ah **kar**-ee-koh dell dess-tee-nah-**tar**-ree-oh
I'll try again later.	Ritelefono più tardi.	ree-teh-**leh**-foh-noh pee-oo **tar**-dee
Can I leave a message?	Posso lasciare un messaggio?	**poss**-oh lash-**ah**-reh oon mess-**sah**-joh?
Hold on.	Un attimo, per favore	oon **ah**-tee-moh, pair fah-**vor**-eh
Could you speak up a little please?	Può parlare più forte, per favore?	pwoh par-**lah**-reh pee-oo **for** teh, pair fah-**vor**-eh?
local call	telefonata locale	te-leh-fon-**ah**-tah loh-cah-leh

Shopping

How much does this cost?	Quant'è, per favore?	kwan-**teh** pair fah-**vor**-eh?
I would like ...	Vorrei ...	vor-**ray**
Do you have ...?	Avete ...?	ah-**veh**-teh.. ?
I'm just looking.	Sto soltanto guardando.	stoh sol-**tan**-toh gwar-**dan**-doh
Do you take credit cards?	Accettate carte di credito?	ah-chet-**tah**-teh **kar**-teh dee **creh**-dee-toh?
What time do you open/close?	A che ora apre/ chiude?	ah keh **or**-ah **ah**-preh/kee-**oo**-deh?
this one	questo	**kweh**-stoh
that one	quello	**kwell**-oh
expensive	caro	**kar**-oh
cheap	a buon prezzo	ah bwon **pret**-soh
size, clothes	la taglia	lah **tah**-lee-ah
size, shoes	il numero	eel **noo**-mair-oh
white	bianco	bee-**ang**-koh
black	nero	**neh**-roh
red	rosso	**ross**-oh
yellow	giallo	**jal**-loh
green	verde	**vair**-deh
blue	blu	bloo

Types of Shop

antique dealer	l'antiquario	lan-tee-**kwah**-ree-oh
bakery	il forno /il panificio	eel **forn**-oh /eel pan-ee-**fee**-choh
bank	la banca	lah **bang**-kah
bookshop	la libreria	lah lee-breh-**ree**-ah
butcher	la macelleria	lah mah-chell-eh-**ree**-ah
cake shop	la pasticceria	lah pas-tee-chair-**ee**-ah
chemist	la farmacia	lah far-mah-**chee**-ah
delicatessen	la salumeria	lah sah-loo-meh-**ree**-ah
department store	il grande magazzino	eel **gran**-deh mag-gad-**zee**-noh
fishmonger	il pescivendolo	eel pesh-ee-**ven**-doh-loh
florist	il fioraio	eel fee-or-**eye**-oh
greengrocer	il fruttivendolo	eel froo-tee-**ven**-doh-loh
grocery	alimentari	ah-lee-men-**tah**-ree
hairdresser	il parrucchiere	eel par-oo-kee-**air**-eh
ice cream parlour	la gelateria	lah jel-lah-tair-**ree**-ah
market	il mercato	eel mair-**kah**-toh
newsstand	l'edicola	leh-**dee**-koh-lah
post office	l'ufficio postale	loo-**fee**-choh pos-**tah**-leh
shoe shop	il negozio di scarpe	eel neh-**goh**-tsioh dee **skar**-peh
supermarket	il supermercato	eel su-pair-mair-**kah**-toh
tobacconist	il tabaccaio	eel tah-bak-**eye**-oh
travel agency	l'agenzia di viaggi	lah-jen-**tsee**-ah dee vee-**ad**-jee

Sightseeing

art gallery	la pinacoteca	lah peena-koh-**teh**-kah
bus stop	la fermata dell'autobus	lah fair-**mah**-tah dell **ow**-toh-booss
church	la chiesa	lah kee-**eh**-zah
	la basilica	lah bah-**seel**-i-kah
closed for holidays	chiuso per le ferie	kee-**oo**-zoh pair leh **fair**-ee-eh
garden	il giardino	eel jar-**dee**-no
library	la biblioteca	lah beeb-lee-oh-**teh**-kah
museum	il museo	eel moo-**zeh**-oh
railway station	la stazione	lah stah-tsee-**oh**-neh
tourist information	l'ufficio di turismo	loo-**fee**-choh dee too-**ree**-smoh

STAYING IN A HOTEL

Do you have any vacant rooms?	**Avete camere libere?**	ah-**veh**-teh **kah**-mair-eh **lee**-bair-eh?
double room	**una camera doppia**	oona **kah**-mair-ah **doh**-pee-ah
with double bed	**con letto matrimoniale**	kon **let**-toh mah-tree-moh-nee-**ah**-leh
twin room	**una camera con due letti**	oona **kah**-mair-ah kon **doo**-eh **let**-tee
single room	**una camera singola**	oona **kah**-mair-ah **sing**-goh-lah
room with a bath, shower	**una camera con bagno, con doccia**	oona **kah**-mair-ah kon **ban**-yoh, kon **dot**-chah
porter	**il facchino**	eel fah-**kee**-noh
key	**la chiave**	lah kee-**ah**-veh
I have a reservation.	**Ho fatto una prenotazione.**	oh **fat**-toh oona preh-noh-tah-tsee-**oh**-neh

EATING OUT

Have you got a table for ...?	**Avete una tavola per ... ?**	ah-**veh**-teh oona **tah**-voh-lah pair ...?
I'd like to reserve a table.	**Vorrei riservare una tavola.**	vor-**ray** ree-sair-**vah**-reh oona **tah**-voh-lah
breakfast	**colazione**	koh-lah-tsee-**oh**-neh
lunch	**pranzo**	**pran**-tsoh
dinner	**cena**	**cheh**-nah
The bill, please.	**Il conto, per favore.**	eel **kon**-toh pair fah-**vor**-eh
I am a vegetarian.	**Sono vegetariano/a.**	soh-noh veh-jeh-tar-ee-**ah**-noh/nah
waitress	**cameriera**	kah-mair-ee-**air**-ah
waiter	**cameriere**	kah-mair-ee-**air**-eh
fixed price menu	**il menù a prezzo fisso**	eel meh-**noo** ah **pret**-soh **fee**-soh
dish of the day	**piatto del giorno**	pee-**ah**-toh dell **jor**-no
starter	**antipasto**	an-tee-**pass**-toh
first course	**il primo**	eel **pree**-moh
main course	**il secondo**	eel seh-**kon**-doh
vegetables	**il contorno**	eel kon-**tor**-noh
dessert	**il dolce**	eel **doll**-cheh
cover charge	**il coperto**	eel koh-**pair**-toh
wine list	**la lista dei vini**	lah **lee**-stah day **vee**-nee
rare	**al sangue**	al **sang**-gweh
medium	**al puntino**	al poon-**tee**-noh
well done	**ben cotto**	ben **kot**-toh
glass	**il bicchiere**	eel bee-kee-**air**-eh
bottle	**la bottiglia**	lah bot-**teel**-yah
knife	**il coltello**	eel kol-**tell**-oh
fork	**la forchetta**	lah for-**ket**-tah
spoon	**il cucchiaio**	eel koo-kee-**eye**-oh

MENU DECODER

l'acqua minerale gassata/naturale	**lah**-kwah mee-nair-**ah**-leh gah-**zah**-tah/nah-too-rah-leh	mineral water fizzy/still
agnello	ah-**niell**-oh	lamb
aceto	ah-**cheh**-toh	vinegar
aglio	**al**-ee-oh	garlic
al forno	al **for**-noh	baked
alla griglia	ah-lah **greel**-yah	grilled
l'aragosta	lah-rah-**goss**-tah	lobster
arrosto	ar-**ross**-toh	roast
la birra	lah **beer**-rah	beer
la bistecca	lah bee-**stek**-kah	steak
il brodo	eel **broh**-doh	broth
il burro	eel **boor**-oh	butter
il caffè	eel kah-**feh**	coffee
i calamari	ee kah-lah-**mah**-ree	squid
i carciofi	ee kar-**choff**-ee	artichokes
la carne	la **kar**-neh	meat
carne di maiale	**kar**-neh dee mah-**yah**-leh	pork
la cipolla	la chip-**oh**-lah	onion
i contorni	ee kon-**tor**-nee	vegetables
i fagioli	ee fah-**joh**-lee	beans
il fegato	eel **fay**-gah-toh	liver
il finocchio	eel fee-**nok**-ee-oh	fennel
il formaggio	eel for-**mad**-joh	cheese
le fragole	leh **frah**-goh-leh	strawberries
il fritto misto	eel **free**-toh **mees**-toh	mixed fried dish
la frutta	la **froot**-tah	fruit
frutti di mare	froo-tee dee **mah**-reh	seafood
i funghi	ee **foon**-ghee	mushrooms
i gamberi	ee **gam**-bair-ee	prawns
il gelato	eel jel-**lah**-toh	ice cream
l'insalata	leen-sah-lah-tah	salad
il latte	eel **laht**-teh	milk
lesso	**less**-oh	boiled
il manzo	eel **man**-tsoh	beef
la melanzana	lah meh-lan-**tsah**-nah	aubergine
la minestra	lah mee-**ness**-trah	soup
l'olio	loh-lee-oh	oil
il pane	eel **pah**-neh	bread
le patate	leh pah-**tah**-teh	potatoes
le patatine fritte	leh pah-tah-**teen**-eh **free**-teh	chips
il pepe	eel **peh**-peh	pepper
la pesca	lah **pess**-kah	peach
il pesce	eel **pesh**-eh	fish
il pollo	eel **poll**-oh	chicken
il pomodoro	eel poh-moh-**dor**-oh	tomato
il prosciutto cotto/crudo	eel pro-**shoo**-toh **kot**-toh/**kroo**-doh	ham cooked/cured
il riso	eel **ree**-zoh	rice
il sale	eel sah-leh	salt
la salsiccia	lah sal-**see**-chah	sausage
le seppie	leh **sep**-pee-eh	cuttlefish
secco	**sek**-koh	dry
la sogliola	lah **soll**-yoh-lah	sole
i spinaci	ee spee-**nah**-chee	spinach
succo d'arancia/ di limone	**soo**-koh dah-**ran**-chah/ dee lee-**moh**-neh	orange/lemon juice
il tè	eel **teh**	tea
la tisana	lah tee-**zah**-nah	herbal tea
il tonno	eel **ton**-noh	tuna
la torta	lah **tor**-tah	cake/tart
l'uovo	loo-**oh**-voh	egg
vino bianco	**vee**-noh bee-**ang**-koh	white wine
vino rosso	**vee**-noh **ross**-oh	red wine
il vitello	eel vee-**tell**-oh	veal
le vongole	leh **von**-goh-leh	clams
lo zucchero	loh **zoo**-kair-oh	sugar
gli zucchini	lyee dzu-**kee**-nee	courgettes
la zuppa	lah **tsoo**-pah	soup

NUMBERS

1	**uno**	**oo**-noh
2	**due**	**doo**-eh
3	**tre**	treh
4	**quattro**	**kwat**-roh
5	**cinque**	**ching**-kweh
6	**sei**	**say**-ee
7	**sette**	**set**-teh
8	**otto**	**ot**-toh
9	**nove**	**noh**-veh
10	**dieci**	dee-**eh**-chee
11	**undici**	**oon**-dee-chee
12	**dodici**	**doh**-dee-chee
13	**tredici**	**tray**-dee-chee
14	**quattordici**	kwat-**tor**-dee-chee
15	**quindici**	**kwin**-dee-chee
16	**sedici**	**say**-dee-chee
17	**diciassette**	dee-chah-**set**-teh
18	**diciotto**	dee-**chot**-toh
19	**diciannove**	dee-chah-**noh**-veh
20	**venti**	**ven**-tee
30	**trenta**	**tren**-tah
40	**quaranta**	kwah-**ran**-tah
50	**cinquanta**	ching-**kwan**-tah
60	**sessanta**	sess-**an**-tah
70	**settanta**	set-**tan**-tah
80	**ottanta**	ot-**tan**-tah
90	**novanta**	noh-**van**-tah
100	**cento**	**chen**-toh
1,000	**mille**	**mee**-leh
2,000	**duemila**	**doo**-eh **mee**-lah
5,000	**cinquemila**	**ching**-kweh **mee**-lah
1,000,000	**un milione**	oon meel-**yoh**-neh

TIME

one minute	**un minuto**	oon mee-**noo**-toh
one hour	**un'ora**	oon **or**-ah
half an hour	**mezz'ora**	medz-**or**-ah
a day	**un giorno**	oon **jor**-noh
a week	**una settimana**	oona set-tee-**mah**-nah
Monday	**lunedì**	loo-neh-**dee**
Tuesday	**martedì**	mar-teh-**dee**
Wednesday	**mercoledì**	mair-koh-leh-**dee**
Thursday	**giovedì**	joh-veh-**dee**
Friday	**venerdì**	ven-air-**dee**
Saturday	**sabato**	**sah**-bah-toh
Sunday	**domenica**	doh-**meh**-nee-kah

COUNTRY GUIDES

AUSTRALIA • CANADA • CRUISE GUIDE TO EUROPE AND THE
MEDITERRANEAN • FRANCE • GERMANY • GREAT BRITAIN
GREECE: ATHENS & THE MAINLAND • THE GREEK ISLANDS
IRELAND • ITALY • JAPAN • MEXICO • POLAND
PORTUGAL • SCOTLAND • SINGAPORE
SOUTH AFRICA • SPAIN • THAILAND
GREAT PLACES TO STAY IN EUROPE
A TASTE OF SCOTLAND

REGIONAL GUIDES

BALI & LOMBOK • BARCELONA & CATALONIA • CALIFORNIA
FLORENCE & TUSCANY • FLORIDA • HAWAII
JERUSALEM & THE HOLY LAND • LOIRE VALLEY
MILAN & THE LAKES • NAPLES WITH POMPEII & THE AMALFI
COAST • NEW ENGLAND • NEW ZEALAND
PROVENCE & THE COTE D'AZUR • SARDINIA
SEVILLE & ANDALUSIA • SICILY • VENICE & THE VENETO

CITY GUIDES

AMSTERDAM • BERLIN • BOSTON • BRUSSELS • BUDAPEST
CHICAGO • CRACOW • DELHI, AGRA & JAIPUR • DUBLIN
ISTANBUL • LISBON • LONDON • MADRID
MOSCOW • NEW YORK • PARIS • PRAGUE • ROME
SAN FRANCISCO • STOCKHOLM • ST PETERSBURG
SYDNEY • VIENNA • WARSAW • WASHINGTON, DC

NEW FOR AUTUMN 2001

EGYPT • EUROPE • A TASTE OF TUSCANY
NEW ORLEANS • SOUTHWEST USA & LAS VEGAS

FOR UPDATES TO OUR GUIDES, AND INFORMATION ON
<u>DK TRAVEL MAPS</u> & <u>PHRASEBOOKS</u>

VISIT US AT
eyewitnesstravel.dk.com

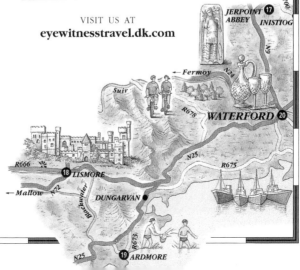

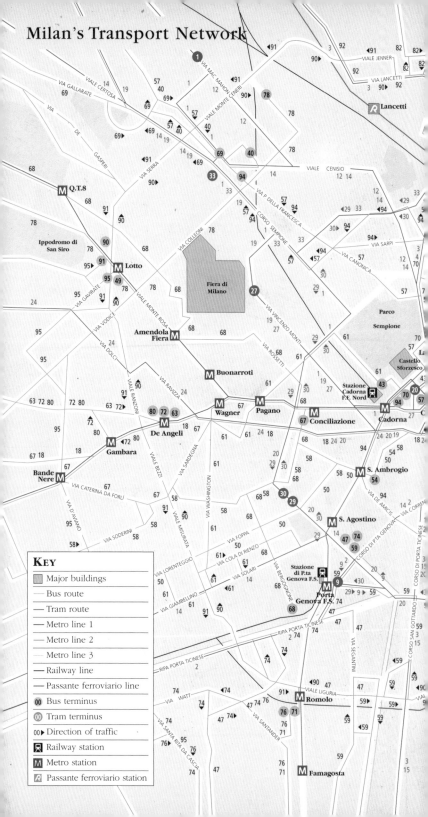

Milan's Transport Network